GLOBAL SOUTH ASIA

Padma Kaimal

K. Sivaramakrishnan

Anand A. Yang

SERIES EDITORS

Mobilizing Krishna's World

The Writings of Prince Sāvant Singh of Kishangarh

HEIDI R. M. PAUWELS

A Samuel and Althea Stroum Book

UNIVERSITY OF WASHINGTON PRESS
Seattle and London

Mobilizing Krishna's World is published with the assistance of a grant from the Samuel and Althea Stroum Endowed Book Fund.

Printed and bound in the United States of America
Composed in Minion, typeface designed by Robert Slimbach
21 20 19 18 17 5 4 3 2 1

UNIVERSITY OF WASHINGTON PRESS
www.washington.edu/uwpress

LIBRARY OF CONGRESS CATALOGING-IN-PUBLICATION DATA
Names: Pauwels, Heidi Rika Maria, author.
Title: Mobilizing Krishna's world : the writings of Prince Savant Singh of Kishangarh / Heidi Rika Maria Pauwels.
Description: Seattle : University of Washington Press, 2017. | Series: Global South Asia | Includes bibliographical references and index.
Identifiers: LCCN 2017004042| ISBN 9780295742229 (hardcover : acid-free paper) | ISBN 9780295742236 (pbk. : acid-free paper)
Subjects: LCSH: Nagaridasa, 1699–1764. | Hindi literature—History and criticism. | Literature and society—India, North—History.
Classification: LCC PK1967.9.N25 Z83 2017 | DDC 891.4/3809 [B] —dc23
LC record available at https://lccn.loc.gov/2017004042

Cover artwork: *Radha Offering Flowers to Yogi Krishna*, Kishangarh school, ca. 1750–60. National Museum, New Delhi, accession no. 63.1769. Courtesy National Museum (New Delhi).

All photos by the author unless otherwise credited.

The paper used in this publication is acid-free and meets the minimum requirements of American National Standard for Information Sciences—Permanence of Paper for Printed Library Materials, ANSI Z39.48–1984. ∞

For Monika Horstmann

Contents

Acknowledgments ix
Notes on Texts, Transliterations, and Dates xiii

INTRODUCTION: Rādhā-Krishna Devotion in Kishangarh 3

1 Soldiers Marching: Kishangarh at the Crossroads 13

2 Gods and Saints Relocated: Sectarian Rivalries and Hinduism in the Making 29

3 Devotees on the Move: *The Pilgrim's Bliss* 71

4 Legends Mobilized: *Garland of Stories and Songs* 107

5 Myth Retold: *Garland of Rāma's Romance* 162

CONCLUSION: Pilgrimage, Hagiography, and Scripture 197

Notes 205
Bibliography 235
List of Illustrations 251
Index 253

Acknowledgments

WHILE WORKING ON THIS BOOK OVER THE PAST TWO DECADES, I had the great privilege of returning like a pilgrim to Braj and Kishangarh, to savor the joy of immersion in the sacred stories and songs of Śrī Rādhā-Krishna and Śrī Sītā-Rāma and enjoy the good company (satsaṅga) of many devotees. Along the way in India, I received invaluable help and support from many generous scholars and enthusiastic *bhakta*s, who made the project come alife. First of all I want to express my gratitude to H. H. Maharaja Brajraj Singh and Maharani Minakshi Devi of Kishangarh, who generously shared with me their deep knowledge of their family traditions and kindly allowed me to consult the non-illustrated manuscripts in the royal collection. Śrī Madan Mohan Ācārya, Mukhiyā of the Śrī Kalyāṇarāya jī temple in Kishangarh, enthusiastically read or sang out the manuscript texts I was reading with him, so that I could not only compare them efficiently with the printed editions but also get a firsthand taste of the emotional fervor, or *rasa*, involved. The monsoon mornings and evenings spent in the lounge of the Phoolmahal hotel in Kishangarh provided the ideal setting for reading the seasonal poetry. I am grateful also to Shahzād Citrakār Alī, who shared stories about his late father, Dr. Faiyāz Alī Khān, an authority on Kishangarhi culture. He graciously allowed me to consult and photograph his father's works and the manuscripts preserved by the family. Dr. Jaykrishna Sharma, the ācārya of the Kacariya Nimbārka Pīṭh, was always prepared to provide background, explain difficult passages, and give tips for pursuing manuscripts. I also had the privilege of enjoying the singing of Pandit Hīrālāl Kīrtaniyā and the company of Bhagadcand jī Somani and his family. During my frequent trips to nearby Salemabad, I enjoyed the expert guidance of Pūjārī Ravi Sharmā. At the National Museum in New Delhi, Dr. Vijay Mathur very graciously shared his knowledge about Kishangarh with me.

I am very grateful to Dr. Swapna Sharma of Vrindavan, now at Yale University in New Haven, for many delightful hours in Vrindavan and on the road, reading through *Tīrthānand* and selections of *Pad-prasaṅg-mālā*; to

Śrī Shrīvatsa Gosvami, who knows the tradition and the region inside out and who together with his wife, Sandhya Gosvami, was, as always, a most gracious host, welcoming me into their wonderful family. I want to thank the staff of the libraries I worked in, the Vrindavan Research Institute, the Mathura Janmabhumi Library, and the Rajasthan Oriental Research Institute in Bharatpur and Jaipur, and Giles Tillotson and Chandramani Singh at the Jaipur City Palace. A special thanks to Jayesh Khandelval of the Ras Bhāratī Sansthān in Vrindavan, for date estimates of his manuscripts and for sharing his extensive knowledge with me.

In the United States, I am particularly grateful to my historian colleague at the University of Washington, Purnima Dhavan, for many stimulating conversations on the history of the period and for our near-weekly reading sessions of Braj and Persian texts of the time, and to Navina Najat Haidar from the Metropolitan Museum of Art in New York City, who very generously made time to share her insights on Kishangarhi art and history. I cannot thank enough Susan Miller, expert on Thai literature from Anacortes, Washington, for her excellent advice on the translations and the chance to rediscover all over again the poetry included here as we discussed its translation together.

I also want to thank the hosts and audiences at the talks I had the opportunity to give, "to test the waters": to Sally J. Sutherland Goldman and Robert Goldman for inviting me to their conference "New Directions in the Study of the Epics of South and Southeast Asia" at the University of California, Berkeley, in October 2012, where I first presented on *Rām-carit-mālā*, a paper now appearing in the *Journal of Hindu Studies*; to Tyler Williams, who organized the "Bhakti Conference" in Shimla in the summer of 2012, where I presented a paper on *Tīrthānand*, now coming out in his edited volume; and to Monika Horstmann, who hosted an earlier chapter of the same conference in Heidelberg in 2003, where I first presented on *Pad-prasaṅg-mālā*. Many colleagues at these venues, and elsewhere, made excellent suggestions, but all remaining shortcomings are my own.

A major source of inspiration has been the work of Monika Horstmann, with whom I had the privilege of studying when she was heading the Institut für Indologie at the Universität zu Köln in 1989–90. I admire in particular that her work spreads over the whole range, from manuscript and archival research to careful philological work and interpretations for history and religious studies. It was a special treat to make my first visit to Galta in 2011 under her expert guidance—topped off with an unforgettable *raj kachauri*. This book is dedicated to her.

I want to thank Lorri Hagman of the University of Washington Press and her stellar team for wonderful editorial support and excellent advice and the anonymous reviewers for excellent suggestions. Thanks also to Jane Lichty for her keen eye and top-notch copyediting. For the images reproduced in this book, I gratefully acknowledge the National Museum in New Delhi, the Cleveland Art Museum, and especially Mr. Eberhard Rist from Stuttgart, to whom I am grateful also for helpful correspondence; for funding the project, I thank the National Endowment for the Humanities, the Guggenheim Foundation, the Royalty Research Fund and the Simpson Center for the Humanities of the University of Washington in Seattle, and the American Institute of Indian Studies. I am particularly grateful to Philip Lutgendorf and Purnima Mehta, for performing Hanumān-like feats in building bridges and moving my paperwork along to make my research trips possible.

Last but not least, I wholeheartedly thank my family: my son, for his humor that helps keep things in perspective; my little daughter, for sharing my enthusiasm for *Rāmāyaṇa* movies and for giving me a taste of Rās-līlā at home by dressing up as Śrī Rāma and Śrī Krishna with crowns and weapons she made herself; and my husband, whose loving intellectual and practical support in so many ways means more than I can say.

Notes on Texts, Transliterations, and Dates

THIS BOOK IS BASED ON THE WORKS OF SĀVANT SINGH OF Kishangarh, alias Nāgarīdās. There are three major editions of his work available, with in-depth introductions in Hindi on his life and literary accomplishments. The first edition is still the one that is used the most, the "Vulgate," published by the prestigious Nāgarī Pracāriṇī Sabhā of Benares and edited by Kiśorīlāl Gupta in two volumes in 1965. All references to Nāgarīdās's work in this book are to this edition, unless otherwise specified. A very solid and scholarly edition, it has many helpful notes, glosses, and other apparatus at the end. Nevertheless, it was challenged right away, the very next year: in 1966, a second edition was published, this one with a Nimbārkan sectarian agenda, by the scholar Vrajvallabh Śaraṇ from Vrindavan's Śrī Sarveśvar Press. Then again, this Nimbārkan challenge was met by the royal court of Kishangarh with a defense of its Vallabhan sectarian agenda. Kishangarhi scholar and courtier Dr. Faiyāz Alī Khān, who had written an impressive PhD dissertation on Sāvant Singh in 1962, summarized his main findings and brought out a new edition, which was published by New Delhi's Kendrīya Hindī Nideśālay in 1974. This work, too, is very scholarly and well annotated. The latter two editions are more difficult to obtain, but they can be consulted in some US libraries. All three editions made use of a yet older one, a microfilm of which is preserved in the New York Public Library. This late nineteenth-century edition was prepared by Pandit Śrīdharātmaja Kisanlāl Gauḍ under the title *Nāgara-samuccayaḥ*. It was published in 1898 under the auspices of the then Kishangarh king, Śārdul Singh, on the initiative of his younger brother Javān Singh. It was printed by Shrīdhar Shivalāljī of the Jñānsāgar (Dnyansagar) Press in Bombay. This lithograph edition looks like a facsimile of a manuscript dated 1883 (1940 VS), preserved in the royal library in Kishangarh, on which it was based.

Hardly any of Nāgarīdās's works have been translated. The fragments that I quote here draw on my own scholarly edition and translation of the texts. The fully annotated translation and text based on a comparison of the aforementioned editions with the manuscripts that I collated will be available separately. For polishing of the English translations, I consulted with Susan Miller, an expert on Thai literature, living in Anacortes, Washington.

At the outset, a clarification of the terms used throughout is in order. I use the term *God* often as a shorthand to refer to the god-images worshipped by the poet and different sectarian groups, because they regarded these images to be manifestations of God himself. They are called *svarūpas*, or "true forms" of God, and are considered able to speak and act, and they thus have a certain agency. In that respect, it is justified to talk about "gods on the move" and similar expressions. I use "sect" to translate *Sampradāya*, because of the lack of a better, shorthand English alternative. It should be understood not in the Occidental sense of "secessionist movement" but in the Indian context as a "succession of preceptors embedded within a larger tradition."

My transliteration policy follows the standard method for transliterating Devanagari (in accordance with the influential *Oxford Hindi-English Dictionary* [OHED]). All text quoted from Old Hindi has the neutral vowel at the end (inherent *-a*) because, although this vowel is often not pronounced in modern Hindi, it is in Old Hindi and is also counted in prosody. All Indian terms are given with diacritics and italicized, except for words commonly accepted in English (pandit, yogi, ashram, etc.); terms widely accepted in secondary literature on the topic, such as caste and occupation names (Brahmin, Rajput, Raja); and terms of Mughal office (vazir, subedar, Mir Bakhshi, jagir, subah). Similarly, names of gods are given with diacritics, with the exception of frequently occurring names, where for ease of readability I write *Krishna* instead of *Kr̥ṣṇa*, *Vishnu* for *Viṣṇu*, *Vrishabhānu* for *Vr̥ṣabhānu*, and so forth. I have opted to transliterate all technical terms and names of images (*mūrtis*), gods, mythical characters, and sects with inherent neutral vowels, to avoid the potential problem of having a single term romanized differently in Sanskrit and Hindi contexts. However, for the names of "Hindi" poets, groups of poets, and their works, I follow the generally accepted model of R. S. McGregor's standard encyclopedic work (published in 1984), where they are transliterated without the neutral vowel, in contrast to their Old Indo-Aryan and Middle Indo-Aryan counterparts. As a consequence, there is unavoidably some inconsistency, when, for instance, I use *pada* to refer to a song, but in titles the silent final vowel is dropped in accordance with McGregor's system, hence *Pad-prasaṅg-mālā*.

Similarly, I use *bhakta* but also *Bhakt-māl*. I spell place-names without diacritics because of the wide currency of anglicized names such as Benares, Allahabad, Delhi, and Lucknow. However, rivers, especially when seen in the text as goddesses, such as Gaṅgā, have full diacritics.

All dates are CE (Common Era), except where otherwise indicated. Conversion of dates from the Hindu calendar in *Vikram Saṃvat* (VS) to CE has been done by the admittedly imprecise method of subtracting the number 57 from the VS date. In the list of references, the same procedure has been followed, except when the CE date is provided in the source itself. The VS date has been included in parentheses in the bibliography, but not in the reference citations in the notes.

Conforming with Indian manuscript-writing practice, I end by begging the forgiveness of the critics whose sharp eyes undoubtedly will detect many infelicities in this work and by expressing my hope that the joys of discovery of Nāgarīdās's works may outweigh such flaws. *Jay Śrī Krishna*.

Mobilizing Krishna's World

Introduction

Rādhā-Krishna Devotion in Kishangarh

IN THE MID-EIGHTEENTH CENTURY, ARMIES OF ALL DENOMINATIONS marched over North-West India, often sowing terror and destruction: Afghans descended from the mountains into the plains out for spoils, Maratha armies moving north extracted tribute, Sikh Misals waged guerrilla war, Rajput rulers fought rivals, regional secessionists arose nearly everywhere, and Mughal armies pathetically tried to meet these threats. All sought to take advantage of the political situation to carve out some profit for themselves.[1]

At one of the military crossroads, an exquisite work of art depicting the arch-lovers Rādhā and Krishna was painted in the ateliers of Kishangarh, a small principality in Rajasthan. This painting (fig. I.1, also reproduced on the cover) bears the hallmarks of its school, which had arisen a few decades earlier: elegant, tall, slender, and haloed figures of Krishna and Rādhā, with curved brows and elongated eyes. They strike a pose in a bucolic setting on a sandbank in a deep-blue river, dotted with elegant pleasure boats, and against a background of shining white domes of pavilions in pleasure gardens and a terrace with merrymakers.[2]

Why was this painting produced in the midst of all the military mayhem? It is tempting to see here an example of escapism, of religion as a refuge from political vicissitudes. Did the romance of Rādhā and Krishna serve as escape from the violence of the time, their paradise of Vrindavan a haven for the world-weary? That would justify the stance of scholars of religion who conveniently bypass the here and now, ignoring the political circumstances of the "real world" and focusing on static and timeless categories.

Perhaps the painting warrants a closer look: there is something unusual about this scene. Rādhā and Krishna are not, as usual, depicted engaged

FIG. I.1 *Radha Offering Flowers to Yogi Krishna*, Kishangarh school, ca. 1750–60. Ink, color, and gold on paper (30.5 × 20.5 cm). National Museum, New Delhi, accession no. 63.1769. Courtesy National Museum (New Delhi)

FIG. I.2 *Portrait of Maharaja Savant Singh with Consort, Bani Thani*, attributed to Nihālcand, Kishangarh school, mid-1700s. Ink, color, and gold on paper (image: 21.6 × 14.0 cm; mounted: 42.5 × 33.0 cm; with borders: 27.4 × 20.0 cm). The Cleveland Museum of Art, gift of Norman Zaworski 2001.172. Courtesy Cleveland Museum of Art. © The Cleveland Museum of Art

in love-play; rather, Krishna's matted hair is that of an ascetic. His arm is supported by a tree, in the way ascetics use a crutch to keep a vow not to sit down. Rādhā is humbly making an offering to him. Have these deities of love-play taken their leave of worldly distractions?

A fascinating aspect of the Kishangarh school of painting is its portrayal of Krishna with the traits of its crown prince, Sāvant Singh (1699–1764), and in the style of Sāvant Singh's poetry. Sāvant Singh was a patron who inspired the local painters, most famously Nihālcand, to develop the new, exquisite style dominated by the depiction of Rādhā-Krishna vignettes, frequently for illustration of his own poetry. As an ardent Rādhā-Krishna devotee, he composed, under the pen name Nāgarīdās, or "Servant of Rādhā," two volumes of poetry in praise of the divine pair. In the commissioned paintings, Krishna often has the same facial features as Sāvant Singh in his (probably flattering) portraits.[3] Some believe that the long-nosed and elongated-eyed Rādhā, too, is based on a real person at the court: Sāvant Singh's young mistress, nicknamed Banī-ṭhanī, or "Miss Makeup" (fig. 1.2).[4]

Whether that is correct or not, she was a devotee who composed poetry under the pseudonym Rasik Bihārī.[5] Both of them celebrated their own love and that of Rādhā and Krishna in their poetry. The boundaries between temple and court were fluid: as God was modeled after royalty, the royalty modeled themselves after God.[6] If the Kishangarhi lovers went boating on a lake, so did Rādhā and Krishna in Nāgarīdās's poem *Love-Play's Moonlight* (Bihār-candrikā) and the matching painting *Boat of Love*.[7] And if Krishna dallied in the bucolic Vrindavan with Rādhā, so did the humans. Sāvant Singh went on frequent pilgrimages to Vrindavan and eventually retired there toward the end of his life, and we know that Rasik Bihārī accompanied him. With that information, we can look at the painting in a new light: like Krishna, Sāvant Singh became a yogi, and at his side, like Rādhā, was his loyal Rasik Bihārī (fig. 1.1).

Two poems on a yogi theme are included in Nāgarīdās's *String of Song-Pearls* (Pad-muktāvalī). Both voice a woman's fascination with a yogi:

> "My eyes thirst for the nectar of the yogi's beauty:
> Ashes on his body, a crown of leaves on his head, his face is like a sliver
> of the moon.
> Unable to turn from this unusual yogi, my eyes betray their love."
> Nāgara: the god of love himself is worshipping the divine pair in the city
> of love.
>
> (PMĀ 66)[8]

"Dear yogi, what's that stubborn wont of yours?
I offer alms, but you refuse them. Yet you come to my door again
and again.
You do not waste a moment! You keep staring at my face, your eyes
betraying greed.
You're worldly wise (*nāgara*), Dark One! People will talk! That's what's bad
about this town."

(PMĀ 219)[9]

Both poems present a scandalous paradox: the yogi should be the symbol of world-weariness and inspire asceticism, yet the opposite is the case. He and the woman whose voice we hear find themselves fatefully attracted to each other. They are unable to keep up pretense and abide by rules of etiquette and propriety. Already the neighbors are gossiping about them. Both poems foreground how their eyes betray their state of mind; the painting does likewise in prominently displaying the Kishangarhi elongated eyes. In the picture, too, nothing is as it seems: his yogi garb is a sham and so is her submissive offering. They both hunger for something else. If the yogi and the lady are really Krishna and Rādhā longing for love, perhaps Nāgarīdās and his lady are lovers longing for spirituality?

The prince and his concubine make for a romantic tale indeed, but this, too, may not be the whole story.[10] If we delve deeper, we discover that behind the idyllic picture and poem lies a world of political intrigue and religious tension. Why did the prince become a yogi? Why did Sāvant Singh retire to Vrindavan? It turns out this move was not totally voluntary; perhaps it is better characterized as exile rather than retirement. When his father died in 1748, Sāvant Singh was in Delhi. Before he could reach home, his brother usurped his throne. Suddenly, this Krishna devotee found himself in a *Rāmāyaṇa*-like scenario: his father deceased, his own brother on the throne. Where to turn? He went on an extended pilgrimage; perhaps Vrindavan and the idyllic woods of Braj looked to him more like the Daṇḍaka forest, where Rāma went into exile. Not coincidentally, during exactly this period Nāgarīdās compiled his own version of the *Rāmāyaṇa*. Yet, contrary to his mythological counterpart, Rāma, Nāgarīdās did not immediately acquiesce, but made efforts to regain his lost kingdom. He and his party joined the armies marching at the time, and after allying with the Marathas, he eventually regained half his kingdom. By that time, though, utterly weary of war, he abdicated in favor of his son and finally settled in Vrindavan. The picture may look static, but behind it is hidden a story of many peregrinations, before the happy ending in Krishna's land.

The conflation of mythology and real life is a fascinating phenomenon. Has the prince molded himself in God's image, or is God molded in the prince's? Should we see this as hubris, a perversion of the rich's prerogative to commission imagined likenesses of themselves, or as an expression of dharmic kingship?[11] Perhaps in the context of *bhakti* (devotion), the phenomenon can be understood as part of the technique of *Rāgānugā bhakti*, or devotion fostered by imitating characters in Krishna's world.[12] Whatever be the case, Nāgarīdās clearly saw and actively made connections between the Krishna and Rāma story and his own personal life. Did he write his life into the mythology, or did the myth intrude in life? Boundaries of myth and history became blurred, as mythological narratives influenced how he scripted his "real life."

This book pieces together the historical record and studies it in conjunction with the works Nāgarīdās composed in this later phase of his life. Unlike for many patrons of painting, for Sāvant Singh we have his works to consult to better understand the pictures. His works make for an excellent case study of how devotion shapes understandings of life events, how mythological patterns impose themselves on human agency, and how myth intersects with life narratives and discourses of legitimation. In short, they demonstrate how myth is mobilized. They reveal not a static world but a dynamic interchange of ideal and circumstances, of divine patterns and human disruptions. We recover a balancing act in a political and social world full of tensions. As it turns out, the dreamy Kishangarhi images are not floating beyond time and space. Nor are Nāgarīdās's poems. If we listen and look carefully, we can glimpse the struggle to cope with an existential crisis and see him at work crafting narratives to capture the meaning of a life suddenly blown off course.

This is not just a private life. Sāvant Singh's exile coincides with a major crisis in the Mughal empire: Afghan invasions from 1739 onward hastened the end of the culturally splendid reign of Muḥammad Shāh "Raṅgīle," or "the Merrymaker" (r. 1718–48). Muḥammad Shāh reportedly issued this edict: "[Historians] should refrain from recording the events of my reign, for at present the record cannot be a pleasant one."[13] The concomitant rise of regional powers led to the decentralization of the Mughal state. For Sāvant Singh, as for many other vassals of the Mughals, it must have seemed like the end of the world as he knew it. What did such vassals make of this change?

Did they see it as an opportunity to reassert their Hindu identity? Or were things more complex than that? The efflorescence of art and culture at this twilight of the Mughal dynasty has lately attracted scholarly attention. What previously was brushed off as a self-destructing overrefinement, or as escapism, now is being reassessed.[14] If we take seriously the works of literature produced in this period, we can study how reactions to political events are intertwined with religious categories, but perhaps in a way different from what the hindsight of twentieth-century events might assume.

Our goal here is to explore beyond the pretty picture, "beyond the beautiful forevers" of the mythic world of the gods. Why did the (all-too-human) creators of pictures and poetry depict the gods and tell the stories the way they did? What happened as they re-created the old myth? What were the real-world intrigues and politics behind them?

TEMPLES AND COURTS

This book is about movements between temples and courts, about the interconnections between the religious and the political in early modern India. The purpose is to uncover both the politics in apparently atemporal religion and the neglected religious in political history. As a contribution to religious studies, the goal of this book is to historicize, politicize, and bring a dynamic aspect to what is often treated as a static, timeless strand of Hinduism that is Krishna *bhakti*. The analysis emerges from primary sources and is organized accordingly, focusing on a pilgrimage report, a hagiography, and a rewriting of scripture in devotional Hinduism. As a contribution to the history of the pivotal eighteenth century in India on the eve of colonialism, the book joins recent efforts to shift focus from great men and great political events at the center to the periphery. It does so with a case study of a Rajput in a provincial center, who proudly participated in cosmopolitan Mughal culture. It aims for a "thick" historical narrative of literary culture in the period, not so much the nascent Urdu literature (as in my 2015 book), but rather the devotional literature. In particular, it investigates how religious paradigms, myth, hagiographical stories, and rituals connected with pilgrimage were mobilized in shaping political agency. In short, this book is about the personal mobilization of myth and religious song and story in the midst of the eighteenth century's complex political developments.

The first locus is the temple and its *bhakti*, arguably still at the heart of contemporary mainstream Hinduism. Devotion for Krishna Gopāla, the "Cowherd God," is centered in the pastoral land of Braj, just downstream on the Yamunā from Delhi. This area developed into a bustling pilgrimage center in the sixteenth century, partly thanks to its new accessibility by road from the imperial twin towns of Agra and Delhi at the time. It has undergone boom cycles ever since, most recently due to the increasing mobility of the middle classes from Delhi, who cause huge traffic jams with their minivans and microcars in pursuit of pilgrimage tourism. Whatever the pollution damage done to the bucolic, idyllic environs of Braj, the mythic location remains an ever-green, ever-popular destination. Likewise, the many songs of devotion to Krishna in Old Hindi (Braj) created in this area starting in the sixteenth century still reverberate, as they continue to be widely performed all over India, from the temple and salon to the international concert stage.

Ever since its scholarly "discovery," the Krishna cult has attracted attention from Western scholars.[15] There have been studies of Krishna himself, of course, of the arts his myth has inspired, including the "mystery plays," or Rās-līlās.[16] Among the studies on Braj as a pilgrimage center is, most notably, the magisterial work by the textual scholar Alan W. Entwistle published in 1987. There also has been a spade of studies on Krishna *bhakti* and its songs in a form of Old Hindi called, after the area, "Braj."[17] These studies focus on the work of individual poets, while also taking care to show their contemporary relevance, and tend to see, to greater or lesser degree, the poets in isolation of their historical context.[18]

There are a few important studies that critically rethink the concept of a *bhakti* movement and its geographical spread, but what has been relatively neglected is an investigation of (i) the pathways of transmissions of the popular songs in view of their ritual or devotional setting; (ii) how the different authors or singers are in dialogue or rivalry with one another, in other words, intertextuality; and (iii) the macro- and micropolitics at work behind the process.[19] This book brings the dynamism of circulation into the sometimes static world of scholarship on Krishna devotion and infuses the somewhat isolated religious imaginings with background on political and religious strife, focusing on not only saints in centers of devotion but also pilgrims and soldiers moving around the area at the time. It studies the circulation of ideas and culture by examining the movement of vernacular devotional songs during the seminal period of the sixteenth through the eighteenth century in North India.

The second locus is the court. The proximity of the center of Krishna devotion, Braj, to the seats of Mughal power in Agra and Delhi and the Rajput courts of Rajasthan allowed for intense interchange. Indeed, stories abound of Rajput kings, Mughal nobles, and even the emperor himself visiting the holy land of Braj and sponsoring its holy men. Provincial rulers from all over India, in particular nearby Rajasthan, made frequent pilgrimages to the area and participated in its local rituals. Temples and monasteries stand as enduring witnesses to sponsorship by regional power centers, as confirmed by inscriptions and documents of land grants. This was not a unidirectional process. Provincial rulers worked closely with local agents. Priests and holy men from the pilgrimage center in turn visited the courts, sometimes to celebrate specific rituals, sometimes even moving there permanently and bringing their Krishna images with them. Thus, not only did the kings visit God, but God paid return visits to the kings. The milieus of court and temple were not isolated from one another: there were multiple channels of exchange back and forth.

Central in this book is movement between these loci, circulation of ideas between the temples of Braj and the palaces of Rajasthan. This case study involves the transactions of Braj with the provincial court of Kishangarh near Jaipur, which in turn had close relationships with the Mughal court in Delhi. It is based on little-studied primary sources by Sāvant Singh, few of whose works have been translated.[20] The Kishangarhi paintings that were commissioned to illustrate the poetry may give the impression of a pretty world of little dreams, but Kishangarh was hardly a Brigadoon unencumbered by the vicissitudes of time. As it turns out, Sāvant Singh was fully immersed in the political and religious reform movements around him. This study peeks behind the purdah of the paintings to reveal his multifaceted personality.

ORGANIZATION AND SCOPE OF THE BOOK

The case of Kishangarh's Sāvant Singh illustrates wider trends in eighteenth-century North India, since Kishangarh can be regarded as a microcosm of the time. *Mobilizing Krishna's World* begins with a sketch of the wider historical canvas of Rajasthan, and of the Kishangarh house and Sāvant Singh in particular. The opening chapters, on political and religious history, will prepare the reader to understand the full impact of Nāgarīdās's literary works.

The three works selected for this book were all authored in the mid-eighteenth century, the time of crisis in the empire. They are from the later stage of Sāvant Singh's life, when he was coping with the crisis in his home state and between efforts to regain his kingdom, he found refuge in Braj. These works thus are particularly relevant to the study of exchanges between temple and court and the interplay of politics and religion.

The Pilgrim's Bliss (Tīrthānand) is a first-person account of events during this period, presented as a pilgrimage narrative. Finished in 1753 (1810 VS), it describes at length Sāvant Singh's peregrinations and the interactions he had in the Braj area, providing us with lively vignettes of exchange between kings and holy men.[21] In its extended descriptions of religious festivals and rites, and even transcriptions of excerpts of Rās-līlā performances, this work provides a wealth of historical information on the religious scene at the time.

Garland of Stories and Songs (Pad-prasaṅg-mālā) is a hagiographical anthology about the power of song and the inspiration of saints. Internal evidence dates it to the same period. Nāgarīdās presents several of his favorite devotional songs and contextualizes them with anecdotes that provide biographical information about the poets who wrote them or the singers who performed them. This work sheds light on the circulation of poems and holy men from the sixteenth through the eighteenth century. It gives us keen insight into the reception history of many famous and beloved *bhakti* songs, including by Sūrdās and Mīrābāī. At the same time, it brings alive the intellectual climate that this patron of art partook in and helped shape.

Garland of Rāma's Romance (Rām-carit-mālā) constitutes Nāgarīdās's own version of the *Rāmāyaṇa* through a compilation of poems by himself and others, including the famous Rāma devotee Tulsīdās and other Krishna poets, such as Sūrdās and Nanddās. This work was compiled in 1749 (1806 VS), while Sāvant Singh actively sought alliances to regain his throne. It thus provides a window into how the mythic story of a struggle for the throne of Ayodhya could have real-life significance for the one who retells it, himself engaged in a struggle for his own throne and a fight with his own brother. It is rare that we have this kind of background information to study a *Rāmāyaṇa* retelling.

These three works are explored not in the chronological order in which they were written, but starting with straightforward narration of real-life events, venturing into the realm of legendary saints interacting with Krishna, and ending with the mythology of Rāma. From life to myth, by the end of the book, we will have come full circle, back to the myth as depicted in the paintings, but now with full understanding of its impact. Along the way, insight is gleaned from several Kishangarhi paintings.

Each of these three works highlights a different area of religious studies, namely, pilgrimage, hagiography, and reworking of sacred scripture. Read together, they bring a new understanding of circulation of people and ideas in the eighteenth century. This Kishangarhi case study provides a snapshot of what was going on in the pilgrimage center of Braj and the nature of exchanges and interactions with regional Rajput courts and the military powers at the time. It maps the channels of transmission of devotional songs, their performance context, and their reception in a real world of political intrigue and military maneuvers. It also speaks to how people in crisis saw the gods participate in their own world and how they modeled their life narratives after mythological patterns and, vice versa, retold stories of the gods after their own lives.

1 Soldiers Marching

Kishangarh at the Crossroads

THE MID-EIGHTEENTH CENTURY SAW SOLDIERS MARCH ALL OVER North India. This military activity was precipitated by both internal and external threats to the Mughal empire. In the hindsight of Partition, Rajputs and Marathas, who were the rising power at the time, are often construed as Hindu allies against Muslim enemies, but to what extent did religion figure into the conflicts? This case study of the Kishangarh house and its complex interactions with the Mughal court, other Rajput principalities, and different Maratha factions reveals some of the factors at play.

Warrior elites, in particular Rajputs, and their upward social mobility and cultural values, have been the subject of recent scholarship that nuances the now-popular colonial and nationalist constructs of them as staunch defenders of Hinduism.[1] Such constructs were inspired by the colonial scholar James Tod's seminal work, beginning with the publication of the first volume in 1829.

Rajput elites sponsored Hindu religious expression of all kinds, promoting literature, recitation and explanation of sacred scripture, and ritual; financing temple building, sculpture, and miniature painting; and supporting music, dance, and performing arts. During various periods, different forms of Hinduism were promoted over others, often at the same time that diverse expressions of Jaina and Muslim religiosity also received financial backing.[2] In short, Rajput religious affiliations were multiple and complex and often changed over time with political alliances and internal rivalries. Far from provincial, Rajputs partook in a multicultural, cosmopolitan world. The kingdom of Kishangarh is celebrated for its transcendental Rādhā-Krishna paintings, but there is more to this small Rajput principality than its paintings.

KISHANGARH, A MUGHAL VASSAL STATE

A historical study of Kishangarh has yet to be written, and archival material is not easily accessible.[3] The main available source is a manuscript preserved

FIG. 1.1 Kishangarh fort

in the Kishangarh Royal Collection, *Administrative History* (Tavārīḳh Maḥkamah), authored by Mathurādās Gūjar Gauḍ in 1913 (1970 VS). This work is subdivided into sections organized by king or prince.[4] Most material cited here is from the *History of Sāvant Singh* (Tavārīḳh Sāvant Singh jī kī). Primary evidence from Nāgarīdās's own work and other literary and historical texts from the period provides additional information.

As a vassal state of the Mughals, Kishangarh was in the middle of the political happenings of the time. This small principality, its fort (fig. 1.1) with prime location on the busy road from Agra to Ajmer (and on to Jodhpur and eventually Ahmedabad), was founded by a Rathor prince of Jodhpur, Kishan Singh, in 1611.[5] He came to the Kishangarh area in 1596, after joining Akbar's service in Agra, for which he received nearby Hindaun as a principality (jagir). He attended the Mughal court and was close to prince Salīm, the later emperor Jahāngīr (r. 1605–27), who confirmed him in his position.[6] Jahāngīr mentions Kishan Singh repeatedly in his memoirs, recording his rise in administrative rank. He also describes his fight with the Rāṇā of Mewar and his gruesome death in pursuit of a vendetta.[7] Later Kishangarh rajas, too, were close to the Mughals and are on record as having fought valiantly in the Deccan against the Marathas, in the North-West Frontier against the Iranis and Afghanis, and in Bengal throughout the seventeenth century.[8]

Rūp Singh (r. 1643–58), the fifth ruler of Kishangarh, is listed as one of the great nobles of the empire.[9] He shifted the capital to Rupnagar, a city named after him and founded at the locale where he grew up.[10] There he installed a Krishna image that he brought from Braj. Devotional sources portray him as a saint in his own right, as in Nāgarīdās's hagiographic anthology (PPM 59). At the same time, Rūp Singh was a general in the Mughal army, battling in Balkh and Qandahar for Shāh Jahān.[11] His victories for the Mughals are celebrated in the epic poem *Exposition on Rūp/Beauty* (Rūp-vacanikā), commissioned by his successor and written by the court poet Vrind in 1705 (1762 VS).[12]

Kishangarh had supported the losing side during the succession battle toward the end of Shāh Jahān's reign (1657–58) and fell temporarily out of favor after Aurangzeb assumed authority. However later, Kishangarh's ruler Mān Singh (r. 1658–1706) served in the Deccan and rose rapidly in Aurangzeb's service. Aurangzeb's son Muḥammad Mu'azzam Shāh 'Ālam was married to a Kishangarhi princess.[13] Their son, 'Azīm ush-Shān, was taught by Vrind, who was in the young prince's service before moving to Kishangarh.

In the battle for the empire that ensued after Aurangzeb's death in 1707, the then ruler of Kishangarh, Rāj Singh (r. 1706–48), supported his relative by marriage, Mu'azzam Shāh 'Ālam, who became the next emperor, Bahādur Shāh (r. 1707–12). Rāj Singh reportedly was rewarded by securing the services of Vrind, who from then onward became attached to the Kishangarh court.[14] Rāj Singh was probably also the first Kishangarh king to sponsor a full-fledged painting atelier, and it was during his time that the school developed its distinctive style of Rādhā-Krishna miniatures.[15]

Fortunes at the Mughal court changed fast, and Kishangarh did not always side with the winning parties in the succession struggles, but later in the eighteenth century there was again a close connection with the emperor Muḥammad Shāh (r. 1719–48). This is documented in Mughal court chronicles and illustrated in a painting that depicts Muḥammad Shāh and high-ranking Mughal nobles, together with a prominently featured Rāj Singh.[16] The painting also portrays the Kacchvāhā ruler Savāī Jai Singh II of Amer (soon to be Jaipur in 1727), thus also attesting to the close relationship of Kishangarh with nearby Amer. On at least one occasion they had been military allies in Mughal service: when Jai Singh besieged the Jat fortress of Thun for the Mughals in 1716, Rāj Singh's son Sāvant Singh fought in his army.[17]

THE COSMOPOLITAN PRINCE

Sāvant Singh was the third of Rāj Singh's five sons. The first son, Fateh Singh, who predeceased his father, is depicted in the official painting *Rāj Singh Receiving Fateh Singh* (fig. 1.2).[18] The second son, Sukh Singh, became a yogi against his father's will and, after rebelling against him in 1727, was put in jail.[19] Sāvant Singh thus became the crown prince of the state in the late 1720s.

Sāvant Singh is celebrated as the main sponsor of the distinctive style of Rādhā-Krishna paintings produced during his father's reign, leading some art historians to conclude that he was somewhat other-worldly inclined. While he was a great devotee, that was not the whole story. As his role in the battle of Thun makes clear, he participated in the military maneuvers of his day.

FIG. 1.2 *Rāj Singh Receiving Fateh Singh*, attributed to Dalcand, ca. 1730s. Ink, color, and gold on paper (28.6 × 22.9 cm). Private collection (Germany). Courtesy Mr. Eberhard Rist

FIG. 1.3 Nagari Kunj, residence of the Kishangarh house at Vrindavan

Sāvant Singh was a cosmopolitan man of his times. He had attended the court in Delhi from when he was a young boy, under his granduncle Bahādur Shāh. There are stories that situate him at the Delhi court at the age of ten.[20] Later on, he seems to have taken well to the refined court culture of Muḥammad Shāh "Raṅgīle," as the characteristics of the miniature paintings he commissioned make apparent. Not only their style but also the scenes they depict, including spectacular displays of fireworks on the occasion of Divālī, show the influence of Mughal culture.[21] Sāvant Singh was also inspired by Urdu poetry, popular in Delhi since the early years of Muḥammad Shāh's reign.[22]

Yet it is also true that he had a firm footing in Krishna's world. Under the pen name Nāgarīdās, he produced an enormous corpus of poetry in praise of Rādhā and Krishna. This attraction to *bhakti* is evident from early on in his life. He visited the Braj area several times while he was still young. His mother spent the last days of her life in Vrindavan, and after her death and cremation in 1728, Sāvant and his father are on record as having done a circumambulation (*parikramā*) of the environs.[23] Construction of the family house (*havelī*) in the pilgrimage town was completed in 1730. Nāgarīdās frequently stayed there when he went to the Braj area, and the residence is now known after him as Nagari Kunj (fig. 1.3).[24]

His earliest dated work, *Blossoming Wish* (Manorath-mañjarī), already expresses his desire to spend time in Vrindavan. It was written in 1723 (1780 VS):

> When will my feet thread on Vrindavan's soil?
> When will I roll in its dust, rub it on my head, and find some joy?
> (MM 2)[25]

These lines could be read as foreshadowing his eventual "retirement" to Braj. Similar themes surface in his later works. His *Dejection's Vine in Corrupt Times* (Kali-vairāgya-vallarī), written in 1738 (1795 VS), deals with the maladies of the present age, the sole remedy being refuge in Krishna's Braj. Similarly, Nāgarīdās's *Weighing Braj and Vaikuṇṭha* (Braj-vaikuṇṭh-tulā), penned in 1744 (1801 VS), compares Krishna's earthly Braj with Vishnu's royal paradise Vaikuṇṭha. These works date from before the fatal events of 1748, yet they document the prince's serious interest in Braj.

APOCALYPSE IN THE MID-EIGHTEENTH CENTURY

In 1748, Sāvant Singh's world changed. First, there was his father's death while Sāvant Singh was away in Delhi (on Vaiśākh *badī* 13), by which the prince was very affected.[26] Within a week (on *sudi* 5), he "received *rājatila*," that is, was anointed king, but he would never be able to rule.[27] Before Sāvant Singh could return home, his younger brother Bahādur Singh took advantage of his absence and usurped the throne.[28] Earlier there had been bad blood between the brothers over money. When Sāvant Singh was appointed to manage the financial affairs of Kishangarh while his father was in Delhi, Bahādur Singh was unhappy with the amount allotted to him, as documented in a letter Sāvant Singh wrote to his father, seeking his advice on the matter.[29]

Bahādur Singh, who was proud of showing off his archery skills in paintings he commissioned (fig. 1.4), also proved to be an excellent strategist in his move to take the throne. Sāvant Singh had nowhere to turn. Under normal circumstances, Sāvant Singh would have been able to rally support for his cause from several quarters in Delhi or in Rajasthan. However, in 1748 his personal hardship was dwarfed by the Mughal empire's troubles. While in Delhi at the time of his brother's usurpation, he would have sought help from the Mughals, but they were facing a severe external threat: Aḥmad Shāh Abdālī "Durrānī," the newly chosen leader of the Afghan tribes, who

FIG. 1.4 *Bahādur Singh Showing off His Skill at Archery*, Kishangarh school, ca. 1750. Ink, color, and gold on paper. Private collection (Germany). Courtesy Mr. Eberhard Rist

would prove to be disastrous for the Mughal empire. Immediately after gaining power in 1748, Durrānī invaded India and confronted the Mughals at the battle of Sirhind in March of that year.[30] Though he was defeated there, he would soon return with a vengeance. Meanwhile, this first temporary Mughal victory resulted in many Mughal casualties. Among those killed was the vazir Qamar ud-Dīn, who had been very sympathetic to the Kishangarh family and is portrayed in the aforementioned painting of Rāj Singh and Muḥammad Shāh. Shortly thereafter, the emperor himself died.[31] Sāvant Singh thus could not expect support for his cause from the emperor or from the vazir.

With Delhi now rife with strife, where else was he to turn? The young new emperor, Aḥmad Shāh (r. 1748–54), who only barely won the victory against Durrānī, was preoccupied with securing his own position. The deaths of Qamar ud-Dīn and Nizām ul-Mulk the same year brought about a total change of guard with ensuing court intrigues. Aḥmad Shāh's confidant, the eunuch Javed Ḳhān, was at odds with the new vazir, Safdar Jang, and the Mir Bakhshi, Salābat Ḳhān. When Javed Ḳhān was murdered in 1752, an all-out civil war ensued from May through November 1753.[32] The emperor and his vazir each approached Maratha parties for support, but the Marathas would eventually maneuver their own candidates into the highest positions, with Ġhāzī ud-Dīn as vazir and ʿĀlamgīr II (r. 1754–59) on the throne.[33] Amid this chaos and the uncertainty about whom to turn to, Sāvant Singh retreated to the Braj area temporarily, not yet ready to retire and give up his rights to his throne.

Meanwhile, internal threats to the empire occupied the nobles in power during this period of transition. In the Punjab, decades-long conflicts in which the Sikhs played a role worsened when the strong subedar, Zakarīya Ḳhān, died in 1745 and his sons disputed his succession.[34] Immediately south of Delhi, right in the Braj area, the Jats had reestablished a power base, and their leader, Sūraj Mal, rapaciously took advantage of the power struggles all around him, selling his services to the highest bidder and plundering the losers mercilessly.[35] Owing to his alliance with Safdar Jang, the new vazir, he became faujdar of Mathura in 1752 and received the title "Brajendra," or "ruler of Braj."[36] That did not mean, however, that he would make a natural ally for Sāvant Singh, who perhaps judged that he was too involved in the Delhi intrigues.

East of Delhi, the Rohillas tried to reestablish their power base, while also internally contesting the succession of ʿAlī Muḥammad after his death in September 1748.[37] To stop them, Safdar Jang was forced to enlist the help of Jats as well as Marathas.[38] By 1751, the Marathas drove the Rohillas into the Kumaon hills and took over the Bangash territory in the Doab.[39] Sāvant Singh turned to the Marathas for help, following them all the way to Kumaon to enlist their services. However, the Maratha defeat of the Rohillas had its own repercussions, as the Rohillas sought help from Durrānī, with whom they succeeded in defeating in turn the Marathas in 1761 in Panipat. But who could have foreseen all that in the early 1750s?

For Sāvant Singh, there was nowhere to turn to in Delhi at the imperial court in the years following 1748. Muḥammad Shāh was no longer alive, and the new emperor, embroiled in intrigues in Delhi, soon lost his throne. The old hands of the empire had died, and the new powerful nobles were preoccupied with insurgencies elsewhere in the empire. In the general confusion of where to turn, Sāvant Singh seems to have tried once more to go to Delhi, probably in 1752, but shortly before the civil war broke out, he returned to Braj.

In Rajasthan, too, Sāvant Singh was unable to secure substantial material support for his cause, as nearly all Rajput kingdoms at the time were themselves involved in conflict for their thrones. Indeed, the middle of the eighteenth century was dominated by Rajput succession struggles in which the contending parties were unanimous only in seeking help from the Marathas.[40] With the Marathas emerging as the new power brokers, Sāvant Singh too would appeal to them for help. Several Maratha players had established control over vast areas in Rajasthan and were willing to mediate in local conflicts for a price, extending their influence yet further. Various Maratha factions supported different Rajput parties in the local conflicts, often turning against their former protégés when an expected payment was not received and had to be recuperated by force. Their favorite tactic was to weaken the Rajput kingdoms by promoting their division among the quarreling parties, while at the same time extracting several concessions for themselves.

Sāvant Singh first turned for help to Jaipur, but since Jai Singh II's death in 1743 the Kacchvāhās had been fighting among themselves. The succession of the eldest son, Īśvarī Singh, was challenged by the Mewari queen's son Mādho Singh, who was supported by Mewar and Bundi and had the Holkar Marathas at his side. Īśvarī Singh promptly allied with another Maratha leader, Jayappa Scindhia. After failing to gain the throne in 1744, Mādho Singh tried again in 1748, but this time Īśvarī Singh enlisted the Jat Sūraj Mal and put up fierce resistance. Still, he eventually had to file for negotiations in August 1748.[41] The Peshva, "Nānāsāhib" Bālājī Bāji Rāo, offered arbitrage, which led to the division of the kingdom and a heavy war indemnity imposed on Īśvarī Singh.[42]

Tied up with the events in Jaipur were the affairs of Bundi. In 1729, Jai Singh II, through diplomatic alliances with the Maratha Peshva, at the time Bāji Rāo I, dethroned Buddh Singh to put his own son-in-law on the Bundi throne.[43] Buddh Singh was unable to regain his throne, though he found support from the Holkar and Scindhia Marathas. After Jai Singh's death, Buddh Singh's son, Umed Singh, mounted a challenge and managed to regain Bundi gradually from 1744 through 1748. Īśvarī Singh was eventually forced to recognize him as the rightful ruler, and that established the Marathas firmly in the Hadauti area.[44] In short, Īśvari Singh was preoccupied with his own struggles and Bundi affairs exactly when Sāvant Singh needed help.

Still, Sāvant Singh did receive some help from Īśvarī Singh, who sent him gifts on the occasion of his coronation.[45] But it was only in September 1750 that Īśvarī Singh offered more substantial help and marched with Sāvant Singh to lay siege to Rupnagar. However, due to Sāvant Singh's lack of funds, and because he was cash-strapped himself, the Jaipur king returned home.[46] By the end of 1750, Īśvarī Singh was unable to pay the tribute the Peshva demanded and, confronted with a Maratha invasion, he committed suicide. Mādho Singh became king, closing off any hope for help from Jaipur for Sāvant Singh. Moreover, Mādho Singh, too, had to face the Marathas, who now demanded payment for their support of him.[47]

Likewise, in Marwar a dynastic succession struggle was in progress amid multiple intrigues to secure Maratha help. Abhay Singh of Jodhpur had enlisted support from Malhār Rāo Holkar to squash his brother Bakht Singh's ambitions.[48] After Abhay Singh's death in Ajmer in 1749, his young son, Rām Singh, had to contend with his uncle Bakht Singh, to whom several of his nobles defected. Bakht Singh was strong: he had the confidence of the new emperor, Aḥmad Shāh, and had received the governorship of Gujarat and Ajmer. The new Mir Bakhshi, Salābat Ḳhān, was on his way to help him.[49] Mādho Singh of Jaipur, too, was on his side. Rām Singh, however, was allied with Īśvarī Singh. Both parties vied to secure the assistance of Maratha leaders and worked to undermine the other's alliances. With Holkar's neutrality secured, in 1751 Bakht Singh managed to take over Jodhpur.[50] However, soon thereafter, he died.[51] His son Bijai Singh assumed the throne and was now the one under attack. Rām Singh tried to regain his position with Jayappa Scindhia's help. Things came to a head in 1751, at which point the Kishangarhi house entered into the civil strife in Marwar.

MARATHAS TO THE RESCUE?

Sāvant Singh ended up trying to regain his throne the way most contestants at the time did: by appealing to the Marathas. He must have had prior relations with different Maratha parties, but Maratha sources first mention the rivalries between the Kishangarh brothers Bahādur Singh and Sāvant Singh in a letter dated September 20, 1750.[52] Sāvant Singh approached the Peshva's brother, Raghunāth Rāo, for help as the latter's troops under Jayappa Scindhia and Malhār Rāo Holkar were fighting the Rohillas in the North, driving them to the Terai region and Kumaon. Sāvant Singh followed them to the Himalayan area to negotiate a contract, the terms of which are unknown, but it is briefly alluded to in his *Pilgrim's Bliss* (TĀ 56). The Marathas agreed to place Kishangarh on their agenda as a stop on the way in their more extensive Rajput campaign of 1753–55.

After Sāvant Singh allied with the Marathas, his son, Sardār Singh, became heavily involved in the Marwar civil war, in the camp of the Marathas of Jayappa Scindhia who fought on the side of Abhay Singh's son, Rām Singh. Sāvant Singh's son was confronted with his uncle, Bahādur

Singh of Kishangarh, who had joined the opponent, Bijai Singh. The Kishangarhis reportedly played a major role in determining the outcome in favor of Rām Singh. Bahādur Singh retreated at a crucial moment in the battle. After Sardār Singh spread a false rumor that Bijai Singh had been killed, everyone in the enemy camp fled in a panic. Bijai, still alive, was isolated and retreated to Nagor.[53] Jayappa then laid siege to Nagor, and, confident of a swift resolution, he suggested that his general Raghunāth Rāo not come to his aid but move on to attack Rupnagar on Sāvant Singh's behalf.[54] However, the siege of Nagor was not resolved smoothly. In 1755, probably during a heated argument with the negotiators from Nagor, Jayappa was assassinated. Enraged, the Marathas murdered in revenge all Rajputs in the camp. Sardār Singh narrowly escaped the slaughter.[55] The Marathas clamored for a blood price (*mundkati*) to erect a monument for Jayappa in Pushkar.[56] Negotiations dragged on, and when peace was finally concluded in 1756 by Dattaji Scindhia, Marwar was divided between the two contesting parties and concessions were made to the Marathas, who exacted a heavy tribute and

FIG. 1.5 *Portrait of Sardar Singh, Son of Savant Singh*, Kishangarh school, ca. 1760. Ink, color, and gold on paper (image: 27.9 × 21.9 cm; overall: 34.6 × 26.6 cm). The Cleveland Museum of Art, Edwin R. and Harriet Pelton Perkins Memorial Fund 2001.122. Courtesy Cleveland Museum of Art. © The Cleveland Museum of Art

TABLE 1.1 Chronological Overview of the Second Part of Nāgarīdās's Life

Date	Broader History	Life of Sāvant Singh	Dated Works of Sāvant Singh
March 1748	Battle of Sirhind: Durrānī defeated	Sāvant Singh in Delhi	
April 1748 (1805 VS; Vaiśākh *badī* 13–14)	Death of emperor Muḥammad Shāh	Death of father, Rāj Singh	
May 1748 (1805 VS; Vaiśākh *sudi* 8)		Coronation of Sāvant Singh	
December 1748 (1805 VS Pauṣ *sudi*)			*Pad-prabodh-mālā* (in Delhi)
1749 (1806 VS)			*Rām-carit-mālā* (banks of Hindani)
September 1750		(Unsuccessful) siege of Rupnagar with Jaipur's Īśvarī Singh; first mention in Maratha correspondence	
December 1750	Suicide of Īśvarī Singh of Jaipur; succeeded by Mādho Singh	Sāvant Singh seeks alliance with Marathas	
January–February 1751 (1808 VS Māgh)	Maratha success against Rohillas in Kumaon		*Jugal-bhakt-vinod* (Kumaon)
March–April 1751 (1808 VS Madhu)			*Phāg-vihār* (banks of Gaṅgā)
1752	Sūraj Mal: "Brajendra," faujdar Mathura; Jayappa assassinated	Sāvant Singh in Delhi	
March 1752 (1809 VS *badī* Madhu)			*Van-vinod*
June–September 1752 (1809 VS Asāṛh–Bhādon)		Sāvant Singh settles in Braj	*Vṛndāban-abhilāṣ-pūran-pad-prabandh*
October 1752 (1809 VS Āśvin *sudi*)			*Bāl-vinod* (Nandagaon)
May–November 1753 (1810 VS)	Civil war in Delhi		*Tīrthānand* (Vrindavan)
January–February 1754 (1810 VS Māgh)			*Sujan-ānand* (Barsana)
1753–55	Maratha campaign in Rajasthan	Sardār Singh fights with Marathas	
March 1755		Raghunāth Rāo camps in Rupnagar	

TABLE 1.1 Chronological Overview of the Second Part of Nāgarīdās's Life (continued)

Date	Broader History	Life of Sāvant Singh	Dated Works of Sāvant Singh
May 1756		Dattaji Scindhia marches toward Rupnagar to lay siege	
June–July 1756 (1813 VS Āsāṛh):		Peace between Bahādur Singh and Sāvant Singh	
February–March 1757	Durrānī's bloodbath in Braj		
October 1757 (1814 VS Āśvin *sudi*)		Motion of understanding between Bahādur Singh and Sāvant Singh (Salemabad)	
January 1761	Durrānī defeats Marathas at Panipat		
January–February 1763 (1819 VS Māgh)			*Ban-jan-praśaṃs-granth*
September 1764 (1821 VS Bhādon *sudi*)		Death of Sāvant Singh (Vrindavan)	

stationed a contingent in Ajmer.[57] Meanwhile, Maratha military support for Sāvant Singh's cause was delayed.

Kishangarh was only incidental in this Maratha Rajasthan campaign. Raghunāth Rāo did not arrive at Rupnagar until 1755, as his encampment itinerary indicates.[58] It is unclear what the outcome was, but for Kishangarh a resolution came only later. With the Marwar treaty signed, Dattaji Scindhia reports that in early May 1756 he moved toward Rupnagar to wage war.[59] According to Kishangarhi sources, peace was concluded by June 1756.[60] The outcome was much the same as in Marwar, with the peace treaty dividing the kingdom in two, Kishangarh for Bahādur Singh and Rupnagar (with the nearby Nimbārkan seat of Salemabad) for Sāvant Singh's son, Sardār Singh, who was installed on the throne (fig. 1.5).

Finally, after a long, drawn-out war, Sāvant Singh's party thus secured, at best, a Pyrrhic victory. Still, as it turned out, the belated peace deliberations saved Sāvant Singh's life. To lend his presence to the official ceremonies, he returned home and, in doing so, escaped the marauding armies of Durrānī that plundered the Braj area in Mathura and Vrindavan in February–March 1757.[61]

Later that year, in October (Āśvin *sudi* 9, 1814 VS), a motion of understanding between Sāvant Singh and Bahādur Singh was signed in Salemabad in the presence of the Nimbārkan abbot Govinddev Ācārya. The two brothers traveled together in a chariot to Kishangarh, where the next day a ceremony took place and Sāvant Singh recognized his brother's son Birad Singh as the legitimate heir of Kishangarh.[62] The brothers also made provisions for their stepmother, "Brajdāsī." Thus concluded, the Kishangarhi case seems to have ended with less bloodshed and enmity than many others in Rajasthan.

RETIREMENT TO VRINDAVAN

During these eventful years, with help from the Marathas, Sāvant Singh managed to recover only the area around Rupnagar in 1756. Shortly after securing the alliance with the Marathas, Sāvant Singh retired to Braj, leaving Sardār Singh to take on the cause. His retreat can be dated as 1752, between the months of Āsāṛh and Bhādon (see chapter 5). He died in Vrindavan in 1764. His *samādhi* (memorial) is located near Nagari Kunj, his residence (fig. 1.6). The inscription reads as follows:[63]

> Śrī Nātha Jī
> Rādhā's Krishna, Mountain-Holder, roaming on Vrindavan's riverbanks,
> Darling of Lalitā and other friends, Lord Viṭṭhala, Mohana, let your mercy flow.
> Sāvant Singh was king in Kali Yuga, yet set an example for all:[64]
> He gave his son the kingdom, while he himself retired to Vrindavan.
> The Lord of Rupnagar had a flock of devotees, whom he cherished lovingly.
> He was a hero, profound in thought, and he delighted devotees.
> As a rule, he humbly drank water used to wash the feet of holy men.
> The sacred songs he sang amount to an ocean.
> Famous to the world as Nāgarīdās, he was handsome by the flowing grace of Rādhā (Nāgarī).
> In 1821 VS, on the second day of the bright half of Bhādon, Mahārāja Nāgarīdāsjī reached (the divine) Vr̥ndāvana.
>
> Craftsman: Khuśāl.

What was Sāvant Singh doing while his son fought with the Marathas? Do his works in the period express his worries? In some "stray" poems he reflects on his lot, somewhat bitterly:

FIG. 1.6 Sāvant Singh's *samādhi* at Vrindavan

Where there is strife, there cannot be happiness—strife stabs all joy in
the heart.
Of all strife in a kingdom, strife's basic cause is the throne.
(*Chūṭak-dohā* 12)[65]

You do not rejoice in love for God, the essence of all bliss.
Even if you are king, so what? A slave you are, shouldering the
country's load!
(*Chūṭak-dohā* 18)[66]

Both these verses illustrate the weariness of his strife for the throne. The latter verse doubts even the value of a successful outcome, for were he to regain his kingdom, he would remain distracted by worldly affairs, secondary to life's real purpose. This verse perhaps anticipates the solace that he was to find later in devotion.

Notwithstanding all the hardship in his personal life, Nāgarīdās wrote several works after 1748 that celebrate the joyful aspects of Rādhā-Krishna devotion, giving them titles that end in *-vinod* or *-ānand*, both words for "bliss." In addition to the pilgrimage report he penned in 1753, *The Pilgrim's Bliss*, he wrote *Amusements of Two Devotees* (Jugal-bhakt-vinod; 1751), *Amusements in the Woodland* (Van-vinod; 1752), *Childhood Amusements* (Bāl-vinod; 1752), and *Gaiety on the In-Laws' Get-Together* (Sujan-ānand; 1754).[67] Rather than writing works in a world-weary tone, Nāgarīdās concentrates on celebrations of *bhakti*. Nearly all of these works are in a lighter tone, and the latter three relate incidents in Krishna's early life, replete with laughter and banter. *Childhood Amusements* and *Amusements in the Woodland* center on practical jokes Krishna played on his friends, and *Gaiety on the In-Laws' Get-Together* focuses on the joyful meeting of Krishna's and Rādhā's parents, with ample room for the teasing and joking (*gālī*) that such gatherings occasion. All three works are permeated with *hāsya rasa*, or "comedy," and were inspired by folksy plays performed during religious festivals in the Braj area.[68] If this literary output is an indication, Sāvant Singh found peace and bliss by moving to the pilgrimage center of Braj and by relocating the purpose of his life firmly in the divine.

While much of the contemporary Mughal elite wrote about doomsday scenarios, exile from Delhi, and nostalgia for the past, in works that fall under the genre of "the city destroyed," or *śahr āśob*, Nāgarīdās wrote works of "bliss."[69] As a devotional poet, he turned to a genre of poetic expression that encouraged immersion in a joyful celebration of divine love. The genre of *śahr āśob*, too, grew out of a celebration of a "continual dalliance" but of "all the beautiful people in the city" with the narrator. In the eighteenth century, though, *śahr āśob* authors "chose to articulate their feelings . . . by lamenting or lampooning the state of cultural decline and an absence of commerce and love in a darker mode of expression, thus working within the same tradition by reversing it."[70] In short, in *śahr āśob*, a riotous celebration of love turned into a genre of nostalgic longing or bitter lampooning. In contrast, Nāgarīdās did not allow the military tumult of the eighteenth century to cast its shadow on the eternal bliss of the *līlā* of Braj.

While Krishna devotional poetry often is otherworldly and conventional, in this rare case we have a wealth of information on the life of the individual devotee who created the poetry. By tracing the effect of Nāgarīdās's personal circumstances in his work, we can see how religion helped him cope with crisis as he reconstructed his identity by rewriting his life narrative into the world of sages and gods.

2 Gods and Saints Relocated

Sectarian Rivalries and Hinduism in the Making

AFTER BEING SWEPT UP IN THE MID-EIGHTEENTH-CENTURY political developments, Sāvant Singh must have found relief and solace in Krishna's world in Braj. The painting of Sāvant Singh as Krishna, who in turn is playing yogi (fig. 1.1 and book cover), could well deceive us into thinking that he safely arrived in a religious haven and retired from the world of politics (if not from that of beautiful women). However, the Braj at the time was not a sleepy, idyllic forest island isolated from the world. Far from being lost in devotion to Krishna, immune to the eventful shifts of the eighteenth century, it found itself in the midst of lively (sometimes bitter) controversy.

In the first half of the eighteenth century, momentous religious changes were in the offing. Political events had repercussions everywhere. There was an exodus of the gods themselves, their images carried from Braj into safety to other surrounding areas, escaping the marauding armies of Muslims and Hindus alike (usually mixed anyways). One could say it was a time during which gods were on the move. Following these images, saints were on the move, too. Thus the Kishangarh prince could not escape politics. His location in Kishangarh was close to important Sufi and Jaina shrines, all part of the cosmopolitan Mughal world. Now in Vrindavan he found himself in intersectarian struggles between different Vaishnava groups. Yet what was taking place was not just regional sectarian squabbles but an important moment in the formation of Hindu orthodoxy. Behind much of the upheaval were the reform policies that had been introduced by his senior colleague, the Kacchvāhā ruler of Amer (later Jaipur), Savāī Jai Singh II (r. 1700–1743). This king had mobilized the different sects at his court to come up with a consistent formulation of Hindu orthodoxy. Due to his influence, which extended well beyond Jaipur, these reforms had far-reaching effects. It could be argued that this was a foundational phase in the formulation of Hinduism as we know it.

JAIPUR MOBILIZATIONS TOWARD ORTHODOX HINDUISM

Jai Singh II held a high position at the Mughal court, yet all the while he maneuvered to ensure his independence and the enlargement of his own sphere of influence. It was his religious reform policy that led to a grand-scale reform movement in Vaishnavism.[1] His case is not that of a "Hindu" ruler legitimating his participation in a "Muslim" imperial formation, as the hindsight of the twentieth century might see it, but rather one of a ruler justifying his personal preference for one Hindu group within the tradition of *bhakti*. The orthodoxy of this group was questioned by the traditional Hindu power brokers at his court, thus challenging the ruler's legitimacy. Significantly, as the king worked with his advisers to formulate what constitutes ritual orthodoxy, he furthered the construction of what is now understood as "Hinduism."[2]

Jai Singh II instituted theological, social, and military reforms, sponsoring conferences on these topics.[3] His theological reform forced all sects to make their philosophical position explicit and establish their orthodoxy by aligning themselves with one of the four major orthodox sects (Catuḥ-sampradāya), that is, the Rāmānuja-, Mādhva-, Viṣṇusvāmī-, or Nimbārka-Sampradāyas. To this effect they had to submit commentaries on the classical scriptures, such as *Brahma-sūtra*. Not satisfied with such a show of philosophical self-definition, the king meddled in all kind of sectarian scholastic debates. By making royal patronage contingent on the ability to prove one's theological credentials, he caused an uptake in the eighteenth century of the production of theological digests and commentaries, as well as hagiographies that aimed to forge links with the orthodox Sampradāyas and to take distance from suspect tenets and practices that had fallen out of favor.

Jai Singh II instituted social reforms to make *bhakti* sects comply with caste orthopraxis, or *varṇāśrama-dharma*.[4] In particular, he discouraged interdining between different castes and forbade gurus to be ascetics (*sanyāsīs*), who fell outside the caste system. The immediate reason was that the king needed orthodox married householders (*gṛhastha*) to officiate as priests at his Vedic rituals, but the consequences went far beyond. Abbots presiding over monasteries came under pressure to marry to prove themselves worthy of royal patronage or else leave Jai Singh's kingdom.[5] Jai Singh's diktats led to several sectarian succession disputes, where ascetic successors were challenged by the king's handpicked orthodox householder candidate. Among the other ritual issues that became controversial were rules of food consumption, such as a ban against eating leftovers of religious leaders, of fasting, such as the accommodation of the *ekādaśī* fast (on the eleventh day of the fortnight), and on initiation practices, especially those involving branding.[6] Much of this revolved around how to reconcile orthodox Smārta rites with Vaishnava devotion. An important consequence was the exclusion of low-castes from monastic orders.

Military reforms included demilitarization of "disorganized elements," counterbalanced with the organization of a coordinated body of warrior ascetics to defend Vaishnavism in North India.[7] While sometimes misunderstood as a defense against Islam, at the time it was perceived as a response to Daśanāmī ascetic warriors' power.[8] Jai Singh, from his side, was keen to limit the influence of the mighty ascetic warrior groups (Rāmānandī, Dādū-panthī, and Nimbārkan) in the Jaipur army and sought to enforce and defend the centralized Vaishnava system he regulated.[9]

While Jai Singh instigated these reforms, many other actors influenced the king's policy, all with their own agendas and patterns of circulation. The Maharashtrian faction of Smārta Brahmins at the Jaipur court insisted on *varṇāśrama-dharma*.[10] Many of them had been recruited from Benares, where they had moved after the fall of the Vijayanagara empire.[11] The Vaishnavas at court played an important role, too. Foremost was the Gauḍīya-Sampradāya, which drew its inspiration from the early sixteenth-century Bengali saint Caitanya and was the king's favorite. The Gauḍīya deity Govindadeva moved from Braj to be installed in Jai Singh's new capital-to-be in 1716. The transfer of the deity also entailed a circulation of people and ideas, as its caretakers hailed not just from the Braj area but also from Bengal. The Gauḍīyas' own internal theological debates were sharpened in the intense efforts to justify their presence at the Kacchvāhā court.[12] At the Jaipur court, interest groups from the past, such as the Vallabhans and Rāmānandīs, keen to preserve their own deities' privileges, took issue with the newcomers' (lack of) theological credentials.[13] The king's reforms thus were influenced by the agendas pushed by several interested parties.

Jai Singh insisted on maintaining the rules of *varṇāśrama-dharma*, which he painstakingly had his advisers work out. Within the king's domain of authority the reforms affected many religious groups. Krishna worshippers (Vallabhans, Gauḍīyas, Nimbārkans, Haridāsīs, and Rādhāvallabhīs), as well as Rāma worshippers (different factions of Rāmānandīs, who were very influential at the Kacchvāhā court), and even groups with Muslim followers (such as Dādū-panthīs and Lāl-panthīs) saw themselves obliged to conform to the new rules. How much this carried over in reality is not always easy to determine, but it resulted in a general shift toward Brahminization and conservatism.

The contentious process of consensus building that went into the formation of modern Hinduism led to new articulations of theological tracts. The increase in production of theological works was due largely to their authors' material dependence on the king, who pressed for orthodoxy. Some works were commissioned by the king to back up his position, and others were responses in opposition to it. Analysis of Nāgarīdās's works helps to illustrate how these reforms were received and what their limits were. By the middle of the eighteenth century, after Jai Singh passed away and was no longer there to push them through, his reforms played out in different ways for different groups.

THE VALLABHA-SAMPRADĀYA AND KISHANGARH'S ŚRĪ NĀTHA JĪ

Most observers have stressed the connection of the Kishangarh court with the Vallabha-Sampradāya, one of the most influential sects devoted to Krishna. The court itself certainly encouraged this strong connection, as it endures even today. The sectarian greeting "Jay Śrī Krishna" is still heard all over the old city of Kishangarh. Most art historians stress the Vallabhan influence in their works on Kishangarh and speculate on the impact of the sect's theology and ritual on the famous Kishangarhi paintings.[14] Three out of four editions of the work of Nāgarīdās also ascribe the influence of the sect to his poetry.[15] In the following background sketch of this particular sectarian tradition and its reception in Kishangarh, the picture turns out to be far from static.

PREHISTORY OF THE VALLABHA-SAMPRADĀYA

The Vallabha-Sampradāya was named after the saint Vallabhācārya (1478–1530), known in the sect as Ācārya jī. He was a theologian, writing Sanskrit works expounding his philosophical understanding called Śuddhādvaita, or "pure monism." The gist of this is that the world is nothing but Krishna, who is also Brahman. Vallabha strongly disagreed with Śaṅkara's Advaita, or monism, which posited that the world was all one single Brahman, but appears manifold due to the mysterious power of *māyā* (delusion). Hence Śaṅkara's followers are denigratingly called *māyāvādins*, or "propounders of *māyā*." Like other devotional thinkers, Vallabha instead allowed for a differentiation between God and mankind, and rather than intellectual grasping of the ultimate reality, he recommended *bhakti*, or devotional love. This does not require an ascetic way of life, but can be realized by householders, within the material world, which is, after all, also part of God. Since liberation is possible only via God's grace, the sect is also called Puṣṭi-mārga, or "path of grace."[16]

While based in Arail and Benares, Vallabha undertook many missionary tours, according to sectarian sources. In the Braj area, he is described as closely involved in the discovery of the deity called Śrī Nātha jī at Govardhan.[17] Under the tenure of Vallabha's son, Viṭṭhalnāth (1516–1586), the sect gained exclusive control over the shrine of this deity, seen to be a *svarūpa*, or full manifestation of the divine. The loving worship offered to the image involves elaborate eight-times-a-day (*aṣṭayāma*) rituals and seasonal festivities throughout the year.[18] All deities of the sect, including those that once belonged to Vallabha, are worshiped following this model.[19] Viṭṭhalnāth, known in the sect as Gusāī jī, resided mostly at Gokul in Braj, where he built splendid *havelīs* for his family and the deities they worshipped. He expanded the sect by securing patronage from rich merchants in Gujarat and was influential enough to obtain land grants from the Mughal rulers.[20]

Descriptions of the sect's recruitment practices and the leaders' preaching appear in the stories about Vallabha's and Viṭṭhalnāth's disciples that initially circulated orally but came to be written down in the seventeenth century, the so-called Vārtā (story) literature in Braj prose.[21] The most famous works are *Story of Eighty-Four Disciples* (Caurāsī Vaiṣṇavan kī Vārtā) and *Story of Two Hundred Fifty-Two Disciples* (Do Sau Bāvan Vaiṣṇavan kī Vārtā). Among the disciples, a group of eight, four of Vallabha's and four of Viṭṭhalnāth's, are called the Aṣṭ-chāp (lit. "Eight Poetic Signatures"): Sūrdās, Paramānanddās, Kumbhandās, Krishnadās Adhikārī (the head of the Śrī Nātha jī temple), Caturbhujdās, Nanddās, Chītsvāmī, and Govindsvāmī. They were assigned to sing for the image of Śrī Nātha jī, and their songs are still sung today in front of the deity. Their poetry testifies to the divine visions they had access to in their roles as friends of Krishna (*sakhā*) by day and girlfriends (*sakhī*) by night.

Viṭṭhalnāth's seven sons inherited the right of initiation in the sect, and it still exclusively rests with their descendants, called Mahārājas. There thus are seven *gaddīs* (seats), or centers of orthodoxy (and an eighth one by an adoptive son). Each son also inherited the worship of one of Vallabha's images.[22] The most prestigious Śrī Nātha jī shrine went to Viṭṭhalnāth's eldest son, and his descendants have controlled it ever since; this house is the foremost and is called Tilakāyat. Most of these images migrated out of Braj, for which the iconoclasm of the Mughal emperor Aurangzeb is often blamed. Some of the images were moved due to internal rivalries between the *gaddīs* (such as Śrī Dvārkānātha jī, the image of the third *gaddī*) or due to political unrest.[23]

Most eventually ended up in Rajasthan, where they were lavishly sponsored by Rajput rulers. In 1671, Śrī Nātha jī came to reside in the Mewar kingdom, in the town now called after him, Nathdvara. He has since been joined by other Vallabhan images. In addition to Vallabha's original treasured images (*nidhi-svarūpas*), Vallabha's descendants consecrated several images and gave them to devotees. Those images are called *puṣṭi-svarūpas*, as they have been consecrated by the "grace" of the important gurus of the sect.[24] It was one of those images that became important for Kishangarh.

A VALLABHAN IMAGE FOR KISHANGARH

The Kishangarh connection with the Vallabhans may have been there right from the start. Its founder, Kishan Singh, worshipped an image of Nṛtyagopāla (in fact two images, one of Krishna and one of Balarāma) that was purportedly Vallabhan.[25] At the same time, Kishan Singh was very close to Jahāngīr, and the later Kishangarh rajas are on record as having fought for the Mughals valiantly in the Deccan, at the North-West Frontier, as well as in Bengal throughout the seventeenth century.[26] Mughal service and Vallabhan devotion were not seen to be in contradiction.

How the Vallabhan image came to be established in the kingdom in the mid-seventeenth century, just before the exodus of the Braj images, was

FIG. 2.1 Temple of Śrī Kalyāṇarāya Jī at Kishangarh fort (photo by Swapna Sharma). Courtesy Swapna Sharma

closely tied up with the Mughal service of the Kishangarh rulers. By this time, Rūp Singh was the ruler. He had strong connections with the Vallabhans in Braj and brought the image, known in contemporary sources as Śrī Govardhananātha jī and now known as Śrī Kalyāṇarāya jī, to establish it in his newly founded capital, Rupnagar (the image is now in Kishangarh; fig. 2.1). Rūp Singh was also a general in the Mughal army, battling in Balkh and Qandahar for Shāh Jahān.[27] The court poet Vrind, in his epic poem on Rūp Singh's life, describes the Mughals' North-West Frontier campaign in which Rūp Singh partook in 1646 (in the text given as 1702 VS).[28] Vrind celebrates the (short-lived) military success[29] and continues in laconic bardic, occasionally rhyming, prose:

> In the world he obstructed his enemies, meeting them metal for metal. His heart remained steadfast through battle after battle. Summons issued from the emperor. Proud of his accomplishments, he paid obeisance. The emperor received him very kindly, gave him a mansab, and let him return to his land. He came by way of Braj. He visited the temple of Śrī Nātha. So pleased he was, joy filled his heart. (RV 143)

He elaborates:

> In the year 1704 VS (1647 CE), he arrived in the Braj area.
> His heart unwavering, he immersed himself in the deepest bliss of
> God's name.
> (RV 144)

> The guru instructed him with the mantra of God's immaculate name.
> Love overwhelmed him, devotion flared up like a flame.
> (RV 145)

The bard does not give any specifics about the guru, beyond that he was located in Braj, but Kishangarhi tradition sees him as Vallabhan.[30] The name of the image he received is now understood to be Śrī Kalyāṇarāya jī, though the bard calls it simply Śrī Nātha jī.[31] Vrind provides more information:

> He received a vision and a command in a joyous dream:
> "Please take Śrī Nātha jī to Rupnagar and install him there."
> (RV 147)

Next, he describes the transformation of Rupnagar into fitting surroundings for a Krishna image, that is, a Braj-like cowherd paradise (RV 148). The year-round project of transforming the urban landscape, described by seasons (RV 149–50), would culminate in the festival of Annakūṭa in Kārtik (RV 151).[32] This transformation of the secular urban into the religious rural space over six seasons is mirrored in a ripening of the king's devotion following the nine-step program of *bhakti*.[33] Finally, the bard concludes:

> Thus he became accomplished in ninefold devotion. He immersed his heart in Śrī Nātha jū:[34] listened to beautiful recitation of *Bhāgavata-purāṇa* and *Bhagavad-gītā*, listened to the (Mahā)bhārata. That way he realized harmony of worldly (*svārtha*) and spiritual goals (*paramārtha*). He was a follower of the Vaishnava path, benefactor of devotees. He was a great patron, like an incarnation of Ambarīṣa.[35] Embodying the whole earth, he was an incomparable king, His Highness Rūp.
>
> (RV 168)[36]

And with that, the devotional interlude is over and the king goes off to his next campaign in Qandahar.[37] Later on, he also fights the Rāṇā of Mewar and destroys the fort of Citaur.[38] The Mewar kings were also Vallabhans, but the alliances were not necessarily determined by religious affinities.[39]

In short, the devotional interlude is sandwiched between two campaigns in the service of the Mughals.[40] The acquisition of the Vallabhan image for Rupnagar occurs en route from Delhi after a campaign in Afghanistan. This story illustrates well the patterns of circulation in the Mughal empire, from provincial center to cosmopolitan Delhi, on to the far West for the campaigns, and back to Delhi, with finally a stop in the pilgrimage center, possibly out of thanksgiving for a successful campaign before returning home to Rajasthan. Far from being isolated, then, the pilgrimage center of Braj was, thanks to its proximity to the imperial capital and its accessibility via roads dating from the sultanate, very much in the hub of things. Significantly, this political appropriation of the Vallabhan image for a new capital predates the installation of the now more famous Śrī Nātha jī image in Nathdvara by nearly a quarter century. While the latter is often said to have "fled" Aurangzeb's iconoclastic zeal, the former image's move to Rajasthan took place in the midst of Rajput-Mughal cooperation.[41]

A similar trajectory is described in a mid-nineteenth-century chronicle regarding Śrī Brajarāja jī's transfer to Kota in the early eighteenth century. Kota's king, Bhīm Singh I (r. 1707–20), had gone to Delhi to congratulate the new emperor Muḥammad Shāh and, on this auspicious occasion, was invited to put in a request for a gift. He asked to be confirmed in whatever land he could conquer by sword. From Delhi he went to Braj, where he was initiated in the Vallabha-Sampradāya and obtained the tutelary image known as Śrī Brajanātha jī (called in the text Śrī Nātha jī). He, too, "transformed" his capital into Krishna's world, renaming it Nandagaon, after Krishna's parental village. But this appears to have been part of an elaborate ruse. The king, immediately after his initiation, is said to have staged his own cremation, which enticed the neighboring king of Bundi to invade Kota. However, Bhīm Singh "as a ghost" drove out the invader and pursued him to Bundi, where he plundered the treasury. With Śrī Brajanātha jī prominently placed at the head of his army, he continued to conquer more territories, in which the emperor was now obliged to confirm him.[42] In the Kota case, there seems to be a felicitous convergence between the king's political ambitions, his devotional aspirations as embodied in the image, and his dealings with the Mughal overlord. For the Kishangarh ruler Rūp Singh, however, a subtle contrast can instead be detected.

SONG FROM THE BATTLEFIELD

Tension between political activity and religious commitment is an important theme in one episode of the hagiographic text ascribed to Nāgarīdās, *Garland of Stories and Songs* (PPM 64), which deals with the close relation of Rūp Singh with the Śrī Nātha jī image he installed in Rupnagar. In this account, Rūp Singh is far away in Balkh and longing for his home. As Nāgarīdās puts it: "Without good company (*satsaṅga*), his mind was distressed." Melancholic, Rūp Singh composed a prayer-song, in which he contrasted home with the "half demons" in Balkh. He sent this plea to bring him back home to Rupnagar, with instructions to the temple servants (*bhītariyā*s) to put this "petition" at the feet of the image. They did accordingly, and on that very day Rūp Singh received the summons to return to his country.

This story also illustrates a come-and-go between temple and battlefield. In the court poet's version, the overwhelming theme is Rūp Singh's *svāmī-bhakti*, defined as loyalty for the feudal overlord, that is, the Mughal emperor. In Nāgarīdās's account, perhaps redacted by the temple priests, Rūp Singh's identity as the Krishna image's devotee is stressed. Even in service of the Mughals, his heart is shown to be Rajasthani and Vaishnava.

This prayer-poem by Rūp Singh is not a sole swan song. His works have not been published, but Sāvant Singh, his grandson, included in his collection *String of Song-Pearls* three other *pada*s by his grandfather.

Attired in forest garb, he returns to Braj from the woods.
His flute play attracts the young girls—irresistibly—singing Rāga Gaurī.
The girlfriends—deeply gratified—gaze at darling Giridhara's lotus body.
As he, from the corner of his eye, steals a glance at his darling's beauty,
Rūp Singh, the girlfriend, approves.[43]

(PMĀ 197)[44]

In this first poem, the poet identifies himself in the last line (*chāpa*) as "Rūp Alī," that is, as a girlfriend of Rādhā. He describes Krishna coming home from herding cows in the forest all day or, rather, the effect he has on the women in the village, especially as he casts a sidelong glance at Rādhā. All the girlfriends, including Rūp Singh, are delighted. The king thus casts himself in a feminine role.

"Mohana with his elongated eyes
Is keen to behold sweet beauty. My heart is attached to him.
To stop me, Mother and Father chide: 'Aren't you ashamed?' Yet not even so.
Crazy for love for my Gopāla, there's none I wouldn't curse!"
In the twilight, as she came out of the shed, milk pail in hand,
Rūp Singh: that Lord, the Clever Mountain-Lifter, raised a brow and stole her heart.

(PMĀ 221)[45]

In this second poem, a Gopī (cowherdess) makes an exasperated comment about Krishna's power over her, which makes her shameless. In the final line, Rūp Singh reveals what happened: she had an encounter with Krishna at the shed after she milked the cows. Here, too, Rūp Singh seems to pose as a girlfriend in the know of Rādhā's secret. Like the previous poem, this one also has the distinctive formula identifying the king in the *chāpa*: "*rūpa singha prabhu nagadhara nāgara*." This reference to his *iṣṭa-devatā* (favorite image) Nagadhara Nāgara, rather than Śrī Nātha jī, detracts from the Vallabhan claim that he was initiated in their sect.

"How could I come? The lightning scares me.
It throws discs with sparklers whenever I leave to meet my love.
He's so clever and eager, O friend, he can halt the night just like that.
The sky thunders, the breeze blows restlessly, I can't keep my shawl in place to cover me."

Hearing the words of his darling, Clever Krishna went to meet her, to please his lady.
Rūp Singh: that Lord, the Clever Mountain-Lifter, joined her to sing the notes of Malhāra.

(PMĀ 622)[46]

In this third poem, Rādhā is afraid to rendezvous with Krishna because of the storm and argues that he should come to her, which he does. That he is coaxed into doing so by the go-between, identified with Rūp Singh, is understood.

There is nothing particularly Vallabhan about these three poems. The king imagined in the role of a *sakhī* in the divine *līlā*, known as *sakhī-bhāva*, is usually seen as characteristic of other Rādhā-centered sects from Vrindavan, notably the Haridāsīs.[47] In Vallabhan sources, the king is interpreted as playing a role in the divine *līlā*, but mostly not as a *sakhī*.

VALLABHAN SECTARIAN VIEWS ON KISHANGARH

The most famous Śrī Nātha jī himself was reputed to have stopped in Kishangarh territory on his journey through Rajasthan, as related in *The Story of the Manifestation of Śrī Nātha jī* (Śrī Nātha jī kī Prākaṭya Vārtā). This Vārtā text, or "sectarian history," is ascribed to the prolific Harirāy (traditional dates 1590–1715).[48] Harirāy was Viṭṭhalnāth's great-grandson and was initiated by his illustrious uncle Gokulnāth of the fourth *gaddī*. The story is supposed to be roughly contemporary with the events of the journey and starts out with the discovery or manifestation (*prākaṭya*) of the image of Śrī Nātha jī and the installation of its worship.[49] The bulk of the text describes the image's journey to its current site in Rajasthan and is somewhat confused, with many stages.[50] Śrī Nātha jī is said to have left Braj in 1669 (1726 VS, Āśvin *sudi* 15), concealed in a cart, with his caretakers Gosvāmīs Govind jī on a horse in front and Bālkrishna jī right behind the cart, fully weaponed. They were accompanied by a third Gosvāmī, Vallabh jī, who was responsible for the cooking, with some help from Bālkrishna and the womenfolk.[51] By the time they reached Kishangarh, they had been on the road for a while, having previously halted in Agra, Dandoti Ghat, Kota, and Bundi. The Kishangarh episode is as follows:

> The king of Kishangarh, Rūp Singh, was a great devotee (*bhagavadīya*), who had become a worshipper (*sevaka*) of Śrī Dīkṣit jī (or Śrī Viṭṭhaleśvar Dīkṣit). But he gave up his body fighting in the battle for the emperor.[52] At

> that time, he had just had an ornament framed. Now he gave it to a barber servant of his who was nearby and said: "Take this ornament and donate it to Śrī Nātha jī, who is housed on top of Śrī Girirāj. Then come back." So the barber went to Śrī Nātha jī and donated the diamond ornament. He had *darshana* of the Rājbhog Ārtī (i.e., the ceremony for the main evening meal), before coming down the hill. Now on top of Dandotī rock he had seen the *svarūpa* of Raja Rūp Singh, who was wearing a yellow sash, with a saffron upper shawl wrapped around him, and with a *tilaka-mudrā* (forehead mark and stamp). That is the Lord's true form with spirtitual power (*teja*). While he had given up his earthly body on the battlefield, he took on a spiritual body that entered the temple of Śrī jī. Everyone had seen him go into the temple, but none saw him come out again. Then all said: "Raja Rūp Singh jī has entered Śrī jī's *līlā*."[53]

Here in the final apotheosis, Rūp Singh is incorporated into the Vallabhan universe, into the divine *līlā* itself. As his mortal body dies on the battlefield, a martyr for the emperor's cause, his spiritual body enters the divine *līlā* via the temple in Braj. Notably, *sakhī-bhāva* is absent in this sectarian account. Instead, the focus is on the costly last gift that the king, as he lay dying on the battlefield, sent via his barber. This focus is in line with the Sampradāya's embrace of the material world. The gift is not considered impure due to the circumstances in which it was sent or the source of the wealth that could afford it. There is no tension between imperial and religious causes apparent from this story.

As is typical of Vārtā literature, this story is told in flashback, as Śrī Nātha jī, en route to his final destination, enters the territory of his devotees, who previously used to come to him. The prior connections with his devotees are related in order to make sense of Śrī Nātha jī's current journey. After this brief prologue, the story continues with Śrī Nātha jī's adventures. By the time Śrī Nātha jī arrives in Kishangarh, Rūp Singh's son Mān Singh is on the throne, and of course he, too, is a devotee, although he is less ardent than expected considering his father's credentials. The Gosvāmī caretakers of Śrī Nātha jī, as is their wont, do not proceed to the capital, but cautiously halt instead in an idyllic place in the wilderness nearby:

> That King Rūp Singh's son, Mān Singh jī, had become the king of Kishangarh at the time that Śrī jī arrived in the land of Kishangarh on his cart. So when Mān Singh jī heard that Śrī jī had arrived, he thought: "Śrī Nātha jī from Braj has come to my country and he is my preferred deity, so it is not

> proper for me to eat or drink before I've caught his *darshana*." So he came for Śrī jī's *darshana*. In the wilderness, there was a jungle of *ḍhāk* trees (*Butea frondosa*). That's where the ruined village by the name of Ajamītī was situated. There was a very beautiful lake and a river and many mountain waterfalls. That is where Śrī jī's cart had stopped. So when he reached there, King Mān Singh had *darshana* of Śrī jī. Taking him to be a Vaishnava, Govind jī gave him *darshana*. Then the king pleaded with Govind jī: "Maharaj, if you would stay here openly, the *mleccha* (barbarian) will know, but please stay incognito in my country, and I will be totally devoted to your service." Śrī Govind jī had the question put to Śrī jī. Śrī jī commanded: "This is a very enjoyable mountain; there are a lot of *ḍhāk* trees here and *kesū* flowers. For that reason we will celebrate the spring season here. Afterward we shall move on. We won't just stay here." Thereafter he celebrated the swing festival (*ḍolotsava*) right there. He was in residence also for the spring season and also some of the hot season. Thereafter they moved on to Marwar.[54]

Mān Singh comes across as somewhat lukewarm about the arrival of what is asserted to be his *iṣṭa-devatā* in his territories. He is unable or unwilling to defy the *mleccha* (said in the footnotes to be Aurangzeb) and suggests only a secret stay. With this proposal of a compromise solution, the Vārtā text betrays a tension between service of God and the emperor, something that was absent from the bardic text from Kishangarh. The hagiography by Nāgarīdās indicated a sense of contradiction in relating Rūp Singh's homesickness during a campaign, but not an intrinsic one in serving God or the emperor. Even in *The Story of the Manifestation of Śrī Nātha jī*, there is no disapproval expressed by the Gosvāmīs about Mān Singh's deferral to the Mughal or by Śrī Nātha jī, who still decides to spend the season on the spot.

NĀGARĪDĀS AND THE VALLABHA-SAMPRADĀYA

There can be no doubt that the Vallabha-Sampradāya had a profound impact on the house of Kishangarh. Yet to ascribe the influence on Nāgarīdās's work as specific to this particular sect rather than more broadly to Krishna *bhakti* in general may be misleading. Nāgarīdās himself did not have a narrow sectarian outlook and associated with *bhakta*s of different denominations (as will become apparent). Arguments about the issue of his initiation are fraught, but a review here of the more convincing points in favor of the Vallabhan connection can be counterbalanced with those in favor of the Nimbārkans in the next section.

The most convincing internal evidence for a Vallabhan connection is the inclusion of poems in praise of Vallabhācārya in Nāgarīdās's *Garland of Festivals* (Utsav-mālā).[55] These poems, though, are not included in all manuscripts.[56] It remains unclear which version came first, the one with the Vallabhan poems or the one without, let alone what was intended by Nāgarīdās. External evidence cited for the Vallabhan initiation is the inscription on Sāvant Singh's *samādhi* in Vrindavan. However, that has to do less with Sāvant Singh's own ideas than with the people who sought to remember him. A second piece of external evidence is a painting purportedly of Sāvant Singh as crown prince worshipping the image of Śrī Kalyāṇarāya.[57] Unfortunately, the identification of Sāvant Singh is not supported by an inscription or resemblance to other portraits. Even so, that Sāvant Singh worshipped the image his ancestor brought from Braj is not a compelling indicator of his own sectarian identity. A more convincing piece of evidence would be a gorgeous painting of Vallabha against the background of Mount Govardhan that has been attributed to Nihālcand and thus would have been sponsored very likely by Sāvant Singh.[58]

Analysis of Nāgarīdās's text does not detect any special Vallabhan bias. His hagiography (*Garland of Stories and Songs*) is influenced by Vallabhan Vārtā literature, but he does not present a sectarian version of the stories. In his pilgrimage account (*The Pilgrim's Bliss*), Nāgarīdās pays very little attention to Vallabhan sites. To be sure, he mentions Govardhan but, remarkably, not *darshana* in the temple of Śrī Nātha jī. He does not mention spending any time at all in Gokul or celebrating the major festivals in any of the Vallabhan temples. Nor does he mention any of the numerous *baiṭhak*s (memorial sites) of Vallabha and his kin in the places he did visit. While there was undoubtedly strong Vallabhan influence in his family, there were other religious influences on Nāgarīdās as well.

THE NIMBĀRKA-SAMPRADĀYA AND THE MONASTERY AT SALEMABAD

In addition to the Vallabhans, another sect devoted to Krishna, the Nimbārka-Sampradāya, was influential at the Kishangarh court in the eighteenth century. Its major seat was nearby, in Salemabad Pīṭh, a monastery situated between Kishangarh and Rupnagar (fig. 2.2), a location that would have allowed intimate connection with the Kishangarh court. During the eighteenth and into the nineteenth century, the resident monks were militant sadhus, who engaged in fighting in Rajput service. While little attention

FIG. 2.2
Nimbārkan monastery at Salemabad

has been paid to this sect, in English or Hindi scholarship, it was equally as influential as the Vallabha-Sampradāya during this period. Attempts by Nimbārkans to remedy this amnesia have included publishing editions of Nāgarīdās's works that counter the claim of Vallabhan influence over Sāvant Singh and the paintings he patronized and establishing instead a claim of Nimbārkan influence.[59] Vrajvallabh Śaraṇ Vedāntācārya, a prominent spokesperson and scholar of the Nimbārkans, spearheaded this effort. In response to his polemics, in turn, the courtier Faiyāz Alī Khān published his own work to reaffirm the Vallabhan credentials.[60] This controversy continues locally today. A look into sources on the Kishangarh court discloses it connections with this lesser-known sect.

PREHISTORY OF THE NIMBĀRKA-SAMPRADĀYA

The founding date of the Nimbārka-Sampradāya is much debated, but it traces its origins to the thirteenth century, which would make it one of the oldest sects worshipping Krishna as Gopāla in North India. It may also have been the earliest to introduce the worship of Rādhā, though this may be a later element.[61] The founder, Nimbārkācārya (Nimbāditya), seems to have been an ascetic Tailanga Brahmin. While asserting the ultimate identity of the universe and man with God, he, too, sought to make room for devotion by introducing a difference between man and God. He developed his own philosophical system, called Svabhāvika-bhedābheda, or "natural difference in non-difference," a response to Śaṅkara's Advaita and Rāmānuja's Viśiṣṭādvaita (qualified monism), and authored his own commentary on the *Brahma-sūtra*.[62] For ascetics, initiation in the sect involves, in addition to the usual Vaishnava elements, also branding on the body the sectarian marks of the disc (*cakra*) and conch (*śaṅkha*) of Vishnu.[63]

The sect's presence in the Braj area dates to at least the sixteenth century, possibly earlier. It established itself first in Mathura and later in Vrindavan, at which point leadership seems to have moved to local Gauḍa Brahmins, such as Śrī Bhaṭṭ (fl. 1525–75). At the same time, literary output shifted from Sanskritic philosophical to Braj devotional textual production.[64] A revival occurred under the charismatic leader Harivyāsdev Ācārya (fl. 1568–1618), who reportedly sent twelve ascetic disciples out to propagate the sect and who also founded householder lineages.[65] The Nimbārkans are organized into different branches (*śākhā*; also called "doors," or *dvāra*), like the Vallabhans, but the difference is that they also have ascetic lineages, two of which are still prominent today.[66]

The branch with its main seat (*pīṭha*) in Salemabad in the Kishangarhi area was founded by Paraśurām. The influential hagiography, Nābhādās's *Garland of Devotees* (Bhakt-māl), says he was a follower of Śrī Bhaṭṭ and Harivyās, proselytizing among "tribals" (*jangalī deśa ke loga*) through his scripture exposition (*kathā*) and singing sessions (*kīrtana*).[67] When Nābhā wrote his account, circa 1600, Salemabad was undeveloped, as Kishangarh was only founded about a decade later. The commentator Priyādās in his 1712 *Illumination of Devotional Emotion* (Bhakti-ras-bodhinī) situates Paraśurām in a mountain cave, where he was tested by a royal temple servant and a merchant, but the geographical area is not specified.[68] By the eighteenth century, though, Salemabad was no longer a backwater. Late in the seventeenth century the sectarian heads, or *mahant*s, of Mathura moved to Salemabad, fleeing the political unrest in Braj.[69]

When Nāgarīdās was crown prince, the abbot Vrindābandev Ācārya (abbot 1697–1740) was very influential. He maintained strong connections with the Amer-Jaipur court and even presided over some of Jai Singh II's conferences (together with the Rāmānandī abbot Bālānand).[70] When Jai

Singh's military reforms instituted eighteen officially recognized training centers of warrior ascetics, or *akhāṛās*, supervised by a suprasectarian head, eight of these were Nimbārkan.[71] Under Vrindābandev Ācārya, Nimbārkan militant ascetics were recruited as mercenaries for battle, and they played an important role in deciding local battles well into the nineteenth century.[72] They were also involved in the succession disputes in Kishangarh after Rāj Singh's death in 1748.

After the death of Vrindābandev Ācārya in 1740, Jai Singh II saw his chance to ensure that the new abbot would not be an ascetic. Driven by the concern that all legitimate gurus should follow *varṇāśrama-dharma*, he put forward for the position a Maharashtrian Brahmin named Jayrām Śeṣ.[73] He was a disciple of Vrindābandev Ācārya, yet not an ascetic. He received official recognition from several other Rajput rulers, including the house of Kishangarh (but not Jodhpur) at a ceremony in Merta organized by Jai Singh.[74] However, the ascetics of Salemabad installed their own candidate. With Jai Singh's death in 1743, Jayrām lost his major supporter, but the conflict continued until 1765. Even so, later abbots of Salemabad continued to be influential in Jaipur, especially with the queens, and often resided for long periods in the city.[75]

SALEMABAD AND THE KISHANGARH ROYAL HOUSE

A close connection has been documented between the Nimbārkans at Salemabad and the royal women of Kishangarh. Nāgarīdās's mother was Rāj Singh's first queen, Catur Kuṃvarī, a Kacchvāhā princess of Kaman. The Nimbārkan abbot Nārāyaṇdev Ācārya had blessed the newlyweds.[76] The influential abbot Vrindābandev Ācārya seems to have been the guru of Rāj Singh's first and second wives. There is evidence of a visit by the abbot to Rupnagar in 1725, which was celebrated with much fanfare.[77] Rāj Singh's second wife, whom he married in 1710, was Nāgarīdās's stepmother. Her given name was Braj Kuṃvarī, but she was known by her patronymicon Bāṅkāvatī and her devotional name Brajdāsī. The Nimbārkans promote the story that she influenced her husband in religious matters.[78] A portrait of Rāj Singh by Bhavānīdās may confirm that he had Nimbārkan sympathies. *Rāj Singh Approaching a Temple* has the inscription "śrī jī dvāra padhārā hai" (arrived at the temple of Śrī jī).[79] The term used for "temple," *dvāra*, and the reference to the image as "Śrī jī" may identify the temple's image as Nimbārkan. It thus would follow that Rāj Singh wanted to have his Nimbārkan connections preserved for posterity. In any case, after his death, his widow Braj Kuṃvarī authored a translation of the *Bhāgavata-purāṇa*, called *Brajdāsī-bhāgavat*. Throughout the work, and also in the final colophon, Brajdāsī invokes Vrindābandev Ācārya as her (initiation) guru, but she also mentions a *vidyā guru*, "instructional guru" Brijnāth Bhaṭṭ.[80] The latter was a famous Vallabhan confidant of Jai Singh, who moved to Kishangarh after Jai Singh II's death, during the reign of his son Īśvarī Singh.[81]

NĀGARĪDĀS AND THE SALEMABAD PĪṬH

Since Vrindābandev Ācārya was important to these two queens, Nāgarīdās would have been in close contact with him, too, especially as a child. There is documentation that his mother had Vrindābandev Ācārya perform a ceremony (possibly but not necessarily initiation) for her young son on the occasion of a visit in 1702.[82] Nimbārkans claim this supports that Nāgarīdās was initiated in their sect.

Some maintain that the young prince studied with Vrindābandev Ācārya together with two other disciples.[83] A painting depicting such a scene is mounted in the durbar room of Śrī jī Mahārāj in Salemabad (fig. 2.3). However, it is clearly modern; it may be a restoration of an older work, but just how old is difficult to say. Nāgarīdās himself is purported to have made a miniature portrait of Vrindābandev Ācārya, as well as the other disciples.[84]

FIG. 2.3 *Vrindābandev Ācārya Teaching Sāvant Singh and Others*, painting framed in living quarters of Śrī jī in Salemabad

Nimbārkans also cite the story of how Sāvant Singh rid the Salemabad monastery's territory of a lion. The hunt is commemorated in a painting by the famous Kishangarhi painter Nihālcand, as well as in a longish (103 *Chand*, or metrical units) poem called "Lion Hunt" (Siṃh-śikār) by Rāo Udaynāth from Narvargarh.[85] The latter mentions it happened on orders of the abbot:

> In the monastery of Salemabad, lived a sage.
> His name was Vrindāban, he worshipped (the sacred stone, or śaligrāma, named) Sarveśu.
> As a rule he practiced with great devotion, gauging the depth of love.
> If sinners came, he would inspire them with devotion and praise (of God).
> Anyone who came and took refuge with him, saw his sins forgiven, became a new man.
> Kings would praise him in poetry. Long live Paraśurām's steady fortress.
>
> A lion gave trouble to his herd of cows.
> The sage sent a message: "Prince, why not gain some fame?
> Follow the ways of your family (*varṇa*), you are a warrior (*kṣatriya*): protect the land.
> Kill this evil monster, this terrible lion."
> As he heard this message, the prince's heart was happy and excited,
> Drums announced: "Sāvant is prepared, genuine and keen is his intent."
> . . . .
> With Krishna and Rādhā, he is known as Nāgarīdās.
> With their help, he was victorious. The prince deserved a seat of honor.[86]

There is corroboration for the incident of the hunt itself. The Kishangarh chronicle (*Administrative History*) of the late nineteenth century specifies that it happened in 1732 (1789 VS). This source has a strong Vallabhan flavor, however, adding that Nāgarīdās after his hunt immediately went to visit the *mūrti* of Śrī Nātha jī.[87] In any case, hunting wild animals and thus assisting a monastery in his territories would have been a normal task for a prince, regardless of whether he was initiated in the Sampradāya or not.

As with the Vallabhans' claim, the texts analyzed in this book fail to support that of the Nimbārkans. If Sāvant Singh were indeed initiated in the Sampradāya, it is remarkable that he does not single out any Nimbārkan to praise in his hagiographic anthology (*Garland of Stories and Songs*). One song he includes is by Paraśurām Ācārya, but he does not comment on the author, focusing instead on the singer, a devotee named Murārīdās in Balonda (PPM 20). The song must have been one of his favorites since he selected it also for collection in his retelling of the Rāma story (RCM 15). From the founder of the Salemabad Nimbārkan monastery, Nāgarīdās thus quotes songs devoted to Rāma, not Krishna. Similarly, a long wedding song of Rāma and Sītā by Vrindābandev Ācārya (with the *chāpa* "Vrindāban Prabhu") is included in *Garland of Rāma's Romance* (RCM 17). Still, that he quotes several Nimbārkan poets in his *String of Song-Pearls* shows that he loved their songs.[88]

Notwithstanding his connections to Salemabad, Nāgarīdās does not report going there to try and enlist the warrior ascetics for his cause against his brother Bahādur Singh. The Nāgās had been at his side during the controversy over Vrindābandev Ācārya's succession. At first, Kishangarh had acknowledged the Jaipur householder Jayrām Śeṣ, under pressure of Jai Singh II. With the death of Jai Singh in 1743, the tide turned and Sāvant Singh supported instead the popular ascetic candidate, Govinddev Ācārya, but Bahādur Singh did not. This disagreement between the brothers escalated. There is an account that Bahādur Singh, with the help of the Merta army, attacked Rupnagar, while the Nāgās from Salemabad and Jaipur rushed to protect the city. The two brothers had to be reconciled by the Jodhpur king, and Sāvant Singh ceded some villages to his brother. It was this controversial *mahant*, Govinddev Ācārya, who would cosign the eventual peace agreement between the two brothers in 1756, shortly before he himself passed away.[89]

According to some scholars, the Salemabad Pīṭh succession incident caused Bahādur Singh to call in the Vallabhans as a counterweight for the Nimbārkans.[90] Bahādur Singh also tried to establish an independent branch of the Nimbārkans in Kishangarh by inviting the eldest disciple of Vrindābandev Ācārya, Bhagavān Dās, who had retired to Braj. He made a grant of a *havelī* in Kishangarh to him in 1766 (1823 VS) and later of land in the village of Kacariya, hence the branch is known as Kācariyā Pīṭh.[91] Bahādur Singh purportedly renamed the Vallabhan image Śrī Kalyāṇarāya in 1772 (1829 VS).[92] A painting depicting Bahādur Singh worshipping Vallabhan images confirms that he promoted a public image of close connection with the Vallabha-Sampradāya.[93] It is rumored that at his court it was obligatory to wear the Vallabhan *tilaka*.[94] However, as for the contract between the brothers, the detail about the villages ceded to Bahādur Singh makes this look like a war less about religious succession than about territorial claims.

Nāgarīdās was close to the Nimbārkans in Salemabad, yet that did not mean he excluded other sects. Why Sāvant Singh did not seek the help of the Salemabad Nāgās to regain his throne is an open question, but perhaps Bahādur Singh foresaw such a move and preempted his brother from approaching the monastery.

OTHER KRISHNA DEVOTIONAL SECTS

Apart from the Nimbārkans, three other Krishna devotional movements were influential in Kishangarh: the Gauḍīya-, Rādhāvallabha-, and Haridāsī-Sampradāyas. Like the Vallabhans, these three Sampradāyas came about in the early sixteenth century and were very prominent in the eighteenth century in Braj. All three are characterized by a strong predilection for the divine love-play of Rādhā and Krishna. They thus are called *rasika*s, or "connoisseurs." Sāvant Singh was well aware of major saints in all three. Of all the Rādhā-Krishna sects, he was perhaps most interested in Haridāsī and Rādhāvallabhīya devotees, whose type of devotion was closest to his own.[95]

GAUḌĪYA-SAMPRADĀYA

The Gauḍīya-Sampradāya looks to the charismatic Bengali saint Caitanya Mahāprabhu (1486–1533) as its founder. He lived part of his life in Jagannath Puri in Odisha, but his disciples established centers in the Braj area, in Vrindavan and Radhakund, causing a stream of devotees, theologians, hagiographers, and ordinary pilgrims to travel from Bengal and Odisha toward Braj and back.

In Braj, Caitanya's "Gosvāmī disciples" dedicated themselves to applying aesthetic theories (*rasa śāstra*) to devotion, most notably Rūpa Gosvāmī.[96] From this inspiration, they wrote dramas and sponsored a technique called *Rāgānugā bhakti*, whereby devotees imagine themselves playing a role in Krishna's world, in particular for advanced devotees to imitate Rādhā's girlfriends (*mañjarī*).[97] They also wrote philosophical treatises about their position on the apparent distinctions between God, the world, and man, which are attributed to the mysterious workings of God's power, or śakti. This view is typified as Acintya-bhedābheda, or "hard-to-fathom difference in non-difference." They codified a system of ritual orthodoxy and helped develop the Braj area into a pilgrimage center for Rādhā-Krishna devotion, with Nārāyaṇ Bhaṭṭ playing an active role in the sixteenth century.[98]

Two of the Gosvāmī disciples, Rūpa and his brother Sanātana, had worked at the Shāhī court in Bengal before becoming Caitanya's disciples.

Some have suggested that their intellectual project may in part have been a way to reclaim their Brahminness.[99] Ironically, this embarrassing past may have been why they were successful in finding patrons for their devotional activity. Thanks to Mughal land grants, they were able to erect lofty temples for their deities in Vrindavan.[100] Like the Mughal imperial forts built in Delhi and Agra, they were constructed of red sandstone. The best known is the Govindadeva temple that was completed at the end of the sixteenth century and sponsored by the Kacchvāhā kings of Amer, who had come to prominence as Akbar's generals.[101] Not just kings, but also merchants contributed: the temple for Madanamohana was sponsored by a Khatrī from Multan.[102] The Gauḍīya presence in Braj, then, involved interchanges with other regional centers, prominently Bengal and Odisha, but also western areas, in particular Jaipur in Rajasthan. During the political unrest of the late seventeenth century, the images were taken to a town on the border with Rajasthan, Kaman, which was ruled by Kirāṭ Singh (d. 1671), a younger brother of Mirzā Raja Jai Singh of Amer (r. 1621–67).

The special relationship with the Kacchvāhā rulers reached a new level in the early eighteenth century when Savāī Jai Singh II initiated his religious reforms. In the upheaval of the late seventeenth century, the Gauḍīya Govindadeva image was moved for safekeeping to Kacchvāhā territories. In 1716, Jai Singh II installed the image prominently in what was to be his newly established capital of Jaipur, perhaps in a spirit of competition with the Mewar rulers' having established the Vallabhan deity Śrī Nātha jī in their capital nearby.[103] The arrival of the image and its Gauḍīya caretakers at court prompted several debates about their orthodox credentials. As the king's special favorites, the Gauḍīyas aligned with him on questions regarding military, social, and theological reforms. They claimed affiliation with the Mādhva-Sampradāya and asserted socially conservative positions. In 1718, they thus obliged Jai Singh at a debate he had organized to force a consensus on the interrelated issues of whether Rādhā was Krishna's adulterous lover (*parakīyā*) or wife (*svakīyā*) and whether the most advanced devotees were still subject to rules of ordinary *varṇāśrama-dharma*.[104] In the wake of this, several works were composed to reinforce the Gauḍīya claim to orthodoxy, including, more broadly, reflections on what constituted Vaishnava orthodoxy.[105] These issues were not limited to Gauḍīyas or even Hindus in Rajasthan alone. Even the Navab of Bengal was involved in disputes regarding the matter of whether Rādhā was Krishna's legally wedded wife or not.[106] Not everyone agreed with Jai Singh II's conservativism, including in Braj the Radhakund party of the *vairāgī* (ascetic) Rūpa Kavirāja, called Sauramya-mat, and in Bengal the faction of Rādhāmohan Ṭhākur. The consequences would be dire: once Jai Singh II became governor of Agra, dissenters were criminalized. Rūpa Kavirāja and his followers were accused of theft and socially excluded.[107]

Without stressing his subjects' sectarian identity, Nāgarīdās quotes in his anthology (*String of Song-Pearls*) and praises in his hagiography (*Garland of Stories and Songs*) several Gauḍīya devotees, namely, Gadādhar Bhaṭṭ, his descendant Vallabhrasik, Sūrdās Madanmohan, and Bhagavān "Hit Rāmrāy." Also corroborating this closeness with the Gauḍīyas is a Kishangarhi sketch depicting Caitanya Mahāprabhu dancing ecstatically, surrounded by disciples (among them Nityānand, Advaitācārya, and the king, Pratāp Rudra, all identified by inscriptions in both Devanagari and Bengali), who are playing instruments, singing, or clapping their hands, one of them prostrated in front.[108] This sketch is estimated to date from 1750, roughly the same period when Nāgarīdās authored his hagiography.

Nāgarīdās also mentions meeting and enjoying the company of a contemporaneous Gauḍīya devotee from Radhakund, Muralīdās, who is also portrayed in a Kishangarhi painting, swooning in ecstasy during a *kīrtan* session.[109] This devotee is mentioned as attending court in Rupnagar (in *Garland of Stories and Songs*) and as inviting Nāgarīdās for *kīrtan* at his house in Radhakund (in *The Pilgrim's Bliss*), together with a Bansīdās. This reference may be to Vaṃśīdās, who was known to be connected with the dissenters from Jai Singh's orthodoxy at Radhakund, the Sauramya-mat. Possibly, Nāgarīdās was associating with people who were *personae non gratae* for Jai Singh II.[110]

RĀDHĀVALLABHA-SAMPRADĀYA

The Rādhāvallabha-Sampradāya developed around deity Rādhāvallabha, installed in Seva Kunj in Vrindavan in 1534 by the Gaur Brahmin Hit Harivaṃś. A grand red sandstone temple was erected for the deity around the same time as the more famous ones of the Gauḍīyas. In this case, the funding came from a Kāyastha in Mughal service of the famous Abdur Rahīm Khānkhānā.[111] This deity, too, left Braj in the political instability of the late seventeenth century for Kaman, but returned to Vrindavan.[112] Kaman was where Nāgarīdās's mother hailed from, so she may well have had some connections with the local Rādhāvallabhans.

The worship of Rādhāvallabha includes songs composed by Hit Harivaṃś, collected as *Eighty-Four Love Songs* (Hit-caurāsī-pad).[113] The work focuses nearly exclusively on the aesthetic enjoyment (*rasa*) of Rādhā and Krishna's bower-sport (*nikuñja-līlā*). Harivaṃś was not interested in philosophy or ritual, and while his descendants (*bindu parivār*) and disciples (*nād parivār*) produced some commentaries, generally the sect avoided exegesis and theology. Famous devotees from the sixteenth and seventeenth centuries are Dhruvdās (who is quoted twice in Nāgarīdās's *String of Song-Pearls*) and Nehī Nāgarīdās (who is likewise quoted twice and also mentioned in *Garland of Stories and Songs*).

The Rādhāvallabhans' aversion to philosophical argument did not place them in good standing at the time of Jai Singh II's reforms. Some sources claim they were persecuted, and, as a consequence, the senior descendant of Harivaṃś at the time, Rūplāl, left Vrindavan and wandered in search of shelter elsewhere.[114] Whether he incurred the wrath of Jai Singh or not, Rūplāl found favor with Nāgarīdās (who quotes him in *String of Song-Pearls*). Two other descendants of Harivaṃś are quoted (thrice and once, respectively, in *String of Song-Pearls*), namely, Hit Kamalnayan and Hit Anūp(lāl).[115] Rūplāl and his entourage, which included his disciple, the prolific Cācā Vrindāvandās, escaped the massacre by Durrānī in 1757. Fleeing Vrindavan, this Rādhāvallabhan group eventually reached Kishangarh, where Bahādur Singh gave them refuge during 1774–75.[116] This visit was commemorated in a painting (ca. 1800) by the Kishangarhi artist Vicitra (Rāy Sevak).[117] Bahādur Singh may well have sought in this way to establish his own credentials as a sponsor of *bhakti* rivaling the memory of Nāgarīdās.

HARIDĀSĪ-SAMPRADĀYA

The Haridāsīs are named after the ascetic singer-saint Svāmī Haridās, a contemporary of Hit Harivaṃś in Vrindavan. Haridās, too, preferred the aesthetic enjoyment of Rādhā and Krishna's bower-sport over philosophy. His songs are sung in the classical musical genre of *dhrupada* and are collected in two anthologies: *Eighteen Songs of Instruction* (Aṣṭadaś-siddhānt-pad) is about devotion to God, and *Garland of Play* (Keli-māl) is exclusively about the love of Rādhā and Krishna.[118] Haridās claimed to be an eyewitness and is understood to be an incarnation of Lalitā, a *sakhī* of Rādhā. Likewise, devotees in this sect are encouraged to model their spiritual lives after Rādhā's *sakhīs*; hence it is also called Sakhī-Sampradāya. Nāgarīdās quotes seven poems by Haridās in his anthology (*String of Song-Pearls*). In addition, Nāgarīdās also quotes four times Svāmī jī's favorite disciple, Viṭhal Vipul.[119] Likewise, quoted seven times in *String of Song-Pearls* is the actual organizer of the sect, Bihāranidās, or Bihārīdās.[120]

Svāmī Haridās was a close friend of Hit Harivaṃś, together with another Vrindavan devotee, Harirām Vyās of Orccha. The three of them are called the Rasika-trayī, a group of three fellow *bhakta-rasikas*, especially devoted to Rādhā. Since their names all contained "Hari," they were also called Hari-trayī.[121] Though Harirām Vyās is much less known than the two others, he was the most prolific of the three. Nāgarīdās is fond of quoting him and devotes more chapters on him than on anyone else in his *Garland of Stories and Songs*.

No grand red sandstone temple was built for the image Haridās worshipped, (Bāṅke) Bihārī. Yet now the image is one of the best known and most visited in Vrindavan. A violent conflict arose about the custody of the Bihārī image in the seventeenth century between the two rival branches of the Haridāsīs, the householders, or Gosvāmīs, and the renunciates, called Ācāryas.[122] The Gosvāmīs are Sārasvat Brahmin descendants of the original caretaker priest of the Bihārī image, whom they say was Haridās's brother, and are currently in control of the image. The Ācāryas control the *samādhi* in Nidhi Ban. Several of them were charismatic figures who composed poetry in Braj, collected as *The Word of the Eight Ācāryas* (Aṣṭācāryoṃ kī Vāṇī).[123]

The two rival branches also disagree about the theological affiliation of the sect: the Gosvāmīs claim that Haridās was Viṣṇusvāmī, whereas the Ācāryas say that he was Nimbārkan. Pītāmbardās defended the legitimacy of the Haridāsī ascetics at one of Jai Singh II's conferences.[124] His disciple Kiśordās produced a controversial hagiography, *Our Sect's Theology* (Nij-mat-siddhānt), which is based on oral traditions about the sect and its founder.[125] The work, aimed at discrediting the Gosvāmīs, accused them of an attack on the prestigious ascetic leader Bihārīdās.[126] In his hagiography, Kiśordās had little interest in philosophy but instead sought to highlight Haridās's exceptional charisma. He thus portrays him as the guru of the *dhrupada* singer Tānsen at Akbar's court.[127] This story is also depicted in a painting of the Kishangarh school and is also taken up by Nāgarīdās in his own hagiography (*Garland of Stories and Songs*). Nāgarīdās may have known of Kiśordās's work, or they may have both reworked a common set of stories current in a Nimbārkan environment.

Nāgarīdās's concubine, who composed poetry with the *chāpa* "Rasik Bihārī," was likely close to the Haridāsī sadhus who professed to be Nimbārkan. Her *samādhi* inscription specifies that her guru was a man named Rasikdās. He has been tentatively identified with the founder of the Rasikabihārī temple in Vrindavan by that name, also known as Rasikdev.[128] He was a controversial figure: after being expelled from Nidhi Ban, he founded the first independent seat of ascetic followers of Haridās. His travels took his deity Rasikabihārī to Udaipur and Dhungarpur, before it returned to Braj.[129] However, the identification of this figure as Rasik Bihārī's guru is not certain.

There is no doubt, then, that in addition to the Vallabhans, Nāgarīdās was close to such more *rasika*-oriented groups. He associated with them not just during his visit in Braj but also welcomed them at court and spent time with them in Kishangarh. Nāgarīdās did not shy away from the sectarian (sub)sects that had fallen out of favor with Jai Singh II in his zeal to make all conform to orthodoxy. While on pilgrimage in Braj, Nāgarīdās associated closely with Gauḍīyas who appear to have belonged to the discredited Sauramya-mat. His concubine seems to have been close to the Haridāsī sadhus who had declared themselves Nimbārkan. In time of need, after the massacre by Durrānī, some Rādhāvallabhans found refuge with Sāvant Singh's brother Bahādur Singh in Kishangarh. While these groups may not have found support from the Jaipur court, they could turn to other courts, such as Kishangarh.

RĀMA DEVOTION AND THE MONASTERY AT GALTA

Since many of the Kishangarhi paintings depict Rādhā and Krishna, very little attention has been paid to Kishangarh's links with Rāma-oriented devotion. However, there are several Kishangarhi paintings depicting episodes of the Rāma story, of which some have come to light recently.[130] Sāvant Singh mentions in his pilgrimage report that he visited the Rāmānandī monastery of Galta near Jaipur, which raises questions about the nature and the extent of Rāma devotional influence on Kishangarh. Rāmānandī history in this period is itself contested.[131] Still, recent research indicates that the perceived boundaries between Rāma and Krishna *bhakti* were perhaps more permeable than once thought.

RĀMĀNANDĪ PREHISTORY

The Rāmānanda-Sampradāya's history is complicated by sectarian controversy. The prevailing scholarly consensus (since the late nineteenth century) was based on assumptions that have proved to be mistaken.[132] The sect is named after Rāmānanda, whose identity is contested. Most agree that he was a Brahmin living in Benares, and some say that he lived in the early fifteenth century and originally hailed from the South. Very little is known about his ideas and his works. The Sanskrit works attributed to him appear to be spurious, and only some songs in Old Hindi with his name are preserved in early sources.[133] Notwithstanding the purported Benares origins of the sect, it seems to have been influential first in Rajasthan.

By 1600, as attested in the guru lineage given in Rāmānanda's great-great-grand-disciple Nābhādās's influential hagiography, some of his followers saw him as a disciple of Rāmānuja, whose philosophical system of Viśiṣṭādvaita is another devotional response to Śaṅkara's Advaita.[134] However, this linking of Rāmānanda with Rāmānuja is highly contested. Since the early twentieth century, Rāmānanda has been claimed to be an independent orthodox Brahmin from the North who lived in the fourteenth century and authored Sanskrit commentatorial texts that justify the heteropraxis of the contemporary Rāmānanda-panth.[135] In fact, the earliest author to confirm a link with Rāmānuja, Nābhādās, had already claimed that Rāmānanda initiated even outcaste figures, such as Kabīr and Raidās, as well as women.[136] He also implied that Rāmānanda had inherited this heterodoxy on social issues from an earlier guru of Benares, Rāghavānanda, who is said to have "firmed up the *bhakti* of everyone, of the four *varṇa*s and āśramas."[137]

The Rāmānandīs have several branches, each defined by descent from one of Rāmānanda's twelve disciples.[138] Most relevant to this discussion is the lineage of Anantānand, whose disciple the Dāhimā Brahmin, Krishnadās Payohārī, established in the early sixteenth century the seat of Galta. This site, in a gorge with a natural water source near modern-day Jaipur, is the monastery Nāgarīdās reports visiting in his pilgrimage report (fig. 2.4).

FIG. 2.4 Water tank at Galta

FIG. 2.5 Guru lineage of Krishnadās Payohārī in his cave at Galta

The sectarian literature situates the founder Payohārī (whose name implies that he subsisted only on drinking milk) originally in Pushkar and proudly proclaims that he was patronized by the Amer Maharaja Prithvīrāj (r. 1503–27).[139] He reportedly prevailed over a Kānphaṭā yogi (later identified as Tārānāth),[140] who is portrayed as adoring Krishnadās Payohārī in the visual depiction of the latter's guru lineage inside his cave (fig. 2.5; the bearded man with hat on the bottom row to the right).

The king may have shifted allegiance from the yogi to the Rāma *bhakta* through the mediation of a queen.[141] In any case, the deity Śrī Sītārāma jī was gifted to the king by Payohārī.[142] It became the Kacchvāhā dynastic deity, and when the king set out for battle, Śrī Sītārāma jī was carried in front of him.[143] The Galta Rāmānandīs were politically adroit and received land grants from the time of Akbar onward.[144] Over the course of the seventeenth century, they were able to build up Galta, constructing water tanks and two temples, one for Raghunātha jī and one for Gopāla jī.[145] The wall paintings, which still survive, are overwhelmingly Krishnaite, attesting to a *rasika* ambience (fig. 2.6).

FIG. 2.6 Krishnaite wall paintings on the exterior of the Gopāla jī Mandir at Galta

This architectural evidence illustrates how the Rāma *bhakti* that prevailed in Galta accommodated or was even modeled after Krishna *bhakti*. The Rāmānandī branch that is closest to the Krishnaite ambience is the Rāma-Rasika sect, which traces its lineage back to Krishnadās Payohārī's disciple Agradās.[146] Agradās's major work, *Handmaiden of Meditation* (Dhyān-mañjarī), focuses on Sītā and Rāma's eternal sporting in Sāket and was influenced by contemporary Krishna *bhakti* works.[147] It seems that many Rāma-Rasikas went to Vrindavan to find preceptors.[148] By the early eighteenth century, the then Galta abbot, Rāmprapanna, organized Rās-līlās—he is even called *rās-dhārī*, or stage manager, in the documents—and was very active in developing the erotic Rāma-Rasika *bhakti*, modeled after erotic Krishna *bhakti*.[149]

MILITANT RĀMĀNANDĪS

The Rāmānandīs also had a military arm, called Laśkarī ("army-related"), which claims descent from Rāmānanda's pupil Sursurānand via his fifth-generation disciple Anabhayānand.[150] These Nāgās, or warrior monks, have their main seat at Candpol in Jaipur. Their leader Vrijānand (d. 1752)

fought on the side of Īśvarī Singh and took part in the Bundi succession wars at the latter's side. There is no record of whether he was involved in the Kishangarhi succession, but it is possible his troops were among those sent by Īśvarī Singh for his short-lived campaign in support of Sāvant Singh in 1750. Vrijānand had strong connections with the Braj area, where he might have resided at the same time as Sāvant Singh did.[151]

Vrijānand's successor, Bālānand (d. 1795), had Rāma-Rasika inclinations: he wrote with the *chāpa* of "Bāla Alī."[152] There is no evidence that Bālānand partook in the hostilities between the two Kishangarh brothers either. He was involved in succession battles of the Jats, and after the Jat defeat by the Mughals in 1773 he turned to Jaipur, partaking in the victorious Rajput-Mughal alliance against the Marathas in 1787.[153]

Another branch of the Rāmānandīs connected with the Kishangarh territory is that of the Khākīs, founded by Krishnadās Payohārī.[154] His disciple Ṭīlācārya, or Ṭīlā Svāmī, a contemporary of the Nimbārkan pioneer Paraśurām, is supposed to have flourished from 1513 to 1610.[155] Today his *samādhi* in Salemabad stands in great neglect, adjacent to the now-flourishing Nimbārka Pīṭh.[156] In short, several Rāmānandī military groups were in the area in the mid-eighteenth century and might have been drawn into the Kishangarhi succession conflict, but there is no documentary evidence to support that this happened.

THE RĀMĀNANDĪS AND JAI SINGH'S REFORMS

Like the Krishna sects, the Rāmānandīs also were affected by Savāī Jai Singh II's reforms, especially the Galta seat and the Nāgās who were heavily involved with the court. The pressure was intense during the early 1730s, leading up to Jai Singh II's prestigious Vedic horse sacrifice of 1734. The Nāgā leader, Vrijānand, played a role in Jai Singh II's reforms.[157] His successor, Bālānand, actively promoted the Rāmānandī link with the Rāmānuja-Sampradāya and is remembered as the main force behind Jai Singh II's organization of Vaishnavas in military orders, or *akhāḍās*.[158] The sect portrays this as a defense against Shaiva orders, and, indeed, Rāmānandī Nāgās in Ayodhya were involved in fighting Shaiva *sanyāsīs*, driving out the Daśanāmī ascetics, so that the Nirvāṇī ākhāḍā could build Hanuman Garhi.[159] Yet Bālānand's military activities were also employed in the major political battles of the time.

Jai Singh II's reforms had a strong impact on the Galta monastery, which sponsored efforts to affirm affiliation with the Rāmānuja-Sampradāya and produced matching genealogies. The eighteenth-century abbot of Galta,

Rāmprapanna, is known to have signed a document forbidding heterodox praxes in his Sampradāya in the early 1730s.[160] A forceful debater, he is depicted by the sect as traveling to defend the Rāma-Rasika sādhanā (discipline) against its opponents.[161] He changed his name to Madhurācārya, adopting at least in name the Rāmānuja southern tradition of spiritual authority via householder *ācāryas*, rather than celibate *mahants*.[162] However, when he came under pressure from Jai Singh to marry (perhaps to qualify to partake in the Vedic rites the king was carrying out), he refused and moved to Citrakut.[163] He delegated the care of affairs in Galta to his disciple Har(i)sevak, who was subsequently forced to renounce *sanyāsa*.[164] It is this disciple, known by his title as Hari Ācārya, whom Sāvant Singh met at Galta. He had become head of the monastery in 1733 and would die in 1756.[165] He was the first householder-abbot of the seat who followed the Rāmānujī model.

RĀMĀNANDĪS AND KISHANGARH

There are currently no records available for the Kishangarh court's relations with the Rāmānandīs. Nāgarīdās's pilgrimage report, though, opens a window onto the matter by describing his visit at Galta in 1748 when Hari Ācārya was in residence at the site (TĀ 6–8).

The freshly dethroned prince and the householder-*mahant* seem to have connected well, perhaps through their shared interests. Hari Ācārya composed poetry with the *chāpa* "Hari-sahacarī," which indicates that he had Rāma-Rasika inclinations, and was heavily influenced by Krishnaite models.[166] An aficionado of theater like his guru, Rāmprapanna, Hari Ācārya started a tradition of organizing Rās-līlās for the festival celebrating Rāma and Sītā's wedding.[167] Nāgarīdās also had an interest in Rās-līlā, which he enthusiastically reports attending once he settled in the Braj area. Perhaps the prince and the abbot enjoyed each other's *satsaṅga*, discussing Rās-līlā scripts and singing devotional songs together, something along the lines of the *bhajana* (communal singing) scene depicted on the murals of the Jñānagopāla temple in Galta (fig. 2.7).

This visit may well have been what inspired Nāgarīdās within a year to compile the *Garland of Rāma's Romance* with verses of other poets, composing a number of verses himself to round it out. This compilation does not contain many quotations from Rāmānandīs,[168] though it features poems from the author so influential in Rāmānandī circles, Tulsīdās. Nāgarīdās included one *Kavitta* (verse) and three *padas* from Tulsīdās's *String of Songs* (Gītāvalī) in the work (RCM 4, 6, 9, 11). In his *Garland of Stories and Songs*,

FIG. 2.7 Wall painting of *bhajana* at Galta

Nāgarīdās devotes several chapters to the great master of Rāma *bhakti* (PPM 22–24). Stories about and songs attributed to Kabīr and Raidās, regarded by some as Rāmānandīs, are included in the longer version of the work (PPM 10–11). This hagiography also features a story about the Rāmānujī (in some recensions called Rāmānandī) Caturdās Khojī (PPM 19), the crux of which has to do with the ability to see God even in a low-caste man. In short, Nāgarīdās's tastes tend toward the heterodox Rāmānandīs. More generally, in writing his hagiographic work, Nāgarīdās was inspired by Nābhādās's influential *Garland of Devotees*, which he gives as a source (PPM 19).

Thus Rāmānandī influence in Kishangarh can be seen in a closer look at Nāgarīdās's work, revealing possible channels of communication and a significant degree of intertextuality between Rāma and Krishna devotees.

THE DĀDŪ-PANTH AND THE MONASTERY AT NARAINA

Nāgarīdās was involved with the so-called *saguṇa bhakti* groups, devoted to gods "with qualities," such as Krishna and Rāma. However, he must have also come into contact with *nirguṇa* groups, who worshipped God in the abstract, "without qualities." Among them, the Dādū-panth was

FIG. 2.8 Dādū Pīṭh monastery at Naraina

very influential in Rajasthan. This sect, too, had its headquarters not far from Rupnagar, in Naraina Dādū Pīṭh (fig. 2.8). The sect is named for the sixteenth-century poet-saint Dādū Dayāl (d. 1603), probably a Muslim cotton-carder (*dhuniyā*), who preached throughout the region, notably in Sambhar, Amer, and Naraina.[169] He did not work out a philosophical system of his own but incorporated elements from both Hinduism and Islam into the devotional hymns he created and collected as *The Word of Dādū* (Dādū-vāṇī).[170]

Like the Rāmānandī Krishnadās Payohārī before him, Dādū found a congenial audience with the rulers of Amer, in his case with Raja Bhagavāndās (r. 1574–89). Dādū's hagiography, authored by his disciple Jan Gopāl, claims also that Kishan Singh Rathor, founder of Kishangarh, was Dādū's disciple.[171] The involvement of the Kishangarh rulers with the Dādū-panth afterward, though, seems to have been relatively minimal. Two generations after Sāvant Singh, the then Ācārya of the Naraina Dādū Dhām, Nirbhayrām, was received in Kishangarh by Maharaja Pratāp Singh (r. 1788–97), who also donated land to his disciple Bihārīdās.[172] The Kishangarh rulers made donations on the occasion of the yearly festival (*melā*) to the Naraina abbots, and in 1898 (1955 VS, Phālgun *sudi* 9) Śārdul Singh of Kishangarh donated a pair of shawls (*dusālo joḍo*) worth ninety rupees.[173] Still, Kishangarh was a minor donor compared not just to Jaipur but also to Jodhpur, Udaipur, and Bikaner. Notwithstanding the proximity to Rupnagar, the Dādū-panth's seat was actually located within the Amer/Jaipur territories, and it is with the house of the Kacchvāhās that it enjoyed a special relationship.

The Dādū-panth produced its own hagiographies, one of which, Rāghavdās's *Garland of Devotees* (Bhakt-māl), could have been a model for Nāgarīdās. It was itself clearly inspired by Nābhā's work of the same name, but Rāghavdās inserts within the wider Vaishnava framework the concerns of his own subsect, the Dādū-panthī Nāgās, or warrior sadhus.[174] He was Rajput by caste and a disciple of Hāpaujī (Hari Singh), the half-brother of Mān Singh of Amer (r. 1589–1614). At this time, a marked Rajput ethos prevailed among Dādū-panthī Nāgās, who had numerically become more and more important in the Panth.[175] The commentary on this work, written circa 1800 by Caturdās, was even more outspoken that way.[176] Yet Nāgarīdās does not seem to be aware of the Dādū-panthī *Garland of Devotees*. Nor does he refer to Dādū or any of his followers in his own work, even though he mentions other *nirguṇīs*, such as Kabīr and Raidās, but it is possible that he saw the latter two low-caste saints instead as Rāmānandīs.

Jai Singh II's reforms also affected the Dādū-panth, which underwent a process of Sanskritization. In 1733 (1790 VS, Śrāvaṇ *sudi* 9), several Dādū-panthī sadhus signed a statement to the effect that they would follow *varṇāśrama-dharma* principles to comply with Jai Singh's diktats. In particular, they would no longer associate with Muslims, ban Śūdras from initiation ceremonies, and prohibit non-Brahmins from becoming abbots (*svāmīs*).[177] The then abbot, Kishandev, was under threat of a coerced marriage and left for voluntary exile in Merta.[178] Upon his death, a drama of succession ensued, where not unlike the earlier Nimbārka Pīṭh succession in Salemabad, the Jaipur ruler Mādho Singh (r. 1750–67) intervened in favor of one of the candidates.[179]

The Dādū-panthīs also participated in the military reorganization of ascetics into warrior groups. Weapon-carrying Dādū-panthīs were early on involved in revenue collection and settlement of local disputes, including perhaps the succession war after Jai Singh's death. They formally organized only in the mid-eighteenth century (1756) during a conference in Galta, under the influence of Bālānand's Rāmānandī order.[180] They built a *havelī* in Jaipur that was the seat of one of their major abbots beginning in 1786. All this was slightly too late, though, to be of help to Sāvant Singh when he found his throne usurped. Though he reports visiting Devyānī near Rupnagar, he does not mention visiting nearby Naraina or any of the other Dādū-panthī sites.

SUFI SHRINES IN AJMER AND KISHANGARH-RUPNAGAR

Kishangarh was on the busy road from Delhi to Ajmer, site of the famous tomb of the Sufi master Khwājā Mu'īn ud-Dīn Chistī (d. 1230). This shrine, known for its openness to all religious communities and to "acculturated" forms of Sufism, such as the celebration of the Hindu festival of Vasant, is patronized by Muslims and Hindus, of all ranks, and has been throughout its long history.[181] Raghunāth Rāo of the principality of Vincur in Maharashtra stopped at the site on his pilgrimage in the mid-nineteenth century.[182] Some of the more famous Rajput sponsors of the Dargāh Sharīf were Hindu rajas, such as Raja Ajit Singh of Jodhpur and Savāī Jai Singh II of Jaipur, who presented a silver archway.[183] Not coincidentally, the rajas of these capitals, roughly equidistant from the holy city, vied for control of the lucrative post of subedar of Ajmer, and on occasion the house of Kishangarh-Rupnagar was involved in such scuffles.[184]

Most secondary literature on Kishangarh does not link the court with Ajmer, but historians of the Ajmer shrine have unearthed some documentation connecting the Rathors of Kishangarh to *vakīls* (intercessors) or *ḳhuddam* (servants) of the Dargāh. One document seems to indicate that Mān Singh of Kishangarh (r. 1658–1706) used the services of a family of *ḳhuddam* and gave them a land grant. A request from the year 1764 (AH 1177) confirms the original *sanad* (grant document).[185] This petition claims that a prince of Kishangarh had granted land in Narvar village (north of Ajmer) to a Syed Ināyatullāh, but the original was lost and his descendants wished to see it confirmed by the then emperor Shāh 'Ālam II.[186] Reversely, one family of *ḳhuddam*, related to a Mīr Syed Zaimullāh, apparently took refuge in Kishangarh state at the end of the 1780s until 1790, fleeing the Rathor "occupation" at the time, returning only when Mahadaji Scindhia regained control over Ajmer.[187]

In the visual record, there is firm evidence that the house of Kishangarh welcomed the official government appointee, or *mutavallī*, of Ajmer. In a painting of a hot-season soirée sponsored by Sāvant Singh, the central figures are Vaishnava, but among the attendees are also court poets and Muslims; directly beneath Nāgarīdās is a figure identified in the inscription as Khān Muḥammad.[188] It is not impossible that he is the Muḥammad Khān who

FIG. 2.9 Tomb of Sultān Pīr at Rupnagar fort

was subedar of Ajmer and for whose granddaughter the court poet Vrind wrote an instructional manual.[189] A painting by Amarcand of Kishangarh depicts Mīr 'Umar, who is designated *mutavallī*, attending a "moonlight party" (*jalas mahtābī*) by Sāvant Singh's son, Sardār Singh, in Rupnagar.[190] Another Kishangarhi painting dated tentatively to circa 1760 shows six Sufis, inscribed with their names, including Mu'īn ud-Dīn of Ajmer.[191] This depiction confirms at least a positive awareness, even a celebration, of the nearby holy man's shrine. Taken together, the evidence seems to confirm close connections between Ajmer and Kishangarh.

Finally, the forts of Kishangarh and Rupnagar are both located near a tomb (*mazār*) of a Sufi saint, remembered as Sultān Pīr.[192] In the case of Rupnagar, the shrine clearly predates the fort, for it is incorporated in the fort's inner area, which had to be designed so as to accommodate the site of the shrine undisturbed (fig. 2.9). According to a local legend, the founder of Rupnagar, Rūp Singh, after once witnessing sheep being saved from a wolf thanks to the power of the Pīr, decided to build the fort on the very site of the miracle.[193] The rulers of Rupnagar are said to have always sought the blessing of Sultān Pīr before setting off to war. A Kishangarhi painting depicting a raja and a Sufi saint against battle scenes in the background (dated to ca. 1725–30) could possibly be interpreted as the king seeking the Pīr's blessing before battle.[194] Sāvant Singh, too, may have done so multiple times, but he did not have the opportunity to do so when he came back from Delhi after his father's passing. While he engaged in multiple relations with Islamicate culture, he does not dwell on it in the works studied here.[195]

JAINA MOVEMENTS IN EASTERN RAJASTHAN

Finally, Jainism has been influential in this region of Rajasthan and it, too, was undergoing change during this period.[196] The eighteenth century saw lively debate between different Jaina sectarian groups, especially in western India. Jaipur was one of the centers, with substantial communities in nearby Sanganer and Kaman, the hometown of Nāgarīdās's mother, as well as in Kishangarh and Rupnagar.

At this time, the Jaina community was riveted by controversy over the legitimacy of image worship and the related issue of the perceived laxity of Jaina Śvetāmbara ascetics. The Sthanakavāsī ("hall-dweller") protest movement rejected image worship and called for stricter rules for monks. It can be traced to the fifteenth-century Gujarati reformer Loṅkā Shāh, who, as a copyist of manuscripts, noticed discrepancies between the scriptural injunctions he copied and the practice of contemporary monks.[197] His reform movement soon led to the creation of a separate sect, the Loṅkāgaccha mendicant tradition, which has had a branch in Nagor in Rajasthan since the early sixteenth century. A renewed vigorous reformation took place within the tradition mainly in Gujarat during the sixteenth century, with the white mouth mask becoming the external marker of identity for mendicants.

Similarly, the Digambara community saw major protest movements. Due to Mughal restrictions on public nakedness, Digambara monks were compelled to wear orange robes. The *bhaṭṭāraka*s, or domesticated monks, who often controlled temples and monasteries, were implicated in local politics, often functioning as close advisers to kings.[198] The *bhaṭṭārakas* of the Amer seat thus were close to the Kacchvāhā royalty.[199] Along with the Digambara courtiers and merchants, they followed to Jaipur when the Kacchvāhās shifted their capital to the newly founded city. Their ostentatious religiosity included image worship with great pomp, which caused negative reactions from some of the laity.[200]

During the seventeenth century, the Adhyātma, or "spiritual," movement rejected rituals. Led by laymen from both the Digambara and the

Śvetāmbara communities, with major centers in Agra and Jaipur, this movement was critical of "ascetics," stressing instead philosophical contemplation of *bheda-jñāna*, or distinction between the soul and the world.[201] The movement's propounders were little concerned with sectarian community formation or ritual niceties, and out of it grew, by the end of the century, the Terah-panth.[202]

The foundation of the Terah-panth was laid in the mid-seventeenth century in Sanganer in Rajasthan by the son of a rich merchant, Godīkā.[203] It followed in the wake of a negative reaction against a *bhaṭṭāraka*, Narendrakīrti of Amer (1634–1665), who (or whose disciple) preached in Sanganer during the rainy season.[204] It thus split the Digambara community by rejecting the authority of the *bhaṭṭāraka*s and the type of rituals they stood for and by stressing the removal of elements of violence (*hiṃsā*) from ritual. In Kaman, another powerful branch of Terah-panthīs was established.[205] With the foundation of Jaipur, it set up a seat in the city in the Baṛā Terah-panth temple, built in 1735, and slightly later another influential seat, Dīvān Badhīcand jī Sāh temple, was built. At the latter site, Pandit Toḍarmal (ca. 1719–1766) authored his foundational texts for the sect in the vernacular.[206] This sect rejects "false" teachers, such as Kabīr, Dādū, Nānak, and Muslim holy men, or *pīrs*, and the worship of "unliberated deities."[207] Some of its followers were very influential not just in the Jaipur court but also in Udaipur. Pandit Toḍarmal would preach at elaborate festivals that were organized in order to foster a sense of community among its followers, who were spread all the way to Multan and Aurangabad.[208] The sect is associated with the Agravāl caste. There was also a Śvetāmbar Terā-panth in Marwar in the early eighteenth century, but its connection with the Digambara sect is unclear.[209]

The rival sect, associated with the Khaṇḍelvāl caste, and now in the majority in Jaipur, is the Bīs-panth.[210] It had a center in Sanganer, where one of its leaders, Kiśan Singh, composed several sectarian texts between 1703 and 1727.[211] It was promoted by the eighteenth-century *bhaṭṭāraka* Mahendrakīrti, who was consecrated in Delhi in 1735. He was sponsored by the Jaipur king Īśvarī Singh. By the middle of the century, the Pāṭodi temple in Jaipur (built in 1727) had become a center of Bīs-panthī activity. One of its great propagandists, Surendrakīrti (1765–1795), authored many works, and he organized community-building festivals after the model of the Terah-panthīs and sent out images consecrated on such occasions. He was influential with high officials at the Jaipur court.[212] While the inter-sectarian strife was fierce, further sectarian rivalry occurred between Jainas and

Shaivas, which eventually led to their persecution under Mādho Singh.[213] A Vallabhan Gosvāmī also had a hand in the Jaina persecutions.[214]

In contrast to Jaipur, little has been written on the role of Jainas in Kishangarh history. Already the founder, Kishan Singh, employed Oswal Jaina divans, who erected the Cintāmani Pārśvanātha Mandir in town. Their lineage continued to serve the Kishangarh rulers.[215] Invitations for monks to spend the monsoon months in town were apparently cosigned by the royalty, and Jaina scholars, such as Upādhyāy Megh Vijay and Jinraṅg Sūri (of the Khartaragaccha, which flourished at the end of the seventeenth century), spent time in Kishangarh, where their works are preserved in the Royal Collection.[216] Kishangarh was also a center of the iconoclastic Loṅkāgaccha. When the capital of Kishangarh moved to Rupnagar, there was already a strong Jaina presence there, as witnessed by three Jaina memorial pillars near Rupnagar from the tenth and eleventh centuries.[217] To this day, Rupnagar has a strong Jaina contingent. The two main temples in town, in Sadar Bazaar, are Digambar Jaina temples of the Ajmer Āmnāya and Nagor Āmnāya. The latter houses an old image of the eight Tīrthaṅkara Candā Prabhu.

The court in Rupnagar seems to have employed Śvetāmbara Jainas as scribes. Long active, they created huge storehouses (*bhaṇḍārās*) of manuscripts, such as that of the Baḍā Dhaḍā Jaina temple in Ajmer.[218] They collected not only books on Jaina topics but also *belles lettres*, or Kāvya, including works by Tulsīdās, Bihārī, and Keśavdās.[219] Thus several manuscripts of Nāgarīdās's poetry manuscripts were written by Jainas working in Rupnagar . An old manuscript of Nāgarīdās's works dated 1739 (1796 VS, Śrāvaṇ *sudi* 8, *budhavāsare*) was written by "Svetāmbra Nānig" in Rupnagar. Another manuscript, dated 1751 (1798 VS), may have been written by the same scribe, but here the name is spelled as Śvetāmbar Nānāgrām.[220] Poems of the Braj poet Ānandghan, who was a contemporary of Nāgarīdās, also were written in Rupnagar in the same period by a Jaina scribe, Śvetāmbar Hemrāj, who took pains to "correct" Ānandghan's poetry by substituting the references to his alleged sweetheart Sujān with references to Rādhā or Krishna.[221] We thus have an example of a Jaina turning secular poetry into more acceptable Rādhā-Krishna verse. All this seems to be evidence not just of a thriving business of scribal services of Śvetāmbara Jainas but also of a strong interest in Rādhā-Krishna poetry in the Jaina community of Rupnagar at the time. More broadly, Nāgarīdās's *Garland of Stories and Songs* (PPM 25) includes a story about a Delhi Jaina (*saravāgī* or śrāvaka) who, after converting to the Vallabha-Sampradāya, turned his poetic powers immediately to the service of composition of sectarian Krishna devotional poetry.[222] This story illustrates the broader phenomenon of fluidity of boundaries between Jaina vernacular output and Rādhā-Krishna devotional literature and of the "open boundaries" of the Jaina community in general.

CONCLUSION: HINDU KINGS AND MUGHALS, SAINTS AND SOLDIERS CONTESTING LIMITS

The religious landscape in the first half of the eighteenth century was complex and dynamic with rapidly changing political, religious, social, and military factors that were often interconnected. Major agents were religious leaders, such as *mahants*, sadhus, and different groups of Brahmins, but also kings and contenders for the throne, military generals, merchants, and many others. Central in all this activity were the god-images that often became focus points of inter- or infra-sectarian strife and were frequently relocated. They also provided political legitimation of contenders for the throne or regional power brokers. Religious sects sanctified images to gain symbolic capital by the patronage of kings, many of whom were in Mughal service. This could be seen as contradictory, but in fact the proximity of Braj to the Mughal power centers and its location near major roadways made it conveniently accessible for Mughal vassals traveling to the capital and back.

The Jaipur king Savāī Jai Singh II played a crucial role through his religious, social, and military reforms. His influence prompted several religious groups to reflect on their orthodoxy and orthopraxis, inspiring much religious literary output. For one, theological works were written that challenged Śaṅkara's Advaita, or monism. Sects produced philosophical tracts and commentaries, aligning themselves with the positions of the prestigious Catuḥ-sampradāya. Several dogmatic issues were contested, including the marital character of Rādhā and Krishna's relationship. Further, genealogies and hagiographies were composed to forge sectarian links with prestigious groups and to assert different sects' and subsects' superiority over one another. They also were edited to show social practices conforming with the king's conservative rulings. All along, though, devotees kept composing songs, which circulated widely via pilgrimage circuits, seasonal festivals, and theatrical performances of the Rās-līlā. The songs transcended sectarian boundaries, with a considerable amount of overlap even between Rāma- and Krishna-*rasikas*.

In response to Jai Singh II's military reforms, several religious groups organized branches of warrior ascetics. Rather than a defense against Islam, as is sometimes asserted, the rhetoric was against militant Shaiva sadhus. Mostly, these warriors formed alliances on a nonreligious basis, following political expedience. This military role was not thought to contradict with the sadhus' religious focus on the divine love-play, whether that of Rādhā and Krishna or of Sītā and Rāma. Sadhus frequently combined the role of soldier and *rasika*.

In short, the period was characterized by intense sectarian strife. The Gauḍīyas and other parties, such as the Vallabhans and Rāmānandīs, were competing at the Jaipur court. In Kishangarh, Vallabhans and Nimbārkans vied for power. Often sadhus wielded considerable influence over the ladies of the court, and their sectarian disagreements then played out in court politics. Notwithstanding all the strife, though, there was also a fair amount of interchange.

In the end, then, it is a fallacy to think of Sāvant Singh's "retirement" in Vrindavan as a move into a transcendental realm beyond the vicissitudes of the times. There was plenty of inter- and infra-sectarian debate going on at the time, and Braj was at the center of it. To be sure, Nāgarīdās had already had a taste of this when he was still prince of Kishangarh. Notwithstanding all the intense rivalry, his works bespeak no specific preference for any sectarian group. He included both Rāma and Krishna *bhakta*s of all denominations, though fewer *nirguṇī*s and no Jainas or Sufis. Nor does he seem to engage at all with Shaiva or Devī worship or Vedic ritual as practiced at the nearby *tīrtha* (sacred locale) of Pushkar or as put to political use by Jai Singh II of Jaipur. His literary works also fail to mention folk religion, such as the hero cult of Tejā jī, who is associated with snake worship. Since the Tejā jī shrine at Sursurā is near Rupnagar, and there were annual fairs that attracted huge crowds, Sāvant Singh must have been aware of this cult, but it does not make an appearance in his works.

Sāvant Singh's inclusion of *saguṇa bhakta*s of all stripes shows in his writing as well as his social engagements. In his *String of Song-Pearls*, he quotes freely songs by *bhakta*s of all denominations, including Rāma *bhakta*s. In his hagiography, he shows very little interest in the sectarian appropriations that were then so prevalent. According to his pilgrimage report, he associated with holy men and visited holy sites without regard for Sampradāya. He even sought the *satsaṅga* of what seem to have been dissenters from Jai Singh's reforms. After understanding the complex religious landscape of the times, we can appreciate all the more how Nāgarīdās steered a course away from these fights.

More broadly, the study of Sāvant Singh's interactions with the diverse *bhakti* Sampradāyas shows that Jai Singh's project for orthodoxy did not go uncontested. While his was a decisive move in the history of Vaishnava *bhakti*, anticipating what happened later in the formulation of orthodox Hinduism, there were limits to the scope of the project. Nāgarīdās's works show that not all Rajput rulers agreed with all his points. What caught on was the development of a strong Vaishnava flavor to what in retrospect can be called "Hinduism" in the making.

3 Devotees on the Move

The Pilgrim's Bliss

We saw the woods of Vrindā at the other side, but in between flowed a
  river deep.
No boat, no other means, O God, how to get across?
Staying at this side, would bring shame to our zeal,
Crossing would fulfill all our intentions.
. . . .

By the time I had contemplated all this,
I had jumped in the water, in the middle of the stream.
As my feet kicked frantically, my zeal became my buoy . . .
Then the affairs of the kingdom swept us away on a wave.
To Indraprastha we went, fire of separation consuming our hearts.
Where are Delhi's walls? Where begins the Holy Land?
In the end, Shyāma brought me back from there.
I left Delhi and with it, left all worldly worries behind.
With mounting excitement, I turned back toward Braj.

—TĀ 61–62, 64, 69

THE PILGRIM'S BLISS (TĪRTHĀNAND) IS IMPORTANT AS AN EARLY autobiographical document in Braj. The fragment quoted above shows the tension between the (covert) political goals that prompted the journey in the first place and the stated goal of a pilgrimage visiting holy places. After negotiating with the Marathas in Kumaon, on his way to seek political alliances in Delhi, Nāgarīdās passes by the Yamunā River and sees the land of Braj at the other side. Unable to resist the pull of the *tīrtha* of the title, the place of crossing, that is, where one can "cross" not just a river but "cross over to the other side of existence," he wades across the river when no boats are available (as depicted in a Kishangarhi painting [fig. 3.1]).[1] He puts it as a choice between "this side" (*vāra*) and "the other side" (*pāra*), consciously privileging the bliss of pilgrimage over politics. Even as next he is called away for the affairs of the kingdom, he longs to return. For the homeless king, the question of his

FIG. 3.1 *Krishna Swimming*, Kishangarh school, ca. 1770–75. Ink, color, and gold on paper (19.0 × 34.2 cm). National Museum, New Delhi, accession no. 63.1770. Courtesy National Museum (New Delhi)

true residence takes on new existential dimensions: Is it within Delhi's walls or in the Holy Land? At Krishna's calling, all ends well, and he settles in Braj.

Nāgarīdās's pilgrimage report is fascinating in several respects. First, it affords a rare glimpse into the author's mental world. Composed during his "exile" after he left his home country, it has a poignant *Sitz im Leben*. Further, it provides a wealth of information on networks and itineraries, local rituals and festivals as celebrated in Braj in the eighteenth century, with vivid vignettes of the gatherings of devotees in which religious songs were composed and transmitted. Against this background, we can understand several of Nāgarīdās's later works. Most of all, we witness a rare personal experience record of the meaning of pilgrimage. If "the real meaning of these journeys lies in people's individual experiences, in the depth of meaning with which they invest them," *The Pilgrim's Bliss* is a rare source text for the eighteenth century. If people "categorize their experience by using culturally mediated categories," then we see here how the framework of the pilgrimage account is used to justify a trip undertaken to rally support for a political cause.[2] Yet we also see how the religious narrative overtakes the political motivations. In any case, it gives us a sense of the problems in reconstructing an elusive category such as "individual experience," for the historian as well as the contemporary anthropologist.

A PILGRIMAGE ACCOUNT BETWEEN OLD AND NEW

The practice of pilgrimage is a crucial feature in Hinduism and the subject of much scholarly interest.[3] Many of the initial studies of pilgrimage centers focus on Sanskrit texts.[4] Studies of the pilgrimage experience tend to be anthropological.[5] *The Pilgrim's Bliss* is a vernacular autobiographical account, simultaneously a report of the experience and a description of mainly one pilgrimage site, Braj.

The Pilgrim's Bliss is a text in between two worlds, the modern and the traditional. It has one leg in traditional pilgrimage accounts, in that it is solely focused on the religious aspect of the journey. There is none of the modern attention to the practicalia and hardships of the journey, nor does it proffer ethnographic musings on the curiosities of the new places visited or reports of official meetings and economic transactions.[6] Whereas travelogues tend to center on the bazaar, *The Pilgrim's Bliss* centers on the temple and fails to mention the cost of the journey, money tranfers, commercial exchanges, or purchases made along the road.[7] Little is even known about how big Nāgarīdās's party was, yet he must have traveled with a group of followers, possibly some soldiers loyal to his cause, but the only references are to his "camp" (*śivira*, at TĀ 18, 44, 60).[8] Modern travelogues often (if implicitly) critique pilgrimage as they report money demands by religious specialists.[9] Though Nāgarīdās must have encountered the notoriously persistent Caubes of Mathura, his report of a visit to Vishram Ghat remains silent on the topic (TĀ 19). *The Pilgrim's Bliss* thus can be characterized as largely traditional.[10]

Yet it also has one leg in the "modern" and differs from other traditional pilgrimage accounts, because it is autobiographical and descriptive. This heralds a shift from the prescriptive accounts of the Māhātmya (Glorification) genre, which were produced in Sanskrit by local Brahmins with a stake in promoting travel to their area and gift-giving in their temples.[11] Such texts are idealized and atemporal and thus promote a mythic perspective of the place described. Nāgarīdās's work also differs from the descriptive but often retrospective and fictionalized third-person accounts of the pilgrimages of holy men.[12] The work is not hagiographical; the closest Nāgarīdās comes to depicting himself as a "saint" is when he relates the warm welcome he received upon arrival in Vrindavan (TĀ 28–33). *The Pilgrim's Bliss* differs also from pilgrimage accounts of royalty that were composed in the third person by a courtier to commemorate auspicious occasions for merit (*puṇya*) and to record for posterity the king's meritorious religious gift-giving.[13] They thus detail the king's donations and acts of charity, foregrounding Brahmins and the Sanskritic rites they performed for the king. They sometimes served to legitimize a new king's tenuous position, as was the case for the Tanjore Maratha ruler Serfoji Bhosle II, who was adopted on the deathbed of the previous king and whose coronation with British support was much contested.[14] Sāvant Singh was in a comparable situation, with a need to justify his case of succession, yet *The Pilgrim's Bliss* bypasses practically all Brahmins, ritual detail, and gift-giving. Possibly, Sāvant Singh did not have much charity to offer as a king in exile, but it seems rather an omission due to a different emphasis of what pilgrimage is about. *The Pilgrim's Bliss* shows no trace of aspiring to gain worldly prestige through lavish display of wealth. Rather than royal self-aggrandizement, Sāvant Singh was interested in personal experience and partaking in mythological events.

This is not to claim any firsts for *The Pilgrim's Bliss*; there are some earlier first-person pilgrimage accounts, such as the description by a (probably Vallabhan) pilgrim from Bikaner, Maheśvarī, of a trip to Braj, undertaken in 1656 (1713 VS).[15] While the itinerary is similar to Nāgarīdās's, it lists mainly places where the pilgrim bathed, in which temples *darshana* was had, and what food was offered, with little personal commentary.[16] Other such reports may have been written but not been preserved or cataloged. Nāgarīdās's account is unique for its tone of intense engagement and joy in the various activities described, hence the aptly chosen title *Tīrthānand*, which literally means "The Bliss of Pilgrimage."

This autobiographical work might seem out of place in Nāgarīdās's oeuvre. Yet its second part, which in following roughly the seasonal calendar, documents not just sacred locale (*tīrtha*) but also sacred time (*utsava*), fits seamlessly with Nāgarīdās's poems that celebrate the Braj area and seasonal festivals. It seems a natural outgrowth of his lifelong production of such poetry, only now tied together as an actual journey in historical time. Unlike the somewhat impersonal style of the seasonal poetry, which presents mainly the mythic realm, the pilgrimage account is shot through with personal experience.

Sāvant Singh undertook his pilgrimage for both sacred and profane reasons. Even if downplayed, there are repeated references to the military objective of the trip, namely, to muster support for his cause in the succession of his throne from the Marathas in Kumaon and from the Mughals in Delhi. This highlights the connection between military maneuver and pilgrimage, which is often overlooked in pilgrimage studies. Braj was located near the route that armies frequented in this period of major power changes: the end of the Lodi Sultanate, Bābar's invasion, Sher Shāh Sūr's short-lived reign, and, again, the return of the Mughals, plus several internal struggles that accompanied these new state formations. It was also exactly in this period that the Braj area experienced a "renaissance." Through new roads, like the ones built by Sher Shāh Sūr, that allowed military movement as well as mercantile travel and pilgrimage, Braj became connected with the twin capitals of Delhi and Agra.[17] To focus on a pilgrimage center in terms of theologians' and saints' discourses as if these took place in splendid isolation from military activity is therefore misleading. Nāgarīdās's pilgrimage report, when contextualized, illustrates vividly how campaigns to seek military help could be combined with pilgrimage. Not incidentally, the latter could serve as a cover for the former. Scholars of the phenomenon of pilgrimage have argued in favor of seeing pilgrimage as "a polysemous way of acting," which "contains multiple meanings and cannot be rendered intelligible by any single explanation."[18]

Nāgarīdās's work provides valuable documentation of itineraries of pilgrimage travel, an eyewitness account of the festivals and rites of Braj, and transcriptions of Rās-līlā performances, offering a lively glimpse of the culture in the mid-eighteenth century, just before things were to change. The work was written in 1753 and gives a vivid description of the Holī festivities of the preceding year. That was just five years before the horrible massacres by Durrānī in 1757, which turned that year's Holī into an orgy of blood rather than red powder.[19]

PLEASURE AND PILGRIMAGE

Pilgrimage accounts are usually very specific about the date of departure because of the formal "declaration of intention" (*saṅkalpa*) expressed typically at the outset. Nāgarīdās, though, does not specify when or where he started the trip, perhaps because his pilgrimage was actually more a forced journey into exile. Instead, he starts out with a contrast between the mundane homeland and the sacred pilgrimage center, anticipating somewhat bitterly the bliss of arriving in the latter. Fittingly for a Rajasthani, he contrasts the dry desert land with the "green, green Tamāla trees" of Braj, anticipating the pleasure of their verdure:

> The more one sees these foolish people here, spurning grace,
> The more the blissful folk of Braj delight the heart.
> Here, ponds are brackish and wells are sadly parched.
> How my heart longs for the sweet Kālindī (Yamunā) River's waters!

The way I live my life now, I cannot describe in words:
Nāgar: no respite in sight, just writhing in despair.
Thorny cactus shrubs and prickly acacia trees, as far as the eye can see.
But oh, how those green, green Tamāla trees fill my mind.

(TĀ 1)[20]

In referring to "foolish godless people" (*mūrakha vimukha loga*), Nāgarīdās may well have had his brother and his party in mind. The work thus begins not just by formulaically contrasting mundane and religious realms, but with a real frustration behind it. This lived experience is also behind the next verse with joyful anticipation of Braj, contrasted with Vishnu's highest heaven of Vaikuṇṭha:

Nothing can compare to Braj
Even Vaikuṇṭha's bliss falls short.
Comfort and rest are found
In the shade of the Mountain-Lifter's protecting arm.
Nāgar who spurned it, now has regrets,
Doomed to wander in distress.
From foreign land to foreign land, the hapless roam.
But rest in Braj and find true joy.

(TĀ 2)[21]

Only a few years before, in 1744, Nāgarīdās composed a lengthier work on the topic, *Weighing Braj and Vaikuṇṭha*, but the verse quoted here is not from that work. The theme of the contrast between royal splendor and bucolic charm takes on special poignancy given his drastically changed living circumstances. The reference to Krishna's "protective arm" evokes Sāvant Singh's real-life quest to find a supporter for his cause. The exhortation not to roam around aimlessly but instead to settle in Braj recalls Sāvant Singh's efforts to find allies, on his fruitless journey over North India around 1750–52. This appeal not to travel but to settle down is unusual, as pilgrimage texts typically foreground the journey. But after his lengthy travel to the Himalayan foothills in pursuit of an alliance with the Marathas, he must have longed to finally settle down. It is as if he was taken up literally on his statements in *Weighing Braj and Vaikuṇṭha* and called to prove that his commitment went beyond poetic convention.

THE PILGRIM'S BLISS

A striking characteristic of this work is that it revolves around *ānanda*, or spiritual bliss, which results from participation in ceremonies at holy places (*tīrtha*) and, for the listener, in Nāgarīdās's singing its praise. The title delivers on its promise, providing "The Bliss of Pilgrimage." Given the existential situation of the author, namely, his exile as a consequence of having his throne usurped, the title might be read as "The Bliss of Pilgrimage in a Time of Distress." However, the work does not bear that out. Nāgarīdās's report is light on the worries about money and alliance-seeking that the journey must have entailed. Such hardships are barely broached: there is only a passing reference to the difficult mountainous territory (TĀ 55). What was in effect a quest for political help from the Marathas and Mughal officials (and possibly the ascetic warriors of Galta) is recast as a pilgrimage with alliance-seeking a mere diversion. Political affairs are dismissed as unpleasant distractions (TĀ 69 and 73, respectively). That contrasts with his eagerness to visit Vrindavan, to the extent that he wades across the Yamunā when no boats are available (TĀ 61–68). Overwhelmingly, the work breathes the bliss of the title. If there is a note of sorrow in the work, it is the sorrow of parting, of leaving the hallowed grounds of Braj (TĀ 18, 39).

Our text bears witness that the combination of pilgrimage and tourism is not a modern phenomenon, as pilgrimage in the mid-eighteenth century was accompanied by leisure activities. No sooner does the Kishangarhi prince reach Mathura than he goes boating (*naukā vihār*) opposite Vishram Ghat at dusk (TĀ 19). The pleasures of travel are described in a tactile way: one can feel the refreshment of the beautiful bucolic setting of Devyānī (TĀ 5), cool Galta (TĀ 6–7), and tree-shaded Braj upon arrival (TĀ 10). Especially attractive are the evocation of the view of Barsana's temple on the hill from a distance (TĀ 71–73) and the *darshana* of the deities (in Vrindavan [TĀ 33] and in Barsana [TĀ 74]). When having *darshana* of Bihārī, Nāgarīdās also expresses his aesthetic delight at hearing his well-dressed concubine, Banī-ṭhanī, whose pen name was Rasik Bihārī, sing before Bihārī's image:

> Passionately, Bihārinī, fully adorned (*banī*),
> Approached her beloved Bihārī.
> With these very eyes, I drank in
> Their exquisite and incomparable loveliness.
> Thereupon we sang songs of reunion
> And in between, songs by Rasik Bihārī.
>
> (TĀ 33–34)

The word *banī* in the first verse is likely an oblique reference to Banī-ṭhanī, his mistress.[22] This passage could be seen as the literary equivalent of Rasik Bihārī accompanying Sāvant Singh in his exile in the picture on the cover of this book.

Similarly, the author includes a loving portrait of the setting for a singing session with the flower ladies at Jñān Gudarī in Vrindavan (TĀ 35–38). In good calendrical fashion, he describes the joys of the seasons of the monsoon (TĀ 76ff.), autumn (TĀ 120ff.), the cold season (TĀ 160ff.), and spring, especially Holī (TĀ 164ff.). A beautiful description of the āratī (fire worship) of Yamunā at dusk in Mathura reveals the author's voyeuristic pleasure in seeing local women participate in the rites with abandon:[23]

> The āratī's bliss is hard to describe.
> . . . .
> Men and women arrive in large groups:
> Hymns in Rāga Gaurī arise from the crowd.
> Even noble ladies dance, suffused with love,
> All shyness gone, proper manners forgotten.
> Hair coiffed artfully on their heads,
> Bodies adorned with golden necklaces and jewelry,
> They wear flower garlands with basil leaves.
> Waterspouts in hand, refined markings on their foreheads,
> Arm in arm, they have gathered for worship, leaving their household
> tasks behind,
> Their bodies divine, like the mythic Brahmin women.[24]
> Their white attire sparkles splendidly;[25]
> They cannot hide their shapely bodies.
> At one side, near the river steps—these women,
> On the other—the devotees of the city gathered.
> Melodious singing rises to the sky,
> With clanging of cymbals (*jhāñjha*), and beating of drums.
> Sweet dishes make the rounds at the time the āratī is blazing,
> A shout of "Hail, hail" arises as flowers rain down.
>
> (TĀ 20–24)

The joy and beauty of musical gatherings is repeatedly expressed throughout the work (TĀ 12–13, 16–17, 35–37, 67–68). This sense of joy is not trivial, as Nāgarīdās explicitly elevates enjoyment above liberation (*mukti*) (TĀ 37).

PILGRIMAGE AS ESCAPISM?

One could look on the journey to Braj as escapism. The postulation that it functions as an escape, as a comfort for the world-weary, is reinforced by the above-quoted first verses of the work, with the contrast of Rajasthan's prickly cactus vegetation with the greenery of Braj (TĀ 1) and the dismissal of majestic Vaikuṇṭha as no match for bucolic Braj (TĀ 2). A similar interpretation might be given of Nāgarīdās's remark that beholding the ashram of Galta "destroys the pride of the world" (TĀ 7). After negotiating with the Marathas, Nāgarīdās rushed down the mountains, eager to make it to Braj (TĀ 56–57). This seems quite literally a case of running away to Braj (even if he does not make it in time to celebrate Holī).

It may be more fruitful to look on it positively, as a quest for psychological relief and healing. What pilgrimage studies usually foreground is the pilgrims' practical goals of life-cycle rituals, the "transactional" vow fulfillment, fertility concerns, the more general acquiring of merit, and the overarching (but, by informants, rarely expressed) desire for release (*mokṣa*).[26] To complement these, it could be added that in a very practical and immediate sense, there is also the desire for relief and for healing in a situation of crisis.[27] The process of going on pilgrimage represents a change of scenery, and the travails of the journey distract the mind from whatever hardships one was working through at home.[28] Once one starts looking for it, one may well find this motive underlying a good many resolves to depart on pilgrimage, or encouraging relatives to do so.

THE ITINERARY: PILGRIMAGE ROUTES IN THE EIGHTEENTH CENTURY

Because of the religious interests of the Kishangarh house, the Braj area figured importantly on their pilgrimage itineraries. *The Pilgrim's Bliss* provides specifics of routes and stops on the way, in particular in the first section (up to verse 69), which is a travelogue, perhaps based on the author's notes of the journey he undertook a few years before finalizing the work.

FROM RAJASTHAN TO BRAJ

Nāgarīdās describes shrines he stopped at on the way from Rajasthan to Braj. What reads as a placid progress of a pilgrim covers up quite a bit of military activity. He started out from Rupnagar toward Sambhar Lake, a mineral-rich area the control of which was contested between different parties at the

TABLE 3.1 Overview of the Pilgrimage Trajectory of *The Pilgrim's Bliss*

Verse Number	Content / *Tīrtha (Utsava)*
1–3	Introduction
	Rajasthan
4–5	Devyānī
6–9	Galta
	Braj
10–13	Govardhan
14–17	Radhakund and Krishnakund
18–27	Mathura (Vishram Ghat)
28–40	Vrindavan (Bihārī; Jñān Gudarī)
	Gaṅgā
41–49	Soron
50–53	Kapilāśram
	Kumaon
54–56	Rāmgaṅgā; Dhavalāgiri; Kauśikī river
57–59	Gaṅgā banks (Holī)
	Braj
60–68	Vrindavan
69	Delhi
70–81	Barsana (monsoon festivals; Tīj)
82–86	Unchagaon (Balarāma Janmotsava)
86–89	Prem Sarovar (Rakṣā-bandhana)
90–95	Nandagaon (Krishna Janmotsava)
96–98	Karhara (Lalitā Janmotsava)
98–100	Kadamkhandi (Dān-keli-līlā)
101–12	Barsana (Vilās Gaṛh; Mor Kuṭī) (Rādhā Janmotsava)
113	Kokila Ban / Jāvak Vaṭ (Rās-līlā)
114	Unchagaon (slippery rock)
115–19	Barsana (Mān Gaṛh; Dān Gaṛh; Sāṅkarī Khor)
120–27	Vrindavan (Sāñjhī; Śarad Rās-līlā)
128–34	Radhakund (Kārtik bathing)
135–43	Govardhan / Mānasī Gaṅgā (Dīpāvalī and Annakūṭa)
144–59	Nandagaon-Kadamkhandi-Nandagaon (Gopāṣṭamī)
160–61	Braj (Māgh–Pauṣ)
162–81	Barsana (Vasant–Holī)
182–205	Nandagaon (Holī)
206–11	Praise of Holī
212–13	Envoi

FIG. 3.2 *Chatrī* at Kup Ghat in the pilgrimage center of Devyānī

time.[29] Facing Sambhar Lake is a pond dedicated to the mythical Devyānī, the daughter of Śukrācārya, the guru of the demons, who married Yayāti.[30] The pilgrimage site, built around this pond, has many buildings from the eighteenth and nineteenth centuries, an indication that it was an active pilgrimage center during that period, though nearly all are in ruins now (fig. 3.2).[31]

The idyllic description of the pilgrim's progress sidesteps significant military activity in the area at the time. It is not entirely clear when exactly Sāvant Singh traveled the area, but it was unsafe. The ongoing Jaipur dynastic struggle had fallout in the form of the battle of Bagru between the two Jaipur half-brothers in August 1748. Īśvarī Singh had the Jat ruler Sūraj Mal on his side and the contender Mādho Singh, the Peshva Bālājī Bāji Rāo. The Marathas, dissatisfied with payments for their support, plundered the area around Sambhar Lake throughout August.[32] Later, by April 1750, the Jaipur contenders were involved in the succession war of Marwar at Raona (south of Merta).[33]

Sāvant Singh's venturing near Sambhar Lake may have been to visit the nearby Dādū-panthī seat of Naraina to enlist the help of the warrior ascetics there for his cause. These ascetics fought in the Jaipur succession war on the side of Īśvarī Singh, but they were nearly annihilated in a surprise attack.[34] Perhaps that preempted Sāvant Singh's mission; in any case, he does not mention the monastery.

Sāvant Singh does mention that, on leaving Devyānī, he made obeisance to "Govinda, the Lord of Gokul." Possibly this was the famous Govindadeva image that, by this time, was installed in Jaipur in the Jaynivās.[35] If he did pay a visit to Jaipur, it may have been a hasty one during 1748 or upon his return to the area in the summer of 1750. Maratha sources indicate that around September 1750 he marched with Īśvarī Singh's help to Rupnagar, to lay siege to the city occupied by Bahādur Singh, but this attempt was ineffectual.[36] Could all that martial activity be hidden in that simple "making obeisance to Govinda"?

Sāvant Singh next mentions a site just outside Jaipur, the monastery of Galta. It is referred to by its Sanskritic name Gālavāśram, after the ashram of another Vedic sage, whose shrine is part of the complex (fig. 3.3). This again contributes to an otherworldly image of the pilgrim's progress, yet Sāvant Singh's objective may have been to muster support for his cause, perhaps from Vrijānand, the abbot of the warrior or Nāgā Rāmānandīs of Jaipur, who supported Īśvarī Singh's cause. What transpired is not known, but Sāvant Singh likely felt at home in Galta, with its distinct *rasika* ambience in the mid-eighteenth century. Nāgarīdās mentions by name Hari Ācārya, the first householder-abbot of the seat after Jai Singh's reforms (r. 1733–56):

> Then came the ashram of Gālava, full of pleasures,
> But forbidden to nonbelievers,
> Where hover large swarms of intoxicated bees.
> The breeze thrice pleasant, the pool pure water-filled,
> Wooded mountain, waterfall, and cowshed,[37]
> One look at the place brings liberation: all false pride disappears.
> We visited this sanctuary worthy of
> Hari Ācārya, the wise sage,
> Fortunate, friendly, peaceful, and serene by nature,
> Meditating on Rāma, bliss incarnate.
> He obliged us with his gift of honor,
> The perfect farewell gift: meditation on Raghunātha (Rāma).
>
> (TĀ 6–8)

FIG. 3.3 The shrine for Gālava Rishi at Galta

Hari Ācārya organized Rās-līlās for the festival of Rāma's wedding. Like Nāgarīdās, he was a poet, with the *chāpa* "Hari-sahacarī," and he was heavily influenced by Krishnaite models. From his description in *The Pilgrim's Bliss*, Nāgarīdās seems to have been very positively impressed by him.

Whether any military support was discussed is unknown; but if so, he was not successful, because next Sāvant Singh turned again to Delhi, as the colophons of two of his works make clear: by the end of 1748 (Pauṣ 1805) he writes at the banks of the Yamunā and in 1749 (1806 VS) on the bank of the "Hindani" (Hindon) River. If Sāvant Singh stayed outside Jaipur, he had good reasons. By the end of 1750, Īśvarī Singh had committed suicide. Mādho Singh then occupied the throne of Jaipur, and since he was an ally of Bahādur Singh, Sāvant Singh would not have met with him. Remarkably, all this political strife of the times is simply bypassed in the pilgrimage narrative.

BRAJ FOR RAJASTHANI PILGRIMS

The first stop in Braj for the party traveling from Rajasthan was Govardhan.[38] Sāvant Singh's party circumambulated the mountain (TĀ 10, 12) and stopped at the nearby adjacent ponds of Radha- and Krishnakund (TĀ 14). This route is very similar to what the Bikaneri pilgrim Maheśvarī reports of a 1656 trip, with the exception that there the *darshana* of the image of Śrī Nātha jī is mentioned.[39] Nāgarīdās does not report visiting the famous Śrī Nātha jī temple, which is a significant omission. The original image was already in Nathdvara by then, but there is evidence that the temple back in Braj was open for *darshana* by the time of Jai Singh.[40]

Next on the itinerary was Mathura, referred to by its Sanskritic name Madhupurī (TĀ 18), and the only specific site mentioned is Vishram Ghat (TĀ 19). In contrast, Maheśvarī dwells quite elaborately on the Mathura scene, listing all the temples and ghats.[41] The next stop was Vrindavan, where the Kishangarh family possessed a residence, Nagari Kunj. Like a modern-day pilgrim, Nāgarīdās had *darshana* in the Bihārī temple (TĀ 33), though the reference may be to another image named "Bihārī."[42] Maheśvarī also mentions having *darshana* of Bāṃko Bihārī jī, in addition to many others, including two other "Bihārīs."[43] By contrast, the only other site Nāgarīdās describes in Vrindavan is that of Jñān Gudarī near the river (TĀ 35).

From Braj, he reluctantly traveled onward, stopping first at Soron, an ancient pilgrimage center on the west bank of the Ganges, east of Aligarh, which makes sense in terms of Rajasthani pilgrimage patterns. Maheśvarī did the same, and also Rajput royal families tended to go there.[44] For example, in 1648, the Mewar royal family made an extended pilgrimage trip from Mathura and Gokul to Prayag, Benares, and Ayodhya, with a stop in Soron (Sukara) on the way. The party included the young prince, future ruler Rāj Singh (r. 1652–80), who later commissioned an illustrated manuscript (finished in 1655) of the Sanskrit *Sukarakṣetra-mahāpurāṇa*, a text celebrating the miraculous power of the Soron *tīrtha*.[45] In 1724, Savāī Jai Singh II, while he was governor of Agra and engaged in a campaign against the Jats, also extended his pilgrimage to Braj with a journey to Soron.[46] Pilgrimage to Soron serves funerary purposes (people immerse the ashes of their deceased family members), but Sāvant Singh does not mention disposing of his father's ashes. It is possible that he had intended to set out to Prayag, as the Mewar family did, but instead he turned north to meet the Marathas.

NORTHERN SITES

Sāvant Singh found opportunities for pilgrimage even as he followed the Maratha troops under Jayappa Scindhia and Malhār Rāo Holkar, who had driven the Rohillas to the Terai region and Kumaon.[47] Ironically, the Rohillas themselves had used existing pilgrim routes to Haridwar to connect their lands with the hill trade of Garhwal and Kumaon and specifically to take advantage of the horse trade at the fairs en route, and the Marathas, who equally sought to safeguard a secure supply of warhorses, did the same.[48] Sāvant Singh again bypasses the military activity and reports just on pilgrimage activity at Rāmeśvaram and the ashram of Kapila.[49]

After crossing Rāmgaṅgā, he may have visited a shrine of Narasiṃha, the man-lion incarnation of Vishnu, possibly Narsingh Badri in Joshimath.[50] This is part of an area known as Vaishnava Kṣetra, which is also the winter home of the Badrinath priests. If that is where he went, he must have traveled via the ancient road through Almora, crossing Rāmgaṅgā north from there.[51]

Sāvant Singh mentions approaching Dhavalāgiri,[52] "where not even birds fly" (TĀ 55), and bathing in the Kauśikī River, supposedly the modern Kosi River, though its course may have been different. The colophon of one of his works locates him near the Kumaon mountains on the banks of the "Kosakī" River in January–February 1751 (1808 VS, Māgh), thus providing an anchor in time for his stay in the North.[53] He gives very little description of the Himalayan sites, and he did not go to Badrinath, probably because the roads were still not open. Instead, he rushed back down the mountains, keen on visiting Braj again, even though he actually ended up first going to Delhi, where he probably arrived shortly before the civil war of 1753.

THE BRAJ REAL ESTATE BOOM

On the next visit, Nāgarīdās approached Braj from Delhi, so the party's first stop this time was not Govardhan but Barsana. Vividly described is the road to Barsana, with the white palace temple in the distance (TĀ 71; fig. 3.4). He also says that lakes everywhere were "brimming with fresh water," probably a reference to the many tanks on the circumambulation path.[54] That fits with the colophons in his works that indicate he returned to settle in Braj during the rainy season of 1752.[55] He continues by mentioning a visit to "Vrishabhānu's durbar," probably the temple at the foot of the hill, before reaching that of Rādhā, the Lārilījī temple on the top.

Any impression that Braj was a bucolic refuge for retirement from politics is belied by the real estate boom it experienced during this period. The Jats were intensely involved: in 1752, Sūraj Mal became faujdar of Mathura and received the title of Brajendra.[56] Barsana was being built up under the influence of Rūp Rām, a Brahmin who served as priest and negotiator of the Jat rulers Sūraj Mal and Javāhar Singh.[57] Rūp Rām built the Lārilījī temple on the hill, which superseded the earlier one sponsored by Vīr Singh of Orccha,

FIG. 3.4 Approaching Barsana

and this is probably the one that Nāgarīdās saw as he approached from a distance. Many other wealthy families chose to reside in Barsana, including a Ṭhākur (landlord) who is said to have made his fortune in Lucknow.[58] Barsana was something of a cosmopolitan hub. A Barsana-centered description of Braj in a contemporary work, written by Sudān at the Jat court of Digh, is put in the mouth of Rūp Rām himself, as he is negotiating with the Maratha Malhār Rāo to prevent him from attacking Braj.[59] To think of Barsana and its environs at the time as provincial and isolated would be a fallacy.

For his second, lengthy stay in Braj, Sāvant Singh seems to have been based in Barsana rather than Vrindavan. It seems less likely that he was seeking Sūraj Mal's support, but rather that he wanted to be in a vibrant, "happening" place. The rites he describes may represent less time-honored traditions than what was "in" for the new elites that were involved in the Barsana boom. All festivals were celebrated in locations near Barsana: Nandagaon, Unchagaon, Karhara, and Kadamkhandi. Mor Kuṭī, which is right on the Barsana hill, is not mentioned here, however; but in his *Garland of Stories and Songs*, Nāgarīdās refers to it as a site on the Parikramā Mārg (circumambulation path) near Barsana, where his namesake, the saint

Nehī Nāgarīdās, used to live (PPM 53). The other places mentioned were trendy at the time and being built up by those associated with the Jats. Still, the deciding factor must have been the primacy of the "urbane" Nāgarī, or Rādhā in Barsana, to whom he felt a special devotion; after all, his pen name, Nāgarīdās, means "Rādhā's servant."

RITES AND FESTIVALS OF THE MID-EIGHTEENTH CENTURY

The Pilgrim's Bliss can also be read as a gazetteer-style overview of rites and festivals of the mid-eighteenth-century Braj, allowing for comparison with the contemporary situation and affording a sense of the historical depth of current practices. The first-person account shares the experiences of the pilgrims and tells of how they construed the meaning of these rituals and festivals.

TĪRTHAS AND *LĪLĀ*: PARTICIPATORY RITES, PROCESSION, AND *SATSAṄGA*

At the more traditional *tīrtha*s outside of Braj, the main ritual activity of the pilgrim is bathing. At the beginning of his trip, Sāvant Singh mentions visiting *tīrtha*s that are built around tanks, such as in Devyānī (TĀ 4–5) and Galta (TĀ 6–7), but also on rivers, such as the Ganges in Soron (TĀ 42, 45) and Kapilāśram (TĀ 51, 53), Rāmgaṅgā (TĀ 54), and the Kosi River near Dhavalāgiri (TĀ 55). Again, pleasure comes into play, here as a refreshing bath after an exhausting journey.

Upon Sāvant Singh's reaching Braj, the ritual bath seems less important; it is the sacred dust of the place that is foregrounded in Sakaran (TĀ 9), near Radhakund (TĀ 15), in Vrindavan (TĀ 31), and upon return in Barsana, when he rolls in the dust (TĀ 73). The only exception is in Mathura, where Nāgarīdās mentions taking a morning bath (TĀ 18), and also upon leaving the area, when he bathes in the Yamunā (TĀ 41). Perhaps the old *tīrtha* of Mathura is an exception in the Braj area. Otherwise, the evidence can be taken to confirm the classification of places of pilgrimage that distinguishes between *jala tīrtha* (primacy of bathing), *mandira tīrtha* (primacy of *darshana*), and *kṣetra* (sacred area), with Braj fitting more the last category.[60] To accommodate the case of Braj, one could nuance the last category by alternatively calling it *līlā tīrtha*, since participation in the divine *līlā* is primary.

Nāgarīdās's account provides evidence for performance of some important daily rites already in the eighteenth century, notably the āratī of the Yamunā in Mathura at dusk (TĀ 20–25). Nāgarīdās vividly describes the spectacle of the local worshippers and their hymn-singing, which he seems to consider more important than the pomp of the priests.[61] Another rite is the daily gathering at dusk of flower ladies at Jñān Gudarī in Vrindavan (TĀ 35), which may also be linked with the procession of flower-decorated carts, celebrated on Śravaṇ Pūrṇimā.[62] Nāgarīdās also describes evening rites involving the floating of lamps in the river Ganges at Soron (TĀ 45–46) and bathing in the Ganges there, accompanied by hymn-singing:

> On the second day, we made offerings of oil lamps
> Till her banks shone like wondrous gold.
> As if fallen from heaven, softly,
> The stars settled down, row after row,
> Adding sparkle to Śrī Gaṅgā's banks
> Like a golden border to her garb.
> Lamps floated midstream, waves aglow,
> The river of the gods, lit up with jewels.
> Feasting our eyes, we spent a happy night on the banks.
> At daybreak we bathed, sanctifying our bodies.
> With bowed head and folded hands we repeated:
> "Please grant me this, Gaṅgā: Deliver me from orphanhood."
> My prayer:
> . . . . .
> "O Gracious One, how many prayers of Nāgar
> Should I utter as I fall at your feet?
> What impedes my residence in Braj?
> O Gaṅgā, please absolve this sin of mine."
>
> (TĀ 45–48)

Here is a sample of a hymn sung for the occasion. It is one of his own making, with a rather personal theme: he seeks access to residence in Braj.

An important aspect of pilgrimage is meeting with holy men and women, or *satsaṅga*. Nāgarīdās's travels frequently involve contact with the residents of sacred places, facilitated through participatory rites, such as procession. Upon arrival in Braj, Nāgarīdās undertakes the circumambulation (*pradakṣinā*) of Mount Govardhan, which turns into a procession:

> We set out on foot, on the path around the mountain.
> On the way many virtuous *rasikas* joined us
> With beautiful singing and *kīrtana*, emotions streaming freely,

Many a cymbal clanging, and many a drum banging.
Cows and cowherds emerged from the forest to listen along,
All ears, imbibing the nectar of Krishna's song.
A devoted (*ananya*) group was intoxicated with love—
Enthralled, concern for body and soul forgotten.
The group of *rasika*s arrived at the spot
Where the ponds are: Radhakund and Krishnakund.
Here, too, devotees gathered to listen with rapt attention.
They arose and led us around as euphoria increased.

(TĀ 12–14)

Nāgarīdās's party's ecstatic *kīrtana* with musical accompaniment draws a lot of attention and other enthusiasts join in. The procession proceeds to nearby Radha- and Krishnakund for more *kīrtana* sessions with local residents. In Radhakund, this ends up as an all-night singing party with the locals Bansīdās and Muralīdās (TĀ 15–17). A lasting bond was forged here: Nāgarīdās mentions staying again with Bansīdās later, for an all-night singing session during the Kārtik bathing festival at Radhakund (TĀ 133). Significantly, this Radhakund resident Bansīdās may be the Vaṃśīdās who lived at Surma Kunj and was a follower of the unorthodox party that had been socially excluded from the Gauḍīya-Sampradāya for their defiance of Savāī Jai Singh II's measures.[63] This provides a vivid background for Nāgarīdās's own opposition to orthodoxy.

In Vrindavan, too, there is plenty of *satsaṅga*. When Nāgarīdās describes his reception by the local community, he says sadhus came running to meet, not prince Sāvant Singh of Kishangarh, but Nāgarīdās, composer of devotional songs, and they insist that he sing his songs for them:

There, all our sadhu friends were gathered,
Each of them, holy in the three worlds.
My official name was announced, but it left them aloof and cold.
Then, when they heard I was Nāgarīdās, they ran up to me, tears
in their eyes.[64]
Some came running to meet me with open arms,
Others called out to me again and again.
Some were moved and spontaneously
Burst out in song with my signature line.
Even madmen who rolled in the dust
Left their haunts, came running to meet me.

Pleased as well, austere ascetics,
Who do not reckon pauper or prince.
All of them thronged around me.
They insisted that I recite and sing songs.

(TĀ 28–32)

This reception is followed by an all-night singing session at Jñān Gudarī (TĀ 35–37).

More sober is the respectful obeisance to a female ascetic in Mathura, who practiced predominantly asceticism, though mixed with *bhakti*:

There (in Mathura) dwells an older ascetic lady.
Her door thronged with people desirous to see her.
Penitence mixed with devotion's passion,
She drinks only milk, starving her body.
We paid our respects, and she showed us grace.
Then we left, keen to go to Vrindavan.

(TĀ 27)

This scene recalls that depicted in an intriguing Kishangarhi painting of a (younger and more attractive) female ascetic on a terrace along a riverbank, attributed to Bhavānīdās's atelier and dated to circa 1725–50 (fig. 3.5).[65] She is approached by a motley group of visitors, presumably admirers who have come to beseech her. But for the elegance of the yogini, this scene resembles that described by Nāgarīdās in *The Pilgrim's Bliss*.

Nāgarīdās's description of ascetics is decidedly less warm than that of *bhaktas*, presumably because there was no strong bond of emotional devotion. That he appears to be less positive toward asceticism becomes clear when he indirectly criticizes a holy man he visits near Kapilāśram. He describes in some detail the self-mortifications the man had undergone, including taking a vow of silence, emaciating his body, holding a contorted body position, wrapping his hands turned around his chest, and staring constantly upward, to the effect that his neck had grown crooked (TĀ 51–52). He is not unlike the ascetics in the background of *A Yogini at Her Retreat*. Nāgarīdās concludes: "He practiced austerities, personifying the hardship of *sanyāsa*. But without *bhakti*, it's useless" (TĀ 52). It is clear that—in his view—excessive asceticism is not the right path. This meeting, too, lacks the shared understanding of like-minded devotees.

FIG. 3.5 *A Yogini at Her Retreat*, attributed to the atelier of Bhavānīdās, Kishangarh school, ca. 1725–50. Ink, opaque watercolor, and gold on paper (20.5 × 23.5 cm). Private collection (Germany). Courtesy Mr. Eberhard Rist

UTSAVA, OR THE FESTIVAL CYCLE

The second half of *The Pilgrim's Bliss* consists of an extended calendrical cycle, belonging to the genre of *ṣaḍṛtu* (six seasons) or, more precisely, *bārahmāsā* (twelve months).[66] For Krishna devotional works of the type, the seasonal characteristics of the twelve months are often described as a backdrop for the longing (*viraha*) of parted lovers. Nāgarīdās, instead, foregrounds the joyful celebration of each season and its festivals. In that respect, his report is closer to peasants' almanacs and to earlier similar Bengali calendrical enumerations of goddess festivals.[67] However, his calendar is not prescriptive; rather, it is descriptive and, moreover, in the first-person voice. That seems fitting for the *utsavas* of Braj, which even today foreground personal experience and are celebrated in a highly participatory manner. Nāgarīdās focuses on festivities in the Barsana-Nandagaon area, which was burgeoning with building activities at the time. Each season is detailed here with reference to the historical context in the sequence Nāgarīdās describes them.

As is commonplace in this popular genre, Nāgarīdās starts his *bārahmāsā* with the month of Āsāṛh (June–July), though he says only that Rāga Malāra is sung during this time of year (TĀ 76). By contrast, the month of Sāvan (July–August) is busy with festivals. For the feast of the third day, or Tīj (Hariyālī Tīj), in Barsana the image of Lārilījī is taken out for the swing festival (TĀ 78–81). Nāgarīdās notes that she is put on a dais (*chatrī*) and dance troupes perform in front of the image, a practice that continues today.[68]

On the fifth day of the bright half of Sāvan (which is also the snake festival of Nāg-pañcamī), Uncagaon is the place to be for Balarāma's birthday (TĀ 82).[69] The temple there, founded by the Gauḍīya Gosvāmī Nārāyaṇ Bhaṭṭ, dates from the sixteenth century.[70] The festival Nāgarīdās describes involves singing and recitation by *ḍhāṛhī*s (genealogical specialists), as well as merrymaking with milk, turmeric, and *khīr* (rice pudding) and also lots of gift-giving (TĀ 83).

Next, presumably on the full-moon day of Sāvan, is the festival of Salono, better known as Rakṣā-bandhana (TĀ 86–89). The festival is already mentioned by Nārāyaṇ Bhaṭṭ in the sixteenth century, but it became especially popular in the eighteenth century. Here the celebration takes place at Prem Sarovar, where Rūp Rām had newly constructed ghats around the octagonal tank.[71] Nāgarīdās describes the rite of tying the *rākhī* (loyalty bracelet) and mentions that a Rās-līlā takes place at Prem Sarovar on this occasion.[72]

Nāgarīdās continues with Krishna's birthday festival, Janmāṣṭamī, on the eighth day of the dark half of Bhādon (August–September).[73] He attended the festival in Nandagaon (Nandagrāma) near Barsana (TĀ 91–95), also a site of construction activity. One of Sūraj Mal's wives, Rāṇī Kiśorī, constructed buildings for shopkeepers and pilgrims, and another Jat, Rūp Singh from Sinsimwar, built the temple Nanda Bhavana there.[74] As with Balarāma's festival, the mythical events are reenacted, with *ḍhāṛhī*s reciting Krishna's genealogy. The festival of Dadhi-kādauṃ, a raucous celebration where people splash milk products on each other, takes place on the next day (Navamī).

The birth festival of Lalitā is described next, on the seventh of the bright half of Bhādon. This is a minor festival nowadays, but Nāgarīdās says that for this celebration everyone went to Karhara (TĀ 98–100), a village to the east of Barsana, which appears to be modern-day Karhela. In the mid-eighteenth century, Jai Singh II of Jaipur built a mansion there for the leader of a Rās-līlā group by the name of Vikram.[75] After the festivities at Karhara,

FIG. 3.6 The narrow passage at Sāṅkarī Khor in Barsana

Nāgarīdās reports proceeding to Kadamkhandi, presumably Sonehara ki Kadamkhandi, which is about the same distance from Barsana but to the west. He describes there a Dān-keli and Hindorā Rās-līlā.

For Rādhā's birthday on the eighth of the bright half of Bhādon (Rādhāṣṭamī), there is an admiring description of the newly built-up town of Barsana, with its splendidly white, steep mount (TĀ 102), and the festivalgoers climbing up and down, thronging the narrow paths (TĀ 105). The pattern of the festivities is by now familiar, with music making, *ḍhāṛhī*s reciting, and Dadhi-kādauṃ. These pastoral practices fit the Krishna myth, but they also appealed especially to the powerful Jat patrons of these sites at the time. The prevalence of *ḍhāṛhī*s reciting genealogy may indicate a contemporaneous anxiety among the Jats to match their military and economic power with fitting genealogical descent for this upwardly mobile caste.

This is also the theater season: Nāgarīdās documents that on the ninth day there are Rās-līlās in Barsana, at Vilās Gaṛh and then at Mor Kuṭī, with the popular distribution of sweets (*laddoos*) (TĀ 109–11).[76] This practice continues in modern times, as part of the so-called *būṛhī līlā* cycle.[77] On the tenth day Nāgarīdās reports watching another Rās-līlā at Kokila Ban, north from

Barsana, beyond Nandagaon, where Rūp Rām had commissioned masonry work at the local pond.[78] En route, Nāgarīdās's party halts at Jāvak Vaṭ, that is, at the village of Jao, slightly southeast of Kokila Ban, where Rādhā is said to have made marks painting her feet with lac (*jāvaka*) on a *vaṭa* tree.[79] After an all-night festival, the party returns via Unchagaon, where they climb a slippery rock (TĀ 113) on a low rocky hill west of Unchagaon.[80] More Rās-līlā follows in Mān Gaṛh in Barsana and in Sāṅkarī Khor. The latter is a "narrow passage," the site where Rādhā and the Gopīs were harassed by Krishna (fig. 3.6). Fittingly, a Dān-keli is performed, which represents Krishna's extorting favors from them in exchange for passage.

With the coming of autumn, Nāgarīdās briefly describes the Sāñjhī festival (TĀ 120–23), where the Gopīs of Braj gather flowers to make designs in honor of the goddess. This celebration is also illustrated in a Kishangarhi miniature.[81] Nāgarīdās produced several poems on the theme and so may have thought it unnecessary to elaborate in this work. Nearly a century later, Gopāl Kavi attributed to Nāgarīdās the founding of a fair at Brahmakund in Vrindavan.[82] If Nāgarīdās indeed started this festival, perhaps he took this initiative only after he had finished *The Pilgrim's Bliss*.

For the full moon of autumn (Śarad Pūrṇimā), the action moves to Vrindavan, where many Rās-līlās take place and people set up worship of their deities on the top of their houses (TĀ 124–25). This remains a major festival in Vrindavan to this day.

For Kārtik, bathing in Radhakund is popular, with oil lamps set afloat in the pond and an all-night singing session (TĀ 128–34). Nowadays there is a midnight bath on the eighth day of the dark half of the month (Ahoī Aṣṭamī or Bahulāṣṭamī), which is especially popular with couples and women.[83] The Bikaneri pilgrim Maheśvarī, while visiting there in 1656 (1713 VS), also reports that on the ninth of the dark half of Kārtik, nine *lākh* (900,000) people bathed there.[84] Perhaps Nāgarīdās is here conflating several days together, as by now Divālī, the *amāvas* (moonless night), has arrived.

For Divālī, in the early morning after bathing, everyone goes to Govardhan for the "garlanding" of the mountain Girirāja (TĀ 135). Singing parties gather under white canopies (TĀ 137). The oil lamps used to decorate the mountain are compared to the wondrous reviving herb (*sañjīvanī jarī*) from the *Rāmāyaṇa* story, which Hanumān fetched from the Himalayas to revive Lakshmana (TĀ 138–39). Lamps are also set afloat in nearby Mānasī Gaṅgā, while the pilgrims engage in activities such as bathing, prostrating, and watching a Rās-līlā (TĀ 140). The next morning, for Annakūṭa, everyone joins in worshipping the mountain, circumambulating, and feeding the cows (TĀ 141–43), all practices that are still popular today.[85]

Next comes Gopāṣṭamī, during the bright half of the month, for which Nandagaon is the place to be.[86] Here a "processional" play of the first cowherding of Krishna and his brother is enacted. Actors portray Baladeva and Krishna, as well as their parents, Nanda and Yashodā (TĀ 145–49). People participate by dressing up as Gopas, and the local women play the Gopīs (TĀ 147), as they move from Nandagaon to Kadamkhandi and back.[87] The Gopāṣṭamī festival is also popular today in Vrindavan and Govardhan, but no such elaborate processions are reported in the literature.[88]

Nāgarīdās mentions the months of Pauṣ and Māgh, but does not give any festival details (TĀ 160–62). The descriptive festival mode is overtaken here by a poetic interlude with a nature description of the coming of spring. For Vasant in Barsana, he mentions only that young girls come to the house of Rādhā's father, Vrishabhānu, with pitchers on their heads (TĀ 164).

The climax of the work is the extended description of the Holī celebrations in Barsana and Nandagaon. First, the Holī pole is set up with musical fanfare (TĀ 167), and then the people of Nandagaon send a message to Barsana to announce that they are on their way (TĀ 171). They arrive with an actor impersonating Krishna and throw red powder all around (TĀ 172). The women first sing insult songs (TĀ 173) and then, striking sticks (TĀ 174), perform a round dance (TĀ 175). Nāgarīdās describes in graphic detail the groping and smearing with color and collyrium that takes place (TĀ 176–79), before the Nandagaon people are sent off with a gift of betel (*pān*) (TĀ 180). The people from Barsana pay a return visit to Nandagaon, proceeding in procession and performing peacock dances on the way (TĀ 182–84). Actors play the part of Nanda, Yashodā, and Rādhā (TĀ 190). Meanwhile, the party from Nandagaon has come to meet them at Yashodakund (TĀ 185). Chaos ensues as no one recognizes who is on whose side because all are drenched in color (TĀ 186–88). In Barsana, the youngsters have gathered on the roofs to pour down pots filled with red paint and colored powder over the visitors (TĀ 188–90). Amid the singing of Dhamāra songs (TĀ 191) and much tumult, the Barsana party makes its way to Nanda's house, where a Khyāl is taking place in the courtyard (TĀ 191–94). Actors playing Balarāma and Krishna are present, and their party sings insults to Vrishabhānu (TĀ 194). A round dance is performed (TĀ 195). The two parties meet with a big clash, shouting, "Ho, ho, ho!" (TĀ 196–97). At this point, Nāgarīdās personalizes the account, describing how he gets caught up among the women, who give him a rough time and then tie his clothes to those of one lady and sing mock wedding songs (TĀ 198–200).[89] At the end of these festivities, the visitors are sent off with *pān* (TĀ 203–5).

After this elaborate description of Holī, Nāgarīdās seems to lose interest. He skips the festivals of the hot months, which are comparatively insipid, he says, though there are many festivals during this period (TĀ 206–7). He proclaims the festival of Phāga as the essence of Braj and both Barsana and Nandagaon as its essence of bliss (TĀ 208–11). He begs Rādhā and Krishna to keep him in Braj forever, and with that the work ends.

MYTHICAL AND WORLDLY REALMS INTERPENETRATING

Strikingly, all these festivals are celebrated in a highly participatory way. This intense audience participation is designed to foster the feeling of being transported to Krishna's mythical world, as scholars have noted for the contemporary Rās-līlās that figure so prominently in each of the festivals.[90] "Taking on roles inspired by the *līlā* gives them access into it; god's time is reactualized, making it a series of presents happening now, in which to come in and participate, gather and give meaning. By entering these presents the spectators become contemporaneous with god."[91] There is little evidence of this subjective experience in the *līlā* texts surviving for pre-nineteenth-century festivals, but the descriptions in *The Pilgrim's Bliss* indicate as much. Beyond documenting, Nāgarīdās's main contribution lies in personalizing the liturgical template of the seasons, witnessing his own entry into the mythical realm.

A related feature of Nāgarīdās's pilgrimage report is the tendency to ascribe divine agency to events. This is not unlike how Braj devotees today read happenings as miraculous. For instance, in a well-documented modern-day "miracle of a bee," the appearance of a bee during a ritual is understood as a manifestation of Krishna and is attributed to both ritual efficacy and the devotees' devotional fervor. Braj devotees are conditioned to "see Krishna" everywhere, and they understand the world in terms of the philosophical principle of Acintya-bhedābheda, that is, the miracle of God's suffusing the mundane.[92]

Nāgarīdās subscribed to a similar philosophical interpretation.[93] In *The Pilgrim's Bliss*, everything is imbued with divinity; personal experiences are described in culturally conditioned terms. For instance, as Nāgarīdās wades across the river Yamunā, he points out that "Taranijā allowed the crossing; the Lord of the forest grabbed my hand" (TĀ 65), thus casting his experience in mythological terms. Similarly, a freak flood of the Ganges at Soron becomes a manifestation of the river goddess Gaṅgā's anger:

There, Gaṅgā's holy waters' touch
Washed away our sins, purified our bodies.
A man in our retinue committed a crime:
On her banks, he killed a goat, a sinful deed!
Graceful Gaṅgā turned momentarily mad:
She suddenly came upon us, her waters surging.
The earth split, collapsing with great force!
At that very moment, we heard the frightful crash.
Flailing, we fled, driven out of our camp.
Frightened, we all gazed at the sight.
When we praised Gaṅgā, bowed our heads at her feet,
She regained her innate serenity and granted forgiveness.

(TĀ 42–44)

What happened is unclear, but apparently a sudden flash flood forced Nāgarīdās's party to flee the riverbanks. The narrative explains Gaṅgā's anger as related to the slaughter of a goat by someone (unnamed) in Nāgarīdās's company. Nāgarīdās also prays on two occasions to Gaṅgā that he may be able to return to Braj (TĀ 47–49, 59), and he interprets subsequent events in the light of her granting his prayers. Later he ascribes his ability to stay in Barsana to an invitation by Vrishabhānu, mediated by Rādhā herself (TĀ 70–75).

This power of transportation to the world of the gods via participation in rites comes out strongest during the reenactment of the Holī rites between the villagers of Nandagaon and Barsana:

Over here, the Barsana women stand eyeing their in-laws,
Then, all at once, they run up to the women of Nandagaon.
Shouting "Ho, ho, ho!" the young women charge.
How could a stream of such fervor stop and turn back?
Surrounded, they return again, four times
Before some mischievously flee.
They take me for someone of Barsana.
They all grab hold of me, and I am crushed by the crowd.
Grabbing my waist pocket, one gives me a tug.
I am but one, and these ladies of Braj are many!
There is much pulling and tugging,
My feet falter, my strength exhausted.
One of the Barsana crowd fetches someone else,

Ties my clothes to hers, and then pulls and tugs.
On this side, they burst out singing wedding songs.
Both sides relish the mocking merriment.
The women keep rubbing my face with powder (*abīr*)
And smearing collyrium in my eyes.

(TĀ 196–200)

As Nāgarīdās himself joins the Holī fun, he is caught by the ladies of Barsana. Literally swept off his feet and then drenched in colored paint, he has his clothes tied to those of a lady of Barsana. In this confusion, he declares that now he truly has "arrived" in Braj (TĀ 201–2).

Significantly, he had anticipated this Holī celebration in Braj for a long time. The year before, on the way back from Kumaon, he had rushed to Braj but was unable to reach there in time and had to settle for playing Holī on the banks of Gaṅgā, where he prayed to the river goddess to let him "play many Phāgas in Braj":

We stayed many days at Kauśikī's banks.
Negotiations for soldiers concluded, we left.
In a few days we arrived at Gaṅgā's banks,
But our hearts bloomed with desire for Braj.
Here, in the wrong place, Holī came and passed.
Our hearts were overwhelmed with a surge of longing.
We settled for a sandy spot on Gaṅgā's banks
And created a Barsana and Nandagaon.
Playing Holī thus, I folded my hands and confronted Gaṅgā:
"Let me play many Phāgas in Braj—Give me, O Gaṅgā, that gift."
I prayed for that boon again and again, then left.
My mouth had fallen silent, but longing for Braj kept burning in
    my heart.

(TĀ 56–60)

On the spot, Nāgarīdās composed a Holī sequence that later came to be incorporated in his collected works as *Celebration of Holī* (Phāg-vihār).[94] By the end of *The Pilgrim's Bliss*, finally his heart's desire is granted, and he can celebrate the "carnival of color" in Braj.

The pilgrimage report's description of Nāgarīdās's role in the Holī festival strikingly resembles Krishna's in the mythical Holī. Elsewhere, Nāgarīdās quotes in a Holī song:

Mohana and his lady-love splatter and soak each other:
Gulāl and *abīr* (types of red powder) flow, darkening day into night.
Shyāma finds himself alone: "Say—where have my friends gone?"
When, suddenly, all the girls swarm over him and grab hold of him.
From ten, twenty places, the girls throng to surround him,
Spilling yellow perfume from the pots that sit on their lovely heads.
Lalitā grabs his yellow sash and ties it to her blue dress.
She dances with her lover, like lightning in a cloud.
As they are begging for Phaguā, passion mounts beyond all description.
Seeing such merrymaking, who could possibly remain calm?
Men and women play Phāga with much fervor.
To cavort with Braj's ladies is Shyāma's great fortune!

(PPM 57)

In this song, Krishna is caught by the ladies of Barsana and has his clothes tied up with Lalitā's, in a scenario similar to what Nāgarīdās reports with regard to himself. In his pilgrimage account, then, Nāgarīdās identifies with the mythology to such an extent that it becomes reality for him. Or, otherwise put, he casts himself after the Krishna in the song. We get here a glimpse of the literary equivalent of what we see so often in the Kishangarhi paintings: that Krishna is cast in the king's likeness or, depending on your point of view, the king is cast as Krishna. Here Nāgarīdās himself is caught taking on Krishna's role in the reenactment of Holī.

RĀS-LĪLĀ PERFORMANCES: PARTICIPATION IN THE DIVINE PLAY

Nāgarīdās's testimony is particularly valuable for the vivid view it provides of the Rās-līlā scene in the middle of the eighteenth century. It brings historical depth to our understanding of these plays, since what we know now comes to us mostly through twentieth-century eyewitness reports. The performances described are similar to contemporary Rās-līlās in combining ritual with drama. The first Rās-līlā described, held in Unchagaon for the occasion of Rakṣā-bandhana, opens with the rite of tying the *rākhī*, with the main actors playing Rādhā and Krishna consequently being swung on a swing at dusk. After that the Rās-līlā proper starts on the stage (TĀ 88–89). The actors thus play a ritual role even before the play begins.

The most popular Hindu ritual is undoubtedly the wedding ceremony, and hence it is frequently included in Rās-līlās. While most of the Rās-līlā

FIG. 3.7 *Krishna's Nuptials*, Kishangarh school, late eighteenth century. Ink, opaque watercolor, and gold on paper (20.5 × 23.5 cm). Private collection (Germany). Courtesy Mr. Eberhard Rist

performances described are held in the month of Bhādon in connection with the birthday festivals (Janmotsava), several also involve wedding celebrations. For Lalitā's birthday festival there is a Rās-līlā at night in Karhara, after which the actors playing the divine couple are swung at dawn. This is followed by an enactment of the wedding rites, perhaps in a Rādhāvallabhan context (TĀ 96–98). In Kadamkhandi (Sonehara ki Kadamkhandi), a particularly busy place for Rās-līlās in Bhādon, a Dān-keli and Hindorā Rās are staged, as is also a wedding līlā (TĀ 100).[95] Krishna's wedding ceremonies are also a popular subject in painting, as a large late eighteenth-century tableau from Kishangarh demonstrates (fig. 3.7).

A striking characteristic of the eighteenth-century Rās-līlās, but one little remarked on regarding the modern plays, is their mobile character. The performances described combine procession with ritual and drama, similar to contemporary Rām-līlās, though on a more intimate scale.[96] Barsana was then, as it is now, a popular scene for Rās-līlās, known today as the *būṛhī līlā* cycle.[97] Its Vilās Gaṛh was the site of a Rās-līlā on the day after Rādhāṣṭamī, and it seems that the same actors moved in procession to Mor Kuṭī, to put on a show there. Back in Barsana, presumably by now on the twelfth day of the month, there were more Rās-līlās in Mān Gaṛh.[98] The highlight of the cycle is the Rās-līlā at Sāṅkarī Khor, the narrow passageway near Barsana, where fittingly an episode of the Dān-keli is presented in which Krishna demands a tax for letting the Gopīs pass through the narrow path. Nāgarīdās includes a quotation from the dialogue:

> That morning, the young couple descends from the mountain
> And plays the Dān-keli at Sāṅkarī Khor.
> Smiles and wiles, turning and twisting, so pleasing,
> It cannot be described with crafting of words.
> One cowherd was seized, tethered by his rope,
> The women tied him by his braid to the branch of a tree.
> Exasperated, the cowherd called out,
> "Listen, hey, I'm calling Nandalāla!"
> "Who are you, and where are you calling from?"
> Thus says Shyāma, the *rasikas*' jewel in the crown.
> The cowherd replies: "Brother, set me free,
> The Barsana people have tied me up."
> Krishna says, "Why, what's so unusual about what happened to you, friend?
> They tie me up all the time, too!"
> Hearing Shyāma's taunts, all are enchanted.
> Some swoon, others are overwhelmed with love, their body hairs standing on end.
>
> (TĀ 115–19)

In this scene the roles are reversed: instead of the men prevailing over the women, one of Krishna's friends is caught by the Gopīs and tied up. He calls out for Krishna to come and save him, but Krishna replies: "So what? They tie me up all the time." Nāgarīdās reports that the audience enjoyed this moment very much. In the modern version of the play, Krishna himself is unable to come to the rescue because he is literally tied up by the Gopīs, too. In the end, it is Rādhā who is moved to compassion and gives her Gopīs the orders to release their tormentors.[99]

Nāgarīdās also reports on a "processional drama," not a Rās-līlā strictly speaking, enacted for Gopāṣṭamī in Kārtik. Actors portraying Baladeva and Shyāma started out from "Gokul" (i.e., Nandagaon), to be sent off for their first cow-herding experience (TĀ 145–46). Actors portraying Nanda and Yashodā were present and met them along the road, perhaps in Yashoda-kund.[100] The Gopīs gave a speech, which Nāgarīdās reports verbatim:

There, the brothers are stopped (to arrange a tableau).
The brides of Braj give a speech:
"Listen, cowherds of noble name,
These two boys are Balarāma and Shyāma.
In Braj there are lions and tigers and other creatures.[101]
Don't let them roam too far in this remote jungle.
They're their father's and mother's treasures,
The life-breath of this Braj, abode of joy.
Why should I waste more words—
They've been placed in your lap, Mother."[102]
As the audience hears the relatives' sweet words,
Their body hairs stand on end, tears well up in their eyes.

(TĀ 149–51)

The women are worried about the young boys going off into the dangerous woods. Nāgarīdās describes the audience's delight at this emotional climax.

Then the procession moves on to Kadamkhandi for the boys' snack and a musical session, specified to be in Rāga Gaurī:

Yet they set off from there as songs are sung.
This is the first day of splendid cow-herding.
They keep moving till they see Kadamkhandi.[103]
That is where they cavort and enjoy the midday repast.
The crowd assembles in earring-shape
Around the young boys of fair and dark body.
Then the beloved boys return to Lord Nanda (Nandīśvara)
To the beating of drums and the sound of the horns.
In between, the sound of the flute comes and goes;
For the cows' arrival, they sing Rāga Gaurī.
The cows look splendid as they move along.
Stopping over and over, the procession makes its way.

(TĀ 152–54)

At twilight, they return home, where they are eagerly awaited in Nandagaon, and an evening āratī is performed:

When the women (back home) glimpse the shining crowns at nightfall,
They alert each other with hand gestures: "It is evening."
Climbing up to the roofs of their houses,

The women of Lord Nanda (Nandīśvara) are on the lookout.
Then the boys appear, and the women's hearts fill with tenderness
As the boys sing in the streets their melodious songs.
As the young people carry pots on their heads,
People stop on the road, enthralled by the young girls.
The two heroes enter their house,
Where evening āratī takes place before the crowd.

(TĀ 155–57)

This detailed description of the procession homeward correlates well with the painting that has been identified as *Return of the Cattle in the Evening* (Go-dhūli) (fig. 3.8).[104]

Similarly, the Holī festivities involved processional movements, in which actors impersonating Nanda, Yashodā, Krishna, and Balarāma on one side and Vrishabhānu, his wife, and Rādhā on the other went in procession,

FIG. 3.8 *Go-dhūli at Gopāṣṭamī*, Kishangarh school, ca. 1760. Color and gold on paper (31.6 × 37.7 cm). National Museum, New Delhi, accession no. 61.1003. Courtesy National Museum (New Delhi)

while singing seasonal songs. On this occasion, though, there seems much less stress on the actors' performance than on the audience itself. Significantly, this is where Nāgarīdās says that he has truly arrived in Braj. The climax of audience participation in the festivals leads to a breakthrough into the divine world.

The drama scholar David Mason in his book on the Rās-līlā describes how in this theatrical tradition the "acting audience" plays a crucial role in making the performance work, in contrast to the so-called realistic Western theatrical experience where the burden of the cogency of the performance is on the actor.[105] Culturally conditioned to construe the performance as conforming to a mythic paradigm, "the audience's own spiritual proclivities . . . complete the transformation of stage action into otherworldly action."[106] To push this a step further, it is not just the stage action but also the audience itself that is transformed. In the course of watching the Rās-līlā, the spectators construe not only the performance onstage but also their own actions in the audience. Audience participation also involves audience transformation, as glimpsed in Nāgarīdās's description of the riotous climax of the Holī celebrations of Barsana and Nandagaon. In this staged play with full audience participation, audience members are "extras" in the play, but for each participant, his or her own experience is center stage. When Nāgarīdās describes how the women of Braj molest him as part of the Barsana-Nandagaon Holī play rites, he expresses complete acceptance, absorption in the world of myth:

> When you are truly joined to Braj, these women of Braj will tie the knot.
> First the knot of worry must give way, before your garments may
>   be knotted.
>
> The women of Braj must make you their own before you can love Braj.
> When the women of Braj color your eyes, you sense the true essence
>   of Braj.
>
> (TĀ 201–2)

From observer, Nāgarīdās has turned participant, and as participant in the rite, he has been adopted into the mythological "real" Braj. By allowing the boundaries between spectator and participant to blur, this festival can unleash its creative powers, in ways reminiscent of the medieval European carnival.[107] The myth becomes fully mobilized once the audience participates in the dramatic action, which it has already construed as otherworldly, or rather real-worldly. At this point, "real life" has become insignificant, while the reality of Krishna's world shines through. It is via full participation in the play-acting that Krishna's divine play is realized.

CONCLUSION: A PILGRIM'S PROGRESS

The Pilgrim's Bliss can be regarded as a precursor of the later autobiographical travelogue, somewhere between tradition and modernity. Sāvant Singh writes in the first person, yet his focus is on the transcendental. His search for political and military support is transformed into a pilgrimage account, in which his peregrinations in exile become a celebration of the joy of visiting Braj and his stints to Kumaon and to Delhi in pursuit of Maratha and Mughal help, respectively, are cast as distractions intruding on his enjoyment of the eternal bliss of Braj. *The Pilgrim's Bliss* is truly a "pilgrim's progress" account, in the process of which Nāgarīdās writes himself into Krishna's Braj. Instead of mobilizing an army to regain his kingdom, he becomes a pilgrim who mobilizes Krishna's world. Whereas previously he inscribed Krishna into his courtly world in poetry and painting, the tables are now turned. Where earlier Krishna was portrayed as boating on and swimming in Kishangarh's Lake Gundalao, Nāgarīdās now portrays himself boating on the Yamunā and, in eagerness to reach Braj, even wading and swimming across the river. Where previously Braj was moved to court, the court is now moved to Braj. And where previously *bhakta*s came from Braj to visit his court in Rupnagar and partake in his soirées, he now joins them in Radhakund for all-night *kīrtana* sessions.

When Nāgarīdās after many peregrinations finally settled in Braj, somewhat counter to expectations, he did not reside in Vrindavan, where his family had a mansion. Perhaps that residence was now controlled by his brother. Rather, he was based in Barsana, but that did not constitute a retirement to a provincial backwater. Barsana and environs were trendy places at the time, with much of the building activity in the area fueled by the money the Jats were making off their multifarious military adventures. Barsana and Nandagaon were at the heart of the construction boom. Nāgarīdās found himself in good company.

Once he settled in Braj, the tone of his work changed, and it became less a pilgrimage report than a calendrical description of the great festivals of the area. Sāvant Singh enthusiastically participated in the rites of Braj. To be sure, the pilgrimage had not ended; there was still plenty of circulation, but it was now in the Braj area. The seasonal rites of Braj included not just *darshana* and *bhajana* singing but also processions and participatory theater that reenacted Krishna and Rādhā's adventures, all designed to transport the participants to a spiritual plane.

It worked for Nāgarīdās. He describes the riotous climax of the Holī celebrations of Barsana and Nandagaon. By allowing the boundaries between spectator and participant to blur, Holī can unleash its creative powers. When the women of Braj molested him as part of those rites, Nāgarīdās became completely absorbed in the world of myth. Significantly, Nāgarīdās perceived that the women were the agents that controlled his access to this world. True to his name, "servant of Rādhā," Nāgarīdās had arrived in the eternal Braj.

4 Legends Mobilized

Garland of Stories and Songs

In Rupnagar was a two-storied mansion. There, the *kīrtaniyā*s were performing a *kīrtana* session when a certain song stood out. Those who were particularly responsive to it became highly emotional upon hearing it. Then a stranger (*vijātī*) who was a fakir became so enchanted by the song that in a fit of ecstasy he tumbled from the roof. That roof was so high that one could die even before reaching the ground. But the fakir, still singing that very song, survived the fall.

O friend, I do not know the way. Would someone tell me where Krishna lives?

—PPM 64

GARLAND OF STORIES AND SONGS (PAD-PRASAṄG-MĀLĀ) PRAISES several great *bhakta*s or, more precisely, their compositions, or *pada*s.[1] It is exactly what the title promises: a collection of hagiographical stories and anecdotes organized around favorite devotional songs, with specifics about how the songs are understood to have been created or received. These vignettes provide narrative settings in which the songs are embedded. Some of the sixty-seven stories feature more than one song. The work does not include explicit information on its date or place of composition, but it likely was composed toward the end of Nāgarīdās's life, probably after he had lost his throne, and while he resided in Braj.[2]

This work is a treasure trove for studying how devotional stories and songs circulated and were mobilized in early modern India. The fragment quoted above is indicative of the wide audiences among which they circulated. Devotional songs about Krishna and Rādhā were heard and received positively, even ecstatically, here by a fakir, well beyond the Krishna devotional milieu they are typically associated with.

This hagiography represents a vivid sample of prose storytelling of its time. Most of the canonical earlier hagiographies are in verse and hence terse and difficult to understand. They were intended for oral exposition by preachers, or *kathāvācaks*.[3] What we find here is in essence a transcript of one set of such sermons. That does not mean it represents the one correct interpretation of the earlier hagiographies, but it gives us a sample version of such accounts and elaborations, even if limited and colored by the preoccupations of its teller and his audience.

Central in this text are the songs, which are in meter; most of them are short, with a few exceptions, and they are as a rule quoted in full in all manuscripts. Nāgarīdās quotes songs in many different languages, besides Braj. That he starts out with three Sanskrit Aṣṭapadīs from Jayadeva's *Gīta-govinda* illustrates to what extent these songs inspired the vernacular *bhakti* poetry. All the other songs are in the vernacular, but some show features that can be identified as Gujarati (Narsī Mehtā, PPM 10–11), Rajasthani (Mīrā, PPM 14–18), or Punjabi (Bhagvān Hit Rāmrāy, PPM 66).[4] The inclusion of such songs indicates they were at least to some extent intelligible to the intended audience. This confirms there was something like a "*bhakti* language," a shared medium for an area stretching at least over North-West India.

Another point of interest is this hagiography's *Sitz im Leben*. Just like *The Pilgrim's Bliss*, *Garland of Stories and Songs* also has some autobiographical elements. Most of the stories are set in Rajasthan or Braj, and several take place in Rupnagar, the then capital Sāvant Singh eventually regained for his son. By the time Nāgarīdās put together this work, he had come to live in Braj, like the Krishna-yogi of the front cover illustration (fig. I.1): the court literally had been transposed into the sacred landscape of the pilgrimage center. This hagiography, then, embodies the confluence of the milieus of court and temple. How does a king-turned-holy-man speak about other holy men? The intention here is not to read this hagiography statically, mining it for historical facts to assess the veracity of the stories told, which would not accord with the hagiographer's purpose of inspiring belief rather than writing a chronicle for posterity. More importantly for historians, the work documents eighteenth-century attitudes and reconstructions of the past in the milieu of the hagiographer. This reading is dynamic, focusing on interactions and exchanges. It asks how hagiographic stories and songs came to be mobilized for sociopolitical and religious purposes in the mid-eighteenth century.

A HAGIOGRAPHIC ACCOUNT BETWEEN OLD AND NEW

Narratives about holy men, or hagiographies,[5] are an important part of Hinduism, in which veneration of holy men (to lesser extent women) takes an important place. Recently, there has been a lot of methodological progress in studying this genre, as to how to read these hagiographic texts.[6] Particularly interesting are prose stories about saints, which are close to the oral stories still told in the communities that relate to them. Seemingly simple, they are articulations of self-identity and can be fruitfully read as constructs of community formation. *Garland of Stories and Songs* has many characteristics of the genre.[7]

OTHER DEVOTIONAL STORY CYCLES

Comparison with other similar texts brings to light the agenda of *Garland of Stories and Songs*. Nāgarīdās did not work in a vacuum but freely drew on other, earlier hagiographies that circulated in his environment. He mentions (PPM 19) Nābhādās's *Garland of Devotees* (Bhakt-māl; ca. 1600) and Priyādās's commentary (*ṭīkā*) *Illumination of Devotional Emotion* (Bhakti-ras-bodhinī; 1712).[8] His testimony confirms that the two were widely read (or recited) and had obtained already something of a canonical status by the 1750s. Nāgarīdās's work is more limited in scope than these two classics. It also differs substantially from them in that it does not allude to stories in poetry but tells them fully in prose and adds the songs in poetry to prove the point. This renders his hagiography much more accessible and provides an explication of the often cryptic stories in the earlier hagiographies. It also provides a mid-eighteenth-century understanding of these two canonical texts.

The stories in *Garland of Stories and Songs* are also close in spirit and form to those told in another important corpus of hagiographical writings, the Vārtā literature of the Vallabha-Sampradāya. The two main texts are *Story of Eighty-Four Disciples* (of Vallabha) (84VV) and *Story of Two Hundred Fifty-Two Disciples* (of his son Viṭṭhalnāth's) (252VV), dating from the seventeenth century but redacted in their current form by a fourth-generation descendant of Vallabha.[9] Given Nāgarīdās's connections with that sect, they were undoubtedly another major source of inspiration. Structurally, too, *Garland of Stories and Songs*, like the Vārtās, is subdivided into chapters called *prasaṅgas*. However, Nāgarīdās does not retell the stories in the same way, and sometimes there are significant differences. His work betrays a fluidity in the Vārtā literature of this period, with a lack of canonical fixity of the text.

Most notable is the absence of the Vārtās' stern warnings against associating with devotees of other denominations.[10] By contrast, Nāgarīdās glowingly relates stories about non-Vallabhan *bhakta*s, in fact more than about Vallabhans. His outlook is very ecumenical: not just Krishna *bhakta*s but also Rāma *bhakta*s are included, and also the so-called *nirguṇī*s. He has Kabīr visit Vrindavan and be a success there (PPM 11b).

At one point, Nāgarīdās himself broaches the issue of sectarian exclusiveness as he relates the story about Tulsīdās, who is said to have been so devoted to Rāma that he did not prostrate himself in front of images of other gods, even other incarnations (*avatāra*s) of Vishnu (PPM 24). When Tulsī visited Braj to meet Viṭṭhalnāth, Vallabha's son naturally took him for *darshana* of Śrī Nātha jī, but Tulsīdās refused to prostrate in front of the image, that is, until Śrī Nātha jī appeared to him as Rāma, with bow and arrow in hand. Reflecting on this incident, Nāgarīdās defends the Rāma *bhakta*'s exclusive loyalty (*ananyatā*) as appropriate, and, somewhat uncharacteristically, he includes a philosophical excursus on the topic of "difference in non-difference" (Bhedābheda). While all *avatāra*s are ultimately the same and even gods (Shiva, Brahmā, and Vishnu) are in essence the same, Nāgarīdās considers it appropriate for devotees to have an exclusive attachment to one only. He adds an example (*dṛṣṭānta*): just as the king and his ministers are the same as representatives of the government to the people, they are not the same for the queens! The comparison with a wife's fidelity to her husband is fascinating. Still, Nāgarīdās quotes a song in praise of both Rāma and Krishna, thus ending the anecdote in favor of inclusiveness. In this celebration of a community of saints of all denominations, Nāgarīdās is closer to Nābhādās than to the Vārtās and seems to delight in bringing the Rāmanandī's ecumenism to the genre.

Another major difference with the Vārtās is the organization of the stories around songs, as the title indicates. The Vārtās quote songs, but these are secondary to the story. For Nāgarīdās, the songs are primary. The stories are mainly about the way a song was performed and remembered in a local community and therefore often foreground the reception rather than the creation. In the light of this poetry-centeredness, one might venture the hypothesis that Nāgarīdās was influenced by the genre of the Tazkirah, or "biographical anthology," in Urdu poetry. Tazkirahs originated from the individual notebooks (*bāyāz*) of those who attended poetry gatherings. They thus stressed the poems, rather than the poet's biographical information, which remained somewhat idiosyncratic and incomplete.[11] Nāgarīdās was certainly familiar with the Delhi scene and its new rage for Urdu (then called Rekhtā), which he regarded as part of his own poetic world, and it was in this same period that Tazkirahs about Urdu rather than Persian poets were collected.[12] The form of Nāgarīdās's hagiography may thus be explained with reference to Indo-Islamic models. On the other hand, it may also have been inspired by the South Indian world of the *cāṭu*, that is, Sanskrit, Telugu, and Tamil poems "remembered, known by heart, available for oral recall" and "employed in social communication."[13] These were usually contextualized with a story about the poems. Like Nāgarīdās's anecdotes, these poems circulated orally, in milieus of *rasika*s, often kings and poets, but also in middle-level, high-caste educated elites outside royal court centers, in smaller towns.[14] While not as exclusively religious as Nāgarīdās's stories, many *cāṭu*s feature famous devotional poets or include a devotional message.[15] A major difference is the much higher degree of criticism and meta-poetics in the *cāṭu* milieu, but common to both is the phenomenon of *para-pūrita*, "completing verses of others."[16] Nāgarīdās, for instance, relates how the Sanskrit poet Jayadeva hesitated to finish an irreverent verse, which was completed by none other than Krishna himself (PPM 1). He also gives the story of a *bhakta* who died before completing the Dhamāra song he was composing and how his widow finalized the song (PPM 21). Some of Nāgarīdās's anecdotes foreground "the magic of language" as in the *cāṭu* tradition, and others critique traditional structures of authority and their representatives, especially those where saints meet kings or pandits who go on to be victorious in debate.[17] This *cāṭu* system seems to have crystallized around the seventeenth century in the Nāyaka period (but goes back to much earlier traditions).[18] There is no evidence of direct contact with Kishangarh, so it is perhaps more of a stretch than postulating inspiration from the contemporary Urdu Tazkirah tradition as flourishing in Delhi.

ANTICIPATING "BHĀRATENDU" HARIŚCANDRA

As in his pilgrimage account, Nāgarīdās in his hagiography balances the old with the new. Drawing from many traditional hagiographies, he also anticipates a modern one, *Sequel to the Garland of Devotees* (Uttarārdh-bhaktmāl) by "Bhāratendu" Hariścandra of Benares (1876).[19] A comparison shows significant similarities as well as differences.

In both cases, the authors are cast as integral to the world of famous Krishna *bhakta*s. Hariścandra boldly claims for himself nothing less than an eyewitness role in the divine eternal *līlā*: he proclaims himself a new addition to the famous Aṣṭ-chāp.[20] Nāgarīdās does not make any such claims for himself, but he is traditionally regarded as the "ninth" of the Aṣṭ-chāp.[21] Whereas Hariścandra is rather flamboyant about his own sainthood, Nāgarīdās is more subtle in inscribing himself into the world of Krishna *bhakti*: he includes his own songs in the work and gives vignettes of the positive reception of these songs, without emphasizing that they are his own (e.g., PPM 63–65). An example is the anecdote quoted at the beginning of this chapter, where a fakir is ecstatic about a song that carries Nāgarīdās's own signature. Thus he does not explicitly declare himself a saint, as Hariścandra does. The latter sets up his work with a dream in which Krishna says that Hariścandra is to be regarded as a Sant, a *bhakta*. Interestingly, the dream vision comes to his "Kṣatrāṇī," that is, his mistress Mādhavī.[22]

Like Hariścandra, Nāgarīdās had a mistress who was a fellow author and a fellow *bhakta*: Rasik Bihārī. He mentions her obliquely in *The Pilgrim's Bliss* and quotes her work in his anthologies, including in his 1742 *Illumination of the Way to Recite* Śrīmad Bhāgavata(*-purāṇa)* (Śrīmad-Bhāgavat-pārāyaṇ-vidhi-prakāś), where she seems to have assisted at an important religious function at court.[23] However, she is absent from the hagiography. Apparently there was no place for her among the saints. Hariścandra, by contrast, gives his "Kṣatrāṇī" a central role in his own identification as saint in a prophetic dream. Moreover, this dream also causes Mādhavī to reconvert to Hinduism: she was originally Rajput but had converted to Islam in the course of her career as a courtesan. This reference to conversion is another marker of the modernity of the work.[24]

Hariścandra starts his work with a short history of his own family, presented as a tale of religious growth from polytheism to monotheism, in an eminently modern way.[25] Nāgarīdās does not do so (perhaps because that was covered already in the *Exposition on Rūp/Beauty* by Vrind), though he includes the anecdote about his famous forebear, his great-grandfather Rūp Singh, but only toward the end of his work (PPM 59).

Hariścandra's work is reflective of a stage in the construction of nationalist Hinduism.[26] Comparison with Nāgarīdās's hagiography is instructive to determine historical patterns (or disruptions thereof) that led to this construct. Notwithstanding its modernity, the work is closer to both Nābhādās and the Vārtā literature than to *Garland of Stories and Songs*. It is presented as a sequel (*uttarārdh*) to *Garland of Devotees*, and, like that work, it is in poetry, in the same *Chappay* meter as is Nābhādās's hagiography. Thus it presents itself as "traditional." While also invoking the Catuḥ-sampradāya framework of Nābhādās, it is closer to the Vārtās in that it has an outspoken Vallabhan tenor, both of which are largely absent in Nāgarīdās's work. The modernity of Hariścandra's hagiography lies in its incipient conception of a "Hindu" community, including reference to the "rival religions" Buddhism and Jainism, while also distinguishing itself from Shaivism, infusing everything with a superior Vaishnava ethos.[27] The project of Jai Singh II in the early eighteenth century can be considered a forerunner of this Vaishnava construction of Hinduism. The question arises, then, whether Nāgarīdās's work might be a lynchpin between the two, the Jaipur king's efforts at constructing orthodoxy and the Benares merchant's son's broadening of a Vallabhan religiosity to be at the center of a new construct of Hinduism.

THE ATTRIBUTION AND TEXT OF *GARLAND OF STORIES AND SONGS*

Before delving into the details of Nāgarīdās's hagiography, it is important to think about its textual history and to critically reflect on its purported authorship and transmission. There are indeed reasons to problematize the attribution of *Garland of Stories and Songs* to Nāgarīdās, and there are significantly different recensions of the text.

No explicit statement appears at the end of the text to affirm that Nāgarīdās wrote the work. Still, its attribution to him is supported by internal evidence. The two final *pada*s both have the *chāpa* "Nāgarī." In one instance, the author speaks in the first person as the composer of a song, which has the signature of Nāgarīdās (PPM 65).[28] As for external evidence, only a few decades after Nāgarīdās's death, in the manuscripts preserved in the Jaipur City Palace Museum, the colophons attribute the work to Nāgarīdās, crown prince of Rupnagar.[29]

Yet toward the end of the work, the author frequently praises *pada*s by Nāgarīdās, perhaps indicating that these passages were composed for Nāgarīdās, rather than by him. One suspects that Nāgarīdās's expositions on individual songs were collected and redacted with some additions by someone else. Who might that have been? The *kīrtaniyā*s of the temple of Rupnagar's Śrī Nātha jī image figure very importantly in this work, so they might have been involved in collecting the material, probably based on oral sources. Of interest in that regard is the *prasaṅga* about how the *kīrtaniyā*s received their hereditary position, which is justified with reference to a forebear, a Shyāmdās Kīrtaniyā (PPM 57). He was a contemporary of Viṭṭhalnāth and is said to have been ordained by Śrī Nātha jī himself, with the assurance that his descendants would remain *kīrtaniyā*s. *Kīrtaniyā*s would obviously

TABLE 4.1 Comparison of Long and Short Recension of *Garland of Stories and Songs*

Long Recension[a]		**Short Recension**[b]	
Introduction		Introduction	
1–3a–b	Jayadeva (b: song by Vyās)	1–3a–b	Jayadeva (b: song by Vyās)
4	Paramānanddās	4	Paramānanddās
5–9	Nāmdev*	5a–b	Chītsvāmī (with Bīrbal)
(8	with Tilocan*;	6–7	Sūrdās
9	with Kabīr)*	8	Tulsīdās
10a–b	Kabīr*	9	Kabīr in Vrindavan (in two MSS)[c]
11	Raidās*		
12–13	Narsī Mehtā†	10–11	Narsī Mehtā
14–18	Mīrā*		
19	Caturdās Khojī*		
20	Murārīdās	12	Rāghodās
21	Rāghodās	13	Murārīdās
22–24	Tulsīdās†	14	Kharagsen Kāyasth
25	Mānikcand*	15	Nārāyaṇdās Naṭvā
26a–b	Chītsvāmī (with Bīrbal some MSS)[d]		
27–28	Hit Harivaṃś	16	Hit Harivaṃś (initiation of Vyās)
29–35	Harirām Vyās†	17	Harirām Vyās (Rās-līlā story)
36–38	Sūrdās	18	Madhukar Shāh
39	Haridās (Tānsen and Akbar)	19	Narvāhan
40–41	Krishnadās (Adhikārī)	20	Hit Harivaṃś (death; song Vyās)
42–43	Kumbhandās	21–23	Sūrdās Madanmohan
44	Caturbhujdās	24	Krishnadās and Sūrdās
45	Gadādhar Bhaṭṭ	25	Haridās (and Akbar)
46–49	Sūrdās Madanmohan†	26	Muralīdās Kīrtaniyā
50	Kharagsen Kāyasth	27	Shyāmdās Kīrtaniyā
51	Narvāhan (songs Harivaṃś)	28	Sahcarī Sukh
52	Madhukar Shāh (song Vyās)	29	Caturbhujdās
53	Nehī Nāgarīdās (Barsānevāle)	30	Kumbhandās (trip)
54–55	Bhagvāndās (Hit Rāmrāy)	31	Tulārām "Bāvrī Sakhī"
	(Chītsvāmī and Bīrbal in most MSS)	32	Kumbhandās (Gauravā)
56	Kisorīdās	33	Rūp Singh
57	Shyāmdās Kīrtaniyā	34vg	Gadādhar Bhaṭṭ
58	Nārāyaṇdās Naṭvā (song Mīrā)	35	Muralīdās Gauḍiyā (Rupnagar)
59	Rūp Singh	36	Kisorīdās
60	Sahcarī Sukh (Rupnagar)	37	Bhagvāndās (Hit Rāmrāy)
61	Tulārām Bāvrī Sakhī (song Rāmrāy)	38	Sūrdās (and Akbar)

62	Muralīdās Kīrtaniyā (Krishnadās)	39	Harirām Vyās (missing *rasikas*)
63	Rajput in Rupnagar (Nāgarīdās)	40	Fakir in Rupnagar
64	Fakir in Rupnagar (song Nāgarīdās)	41	Bhagvāndās (Hit Rāmrāy) (VRI)
65	Muralīdās Gauḍiyā (song Nāgarīdās)	42	Rajput Rupnagar (Nāgarīdās)

[a] MSS of the long recension: JCPM 903 and 2210 (1792); BRORI 4077; VRS 968 (ca. 1790–1800); both KRC MSS. K. Gupta (1965) and Khān (1974) also have all stories from the long recension, though in different sequences. I am following Gupta.

[b] MSS of the short recension: JCPM 3904 (1792); BRORI 256 (1822); VRS 1019 (ca. 1790–1800); VRI 17136.I.

[c] VRI 17136.I.9, folio 73r–v, and JCPM 3904, folios 30v–31r.

[d] The manuscripts of the longer recension give the story of the meeting of Chītsvāmī and Bīrbal later (VRS 968, folio 50r–v; JCPM 903 and 2210; and both KRC MSS), as do the editions by Gauḍ (1892: 229–30) and Khān (1974: 606). K. Gupta (1965) had chosen to put that story together with the other Chītsvāmī story, and indeed the two stories come together also in the shorter recension. For the reader's convenience, I am following Gupta's text.

* The *prasaṅga* is only in the long recension.

† Not all *prasaṅgas* are in the long recension.

have an interest in incorporating this anecdote in the text. In another story, the servant of Rupnagar's Śrī Nātha jī, the *bhītariyā*, plays an important role (PPM 59). Given their professions, these *kīrtaniyās* and *bhītariyās* may also have been engaged in oral exposé of stories about saints. Since several of the stories are close to the Vallabhan Vārtā literature, it would not be surprising that Vallabhan temple priests played a prominent role in composing some of the stories, perhaps even putting together the collection. In any case, it is safe to say that these stories floated around among Nāgarīdās's entourage: some told by him, some by the priests, some perhaps by courtiers and visiting holy men. Nāgarīdās may well have requested them to be anthologized. In the following discussions, my reference to "Nāgarīdās" as the author thus is to be understood as shorthand for Nāgarīdās and his environment.

The hypothesis that a collection of free-floating stories came to be redacted as *Garland of Stories and Songs* is confirmed by the observation that different manuscript recensions contain some different stories and songs and the sequence is different, too. Moreover, some editions and manuscripts of Nāgarīdās's complete works include a hagiographical story attributed to Nāgarīdās yet not found in *Garland of Stories and Songs*: *Introduction to Govind jī* (Govind jī kī Parcaī).[30] The existence of this short work may indicate that, similarly, the *prasaṅgas* of *Garland of Stories and Songs* may have been free-floating, before they were collected in the larger hagiographical work.

Whether authored by the prince himself or others, *Garland of Stories and Songs* is closely connected with the Kishangarh court for another reason. Several paintings commissioned by the court may well be illustrations of this work. One famous painting portrays the meeting of the saint Haridās with Tānsen and Akbar, and another depicts Mīrā.[31] Both fit well with incidents described in *Garland of Stories and Songs*. If he commissioned illustrative paintings, it would follow that the prince was closely involved with the work.[32]

Manuscript study of the text shows that *Garland of Stories and Songs* was quite popular. It circulated widely in the Rajasthan-Braj area.[33] Not all the manuscripts give the same text, though: there is a longer and a shorter recension of the work. Determining which one was the original and which was secondary is not easy because the oldest dated manuscripts of each recension happen to be from about the same time (early 1792; Māgh and Phālgun 1849 VS). Both are preserved in the Jaipur City Palace Museum. The earlier, shorter version was written in Brahmapuri, a neighborhood of Kishangarh, but not at the royal Kishangarh court.[34] The slightly later one was written for the king Pratāp Singh in Jaipur and thus can be considered an "authoritative version."[35] It is tempting to see the longer recension as the official version and the shorter recension as the original one, but it could also be the case that the longer was the original that was later deliberately shortened. To facilitate a comparison, the table above gives an overview of the stories and indicates the ones that are only in the longer redaction.

STORIES MOBILIZED

Garland of Stories and Songs is a hagiography about saints as well as ordinary men with extraordinary experiences. The category "saint" is fluid: simple villagers, through their devotion, can demonstrate the characteristics of the saints. Nāgarīdās singles out for mention several villagers from small places in Marwar, such as Palari (PPM 19) and Balonda (PPM 20).

To discuss how the stories about specific saints were told and received in the mid-eighteenth century, and how that compares with earlier versions, the saints are organized roughly by sectarian groupings. Doing so is somewhat misleading, since Nāgarīdās does not categorize them that way and, in fact, does not pay much attention to the sectarian affiliation of the saints he mentions. But the goal is to bring Nāgarīdās's stories into conversation

FIG. 4.1 *Jayadeva Worships Rādhāmādhava*, painting framed in the Salemabad temple

with similar ones told elsewhere. It is impossible to do justice to all the variants of the stories, but identifying the main issues of intertextuality is helpful in understanding the discourse of *Garland of Stories and Songs* and its historical relation with other hagiographies. Applying methods of narrative criticism, comparison of "doublets," identification of sectarian redaction, and analysis of the hagiographers' rhetoric conveys much about intertextuality and the circulation of songs and stories from the sixteenth to the eighteenth century.

STORIES ABOUT JAYADEVA

That Nāgarīdās begins with anecdotes about the songs of *Gīta-govinda*, composed by the twelfth-century Bengali poet Jayadeva, makes sense since he is a Sanskrit poet and comes first chronologically. Nāgarīdās is in sync with the times: Mahīpati's *Victory to the Devotee* (Bhakt-vijay), a hagiography from Maharashtra, composed just slightly later (1762), also starts out with Jayadeva.[36] The Sanskrit poet also figures importantly in the 1763 work *Our*

Sect's Theology authored by Kiśordās, one of the Haridāsī sadhus who had aligned themselves with the Nimbārka-Sampradāya.[37] Jayadeva's *mūrti* here is called Rādhāmādhava. Is it coincidence that shortly after the writing of that text, in 1766 (1823 VS), an image called Rādhāmādhava was brought to Rupnagar and then Salemabad under *mahant* Śrī Govind Śaraṇ jī?[38] At some point this image in Salemabad became identified with Jayadeva's, as illustrated by a modern framed painting on the temple walls in Salemabad (fig. 4.1). According to the sect, the image was brought from Radhakund, where Śrīnivās Ācārya had worshipped it, but there is no early evidence.[39] There are also other complications: "rival" Rādhāmādhava images are said to be Jayadeva's. One is worshipped at the Rādhādāmodara temple (of Jīva Gosvāmī) in Vrindavan, and another one in Kanaka Vrindavan near Jaipur, where the deity is said to have been taken in 1713. Nāgarīdās mentions Rādhāmādhava in connection with Jayadeva (PPM 3a), but that may just be an epithet for Krishna, rather than a specific image of Jayadeva, installed in the Jagannātha temple in Puri. For now, any such connection must remain speculative, but we can conclude that Nāgarīdās's foregrounding of Jayadeva coincides with an interest in Jayadeva in Nimbārkan circles at the time.

The main theme in these *prasaṅgas* is the power of Jayadeva's songs, most importantly, that devotion attracts God himself. To be sure, the theme of Krishna's attraction to the Aṣṭapadī songs is already foregrounded by Nābhādās:

> Who practices the Aṣṭapadī songs, will expand his mind.
> Krishna himself, pleased to hear it, will certainly come to him.
>
> (Bhm 44)

The stories told by Nāgarīdās could all be seen as expansions of this theme.[40] The first is the story of Krishna finishing a verse of *Gīta-govinda* with his own hand:

> As Śrī Jayadeva jī was composing an Aṣṭapadī of his *Gīta-govinda*, he wished to include the line "Place your foot on my head—a sublime flower destroying the poison of love!"[41] But then he thought, "How is it possible for the Lord to say something so unorthodox?" Worrying about that, Jayadeva jī went to answer nature's call. After he left, the Lord came and with his holy lotus handwrote that song: "Place your foot on my head—a sublime flower destroying the poison of love!"
>
> (PPM 1)

Priyādās and Kiśordās also tell this story.[42] It illustrates a common hagiographic *topos* where God interferes in the world of men.

Nābhādās had alluded to Krishna's promise to appear wherever a particular Aṣṭapadī is sung. Priyādās tells about a gardener's (*mālī*) daughter, who attracts Krishna by humming this favorite song. Nāgarīdās expands the story:

> Krishna appeared before him (Jayadeva) there in the jungle. He promised, "If anyone sings this Aṣṭapadī, I myself will come to listen, no matter who sings this Aṣṭapadī, whether in a temple or seated in a deserted place." Now a foolish gardener's daughter had learned only this line: "In woods on the windswept Jumna bank, Krishna waits in wildflower garlands." She was singing that line as she strolled in the aubergine garden, and the Lord followed her every step. His trousers got tangled in the thorns of the aubergine plants. They were ripped to shreds. The Lord, enchanted, was also ripped to shreds. Meanwhile, in the Śrī Jagannāthadeva temple, where the body of the image (*ṭhākur*) is his true form, people saw that the Lord's trousers were torn, and they saw the aubergine thorns entangled in them. Then all the priests in the sanctum and surrounding grounds inquired, "Lord, what happened?" The Lord explained everything through the dream of a priest. When the king of the land heard about this, he issued an edict: "No one shall sing an Aṣṭapadī while moving about. If anyone wishes to sing one, he should do so either in the temple or in another suitable place."
>
> (PPM 3a)

Appropriately, Nāgarīdās quotes the song that attracts Krishna as the one with the epithet "*vanamālī*," or "with the forest-flower garland," in its refrain.[43] In Priyādās's version the story ends with the king inviting the girl to perform in the temple.[44] Nāgarīdās's account omits that ending, but tells how the king issued an edict to forbid singing the song while moving about. Priyādās mentions the edict in a separate verse and adds that it was put to the test by a "Moghol," who sang the Aṣṭapadī while on horseback.[45] It seems that Nāgarīdās is interested less in the *topos* of the test than in the power of the song.

Nāgarīdās also tells a story about the miraculous power of the Aṣṭapadī songs to revive the dead:

> One time, Śrī Jayadeva jī was staying with a king, and his wife, Padmāvatī jī, with the queen. Now that queen was into thoughtless backbiting. To test the love of Padmāvatī jī and Jayadeva jī, the queen made up a lie. She said

to Padmāvatī jī: "The Raja has gone out to hunt lions. A lion has killed Jayadeva jī." As she said this, she brought his turban (as proof). No sooner had she heard this than Padmāvatī jī gave up her life on the spot. The queen's mouth became dry with fear. Meanwhile, the king and Jayadeva jī returned home. When he heard what had happened, the king was deeply overwhelmed. Jayadeva sat down near Padmāvatī jī's corpse and started singing an Aṣṭapadī of *Gīta-govinda*. Padmāvatī jī revived at that very moment and joined him in this song.

(PPM 2)

Priyādās tells this story more elaborately, with a focus on the test of Padmāvatī's pure love that proves nearly fatal.[46] He stresses the embarrassment of the king about his wife's behavior, which is what prompts Jayadeva to revive Padmāvatī. The miracle is conveyed in a few rather laconic words: "He melodiously sang an Aṣṭapadī, and revived her corpse." Again, Nāgarīdās chooses to de-emphasize the test and stress the power of song. We thus see a pattern develop that will be confirmed elsewhere: Nāgarīdās selects the episodes that foreground the power of song and makes all other hagiographic concerns secondary to it.

STORIES ABOUT NARSĪ MEHTĀ

In all redactions, Nāgarīdās includes the Gujarati *bhakta* Narsī Mehtā, an early devotee-singer. He is rarely included in the more regionally limited hagiographies, partly because of his region and partly because his fifteenth-century date (traditionally 1417–1480?) makes it difficult for him to be claimed by any of the sects founded in the early sixteenth century. Nābhādās mentions him, but it is Priyādās who foregrounds him in a record twenty-seven *Kavittas*, emphasizing God and his *bhakta*'s boundless generosity within "*bhakti*'s economy of endless abundance."[47] Nāgarīdās illustrates the story with a song. Two of Narsī's "autobiographical" poems are contextualized: *Māmeruṃ-* and *Hārasamenāṃ-pad*.[48] The first one illustrates how God comes to the rescue to help his devotee fulfill his family obligations, in particular, paying his daughter's customary gifts to her in-laws (*māmeruṃ*).[49]

Narsī Mehtā was a Brahmin of Gujarat. He was a great Vaishnava who worshipped with deep emotion (*mahānubhāva*). After his daughter's marriage, he went to visit her in-laws. He had become penniless through his generosity and hospitality to Vaishnavas according to the Lord's wish. So his daughter's in-laws did not respect him. Greedily, they kept thinking

> about the ceremonial gift they felt they were entitled to.[50] But he wondered, how could he give them such a gift? So he composed a song and sang it. Then miraculously the material for the gift appeared, and the in-laws were gratified.
>
> (PPM 12)

Thus when Narsī is in financial straits, God saves his honor. The second poem is contextualized with a test of the veracity of Narsī's sainthood by the king.[51] The same stories are told also by Mahīpati in his *Victory to the Devotee*, which, like Nāgarīdās's version, predates the boost to Narsī hagiography in the late eighteenth century, when one of Narsī's descendants, who was in the service of the Gaekwad Marathas of Baroda, decided to commemorate Narsī by rebuilding, on a grander scale, his ashram in Coro, Junagarh.[52]

STORIES ABOUT THE SANTS

Of most interest, perhaps, are the stories about the Sants: Nāmdev, Kabīr, Raidās (and, in passing, Tilocan).[53] Several of Nāgarīdās's stories are well known from earlier story cycles, such as Anantdās's *Parcaīs*, but are given a new twist and linked with a song by the Sant in question.[54] Strikingly, Nāgarīdās refrains from portraying these Sants as disciples of Rāmānanda, as the Rāmānandīs do. Still, they are seen as a group of contemporaneous, like-minded friends, in fact vying with each other for superiority. Nāmdev is the most influential figure, and Tilocan and Kabīr come across as (perhaps junior) contemporaries, in awe of Nāmdev's visions of the Lord.[55] A story that illustrates this well is the story about the vision of God in a dog:

> The Vaishnava Śrī Nāmdev jū saw only the Lord in all living beings. One time, the Vaishnava Tilocan jū said to Nāmdev jū, "Could you help me out? I am incapable of having a vision of the Lord, but by your grace it might be possible." So Nāmdev jū said, "I always see only the Lord in every being. Why don't you look upon the world that way, too? See that dog standing there? The Lord is in him, too. So by my heart's truth, let me give you a vision of the Lord, even in this dog." Now how could Tilocan jū quarrel with him and dispute his truth? When Tilocan jū heard this, he smiled and remained quiet. Then Nāmdev jū pulled cymbals out of his waistband. He composed a new song describing that dog and started to sing it. At once the dog disappeared from view and in its place, a vision of the Lord appeared.
>
> (PPM 8)

Nāmdev asserts that God is present in all living beings and proves it to Tilocan by showing him the vision of God in a dog. In Mahīpati's *Victory to the Devotee*, Nāmdev shows this not to Tilocan but, perhaps with greater effect, to a Brahmin, Rāmdev.[56]

An important feature that the Sants have in common is their low caste: Nāmdev was a tailor, Kabīr a weaver, and Raidās a leather-worker.[57] One incident that foregrounds the low caste of Nāmdev is not related elsewhere:

> At some point, Kabīr jū said to Nāmdev jū, "When you realize God's *darshana* on your own, you are furthering your own spiritual development, but at some time you should further the highest good for my sake, too." Nāmdev jū replied, "Already you have that knowledge within you. Why make the request of me? There is no dearth of divine manifestation, but rather a dearth of belief in people." Thus did those two great souls converse. A few days later, a Moghol took Nāmdev jū away for forced labor (*begār*).[58] The Moghol put a bag on Nāmdev's head and forced him to go. At that time, Kabīr jū approached from another direction. He asked, "What happened to you!?" Then by way of an answer for the surrounding crowd to hear, Nāmdev jū composed a new song and started to sing it as he went along. When Kabīr heard the last line of the song, he fell at the Moghol's feet. Instantly the Moghol disappeared, and in his place Kabīr experienced *darshana* of Śrī Rāmacandra jū. So the song that Nāmdev jū sang when Kabīr jū received *darshana* of Śrī Rāma jū, is the following song:
>
> *For all I know, this could be Rāma jī.*
> *I was absorbed in devotion, so who else could have taken ahold of me?*
> *With a rosary fit for a god and such fine attire,*
> *He must be the one, the Lord (Moghol) of Dvarka city.*
> *Dark horse, silverwork saddle,*
> *His cap (*kulaha*) is God's crown (*tāja*). He is the merciful one!*
> *Nāmdev says: Listen Kabīr,*
> *Fall at his feet, for he is Raghuvīra (Rāma).*
>
> (PPM 9)

In this anecdote Nāmdev demonstrates the same point to Kabīr as he did to Tilocan in the previous one. This time, God is present in the oppressor "Moghol," who conscripts Nāmdev for forced labor.

In nearly all the stories that Nāgarīdās tells about Nāmdev, his low caste plays a role. Sometimes the moral is the triumph of devotion over caste status, as in the story where Nāmdev is elbowed out of the temple, but God turns the temple around, so he can still have *darshana* (PPM 6).[59] At other times the message seems more conservative and at least implicitly confirms a status quo where low-castes are made to perform forced labor for the powerful, who can be seen as God incarnate.

For the Camār (leather-worker) Raidās, too, the central issue is his untouchability. Nāgarīdās relates the story of Raidās's competition with Brahmins jealous of his success:

> At some point, many people came to praise the excellence of Raidās jū. Seeing this devotion, several Brahmins, proud of their orthodox dharma, became very jealous. Though many wise and well-intended Brahmins who were vigilant in Vaishnava Dharma rebuked them and sang in praise of devotion, still they did not comprehend. That is the reason such a group got together and went to the king exclaiming, "How can this low-caste worship the image of the Lord? It is not allowed according to the *Dharmaśāstras*. His sin affects you as well." Then the king retorted as follows: "The greatness of devotion is not to be underestimated, and at the same time the śāstras should not be overruled. So let us position the image of the Lord in between you and him (Raidās). You sit on one side, and Raidās on the other.[60] You worship your way, and he, his way. If the Lord is pleased with either of you, he will spontaneously move toward you, throne and all." So they arranged to do the king's bidding. On one side sat the Brahmins, all purified. They spent half a day reciting the Vedas. Their throats became hoarse. They were all perspiring heavily and became anxious, but they kept seated. Then Raidās was told, "Now you begin." Not knowing what else to do, he pulled his two cymbals out of his pocket. He composed a new song and began to sing it alone, with breaking voice, filled with humility and sorrow (*karuṇā*). The moment he had finished the signature line at the end, as all looked on, the Lord moved, throne and all, and he settled on Raidās jū's lap to stay.
>
> (PPM 11)

This popular story combines two hagiographic *topoi*: conflict of the devotee with the sage or pharisee and with the king or caesar. As fitting for a "royal" hagiography, the court is the arena where this conflict plays out, and, needless to say, Raidās is victorious. Anantdās told the story in his *Parcaī*,[61] highlighting the debate between Raidās and the Brahmins, but Nāgarīdās focuses on the power of song. Priyādās had linked the incident with the royal support of the Jhālī Rāṇī, but Nāgarīdās's innovation is to connect it with a particular song by Raidās.[62]

For Kabīr, Nāgarīdās tells the story of his attempted seduction by two *apsarās* (nymphs):

> One time Kabīr was sitting in the jungle. There, in that lonely place, two *apsarās* descended from heaven. Kabīr jū thought, "It is not proper to talk to them, just as it would not be good to look upon their seductive forms. It would not even be appropriate to listen to what they have to say." With this in mind he composed a song and began to sing it. In that very song he told them to get up and leave. As the *apsarās* saw their intentions thwarted, they left. The song he sang at that time is this song:
>
> *Please go home, my sisters—there's nothing here for you to give or take.*
> *Without Rāma, without Govinda, you're poison to my eyes.*
> *Your glittering garments with inlaid jewelry, your necks with pearls adorned,*
> *You are on a mission from Indra's world to turn me into a lover.*
> *Leave behind such nonsense. Sing instead Govinda's praise.*
> *Wear basil-beads (*tulsī*) around your neck, so that you'll go to Brahman's heaven.*[63]
> *Is there a shortage (of lovers) in Paradise? Can't you find anyone but me?*
> *You've come to make me waver, but what a waste of destiny that would be!*
> *Many an ascetic you've caused to fall, tying them up in gossamer threads.*
> *But try as you can, you'll find out: water does not catch fire.*
> *You are but an illusion. I've found refuge in Hari alone.*
> *By my guru's power, by communion with the sadhus, I've reached the highest goal.*
> *My name? Kabīr. My caste? Weaver. My house is the forest. Ascetic, I dwell alone.*
> *If you've come to pay a great man your respect, then one (of you) can be my mother—and like a mother, the other.*
>
> (PPM 10)

Kabīr's resistance to female charms is also the subject of one of Anantdās's *Parcaīs* and is briefly alluded to by Priyādās.[64] Again, Nāgarīdās's innovation is to furnish Kabīr's actual words, the song he sang on the occasion.[65]

The manuscripts of shorter recension do not include that story about Kabīr, but instead describe Kabīr's visit to Vrindavan:

One day the Vaishnava Kabīr happened to come to Vrindavan. His heart was immersed in the joy of *satsaṅga* with the learned men, *rasikas*, and Vaishnavas there. There Kabīr composed a new song. Several of the Kabīr-panthīs who were with him heard that song and understood it. And so they even stayed on in Vrindavan. That song became very famous. And here is that song:

Now I have tasted Hari's rasa,
I am burning inside in Brahma's fire, ever since this still has been lit.[66]
When I take in hand the gourd-instrument of the five sounds, I lose myself in my alchemy.
I take in hand the thunderbolt of the eight-petaled lotus; when rubbed, it makes the elixir trickle down.
In the throat of a corpse that is seated down, drips the elixir from the still.
Hold on to devotion in the face of challenge. Drink like an auspicious elephant.
Dhruva drank it; Prahlāda drank it; their suṣumnā *(subtle channel) did not remain obstructed.*
Cutting the flower and drinking (the nectar), all sadhus are in Rādhā's power in Vrindavan.
The distiller fills to the brim the inebriating cup of love.
Kabīr says, "Listen brother sadhu, try as you may, but you cannot get to the end of this drinking party."

(PPM 10b)

Nāgarīdās is looking at Kabīr from a Vrindavan-centered perspective. The song here that functions as "proof" for the story is one of the deliberately mysterious *sandhyā-bhāṣā* (Twilight-idiom) poems by Kabīr, in this case mixing yogic imagery with that of the liquor distillery. The hagiographer interpreted literally the refrain and the reference to Rādhā in Vrindavan. Within the context of the song, *rasa* probably has a tantric hidden meaning, connected with alchemy and sexual yogic practices. In the story, Kabīr's poem receives a warm reception, and consequently his followers, called Kabīr-panthīs, stay on in Vrindavan. Such a view would fit well the ecumenical spirit between Sants and Krishna *bhaktas* that appears in the work of Vrindavan *bhaktas*, such as Harirām Vyās, who is quoted extensively by Nāgarīdās.[67]

For Nāgarīdās's Sants, Rāmānanda is nowhere in the picture.[68] The absence of Rāmānanda defeats any impression that the longer redaction, which includes these Sants and is more radical on caste issues, would be a Rāmānandī redaction. Nāgarīdās has an anecdote about a Rāmānujī, but, remarkably, this one is famous for his lack of conventional consideration for caste. The Marwari villager Caturdās Khojī recognized God when he appeared as a low-caste man, disgusting to all others present:

> In Marwar, there is a village, Palari. There lived a Vaishnava by the name Rāmānujī Caturdās. He became famous under the name Khojī. How he became so famous is told in the *ṭīkā* on *Garland of Devotees*, but it is not described there in detail.[69] In his *Sākhīs* he signed with the name Khojī, and in his *Viṣṇupada* (devotional hymn) he signed it as Caturdās. Now one day, this Caturdās was reciting the *Bhāgavata-purāṇa*. There were many other listeners sitting there, when a low-caste Kañjar, also called Kol, slipped into the crowd, carrying a trap in his hand.[70] He was dirty, his hair hanging over his face and eyes. On his head he had a basket with leftover bread and grain. And from his mouth came the foul call: "Would anyone give me a bag with water left over from boiling rice?"[71] Seeing the low-caste man in such a filthy condition, the listeners all burst out laughing, but Caturdās left his ritual seat and ran to bow his head at the Kañjar's feet. Then the crowd all got together and exclaimed, "The Svāmī has become crazy." So the Kañjar was standing there, surrounded by this crowd and Svāmī lay prostrated at his feet. At that moment, the Kañjar, who was an embodiment of the Lord, disappeared. Then all understood the power of Caturdās. They stopped laughing, stunned. And this story became very famous everywhere. On that occasion, Caturdās composed a song.
>
> (PPM 19)

This disregard for caste seems a bit out of character for Rāmānujīs, otherwise thought to be orthodox. Perhaps for that reason, Khojī is said to be Rāmānandī in some manuscripts that are of the longer redaction, and the *prasaṅga* is omitted altogether from the shorter edition.[72] In any case, the central idea of God appearing in all guises, including the most polluting ones, is clear.

STORIES ABOUT TULSĪDĀS

Nāgarīdās's inclusion of Tulsīdās provides a mid-eighteenth-century source for how Tulsīdās was remembered at the time, shortly before the influential Marathi *Victory to the Devotee*. This is particularly important given the controversial discoveries of other hagiographies in the late nineteenth and early twentieth centuries that purported to be old, even contemporaneous with Tulsīdās himself.[73] If such texts existed in Nāgarīdās's time, he was apparently unaware of them. In Nāgarīdās's version, Tulsīdās's sectarian identity is not an issue: he is consistently called "Vaishnava Śrī Tulsīdās jī, a worshipper of Rāma." That does not mean he is considered a Rāmānandī, as no such formal sectarian link is established.[74] The only point Nāgarīdās's narrative has in common with the spurious hagiographies is establishing a relationship to famous contemporaries.[75] In one anecdote, Nāgarīdās describes Tulsīdās's meeting with the emperor, who is specified here to be Jahāngīr.[76]

There are three stories about Tulsīdās in *Garland of Stories and Songs*, each elaborating on Priyādās's cryptic allusions. The main innovation is again that Nāgarīdās links the stories to songs. In the most famous story, a ghost in a tree refers Tulsīdās to Hanumān, who in turn tips him off about where to get a vision of Rāma.[77] However, Rāma and Lakshmana appear as hunters, and Tulsīdās does not recognize them:

> Hanumān directed him to a higher area in a nearby wood. "Go and sit there, and a vision will come to you." So Tulsīdās sat down and waited there. He kept up his watch and grew anxious.
>
> Meanwhile, Śrī Rāma and Lakshmana jū came by. They had taken the form of humans, but in the following way: their clothes were dirty, they had a bow and arrows in hand, they had killed a deer, and they had put it upside down as they carried it, blood dripping as they went. Tulsīdās jū turned his eyes away from them and looked toward the earth. He said to himself, "I cannot bear to look at such cruel people. They will pass by quickly." So that's how Śrī Rāma jī passed by, and Tulsīdās remained sitting there for a long time after that. He kept on watching the path for Śrī Rāma jū's arrival. Finally, he received *darshana* of Hanumān jū there as before and asked, "When will I get my vision of Śrī Rāma jū? I've been sitting here for a long time!" Hanumān replied, "Those people were Śrī Rāma and Lakshmana themselves. They took the form of young hunters!" Tulsīdās burst into tears. He felt strong remorse, and on that occasion he composed a song. And here is that song:
>
> *I shall hate my eyes as long as I live.*
> *Willfully they have ruined me, burying themselves in the earth.*
> *Not realizing your (Rāma's) ways are inscrutable, I was asleep while awake.*

The ultimate of all phenomena escaped me, though he was
tantalizingly close!
I am a failure: I found a diamond and instantly lost it.
Tulsīdās missed Śrī Rāma! Tell me, how could that be?

(PPM 22)

Nāgarīdās's telling of the story stresses Tulsīdās's aversion to the low-caste and untouchable aspect of the hunters and is reminiscent of the appearance of God as a Kañjar in the story of the Marwari *bhakta* Caturdāsa Khojī (PPM 19).[78] Remarkably, Tulsīdās misses this unique glimpse of God due to his aversion to untouchability, whereas Caturdās, as well as the lower-caste Sants, mentioned above, does not fail to recognize God when he comes in such a disguise. Perhaps Nāgarīdās is here implicitly asserting the superiority of the Sants, devotees of a *nirguṇa* Rāma. Or maybe this is just a move to humanize Tulsīdās and make him more accessible.

The second story is the only one on Tulsīdās in the shorter recension. It is actually two stories in one: the first is the revival of a *satī*'s (virtuous woman's) husband because Tulsī distractedly greets her with a blessing to remain happily married for a long time. This is linked with a second story where the emperor summons Tulsīdās to perform a miracle.[79] Both stories are also told in Mahīpati's *Victory to the Devotee*, the latter with respect to Akbar.[80] Here is how Nāgarīdās tells it:

When this event came to the notice of the emperor Jahāngīr, he called for Tulsīdās jū and commanded: "Show me a miracle." Tulsīdās replied, "But I cannot perform any miracles." So he was thrown in jail. At that time, King Anīrāy Baḍ Gūjar visited Tulsīdās jū and begged him, "Mahārāj, please do something so that the path of the Hindus (*hindavani*) does not seem weak and that in the future no one would dare attempt to torment Vaishnavas." Thereupon, Tulsīdās composed a new song and started to sing it. Immediately, in front of the emperor's eyes, countless monkeys appeared to attack him. The emperor became afraid and fell at Tulsīdās's feet. The emperor asked Tulsīdās to forgive him and to instruct him. As Tulsīdās jī left, he explained as follows: "The retinue of Śrī Rāma jī's servant Hanumān has arrived here. Now that they have conquered this place, you should move elsewhere. Your family members who stay here will remain here only as prisoners." The king took it to heart and left Salimgarh. Even today the family of the emperor remains in jail there.

(PPM 23)

Jahāngīr's memoirs indeed mention a figure named Anīrāy Baḍ Gūjar, whom he especially favored and trusted.[81] Perhaps Nāgarīdās relied here on oral traditions among Baḍ Gūjars, to which he may have had access because of his own family relations with them (his son was married into a Baḍ Gūjar family). The incident is puzzling for the raja's strident tone, which seems to cast the matter as a broad defense of Hindus. Is this evidence for an early communalist attitude?

The coda of the story is that Tulsīdās advises the emperor to desert "Salimgarh" and says it will be a prison for his family members in the future. This remarkable detail, which is not in Priyādās's version, is an example of (chronologically confused) historical etiology of place. The fort was built by another Salīm (Salīm Shāh Surī) in Delhi in 1546, but it was renamed upon the Mughals' return and their victory over the Suri sultans. When the new capital of Shāhjahānabād was built in 1638, it was deserted for the Red Fort, to which it was linked by bridge.[82] An Indian equivalent of the "Tower of London," it later served as a prison for Aurangzeb's siblings.[83] So Tulsīdās is given in hindsight some lines with prophetic views. The incident of the attack of Hanumān's army is eminently believable in view of the persistent presence of monkeys at the place even today. Nāgarīdās thus is working with his own experience of the place in the mid-seventeenth century, linking it anachronistically to the story about Tulsīdās.

Jahāngīr figures elsewhere in divine revenge stories, appearing in a similar plot in the roughly contemporary (1752) Bengali *Praise of Annada* (Annada-maṅgal) by Bharatcandra Ray. This one, though, involves not Hanumān but the Devī, and it is her hordes of blood-thirsty spirits and yoginis that assault the city of Delhi in revenge for the emperor's belittling her. The outcome is that her protégé, the Nadia Raja Bhavanand Majumdar, is liberated from jail and given a mansab, thus founding the dynasty that sponsored this Maṅgal-kāvya (praise poem). The intermediary between the Nadia king and the Mughal emperor is Mān Singh of Amer. Both he and the Mughal emperor end up becoming devotees of the goddess, and Durgā Pūjā is henceforth a feature in the Delhi fort.[84] Rather than expressing Hindu-Muslim antagonism, such stories make a case for the cultural investment of the Mughal empire in Bengal and imply that the Mughal administration was not regarded as an alien regime.[85]

The third story brings Tulsīdās to Braj, where he has *darshana* of a Krishna image, but sees only Rāma. In Nāgarīdās's version, he goes to Govardhan, where Viṭṭhalnāth takes him for *darshana* of Śrī Nātha jī (PPM 24). In the story told by Priyādās, the Gauḍīya devotee, Tulsīdās instead meets with

Nābhādās and has *darshana* of Madanagopāla.[86] The Vārtā version makes Tulsīdās the older brother of the Vallabhan poet Nanddās. Tulsīdās does not actually travel to Braj, but he sends a letter to call his brother back east. According to the Vārtā of Nanddās, Tulsīdās writes to his younger brother to admonish him for straying from loyal *bhakti* to Rāma alone, casting this in terms of a wife's fidelity to her husband (*pativratā dharma*). Nanddās promptly answers that the problem with Rāma is that he vowed to take only one wife (*ekapatnīvrata*) and, moreover, has trouble keeping her. He sees Krishna as the better choice since he can accommodate innumerable wives. Tulsī has to admit defeat and acknowledge Nanddās's choice.[87] This version then also raises the issue of *ananyatā* in devotion, and validates it, unapologetically putting forward the Vallabhan choice of Krishna over Rāma.

VARIANTS OF THE VĀRTĀS

Nāgarīdās frequently quotes the same songs of Vallabhan *bhakta*s as the Vārtās, yet he tends to omit the Vallabhan sectarian frame. Such is the case for the story of the Aṣṭ-chāp poet Paramānanddās (PPM 4). In Nāgarīdās's version, Vallabhācārya hears about his songs and travels all the way to Vrindavan to listen to Paramānand. He is so impressed that he remains in a trance for about a week. In the Vārtā, by contrast, this song comes up only in the second *prasaṅga*, when, Paramānand has already been firmly established as a disciple. Vallabha and his entourage, on the way to Braj, happen to stop at Paramānand's house in Kannauj.[88] When Vallabha loses consciousness upon hearing his song, a frightened Paramānand exclaims that he will never again sing such a song. In the first *prasaṅga*, one of Vallabha's servants from Arail heard about Paramānand's singing and crossed the river to hear him sing in Prayāg. Subsequently, Paramānand had a vision of the Vallabhan image of Śrī Navanītapriyā jī in his dream, and the next morning he crossed the river in the other direction to have *darshana*, sing for Vallabha, and become initiated.[89] In both versions of the story, Paramānand thus is shown to be a specialist in singing about *viraha līlā*; however, the Vārtā stresses that Paramānand is impressed with Vallabha, whereas Nāgarīdās tells it the other way around, and he does not speak about a Vallabhan conversion.

For another Aṣṭachāp poet, Kumbhandās, Nāgarīdās singles out an episode that shows, in this case, Viṭṭhalnāth being impressed with him, rather than the other way around (PPM 43). Nāgarīdās does not even mention that he was among the first generation of Vallabha's devotees in Braj.[90] Like the Vārtā, Nāgarīdās's story mentions that Kumbhandās was from Jamunāvat village near Govardhan, and he adds a song of his vision of Śrī Nātha jī at night from the parapets of his house. In the Vārtā, Viṭṭhalnāth invites Kumbhandās along on a trip to Dvarka to provide him with some income, but at night in his tent Kumbhandās laments his bereavement from Śrī Nātha jī so loudly that Viṭṭhalnāth is moved to send him back home.[91] Nāgarīdās leaves out the issue of financial improvement, instead focusing wholly on the *viraha* experienced by Kumbhandās, who climbs in a tree to catch a glimpse of Śrī Nātha jī from a distance and falls down in ecstasy (PPM 42).[92] Similarly, Nāgarīdās's narrative about Kumbhandās's son Caturbhujdās (PPM 44) also differs from the Vārtā story. In the Vārtā, Caturbhujdās experiences *viraha*, not because of his own travels, but because Śrī Nātha jī had been taken to Mathura for a big Holī festival and failed to return.[93] Upon hearing the same song by Caturbhujdās as reported in Nāgarīdās's text, Śrī Nātha jī himself decides to return so as not to prolong Caturbhuj's sorrow.

Nāgarīdās also tells stories about Viṭṭhalnāth's disciples. He describes the conversion of the Jaina Mānikcand from Delhi (PPM 25), possibly Mānikcand Osvāl Baniyā of the Vārtā, and of Chītsvāmī (PPM 26).[94] The latter is portrayed before conversion as a mischief maker, a Shaiva according to Nāgarīdās and a Caube of Mathura, who visits Gokul with four of his Caube pals, in the Vārtā.[95] In both cases, Chītsvāmī offers a bad coconut (in the Vārtā also fake money) to Viṭṭhalnāth, who sees through the deception. Nāgarīdās also tells the story about Chītsvāmī's quarrel with Bīrbal over a song celebrating Viṭṭhalnāth as identical with Krishna (PPM 26b).[96] In the Vārtā, Chītsvāmī is said to be Bīrbal's *purohit* (priest), and the emperor Akbar himself is also involved in the dispute.[97] In both cases, Chītsvāmī's song demonstrates him to be a firm believer in Viṭṭhalnāth, and, in this case, Nāgarīdās tells the conversion story, whereas the Vārtā takes his initiation for granted. Nāgarīdās also selects for retelling the incident of Viṭṭhalnāth's disciple Krishnadās's engaging a courtesan for service in the temple, which leads to her death:

> One day, Krishnadās jū, the head temple priest (*adhikārī*), left Govardhan for Delhi to bring some necessary items, such as clothes, jewelry, and other things for Govardhananātha jū. There, at night on someone's balcony, he spotted a Rāmjanī who excelled at singing. He saw her singing and dancing. Hearing her voice, he stopped on the road, enchanted. It occurred to him that her voice would be worthy of a performance to enchant Śrī Govardhananātha. But at this point he returned home. Later, by God's

> wish, he was able to give her a sum of money to come with him. He told her, "My boss (*sardār*) is very attractive, generous, and handsome, unlike anyone you have ever known. You will reap many rewards." That was the explanation he gave on the way back to Govardhan. An old memory (of a previous birth), then awakened within her, and her attraction to God through hearsay (*śravaṇānurāga*) began to grow. When they reached Śrī Govardhan, he took her into the temple. Until then, she had not known anything about the mystery of how the Lord is worshipped in his true form (*svarūpa*). The *kīrtana* started. Krishnadās jū had had her memorize a song he had composed, and she sang it. Just then, the curtain was pulled.[98] Seeing God's sweet beauty, she stood there, watching motionless, savoring his beauty as her eyes filled with tears.
>
> Her attendants supported her at her armpits, they kept her body steady.
> But her mind had gone off to taste the nectar of Hari's beauty.[99] Her heart
> ceased to beat.
>
> Such is the way the Lord accepted Krishnadās's gift. Her heart was enraptured. Then, tears streaming, overcome with great love, she performed a mime and sang. When the line with the dedication came, her soul left her body. Everyone was astonished and shouted "Bravo! Bravo!" Many important people disregarded caste rules (*maryādā*) in order to take part in her final rites. Now follows the song that the Rāmjanī was singing as she, by the grace of Śrī Krishnadās jū, gave up her body in *satsaṅga* and united with the Lord.
>
> (PPM 41)

Here Krishnadās witnesses the girl's performance only from a distance, as she is up on a balcony. In the Vārtā, the incident is more scandalous: Krishnadās is quite enchanted and has her privately perform for him first before taking her to the temple. After she dies in ecstasy performing Krishnadās's song, her "mother" successfully presses Krishnadās for restitution money.[100] This problematic incident called for several interpolations of spiritual explanation (*bhāva-prakāśa*). Nāgarīdās in that vein mentions that the girl had an "old memory" of Śrī Nātha jī, that is, she remembered him from a previous birth. He lovingly dwells on her performance in the temple and her death in ecstasy, stressing how several in the audience were so moved that they chose to partake in her last rites, notwithstanding her caste. That Nāgarīdās's courtesan is based not in Agra but in Delhi, where his own concubine Rasik Bihārī was purchased, perhaps made him more sympathetic to the case of the girl's spiritual conversion.

Another touchy issue is the sectarian allegiance of Bhagvāndās (who used "Hit Rāmrāy" in his *chāpa*), a Sārasvat Brahmin, who according to the Vārtā was originally a follower of Caitanya (Mahāprabhu) but later became a disciple of Viṭṭhalnāth.[101] The Vārtā describes how he experienced a life-changing vision on the occasion of Janmāṣṭamī, realizing that Viṭṭhalnāth was God himself. Because Rāmrāy brokered Bhagvāndās's meeting with Viṭṭhalnāth and arranged for his initiation, Bhagvāndās gratefully would sign all his songs with the *chāpa* "Bhagvān Hit Rāmrāy."[102] The Vārtā delights in elaborating that all this displeased the *adhikārī* of the Govindadeva temple, who tried to ban this apostate from *darshana* but eventually had to bow to the will of God himself and allow him in again.[103] Still according to the Vārtā, Bhagvāndās became disillusioned with living in Vrindavan and moved to Agra to become a divan (*sūjā kī dīvāngirī karte hate*); from there he commuted to Gopalpur once or twice a month, and when his end came near, he did not want to be taken to Braj, as he considered himself unworthy.[104] Nāgarīdās starts his stories with Bhagvāndās's death, without specifying where it occurred but instead describing Bhagvāndās's last performance (PPM 54). Skipping all the sectarian quarrels, Nāgarīdās presents Bhagvān as utterly aloof from philosophical debate. Yet he situates him in Vrindavan and has him, in turn, convert a pandit-householder who ends up also living there (PPM 55). Again, the power of song is foregrounded and the sectarian angle is avoided. Instead, Nāgarīdās subtly undermines the Vallabhan move to turn this ex-Gauḍīya *bhakta* away from Vrindavan to Agra and Gopalpur, to the point of denying him a death in Braj. Nāgarīdās's worldview is firmly Vrindavan-centered: in his story Gokul is not mentioned at all.

Another disciple of Viṭṭhalnāth in the Vārtā is Madhukar Shāh, the king of Orccha (PPM 52).[105] Nāgarīdās, without mentioning Viṭṭhalnāth, celebrates this king's devotion for holy men together with that of his famous queen, Ganesh De. He marvels at their jointly worshipping a donkey dressed up with all the hallmarks of Vishnu's devotees. He may have been inspired by Priyādās's story about a crook masquerading as a holy man who tries to rob the queen, stabbing her in the thigh. The queen is unshaken in her belief in holy men and even tries to hide her wound from her husband for fear that he will punish the "holy man." When Madhukar Shāh finds out, he is instead pleased with his queen's devotion to holy men.[106]

We thus can distinguish a pattern in how Nāgarīdās reworks the Vārtās: in nearly every case he drops the sectarian concerns and focuses instead on the power of the *bhaktas*' songs. Even if the final redaction of *Garland of Stories and Songs* was done by Vallabhans, they did not attempt to correct for these revisions.

STORIES ABOUT SŪRDĀS

Sūrdās is seen as a Vallabhan in the Vārtās, but that may be a late development.[107] Nāgarīdās confirms a Vallabhan initiation, but his text differs from the canonical story in that it is not Vallabha but Viṭṭhalnāth who initiates Sūrdās (PPM 36). In the Vārtā, Vallabha had weaned Sūrdās from "whining" songs of petition to the Lord (*vinaya*),[108] and here Viṭṭhalnāth suggests that he stop wasting his talent on hilarious Holī songs. In both cases, Sūr already had a career as a singer but pleads ignorance about the divine *līlā*, which is remedied by Vallabhan instruction. Both versions continue by ascribing specific songs by Sūr to Vallabhan inspiration. Nāgarīdās singles out one of the Vārtā songs as the very first song Sūr composed and which Śrī Nātha jī liked so well that it came to be included in his official liturgy by his demand (PPM 36). This fits with the Vallabhan assertion that Sūrdās was appointed in Śrī Nātha jī's service as a singer. Overall, Nāgarīdās's testimony shows that even by the mid-eighteenth century the story of Sūr's Vallabhan initiation was not wholly consistent yet.

The Vārtā asserts other well-known facts about Sūrdās that have been questioned by scholars. Here Nāgarīdās corroborates those assertions. What about Sūr's purported blindness?[109] By the mid-eighteenth century, this was well established. Nāgarīdās does not repeat the Vārtā stories, but tells an anecdote contextualizing two songs by Sūr, one as a lament of his blindness and the other as testimony that the only vision that matters is that of God (PPM 37). What about Sūrdās's meeting with the emperor Akbar? The court singer Tānsen was the one who put Akbar on Sūr's track in the Vārtās,[110] but Nāgarīdās saves that for the story of Akbar's meeting with Svāmī Haridās. He skips the efforts Akbar went through to get Sūr to come to his court. He also leaves out Akbar's questioning the last line of the poem Sūr sings for him, in which the blind Sūr had said: "My eyes are dying with thirst." Nāgarīdās says only that the emperor was very impressed with this song and has only minimal narration contextualizing the Vārtā song.

The Vārtās also tell about the rivalry of Sūrdās and Krishnadās.[111] Sūrdās explicitly challenges Krishnadās to compose a song that does not show any of his influence (*chāyā*). It seems a rather existential challenge and perhaps was an accusation of plagiarism or at least imitation. The poem Krishnadās comes up with is not his own, but is composed by God to help him save face. Sūrdās sees through this and says: "I had a quarrel with you, not with the Lord. I recognize the Lord's penmanship!" Krishnadās can only remain silent. The issue remains unresolved. In Nāgarīdās's version, by contrast, the challenge seems more of a friendly competition based on an invitation to compose songs on a common theme, in this case, on *godhūla*, or "the return of the cows" (PPM 40). Krishnadās is embarrassed by his inability to create a song *ex tempore*. When Krishna comes to his aid, Sūrdās recognizes the song as the Lord's but praises Krishnadās for having been taken under wing by God himself. This version thus has more of a happy ending.

STORIES ABOUT GAUḌĪYA DEVOTEES

Nāgarīdās rather sparingly relates stories about Gauḍīyas, perhaps because the vernacular output of the sect is overwhelmingly in Bengali, a language into which Nāgarīdās does not venture. Still, he mentions three Gauḍīya devotees: Sūrdās Madanmohan (PPM 46–49), Gadādhar Bhaṭṭ (PPM 45), and the latter's descendant Vallabhrasik (PPM 66). All three are also quoted in Nāgarīdās's anthology.[112] As he does with the Vallabhan saints he mentions, for these Gauḍīya saints he ignores or makes light of sectarian identification.

Nāgarīdās follows Priyādās in telling how one of Gadādhar Bhaṭṭ's songs became so popular in Vrindavan that he was invited to live there,[113] adding the quaint detail that when the invitation arrived, Gadādhar was cleaning his teeth at the village well. As in Priyādās's version, he fainted when he heard the messenger had come from Vrindavan. When he came to and heard the message, he moved to Vrindavan right away, without even returning home. Priyādās says that it was Gusāṃījī who sent the letter, traditionally taken to be the Gauḍīya Jīva Gosvāmī. In portraying it as instead authored collectively by several Vrindavan *bhakta*s, Nāgarīdās decouples the story from its sectarian mode.

Vallabhrasik is not mentioned by Priyādās, but he figures in Nāgarīdās's hagiography. The story somewhat morbidly regards his choice of a funeral hymn, a poem by Bhagvān Hit Rāmrāy. Here Nāgarīdās ignores the sectarian issue of whether Bhagvān converted to Vallabha's sect.

Sūrdās Madanmohan merits three stories that are very similar to the ones told by Priyādās. Nāgarīdās shares with Priyādās the comment on the name "Sūrdās" notwithstanding this *bhakta*'s fine eyesight,[114] which again proves that he regarded Sūrdās himself as blind. Both tell how Sūrdās

Madanmohan, a Brahmin, was a local administrator (from Sandila), who spent the district income on feeding sadhus.[115] Instead of sending the tax to the emperor, he wrote a *Dohā* (distich) by way of inventory (*bījak*) to the empty treasury chests:

> Your tax of thousands from Sandila? Spent to satiate sadhus' appetite.
> Sūrdās ("Madanamohana") was among them. He has now absconded into the night.
>
> (PPM 46)

Priyādās gives the Persian name (*ruq'ah*) for the note and quotes only the rhyme words of the verse. He also describes the aftermath of this scandal in Delhi, and it is not the emperor himself but Toḍar Mal who is the villain keen on pursuing the absconder.[116] Nāgarīdās's second story tests Sūrdās for the sincerity of his self-pronounced humility as a "guardian of the shoes for the Lord's devotees" (PPM 47). Priyādās tells this story in similar terms with allusions to the same song.[117] The third story proclaims the instant, wide-ranging success of one of Sūrdās Madanmohan's songs on the erotic play of the Lord (PPM 48), again based on Priyādās.[118] In addition, Priyādās had also identified him as a Surdhvaj Brahmin and as having the same *iṣṭa-devatā* as "Mahāprabhu," presumably Caitanya Mahāprabhu. True to form, Nāgarīdās neglects to mention the sectarian link, but adds a gossipy incident about a theft of jewelry in the Keśavarāya temple in Mathura not mentioned by Priyādās:

> Once, there had been a theft in the Keśavarāya jū temple in Mathura. The *ṭhākur*'s jewelry and wealth went missing. It became the talk of the town. When Sūrdās Madanmohan jū heard the news, this is what he made of it: "The *ṭhākur* has gone to his in-laws' home. According to local custom, all the son-in-law's jewelry is put on display, to be "plundered" by his women relatives in the inner quarters, to their great mirth (*hāsa*)."[119] With that mood in mind, he composed a new song. It instantly became popular. And here is that song:
>
> *There has been a theft, friend (*mãī*), of Keśavarāya's jewelry:*
> *They took the crown from his head, the studded bracelets from his arms,*
> *Took the flute from his lips, the pair of anklets from his feet.*
> *'Twas to keep the people of Barsana village happy:*
> *They are Shyāma jū's in-laws (*sasurāl*)—it is Rādhā's parental home (*māykā*)!*

Even the thieves' luck turned: it was to give bliss to all,
That Sūrdās's Madanamohana then came home again.

(PPM 49)

It is just this kind of gossipy context for *bhakti* songs that indicates that *padas* did not just float in a lofty realm but were part of a lively mode of exchange, perhaps a public sphere of sorts.

Notwithstanding the relative lack of literary interest in Gauḍīya Vaishnavas, Nāgarīdās seems to have had a very intimate association with a contemporary Gauḍīya named Muralīdās, whom we already encountered (TĀ 16). He indicates that Muralīdās visited the Rupnagar court (PPM 65) and relates that Muralīdās knew one of his newly composed songs even before it had been performed. Implied is that the song was already popular in Krishna's supernatural realm, to which Muralīdās apparently had instant access. In short, Muralīdās is considered a great *bhakta* and "on the same wavelength" as Nāgarīdās. The song he quotes is also included in his anthology written in 1746,[120] so it must have been composed at least by that date, which means that the incident predates Nāgarīdās's exile.

Muralīdās's presence at court is confirmed by a painting of a *majlis*, or poetic gathering, titled *A Night in the Hot Season* (Grīṣma Ritu Rātṛ).[121] Its setting is a pavilion on a terrace overlooking a body of water, presumably the lake in Kishangarh, though possibly the river Yamunā.[122] That the sponsor is "Śrī Mahārāj Kumār Sāvant Singh Bahādur jī" (identified by Devanagari and Nastaliq inscription) makes it possible to date the painting to the time when Nāgarīdās was still crown prince, before 1748. He is depicted in full regal attire, but is holding a rosary in his right hand. The overall scene looks like an ecstatic *kīrtana* party, with several shaven ascetics present. One, swooning and being caught by someone behind him, is identified in the inscription as Vaishnava Muralīdāsjī.[123] This very likely is the same devotee. Nāgarīdās met him again during his pilgrimage to Radha- and Krishnakund in the Braj area. The painting provides a vivid visual illustration of the circulation of devotees from Braj to the court and, vice versa, the king visiting the same devotee in Braj.

STORIES ABOUT THE RASIKA-TRAYĪ AND THEIR FOLLOWERS

Nāgarīdās also sings in praise of the Rasika-trayī, the group of three fellow *bhakta-rasikas*, who settled in Vrindavan in the middle of the sixteenth century and composed poetry that dwelled on the love-play of Rādhā and Krishna: Hit Harivaṃś, Harirām Vyās, and Svāmī Haridās. Remarkably, Nāgarīdās spends more time on Vyās than on anyone else in the work.

Nāgarīdās seems to have considered the Bundela Brahmin Harirām Vyās a kindred spirit. He quotes one of his songs on Jayadeva very early in his work (PPM 3b). There are, in addition, no less than eight anecdotes associated with Vyās's songs in the section about him in the longer recension (PPM 27–35). Nāgarīdās selects several of Vyās's songs celebrating other devotees: two express his respect for the Sants (PPM 29 and 32) and two others his despair at the death of his friends (PPM 27 and 34). Further songs quoted from Vyās's voluminous oeuvre express his love for Vrindavan (PPM 30), his disregard for caste (PPM 31, 32), and spiritual instruction to his family (PPM 33, 35). Vyās's guru is portrayed as Hit Harivaṃś (PPM 27–28), following the claim put forward first in a mid-seventeenth-century hagiography attributed to Bhagavat Mudit, quoting the same "conversion song" by Harivaṃś.[124] Nāgarīdās also tells stories about Vyās's son Kisorīdās (PPM 56) and his patron, Madhukar Shāh (PPM 52). The latter story, again, is illustrated with a song by Vyās approving of the king's worship of devotees.

Nāgarīdās seems to have felt close to the Rādhāvallabhans. He quotes seven poems of Hit Harivaṃś in his anthology, though in his hagiography he mentions him only in connection with others. He is first introduced through the effect his death had on his close friend Vyās (PPM 27) and next as the latter's guru (PPM 28). In the anecdote about his disciple, the robber Narvāhan, Harivaṃś's *Eighty-Four Love Songs* is considered to be a canonical work chanted by his followers (PPM 51). Narvāhan resembles the Jat-brigands who were so prominent in Braj in Nāgarīdās's time when the boundaries between landlord and highway robber were not very distinct. Narvāhan has robbed and imprisoned a merchant, but when he hears his prisoner recite *Eighty-Four Love Songs* he realizes that he is a fellow disciple of Harivaṃś and promptly sets him free. In Bhagavat Mudit's version of this story, the merchant is a Jaina, and the attack on him is partly out of animosity for Jainas. As the man is in captivity, Narvāhan's maidservant feels compassion for him and teaches him the miraculous mantra "Rādhāvallabha Śrī Harivaṃśa," which works its wonder.[125] Nāgarīdās also mentions a disciple of Harivaṃś's eldest son, also named Nāgarīdās, who lived in Mor Kuṭī, on the Parikramā Mārg of Barsana, and is often nicknamed Nehī Nāgarīdās (PPM 53). He had a vision of Rādhā in a dense jungle (or a place near Barsana called Gahvar Ban). Bhagavat Mudit also tells this story, adding that Rādhā herself invited him to stay in Barsana near Sankhari Khor.[126] Mudit also tells stories about another Rādhāvallabhan, the Kāyastha Kharagsen (PPM 50), none of which overlaps with Nāgarīdās's text, however.[127]

Svāmī Haridās figures prominently in the meeting with the emperor Akbar and his court singer Tānsen in Vrindavan:

> One time the emperor Akbar asked Tānsen, "From whom did you learn to sing? Is there someone who sings even better than you?" Now Tānsen answered, "I do not amount to anything. In Holy Vrindavan there is a Vaishnava by the name Haridās jī. In singing, I am his disciple." When he heard this, the emperor got into a boat, took Tānsen with him and headed for Svāmī jū's place in Śrī Vrindavan. First Tānsen sang. Then he asked respectfully, "Mahārāj, would you recite something?" Then Śrī Haridās jū began the prelude (*alāpcārī*) of Rāga Malāra (of the rainy season). It was the month of Caitra or Vaiśākh (springtime). But right at that moment, clouds gathered. The peacocks began to call out. Then Śrī Haridās jū sang a new *Viṣṇupada* that he had composed. And at that very moment it started to rain. And here is that song:
>
> *Such is the season, that always, everywhere, the peacocks keep calling out.*
> *Lush clouds, lush rainbows everywhere, lush deep rumbling clouds.*
> *Lush green, green land, red-velvet monsoon insects on the cactuses burn bright like millions of Kāmadevas.*
> *The Malāra melody of Haridās's Lord Shyāmā-Kuñjabihārī fans the passions of the divine young pair.*
>
> (PPM 39)

Nāgarīdās's story, portraying Tānsen as Svāmī Haridās's disciple, is now famous and widely circulated, especially in music circles, but it can be traced to this work as its original source.[128] It may be an innovation of Nāgarīdās's or based on an oral story circulating in the Haridāsī-Sampradāya at the time. In one variant Vārtā story, Tānsen is linked with the Vallabhan poet Govindsvāmī.[129] However, the Vārtās show disapproval of Tānsen, an artist (*kalāvant*) at the court, stigmatizing him as "seeking refuge in others" (*anyāśrayī*), that is, not a loyal follower of Vallabha. Before he could become a disciple, he had to renounce his Muslim identity and eventually give up working at Akbar's court.

A contemporary variant is found in the slightly later (1763) hagiographic work that polemically defends the Sādhu branch of the Haridāsīs.[130] That version of the story ends with the lines:

FIG. 4.2 *Disguised Akbar with Tansen Visit Svami Haridas*, Kishangarh school, ca. 1760. Color and gold on paper (25 × 31 cm). National Museum, New Delhi, accession no. 48.14/61. Courtesy National Museum (New Delhi)

> Akbar, the embodiment of dharma, came to know well Svāmī Hari(dās)'s heart. Then he called a painter and had him paint a portrait of Svāmī Haridās. (*Nij-mat-siddhānt* 109.4)

This may allude to a contemporary painting depicting Svāmī Haridās, Tānsen, and Akbar (fig. 4.2). In fact, the story may be so widespread because of its depiction in art. One painting, now in the National Museum in New Delhi, is attributed to the Kishangarhi painter Nihālcand and estimated to date from 1760.[131] There are at least two other close copies of the painting, one in the Vrindavan Research Institute and one in Bhārat Kalā Bhavan in Benares, as well as a late eighteenth-century Mughal copy of a detail.[132]

This painting illustrates the anecdote in the *Garland of Stories and Songs* perfectly. Immediately striking is the lush verdure of the setting, as described in the song. Tānsen is portrayed with his instrument resting on his knees, as if he just paused from performing. Haridās is singing, and as he does a peacock calls out, as in the song. The white flowers with yellow hearts and the yellow flowers with white hearts may be the artist's representation of the cactus flowers mentioned in the poem. The now largely forgotten hagiographical work thus may have been foundational for one of Nihālcand's most famous paintings.

STORIES ABOUT MĪRĀBĀĪ

Nāgarīdās's hagiography is an important eighteenth-century source for the famous female saint Mīrābāī's life and the reception of her songs.[133] He elaborates on Nābhādās's work and Priyādās's commentary, but with a twist.[134] Mīrā is persecuted by the Rāṇā (here her brother-in-law), not just because of her association with holy men, but also because she refused to become a *satī* and burn herself on her husband's funeral pyre (PPM 14). Having escaped his plots against her, among which is an attempt at poisoning her (PPM 15), Mīrā defiantly sets off on a pilgrimage, to the Gaṅgā, to Vrindavan, and eventually to Dvarka (PPM 16). Like Priyādās, Nāgarīdās briefly alludes to Mīrā's meeting with Jīva Gosvāmī in Vrindavan, but he does not include the meeting with Akbar.[135] Likewise, Nāgarīdās omits the conflict of Mīrā with her female in-laws who worship the Goddess and press her to do so, too.[136] Nāgarīdās tells how the Rāṇā sends a maid to spy on Mīrā, but she is converted (PPM 18), whereas in Priyādās's account, the spy informs the Rāṇā that there is a male in Mīrā's apartments, who, when the Rāṇā investigates, turns out to be Krishna himself.[137] The story of Mīrā's arrival in Dvarka and final absorption in the Raṇachoḍa temple is told more elaborately than in the terse verse by Priyādās:[138]

> Mīrā arrived in Dvarka. She stayed there for several days. After that, the *purohit* and other servants of the Rāṇā who had accompanied Mīrā said, "Many days have passed now. You must return to your homeland now. It is the Rāṇā's command." They kept saying this to her for a few days, but then they became insistent with Mīrābāī. Then Mīrābāī, under the pretense of bidding farewell to Raṇachoḍa, went alone inside the temple. In an āratī she sang a newly composed song. And here is that song:
>
> *Lord, help your servant.*
> *You kept Draupadī's honor—you lengthened her garment.*[139]
> *For the sake of Dhruva's devotion, you came down yourself in the body of a lion-man,*
> *You killed Hiraṇyakaśyapu and refused to put up with him.*[140]
> *When the elephant was drowning, you grabbed hold of him and saved him, lifting him out of the water.*[141]
> *Mīrā is the servant, the Mountain-Lifter her darling; when one suffers, the other is pained.*

Even when she sang this song, Krishna did not stir from where he was. Then she composed another song and sang it in a surge of love in a grand āratī. Only then did the Lord take her, absorbing her earthly body into himself. Not even a corpse remained. Here is the song she sang when she was merged with Krishna:

My love, as soon as you hear my prayer, take it to heart.
I have no one but you; please be kind and show me mercy.
By day I have no hunger, by night I cannot sleep; this body weakens with each moment.
Mīrā's Lord, Clever Mountain-Lifter, now that we have met, please do not abandon me!

These two songs were memorized and written down by Mīrā's alert Vaishnava ladies-in-waiting who were standing nearby on the porch. These songs became famous.

(PPM 17)

The most important contribution of Nāgarīdās is that he illustrates each story with one of Mīrā's own songs. A corpus of six songs attributed to Mīrā are provided that were popular approximately in the mid-eighteenth century, and several of these are still popular. The two quoted in the story translated here were Gandhi's favorites, "Lord, Help Your Servant" (*Hari hariho jana kī bhīra*) and "My Love, as Soon as You Hear My Prayer, Take It to Heart" (*Sajana sudhi jyauṃ jānaiṃ jyauṃ lījaiṃ*). Others have the refrains "Mīrā is steeped in passion for the Lord" (*Mīrā ke raṅga lagyau hari kau*); "The Rāṇā gave me poison—I knew that is what it was" (*Rāṇaijū viṣa dīnau hama jānī*); "Śrī Raṇachoḍa, please let me stay in Dvarka" (*Rākha Śrī Ranachoḍa dījyo Dvārikā ko bāsa*); and "O friend, I cannot sleep" (*Sakhī merī nīnda nasānī ho*). In addition, Nāgarīdās quotes a Mīrā song in another chapter of his work, the anecdote about Nārāyaṇdās Naṭvā:

There once was a dancer named Nārāyaṇ Dās. He was very fond of Vaishnavas. So wherever there was a congenial Vaishnava gathering that would listen, he would go to do *kīrtana* without requesting any payment (*nirlobha*). So one time, a Navab in Handiya Saray strongly insisted that Nārāyaṇ Dās dance. Nārāyaṇ Dās took a *tulsī*-garland and danced in front it.[142] Even the Navab was spellbound. He was delighted. The song Nārāyaṇ

Dās was singing had a rhyme "steeped in Krishna's passion." He was showing its meaning by performing Krishna's thrice-bent position, and then he froze in that position. In an outpouring of great love, he left his body. And here is that song:

The only true bond is that of love.
This, Vrishabhānu's daughter knows, as does anyone steeped in Krishna's passion.
Love is the strongest chain: even a mad elephant it can restrain.
Mīrā's Lord, Mountain-Lifter, let me dwell in the palatial groves (of Braj).
(PPM 58)

This story features a dancer who, while performing a song of Mīrā's, reaches the highest ecstasy, to the point of dying on the spot. The story indicates that this song by Mīrā was performed as far away as Handiya Saray near Allahabad. It also attests to at least the mid-eighteenth-century popularity of Mīrā's song with the refrain "The only true bond is that of love" (*Sācau prīta hī ko nātau*). The same incident is alluded to in Nābhādās's *Garland of Devotees*, though only the refrain of the song is mentioned, and none of the commentaries make the link with Mīrā.[143] In quoting the full song alluded to in the 1600 work, Nāgarīdās provides evidence that it was attributed to Mīrā by circa 1600, which is well before most of her songs are attested.

The inclusion of Mīrā and her songs is significant also because of the Vallabhan milieu of *Garland of Stories and Songs*. Judging by the Vārtās, the Vallabha-Sampradāya does not hold Mīrā in high esteem. Mīrā is shown in a negative light most famously in the Vārtā of Krishnadās Adhikārī, but also in the Vārtā of Rāmdās, Mīrā's *purohit*.[144] Mīrā is here called names and vehemently dismissed as not exclusively devoted to Vallabha (*anyāśrayī*).[145] Perhaps we should question the extent of this negative view beyond the Vārtās. Additional work on the origin and extent of the Sampradāya's negativity toward Mīrā might clarify whether this reflects sixteenth-century attitudes or might be due to later developments, such as the seventeenth-century power struggle with the *pujārīs* of the Raṇachoḍa temple in Dakor and the subsequent Vallabhan takeover.[146]

Nāgarīdās's celebration of Mīrā is also significant because of its Rajput milieu. Some have assumed that Mīrā is *persona non grata* among Rajputs and even postulated a Rajput attempt to obliterate the memory of Mīrā.[147] Nāgarīdās provides evidence of a positive evaluation of Mīrā, at least in her own clan of Rathors, to which he, too, belonged. Perhaps the enmity toward Mīrā is located mainly in Mewar Sisodiyā circles, in other words, with Mīrā's in-laws.[148]

Some caution needs to be exercised, as not all manuscripts of the text include the anecdotes on Mīrā: they are notably absent from the shorter recension. They are included in both modern editions based on the 1898 edition by Gauḍ, which is in turn based mainly on a manuscript in the royal library predating it by only about fifteen years.[149] The "authoritative" manuscript and the edition thus date from exactly the period that the academic construction of Mīrā began. In the late nineteenth century, a Rajputization was under way that involved a reintegration of Mīrā as a Rajput heroine.[150] Is it coincidental that the date of Gauḍ's edition is the same as that of the first academic work published on the famous poetess?[151] Were the Mīrā *prasaṅgas* part of the newly "invented" Rajput Mīrā story?

Some aspects of Nāgarīdās's story correspond to the Rajput rehabilitation image of Mīrā. For one, the conflict of her devotion with societal norms is downplayed. Foregrounding Mīrā's widowhood gives the impression that her devotion matured only after her husband's death.[152] Yet Nāgarīdās can hardly be suspected of promoting Rajput values, as the whole point of the first *prasaṅga* is to stress that Mīrā refuses to become a *satī* (PPM 14). Also, Nāgarīdās has a defensive attitude about Mīrā's chastity, which has a modern cast to it. He chooses to omit Priyādās's story about the sadhu who challenges Mīrā's chastity.[153] He also singles out the Rāṇā as the sole villain, identifying him as Mīrā's brother-in-law rather than her husband, which aligns with the nineteenth-century views.[154] Finally, the concern with the transmission of Mīrā's songs, tracing the two "last" *padas* by Mīrā to the earwitness reports of her *sakhīs*, feels modern. It seems to anticipate the "academic" construction of Mīrā's *padas* on the basis of the mysterious manuscripts said to be preserved in Dakor, allegedly based on notes made by Mīrā's female attendants.[155]

However, the Mīrā *prasaṅgas* should not be dismissed as modern constructs, for three reasons. First, a manuscript dated 1792 already includes the Mīrā *prasaṅgas*.[156] This manuscript was written for the then king Pratāp Singh in Jaipur, which indicates that these stories were told about her at least by the end of the eighteenth century.[157] That does not guarantee that they were composed by Nāgarīdās, but they are not modern constructs either. Second, Nāgarīdās did not shun Mīrā. He cared enough to quote one of her songs in his anthology *String of Song-Pearls*:

Listen to me, my simple eyes!
Enchanted with Manamohana's beauty, you do not give a wit for humility.
Shrinking in fear of the world, you hide his beauty, till you fill up
with tears.
Mīrā's Lord is the Mountain-Lifter. Even wrapped in a shawl, hidden and
concealed, he knows it all.

(PMĀ 571)

Moreover, *Garland of Stories and Songs* includes the anecdote about Nārāyaṇdās Naṭvā (PPM 58), which quotes a Mīrā song as its crucial point in all manuscripts of the text, both long and short recension. That story unhesitatingly shows a positive reception of Mīrā's song. Though there is some doubt about the authenticity of the Mīrā anecdotes, it thus does not seem out of character for Nāgarīdās to have told them, and they certainly were already told before the end of the eighteenth century.

The third reason for accepting the Mīrā chapters as earlier than the Rajasthani rehabilitation is to be found in visual evidence. A painting preserved in the Kishangarh Royal Collection, attributed to Nihālcand, depicts Mīrābāī performing *pūjā*.[158] The Kishangarh court must have commissioned this work at some point in the mid-eighteenth century, showing that, at least at that time, Mīrā was respected. The painting is rather mysterious and presents a scene with a group of *bhakta*s in the interior of a temple or shrine. The haloed figure Mīrā is seated among white-clad women devotees with rosaries in hand in front of the shrine, which itself is not visible. One of the women holds a musical instrument, and a man with a cap is seated toward the back, playing a drum (dholak), so it looks like a *bhajana* session. In the very back, another man with the same type of cap is seated, holding up one arm, in a singing gesture or possibly defensively. Behind him, a clean-shaven man is entering, respectfully greeting the image or maybe reacting to the central event. One of the women standing around Mīrā peeks from behind a pillar, shyly or fearfully, as opposite her, another woman, also standing, holds on boldly to the pillar with one arm. She stretches out the other arm with a cloth toward Mīrā in what seems to be a dramatic accusing gesture. Mīrā herself is seated with bowed head, defensively, it appears. She stretches one arm in front of her, perhaps with the percussion instrument (*kartāla*) she is popularly depicted with, though she displays an odd turn of the arm. Alternatively, she may be holding a small item that she is turning down. Is this a cup that she shows she has emptied? Or is she emptying poison from a ring into a cup that the lady next to her is holding? An older woman seated in front of the shrine, separate from the rest of the group, is holding up something that looks like a tray. Might this be the tray on which the poison was offered to the deity and then as *prasāda* (distributed offering) to Mīrā?[159] If the event in this painting is Mīrā drinking the poison cup, it could have been intended to illustrate Nāgarīdās's retelling of the infamous incident in the context of Mīrā's persecution by the Rāṇā (PPM 15).[160]

That the chapters on Mīrā were initially part of Nāgarīdās's work is quite likely, but some recensions omitted them and also shortened the work in other ways. If they are original, the question is by whom and why were they later excised. Perhaps current praxis in the Kishangarh temple provides a clue: her songs are not sung in front of the Śrī Kalyāṇarāya image.[161] Were the temple priests behind this revisionist project? Perhaps this happened under the influence of the usurper Bahādur Singh, who associated himself strongly with the Vallabha-Sampradāya after the quarrel about the succession of the Salemabad Nimbārka Pīṭh. If the Mīrā chapters were excised because of sectarian sensitivities, however, one would have expected the short recension rather than the long one to be favored in the Kishangarh Royal Collection, yet it is the other way around. It remains a mystery.

Garland of Stories and Songs' interpretation of Mīrā seems to be halfway between the medieval vulgate and modern Rajput interpretations. Since the chapters date at least from 1792, elements of the Mīrā story that look suspiciously like modern constructs may yet have older antecedents. The account is precolonial, or at least it antedates James Tod's 1820 romantic Mīrābāī by about three or more decades. It also provides a case of a positive memory of Mīrā in Rajput circles, counter to the assumption that Mīrā has always been *persona non grata*. At least in some Rathor circles in the mid- to late eighteenth century, Mīrā was held in high esteem. Her exclusion from some manuscripts may be linked with the fact that her poetry is not performed in the Śrī Kalyāṇarāya temple in Kishangarh nowadays. But even if her memory was suppressed at some point in history, it was celebrated by Nāgarīdās.

NONSECTARIAN AGENDA

At the end of this comparative analysis, one point is confirmed: for Nāgarīdās, sectarian affiliation mattered little. This feature of *Garland of Stories and Songs* in general (both short and long edition) is also articulated elsewhere in his works, perhaps most explicitly in the first song of one of his works, *Garland of Songs of Awakening*, finished in 1748 (1805 VS):

These are my holy sages:
Śrī Harivaṃś and Vyās; Gadādhar, Paramānand, and Nanddās.
Śrī Haridās, Bihāranidās, Viṭhal Vipul, with keen insight (*sujāna*);
Rāmdās, Nābhā, Dāmodar, Ali Bhagvān, Sakhī Bhagvān,
Caturbhujdās, Mehādās, and then again Śrī Bhaṭṭ and Caturbihārī;
Prītam Rasik, Vallabhrasik, and Dhruv, who articulated the rites of *rasa*.
Tulsīdās, Mīrā, Mādhav, and the two other Nāgarīdāses;
Āskaran, Narsī, and Vrindāban, who had a taste for the sweet bliss of the Rās,
Krishnadās, Sūr, Govind and Kumbhan, and Chītsvāmī, the devoted (*anuraktā*):[162]
They are the reciters, I am the devoted listener—their songs are my holy scriptures;
To forsake their songs and follow the exegesis of sundry sects is mistaken.
Why try to establish their authority according to scripture and give up these songs, the highest reward, the elixir of immortality?
May their songs (*pada*) resonate on my tongue and in my ears and purify my heart.
Nāgariyā: may the dust of their feet (*pada*) adorn my forehead.
(*Pad-prabodh-mālā* 1)

This poem enumerates devotees from different sects under one umbrella and stresses that their songs constitute the highest scripture. Nāgarīdās asserts that there is no need to ascertain the orthodoxy of these songs in accordance with scripture. That, of course, was exactly what many at the time were engaged in doing, in adherence to Jai Singh II's project. Nāgarīdās as much as says that such sectarian exegesis is mistaken or, to use his word, "transgressive" (*vyabhicārī*). He may well have composed this song in Vrindavan when he arrived there shortly after the death of his father, given the date of the collection.

In another song he makes the same point:

I don't manage to understand the scriptures
Never did, don't now, but shall act as those who do say.
I'll follow the opinions of the highest learned men, the four Ācāryas:
Taking dips in the Sarasvatī River, I determine not to reemerge.
Now that I've tasted the nectar of love-play in Braj, I won't relapse in philosophical disputation!
Nāgarīdās settles in Vrindavan and won't shy away from the eternal love-play.
(*Chūṭak-pad* 153)[163]

In these poems, Nāgarīdās provides a summary mission statement for his hagiography: to bypass all the sectarian concerns and simply enjoy songs of all denominations without bothering with establishing their orthodoxy and without too much philosophical argument. If the inspiration is true *bhakti*, the songs cannot be wrong. The celebration of the power of the devotional song thus is the real topic of *Garland of Stories and Songs*.

SINGERS AND SONGS ON THE MOVE

Garland of Stories and Songs is a hagiography, but its main concern is actually the reception of the devotional songs it quotes. That the special power of songs is crucial is made clear from the very beginning. The dedicatory verse and the short exposition that follow set the tone:

> Neither in the highest heaven do I dwell, nor in the heart of yogis.
> But where they sing of love for me, there, O Nārada, is where I go to stay.[164]
>
> Śrī Krishna is fond of his devotees (*bhakta-vatsala*)—in fact, their devotion is the only thing that pleases him. Such devotion consists of nine expressions, the most important of which are *śravana* (listening) and *kīrtana* (singing his praise). By *kīrtana*, one accomplishes two tasks: listening as well as singing. Thus *kīrtana* is the heart (of devotion). *Kīrtana* has a subcategory—*kīrtana* accompanied by music. Such *kīrtana* is superior in that it helps concentration of the mind and it provides spiritual stimulation (*udīpana*). The Lord attracted the hearts of the ladies of Braj and drew them to him through music (*gāna*). Nārada invited Śrī Krishna into his heart, attracting him through music. Moreover, enchanted by Shiva's music, Hari melted and water flowed from his feet.[165] Thus songs are dear to clever Shyāma. Vaishnavas from time immemorial have sung songs composed in meter about his *līlā*. I have written some *prasaṅgas* about their *padas*.
> (PPM, introduction)

The central purpose of the text, then, is to celebrate songs, not just through performance but also through singing. Informal singing is often accompanied with rhythmic instruments, such as drums and especially cymbals that the *bhakta* can carry conveniently in his or her "pocket" (Nāmdev, PPM 8; Mīrā, PPM 14). In more formal performances, some singers accompany themselves on the tamboura (Bhagvāndās, PPM 54), and others even dance, as Narsī Mehtā does (PPM 12). Seeing the *bhakta* as a performer, or *kīrtaṅkar*, is crucial.[166]

Only rarely is a song said to be written, and usually that is secondary, after an initial oral composition moment, such as Mīrā's songs memorized to be written down by her friends (PPM 17). Songs may be written down to send to someone else, such as Mīrā's song sent to the Rāṇā (PPM 13), Sūrdās Madanmohan's couplet sent by way of "inventory" with the empty treasury box to the emperor (PPM 46), or Nāgarīdās's ancestor Rūp Singh's song created in Balkh, then written down and sent home as a letter of petition to his image (PPM 64). Nāgarīdās himself indicates that he wrote down his songs, mentioning that he put a composition in his pocket, as the inkholder stood nearby:

> A Vaishnava named Muralīdās Gauḍīya Syāmānandī who lived in Vrindavan was a man of strong devotional emotion. He came to Rupnagar. Now, one time he got up from his spot in a state of ecstatic love to visit me. I had composed a song at the time. No one had yet heard it. As soon as the song was written, Muralīdās came by, so I first kept it in my pocket. The inkwell was still nearby. Now, Muralīdās came humming one verse of that song: "Handsome Hari Lingers in My Heart." Singing it over and over again, he fell into a state of ecstasy (*antaraṅga*). He lost awareness of his body. For a long time he remained in that state. Without even having heard the song, he came singing that verse in an outpouring of love. I was most amazed.
>
> (PPM 65).

While writing is mentioned in this anecdote, it is the oral performance that will signify the "publication" of the song: Nāgarīdās says that "no one had yet heard it." What surprises him is that Muralīdās was already humming a line from the song. The implication is that the freshly composed song was instantly floating around in Rādhā and Krishna's *līlā* world and that Muralīdās had picked it up there. It illustrates how Muralīdās is able to "tune in" to this realm and, at the same time, how Nāgarīdās's songs were liked so well by the divinities that they were instantly popular. This same underlying belief is seen elsewhere, as in a story about Kisorīdās, whose Rās song met with divine approval (PPM 56), and that of a Rupnagar amir singing Nāgarīdās's song during his circumambulation of Govardhan (PPM 63).

The divine world thus is involved in the transmission of songs and in their composition, too. Krishna composed a Sanskrit verse for *Gīta-govinda*. Vernacular songs, too, can be composed by God himself, sometimes to save face for a favorite devotee, as in the story where Krishnadās was challenged by Sūrdās to compose something extemporaneously and Krishna intervened to help him out (PPM 40). *Garland of Stories and Songs* thus illustrates to what specific purposes songs were mobilized in the mid-eighteenth century, and from that, in turn, we can derive something about community identity formation and demarcation in the period.

HOW SONGS CIRCULATE

From *Garland of Stories and Songs* we can study the meaning of songs and also their patterns of transmission. It documents that singers and songs circulated in this early modern period, not just from Braj to Rajasthan, but all over India and not just geographically, but also between different social milieus. Kings may have tried to enforce a prohibition of performing songs while "on the move," as the king of Puri did with *Gīta-govinda*'s songs (PPM 3a, quoted above). Yet the mobility of songs defied such attempts to confine them to house and temple.

Much can be gleaned from *Garland of Stories and Songs* about where and how songs circulated. Pilgrimage provided a major occasion to bring songs not just from their place of origin but from any place on the way to the end destination and back home again. This transmission could happen with lightning speed, or "miraculously" as the text itself has it. One example is Sūrdās Madanmohan's song for the full moon festival of autumn (PPM 48). We learn that Vaishnavas hear a song at a performance in one place, learn it by heart, and transmit it to Vrindavan. But there is a return journey, too, as in the case of Gadādhar Bhaṭṭ in the South, whose songs are such a success that the Vrindavan residents get together and send him a letter of invitation, which Gadādhar promptly accepts (PPM 45). Another example is the case of the amir of Kishangarh who, during his circumambulation of Govardhan in Braj, sings a song composed by Nāgarīdās:

> Among the great amirs was a Rajput who served at Rupnagar. He was a great and loyal Vaishnava and remained a devotee of Vrindavan. So when he would go on a pilgrimage to Vrindavan, he would shave and dress for the occasion, take a gourd-pot in hand, and with a group of ascetics (*virakta*) wander about, experiencing the sweetness of Braj and Vrindavan. Now, on one such occasion, he was circumambulating the Holy Mount Govardhan at night. There was a pool of moonlight of Caitra–Vaiśākh. He happened upon an ecstatic group of four or five Vaishnavas. He joined them and together they went about singing a song in an outpouring of ecstatic love. Then they began to hear that same song coming from the

direction of Govardhan as well. Now they figured that the song they were singing had an echo that was coming from the mountain. So they fell silent. Even then, the sound continued as before. So they set out in the direction of that sound. But as they went, the sound did not get closer; they kept hearing it, coming from the same distance. So first they surmised, "Somewhere some child-ascetics and children of Brajvasis have heard us and started to sing that same song." When they had come halfway around the mountain, they looked everywhere for people but did not find anyone. At that point they became euphoric with ecstasy and swooned. They understood what had happened: it was Krishna's entourage in his eternal play that was singing this song. Then the devotees completed their circumambulation in the same way as before with greater zeal. Meanwhile dawn had broken. Everyone was overjoyed at this extraordinary event. So the song that they had heard being sung from the direction of Govardhan in high childlike voices was from the holy mouths of Krishna's eternal celestial entourage! That song became famous. And here is that song:

Peacocks sing in the pure moonlight.
Over and over the song echoes in Vrindavan; the mountain and all its caves respond—
A symphony that brings great bliss; the last watch of the night remains.
Nāgarīdās sees Shyāma and Shyāmā during their love-play in their unattainably high loft.

(PPM 63)

This contextualization claims for Nāgarīdās's song nothing less than divine approval. It illustrates how songs circulated and specifically how pilgrimage afforded an opportunity for songs to travel, too. One pilgrim would start a song heard elsewhere, another would chime in, and, as they completed the ritual circumambulation, the song would catch on with the crowd. This vivid depiction of a ritual context at a pilgrimage center affording the opportunity of literary exchange is also at work in Nāgarīdās's *The Pilgrim's Bliss*, where he describes the multiple *bhajana* sessions with locals. Such occasions must have afforded opportunity for songs to be exchanged. The story just quoted makes the offhand comment that while the Kishangarh amir actually was a great noble of the empire, he chose to travel incognito, without external evidence of his rank. Songs' potential to travel was not socially restricted: pilgrims shared a sense of community that transcended social boundaries. When Sūrdās Madanmohan absconded from Sandila in the East to

Vrindavan as a sadhu (PPM 46), pilgrimage afforded him the advantage of anonymity, despite his criminal record. In the eyes of faith, such a record was irrelevant, as only devotion counts.

Another way songs circulated was during "promotion tours" undertaken by temple priests and gurus:

> One time, Śrīmad Gosvāmī Viṭṭhalnāth jū, deferring to the Lord's wish, had to go abroad in order to help souls find their way to God (*Brahma-sambandha*) in this Kaliyuga. He also took his servant Caturbhujdās with him. There, far away from home, Caturbhujdās jū composed a song of longing for Śrī Govardhananātha. The Lord Śrī Govardhananātha was so pleased with it that he gave him *darshana*. And the Lord ordained thus: "Anyone who makes a practice of singing this song daily for a year will receive my *darshana*." So from then on, wherever that song was sung with respect to Śrī Govardhananātha, there Śrī Govardhananātha would appear and the singer would receive his *darshana*. Nowadays people sing it in Mewar in the village of Sinhār, in the place where that very *ṭhākur* Śrī Govardhananātha is now enshrined. People go there and receive *darshana*.
> (PPM 44)

Sinhār is the old name of the town now famous as Nathdvara. This story thus is etiological in explaining Śrī Govardhananātha jī's move from Braj: it is a by-product of Viṭṭhalnāth's promotion tours. To the *bhakta*'s understanding, such trips were undertaken for God's cause: "to bring about *Brahma-sambandha* in Kaliyuga." Viṭṭhalnāth frequently travels "abroad" (presumably to Gujarat; PPM 42–44), but this was by no means exclusively a Vallabhan praxis, as there are similar references for the Gauḍīyas in Bengal.[167] Like kings, touring to establish and enforce their authority, religious leaders also circulated to forge and reinforce ties with devotees.[168] Probably not incidentally, such tours were also "money-spinners," as devotees would contribute gifts for the worship of the main image, especially as formal "send-off" presents, given upon departure. This is not a modern observation; it is explicit, for instance, in the Vallabhan Vārtās. Viṭṭhalnāth takes Kumbhandās along with him for such a trip with the explicit purpose of providing him with some extra income.[169] One negative example is the story where Krishnadās Adhikārī visits Mīrābāī but refuses her farewell gift, even though many others present are waiting for just that.[170] In Nāgarīdās's hagiography, sectarian leaders frequently go on these tours accompanied by their temple singers (Kumbhandās and Caturbhujdās, PPM 43–44). These singers performed songs from their repertoire, gaining them wider currency, and the experience of travel, in turn, sometimes became a source of inspiration for them and also gave them the opportunity to learn new songs from others on such tours.

Garland of Stories and Songs also shows that songs from devotional milieus circulated to secular ones. Krishnadās, the *adhikārī*, is portrayed as regularly traveling to get supplies for the deity in nearby big cities and, on one occasion, even brings a singer from Delhi, who is a courtesan (PPM 41). As quoted above, the courtesan is led to believe she will perform for a wealthy patron. Rather than being disappointed upon discovering it is Śrī Nātha jī she is to entertain, she is thoroughly moved and dies in ecstasy singing the song Krishnadās had taught her. This incident illustrates that, however uncomfortable, the devotional and secular performance domains did mix on occasion. The reverse may have been the case in Handiya Saray for Nārāyaṇ Naṭvā when he found himself obliged to perform for a "Navab" and made up for the lack of temple surroundings by worshipping a *tulsī* garland, to render some sacrality to the setting (PPM 58).

Closer to home, in Rupnagar, temples functioned to disseminate songs, and there are several instances in which such songs "caught on." The image of Śrī Govardhananātha (now called Śrī Kalyāṇarāya) was at the time installed in Rupnagar and was the hub of much devotional activity. One story from the Holī season offers a vignette of how the *darshana* and song in the temple cause a stir in town:

> There is a *Viṣṇupada* of Phāga. When the days of Holī would come, the decorations (*śṛṅgāra*) of Śrī Govardhananātha would be carried out according to this song. On that day, Holī in Rupnagar would be celebrated with spectacular display and all devotees would crowd into the temple for *darshana*. And they would run back home telling everyone, "Today they have set up the spectacular display for that special song. Come quick!" So that day, sensitive (*bhāvuka*) people would listen over and over to that song and admire the *darshana* of God's *svarūpa* over and over. Overcome with love again and again, many would fall down swooning. All knew this truth: "This song has pleased God and he has approved of it." Then one year, it so happened that this song was not sung in the Holī season and the decorations were not put up and there was no spectacular display. Then wise Śrī Govardhananātha, that highest *rasika*, in a dream twice commanded that this song should be performed.
>
> (PPM 60)

People would apparently run to tell others about the great "show of the day," and a crowd might assemble with *rasika*s admiring the image and listening to the new song, even swooning, causing something of a mass hysteria. The song might be repeated the next year when the festival season started again. This also illustrates how festivals were important moments for the dissemination of songs, especially seasonal ones. Another example is a song of the swinging season:

> During the days of the swing festival, Rupnagar's Lord, Śrī Govardhananātha, was swinging. In front of him, Muralīdās and other *kīrtaniyās* were singing songs. Now, the Lord became enchanted with one devotional song. Whenever the *kīrtaniyās* sang that song, their singing brought abundant rainfall during the swinging. When they sang another song, the rain would cease. When they would sing this one again, the downpour would return. The devotees and the temple servants all came to understand this effect, so this song came to be requested at the time of the swing festival. Now, there were many festivals, such as the dinner of dedication (*nyauchāvar bhog*), but there was not a chance of a single raindrop from the sky. But then when this song was sung, clouds gathered and there was a heavy downpour. The image became drenched. His little turban with the moon-jewel sagged, and his pearl necklace seemed to drip with rain. His holy body was beautiful. All became carried away in devotion (*vimohita*). So the song that had enchanted the Lord, Śrī Govardhananātha, became famous for this effect.
>
> (PPM 62)

This song is associated with a particular *darshana* of the day, and this time the admired decorations, though, are brought about not by the priests but by the weather conditions. Like the song of Haridās for Akbar (PPM 39), this song has the miraculous power to bring rain, something eagerly awaited especially in the desert area. The narrative of a "miracle" is then, in turn, used to spread the fame of the song. This story seems somewhat "gossipy," straight out of a Rupnagar gazette, as it provides a "weather-cum-*darshana* report" from the temple. Another anecdote could be similarly characterized, the one about the theft in the temple of Keśavarāya in Mathura, which inspired Sūrdās Madanmohan to create a song just for the occasion (PPM 49). While that song's currency value might have been limited to the period when the theft was fresh in people's mind, the seasonal songs had a guaranteed recurrent playtime each year.

Some stories about the Rupnagar image also include the motif of songs cutting across social barriers, as is the case with a song performed in the temple at Janmāṣṭamī:

> It was the day of the birth festival of Rupnagar's *ṭhākur*, Śrī Govardhananātha. A Braj artist (*gunī*) by the name of Tulārām, whose famous pen name was Bāvrī Sakhī, was dancing and singing, full of love, in front of the image. This created a great stir. As he sang the song, he came to the line: "Fortunate Nanda invited the ladies to sit down and they asked their price for the garland." At that point in the song, the Lord became enchanted. A flower garland broke away from his neck and slipped down from his body. An old *bhītariyā* was seated behind the screen that was placed there to keep the sacred area of the image from being defiled. He took it for a miracle, got up, and lifted the garland to put it around the neck of the Braj artist who was dancing and singing. There were other important devotees standing there, but the servant gave the garland of the image to that Braj dancer.
>
> (PPM 61)

This example illustrates how ecstatic singing and dancing while performing a song in the temple on a festival occasion can win special acclaim. The temple servants have the power to indicate God's approval for the song by rewarding God's special *prasāda* to the singer. They preferentially reward the sincere devotee over the higher-ranking officers present. The motif of the "equalizer effect" of true *bhakti* illustrates how songs circulated from one social milieu to another.

Thus not only devotees but also songs circulated from court to temple and from capital to pilgrimage center and back. The religious literary scene had the potential to be an egalitarian environment: the songs that "worked" were the ones that pleased God and his devotees, seemingly independent from the social status of those who composed or performed them.

Nāgarīdās also comments on how songs were received in small villages (PPM 19–21, 67) and, in turn, caught on in elite circles. Some residents, however, were excluded from performance in a temple, the so-called untouchables. Yet while certain settings were thus exclusive, others seemed to have been fairly inclusive, such as the soirée in the two-storied mansion in Rupnagar (for a fine example, see fig. 4.3), where a fakir became ecstatic to the point of falling from the roof, another rather gossipy anecdote quoted at the beginning of this chapter (PPM 64). During pilgrimage, open-air

FIG. 4.3 A two-storied *havelī* in Rupnagar

bathing and circumambulation also allowed for a high degree of mixing of social groups, as with the amir from the court circumambulating Govardhan (PPM 63). In such spaces, there was a certain "equal access" atmosphere. Poetry, even if created in elite circles, did not remain limited to those milieus, but floated rather freely on a broad scale.

Before we ask whether all this amounts to evidence of an early modern "public sphere" in India, we should consider whether the essentially European notion of a public sphere (Öffentlichkeit) as "a realm of our social life in which something approaching public opinion can be formed" and in which "access is guaranteed to all citizens" can be applied to the early modern Indian situation.[171] There have been calls to study early modern Indian "public sphere" precursors to the mid-nineteenth-century consciously nationalist one.[172] Is it legitimate to speak of a "Bhakti public sphere" (*bhakti kā lokvr̥tt*), as some have asserted?[173] A study of Marathi public memory of Nāmdev has preferred to speak of "publics," and another of a North Indian ecumene (after the world of late antiquity, the Greek-Christian *oikoumene*).[174] If the formation of "public opinion" has to include an element of critical reasoned political debate, it is perhaps not so easy to see continuities for the form of cultural and political debate typical in North India before the emergence of newspapers and public associations. One could see evidence of a "Muslim" public sphere in the Tazkirahs, where nobility and common man rub shoulders debating literary propriety, and what constitutes the proper medium for the discourse.[175] For Hindu polity, one could consider the śāstric notion of *apadharma*, or "abuse of power," and the *bhakti* notion of unmediated access to God, as opening up venues of "critical vigilance" over the doings of the state and society.[176] This plays out in debates about public religion, history, and literary propriety, not just debates involving "other religions" but also debates among different rival Hindu groups.[177] An important venue for such debates was cultural performance at festivals.[178] The close connection between literary endeavor for the Hindu performative world and political information systems is well exemplified by the roaming yogis, who were not just preachers and singers but also conduits of political information.[179]

Can *Garland of Stories and Songs* be read for evidence of such an indigenous ecumene? Debate and criticism come to the fore especially in stories about confrontation of saints with kings and the emperor, but also in the references to pandits keen on disputation Sometimes the anecdotes feel like gossipy local gazette items. Most disagreements do not immediately appear to be directed toward representation within the state polity;[180] rather, they manifest disagreements between different religious groups and thus are indicative of another power struggle.[181] There is an argument to be made that, in that way, *Garland of Stories and Songs* provides evidence for a vibrant public sphere. The case could be made that the realm of vernacular *bhakti* discourse was mobilized by Nāgarīdās for a political intervention in reaction to the religious policies of Jai Singh II. We see these debates reflected in *Garland of Stories and Songs*.

FLAUNTING ORTHODOXY TO BEST THE JAIPUR KING?

A recurrent theme in the hagiography is disregard for the orthodoxy that is often called *varṇāśrama-dharma*. There is story after story about disregarding the rules of caste and purity and how this was insignificant in view of love for God. There are the stories about the low-caste Sants: Nāmdev is shooed out of the temple, but God turns the temple around to see him (PPM 6), and Raidās's worship is proved superior to caste Brahmins' Vedic rituals (PPM 11). In contrast, caste Brahmins flaunt the purity rules: Caturdās Khojī bows to a low-caste Kañjar begging for leftovers (PPM 19), and Harirām Vyās takes leftovers from all Vaishnavas and, when scolded for it, defies such concerns in his songs (PPM 32). He even turns his sacred thread into an emergency anklet for the actor dancing Rādhā's role in the Rās-līlā, proclaiming that finally his sacred thread has been of use (PPM 31)!

All this seems less than innocent in the light of the monumental efforts of Jai Singh II to ensure that devotional sects adhered to orthodoxy. His particular concern to preserve orthodox rules of interdining is flaunted frequently in this hagiography. Did a backlash against Jai Singh's orthodoxy surface after his death in 1743? Certainly, the hagiography triumphantly proclaims that *bhakti* trumps all these Vedic rites Jai Singh was so preoccupied with and that the concern for *varṇāśrama-dharma* is irrelevant. While Jai Singh was not strictly speaking the "ruler" of the Braj area, he was subedar of Agra twice during the first half of the eighteenth century.[182] The religious debates he stimulated had repercussions as far east as Bengal. Sāvant Singh certainly would have known of them.

There is another recurrent theme that may point to a backlash of Jai Singh's reforms. Under Jai Singh's regime, the imperative for devotional sects to prove association with the orthodox Catuḥ-sampradāya caused the production of Sanskrit treatises and led to several court debates. Is it coincidental, then, that in *Garland of Stories and Songs*, at a couple of points, philosophical debate is made light of and even pronounced as antithetical to *bhakti*? This is the case when the pandit Vyās arrives in Vrindavan, keen on debate, but after conversion to *bhakti* submerges all his learned books in the Yamunā (PPM 28). Or even more outspoken is the story of the conversion of a pandit by Bhagvāndās Hit Rāmrāy. He had challenged many to debate, and Nāgarīdās specifies the lines along which he was thinking:

> "The Vaishnavas here will bicker in all kinds of philosophical debate. If there is anyone who has been steeped in Vrindavan's true colors, then he will not be willing to engage in a philosophical debate with me. I shall become a disciple of that person." So he engaged in philosophical debate with many people, day after day. In the course of the debates, he even angered several. In his own mind, he did not consider himself to have lost a debate to anyone.
>
> (PPM 55)

This may be an apt picture of Jai Singh–era Vrindavan: many debates, much anger, much competition. Nāgarīdās clearly did not approve.

Remarkably, it seems to be a Vallabhan milieu in which such a resurgence takes place, that is, if we take seriously the possibility of a Vallabhan redaction of *Garland of Stories and Songs*. Vallabhans encouraged *bhakta*s to remain householders (*gṛhastha*), and in that respect they thus were in Jai Singh's "good books," as the Jaipur king discouraged *sanyāsa*. However, the Vallabhans smarted from their loss of superiority at the court under Jai Singh, who favored orthodox Smārta Maratha Brahmins and Gauḍīya *bhaktas*. The latter worked hard to establish their orthodox credentials, even in the minutiae of ritual and theology and to align themselves with the Mādhva-Sampradāya. The argumentation was carried out overwhelmingly in Sanskrit. *Garland of Stories and Songs*, in response, is a vernacular text telling charming stories to make the opposite point.

Rather than foregrounding sectarian affiliation with orthodoxy, Nāgarīdās emphasizes an ecumenical atmosphere, mixing *bhaktas* from all sects. He even includes the low-caste Sants. That he does not claim them to be Rāmānandī is significant; the stories of initiation by Rāmānand are conspicuous by their absence. What counts is that their devotion trumped orthodoxy. An important point is made when the Rāma devotee Tulsīdās is shown to regret lifelong his inability to recognize Rāma when he appeared to him in the form of a low-caste hunter (PPM 22). Where this famous *Rāmāyaṇa*-expounder failed, an obscure devotee, Caturdās Khojī, is celebrated for recognizing God in a disgusting low-caste Kañjar begging for leftovers (PPM 19). Some manuscripts specify that he is a Rāmānandī, but others make him a Rāmānujī, purportedly the stalwarts of orthodoxy. Perhaps there is a subtle anti-Jaipur agenda here.

To back up this thesis, it pays to investigate whom Nāgarīdās chose to keep company with. In *The Pilgrim's Bliss*, Nāgarīdās was very positive about his gatherings in Radhakund with Bansīdās and Muralīdās. In *Garland of Stories and Songs*, he hosted Muralīdās in Rupnagar and praised his ability to tune in to the divine realm. Possibly, both were Gauḍīyas and followers of the unorthodox party of Rūpa Kavirāja, the so-called Sauramya-mat, which was socially excluded for its defiance of Jai Singh's measures. If so, Nāgarīdās was associating with the foes of Jai Singh's policy, the pariahs of the Gauḍīya-Sampradāya at the time.

There is a textual complication: the stories about the low-caste Sants are included only in the longer recension of *Garland of Stories and Songs*. It is curious that the shorter recension omits in many cases exactly those anecdotes that foreground this social permissiveness. Is it coincidental that the story of Tulsī's "missed vision of the hunter-Rāma" is left out in some of the shorter recension versions? And those of Vyās's defiance of commensuality rules? This fuels suspicion that perhaps the shorter redaction is the later one. It may be that parties sharing the sensitivities of the late Jai Singh were involved in this "censorship." Was there a resurgence of Jai Singh's orthodoxy in the later eighteenth century?[183] Or may it simply have been a matter of the personal taste of the scribes and their patrons or audiences? With regard to the puzzle of the two recensions then, one may have to consider the possibility that the shorter recension was the later one, leaving out the parts from the work that offended orthodox sensitivities most.

CONCLUSION: A VERNACULAR ANSWER TO JAI SINGH'S ORTHODOXY

Nāgarīdās's main objective in this hagiography is to contextualize songs within their composition and performance context. This reveals what these songs meant to their authors and audiences. We learn about their hybridity as they were composed and transmitted partly orally, partly written; but even when written, it was the first performance that was regarded as constituting "publication." We learn about the belief in divine intervention in composition as well as transmission of the songs, the belief in a transcendent realm of performance in the divine *līlā*, which devotees "tuned in" to. We learn what were regarded as "classics" and liturgical songs. Without buying into each anecdote having exactly happened as told, we get a fair sense of what individual songs meant at least in some pilgrim circles in the mid-eighteenth century and how songs like these circulated and were received by very diverse audiences, not limited to hardcore Krishna devotees. Perhaps this constituted an early modern "public sphere" or ecumene of sorts.

Most importantly, we learn how the stories about the saints and their songs were mobilized to create interventions in the real mid-eighteenth-century world of sectarian strife and social ferment. Nāgarīdās may have conceived of his project as an answer to Jai Singh II's. The Jaipur king, who was engaged in Vedic sacrifices to establish his legitimacy as a Hindu king, was concerned with bringing the unorthodox devotional sects within the orbit of *varṇāśrama-dharma* and Hindu orthodoxy. In response, this Kishangarh king produced a hagiography that is decidedly more left-leaning, repeatedly foregrounding the heterodox tendencies of a *bhakti* that does not shy away from seeing God in a low-caste. Untouchable and low-caste saints find place of pride in Nāgarīdās's hagiography (especially in its longer recension), and their songs are mobilized through the stories to make a point of devotion trumping concerns of orthopraxis. Likewise, one of the favorites, repeatedly quoted in *Garland of Stories and Songs*, is Harirām Vyās, a Brahmin with outspoken antinomian views. Nāgarīdās's hagiography mobilized Vyās's poems that include the low-caste saints. In its longer recension, *Garland of Stories and Songs* also devotes space to Mīrā, the Rajput princess of Nāgarīdās's own Rathor clan, who dared defy the rules of decorum for devotion's sake; Nāgarīdās perhaps even sponsored a painting of the much-maligned princess. It may be that some of this radicality got toned down, edited out in a shorter recension of *Garland of Stories and Songs* (or, vice versa, that it was amplified in a later, longer recension), but the message of the work as a whole stands in its decisive privileging of *bhakti* over ritual. This mobilization of song and story is all the more powerful because it is done in the vernacular, through an easily accessible medium and the oral transmission of storytelling. Whereas the orthodoxy of the Jaipur king's reformation gave a boost to the production of Sanskrit theological tracts, the Kishangarh king's "contra-reformation" brings a flood of songs and stories that celebrate in the vernacular the devotion of the heart.

The significance of *Garland of Stories and Songs* for the evolution of modern orthodox Hinduism is that it disrupts the notion of direct unbroken progression from Jai Singh II's early eighteenth-century royal decrees to the nineteenth-century construction of "traditionalist Hinduism."[184] In Nāgarīdās's hagiography, we see one of the fits and starts of history at work. His hagiography certainly foregrounds *bhakti* with a Vaishnava flavor, but it is not a lynchpin between Jai Singh's early eighteenth-century endeavor and Hariścandra's late nineteenth-century effort. Rather, it presents a reaction to the orthodoxization of the *bhakti* cults, a turn to the left, which would eventually be engulfed by the broader trend toward the right that we see at work in Hariścandra's modern "sequel" to the story.

5 Myth Retold

Garland of Rāma's Romance

The other stories, those overflowing with sadness (*karuṇā*), I have deliberately not written.
Now I present songs in the heroic mood: the stratagems for killing Rāvaṇa.

—RCM *Dohā* 1

GARLAND OF RĀMA'S ROMANCE (RĀM-CARIT-MĀLĀ) IS AN ANTHOLOGY in which Nāgarīdās compiled his favorite songs on Rāma's story by great devotees and added some of his own, to total thirty-one poems. Like *Garland of Stories and Songs*, it is a "garland," or *mālā*, but he did not provide any commentary or background on the poems because the main goal was to retell the story. As is clear from the quotation above, he collected the poems selectively and deliberately skipped major parts of the story. A close study of what he chose to leave out and what to foreground furthers understanding of the dynamics of *Rāmāyaṇa* retellings in general.

This is one of the few works by Nāgarīdās that centers on Rāma. He composed a handful of poems for the celebration of Rāma's birthday festival (Śrī Rāma–janmotsava) collected in *Garland of Festivals*. Otherwise, only one other poem uses the *Rāmāyaṇa* theme, and that is to make a general point of advice, namely, never to listen to a woman:

On Kaikeyī's say-so, happened terrible things:
Daśaratha died and went to the hereafter.
On Mantharā's say-so, the queen lost everything;
She is forever reviled down in the world.
On Jānakī's say-so, her brother-in-law ran off:
Without him, his sister-in-law was abducted by Rāvaṇa.
Nāgar: this story is so famous in the world!
Say, by women's say-so, has ever come about anything good?

(*Chūṭak-kavitta* 67)[1]

This does not exactly entail a flattering treatment of the *Ramayaṇa* story, or of women, but it effectively makes its point of advising against listening to women. While not politically correct by modern standards, one can imagine a scenario where it might fit in its context, for instance where a ruler might be advised against demands from the harem. The poem belongs to the genre of "*bon mot* for the right moment" that the educated courtier would use to impress his peers and superiors when the occasion would arise.[2]

In any case, *Garland of Rāma's Romance* is an anomaly among Nāgarīdās's works, which otherwise profess exclusive devotion to Rādhā and Krishna. To understand how he might have justified it, we can refer back to his own reflections on the issue of exclusive devotion, or *ananyatā*, in his hagiography. Regarding the great Rāma devotee Tulsīdās's unwillingness to prostrate himself before Śrī Nātha jī, and to compose in praise of Krishna (PPM 24), Nāgarīdās confirmed that while all *avatāras* are ultimately the same, it is appropriate for devotees to feel an exclusive attachment to one only. Still, the Tulsīdās song he quoted to illustrate the story was in praise of both Rāma and Krishna. Similarly, Nāgarīdās presumably understood his Rāma composition not to detract from his devotional profile but to mirror Tulsī's poems on Krishna.

Nāgarīdās's *Rāmāyaṇa* never was as popular as his Rādhā-Krishna poetry, though manuscripts are preserved in places as far as Sitamau (Madhya Pradesh), and it is also included in manuscripts of his complete works.[3] Why did Sāvant Singh turn to the Rāma story at all? In the final verse, Nāgarīdās gives the date as 1749 (1806 VS) and the place of composition as at the banks of the Hindani River, the Hindon, which flows between the Yamunā and Gaṅgā. This means that it was compiled during his exile, while he actively sought alliances in Delhi and Jaipur and with the Marathas for his fight against his brother. Here we have a fascinating opportunity to see the politics at work behind a mythological retelling. Nāgarīdās turns to Rāma's story at the point in his life when he had just lost his throne and the hostilities with his brother were in full swing. Within a year of completing the work, he would (unsuccessfully) lay siege to Rupnagar with the help of the Jaipur ruler Īśvarī Singh. The story of Rāma's exile as a consequence of palace intrigue must have acquired a new existential dimension for Sāvant Singh, as he was now himself a usurped king, exiled from his home, building alliances to fight the enemy. One could say that his retelling of the *Rāmāyaṇa* is emplotted and configured anew in the light of his own new experience. This personalized version of the *Rāmāyaṇa* has the potential to provide a window into how the mythic story of a struggle for the throne of Ayodhya could have real-life significance for the one who retells it. It is rare that we have this kind of background information to study a *Rāmāyaṇa* retelling.

MYTH'S MULTIPLE MOBILIZATIONS

After many decades during which *Rāmāyaṇa* studies were dominated by the Sanskrit version attributed to Vālmīki, political events in India prompted Western academia to shift attention to the vibrant "vernacular" *Rāmāyaṇa* traditions. In particular, the rise of Hindutva in Indian politics and the controversy about Rāma's birthplace (*janmabhūmi*) in Ayodhya led to an academic cottage industry of "many *Rāmāyaṇas*."[4] Many studies, from a gender angle, focus on retellings of the story that are interesting for women studies, others on popular and minority *Rāmāyaṇas*.[5] Yet others focus on the political power of the myth and what it is that makes the *Rāmāyaṇa* story so compelling as historical imaginaire.[6] The *Rāmāyaṇa* analyzed here does not represent such previously underrepresented groups who mobilize the myth for their political ends. This retelling is not one that is "talking back to Vālmīki." Still, it contributes to our understanding of the political power of the myth.

AN IDIOSYNCRATIC *RĀMĀYAṆA* RETELLING

For many medieval *Rāmāyaṇa* retellings, it is possible to argue that the story was employed in a clash of cultures with a Muslim "other," and the narrative's formula, with its divinization of the hero and demonization of his enemies, worked well in that context.[7] Does this hold good for Sāvant Singh's retelling, too? It is a relatively late *Rāmāyaṇa*, but the political circumstances seem ready-made for a retelling that foregrounds the twin themes of divine kingship and demonized threats from outside. As for royal legitimation: Sāvant Singh was in need of a rationale for his succession to the throne in view of the challenge by his brother. A divinization scenario and promise of theocratic rule would suit that need. As for an outside threat: the Afghan armies of Ahmad Shāh Abdālī "Durrānī" had invaded India from the northwest. Though Sāvant Singh did not actually partake in the 1748 confrontation with Durrānī, just one year before his *Rāmāyaṇa* composition he was in Delhi in response to the emperor's call for help to counter the threat posed to the empire. In short, the situation seems an ideal breeding ground for the *Rāmāyaṇa*'s divinization/demonizing narrative to have taken off. Perhaps the crisis of the empire is to be read behind the quotation at the beginning of the chapter: Nāgarīdās says he intends to skip the tragic narratives (of the *Ayodhyā-* and *Kiṣkindha-kāṇḍas*) and move right to the battle with Rāvaṇa.

It seems promising to read Nāgarīdās's work as an example of historical imaginaire. However, once we start looking at the actual text, we find that things are not so clear-cut. When Nāgarīdās portrays Rāvaṇa, we do not necessarily see Durrānī leaping off the page. Perhaps there is a different type of political appropriation going on. Rather than making a public political statement, Nāgarīdās is working through the personal crisis situation by means of mythology. What more apt story than the *Rāmāyaṇa* to turn to when one finds one's throne usurped? The *Rāmāyaṇa* in its Vālmīkian version, contains three reflections on strife for the throne between brothers: apart from the human tussle for the throne of Ayodhya, there is the monkey one, where the Vānara brothers Sugrīva and Vālin are fighting each other over Kishkindha, and the demonic one, where Vibhīṣaṇa will eventually replace his brother, the demon Rāvaṇa, as the king of Lanka. The human drama thus is echoed in a monkey and a demonic scenario. All this mirroring provides extensive occasion for reflection on the main theme of fraternal rivalry for the throne.

Reading Nāgarīdās's *Rāmāyaṇa* against the background of his life and in conjunction with the two other roughly contemporary texts analyzed in this book enhances our understanding of the personal factors behind how such myths are retold. It is rare that we can avail ourselves of other works of different genres by the same author to synoptically read with the *Rāmāyaṇa* retelling. From *The Pilgrim's Bliss* we learned much about Nāgarīdās's personal circumstances. From *Garland of Stories and Songs* we learned who his sources of influence were. As we will see, several of the poems included in *Garland of Rāma's Romance* are by poets praised in the hagiographical text; in one case, there is even the overlap of a poem that occurs in both works. Nāgarīdās's text affords us a unique opportunity to peek behind the curtains of the storyteller. While it may be rather idiosyncratic, it still is instructive to help us think about other *Rāmāyaṇa*s for which there is much less information available.

THE COMPILER AS CREATIVE READER

As the title indicates, the author regards his work as a "garland" of poems that have just been "picked" to make a new version of the story. Nāgarīdās himself puts it this way:

> Let me select ancient verses to weave a garland for the story of Rāma.
>
> (RCM 1)

He thus uses the imagery of a "collection of flowers," the Greek etymological meaning of *anthology*, translated as "florilegium" in Latin.[8]

For the most part, the poems in this work are by others. He picked the very best of *bhakti* literature and included, as one would expect, poetry by the famous Rāma *bhakta* Tulsīdās (four poems). None are from Tulsī's canonical *Holy Lake of Rāma's Romance* (Rām-carit-mānas); they are all from his Braj work *String of Songs* (Gītāvalī). Most of the poems he chose, though, are by famous Braj Krishna poets, especially Vallabhans, with eleven poems by Sūrdās and one poem by Krishnadās and Nanddās each. One poem is by Krishnadās Kaṭahariyā, perhaps the Kaṭaharīyā claimed to have been converted by Viṭṭhalnāth from his old occupation of robbing caravans on the road between Braj and Gujarat.[9] Nimbārkans are represented with one poem by Paraśurām and one long wedding song by Vrindāban Prabhu, both abbots of Salemabad.[10] The testimony of these songs in Nāgarīdās's work helps in understanding their reception history and gives us a snapshot of what Rāma poems, for instance by Sūrdās, were already popular in the mid-eighteenth century.[11]

Apart from these poems compiled from other poets, the remaining poems of the work (twelve in all) were composed by Nāgarīdās himself. For an anthology, that is a relatively high personal input.[12] In addition, Nāgarīdās provides classificatory categories in the form of subtitles and one explicatory verse at the beginning, middle (quoted above), and two at the end. He states his purpose, or at least the desired effect of the work, at the end:

> If you listen to or recite this book for an hour one watch of the day,
> Handsome Siyā-Rāma will dwell forever in your heart.
>
> (RCM 32)

This anthology thus was intended for "religious reading," a deep reading of the meditative and transformative type.[13]

This remarkable work is just under two-thirds anthology, just over one-third compilation. Perhaps it is more precisely an annotated selective reading of the *Rāmāyaṇa*. This is particularly pertinent in view of recent theories of reading that highlight that reading also involves an act of composition. Nāgarīdās's composition-cum-compilation illustrates that reading is a "constructive act done in conjunction with mediating texts and the cultural-historical context in which [the] reading takes place."[14]

WORKING THROUGH SCRIPTURE

Nāgarīdās's work contains many variants on the *Rāmāyaṇa* theme. The table of contents of *Garland of Rāma's Romance* will immediately strike connoisseurs of the *Rāmāyaṇa* with some important omissions and additions.

TABLE 5.1 Overview of the Headings of *Garland of Rāma's Romance*

Verse Number following K. Gupta (1965)	**Introduction: An Anthology**
	Bāl-kāṇḍ
1–2	Songs of Rāma's Birth
3–5	Songs of Childhood Play
6–9	Polo (Horse and Ball Play)
10–14	Rishi Viśvāmitra's Arrival in Ayodhya: Fulfilling the Beggar's Command
	Adventures in Viśvāmitra's Company
	First the Killing of Tāḍakā for the Protection of the Sacrifice and So Forth
	Ahalyā and the Boatman
15	Entering Janaka's Capital, and First Sight When Roaming in the Garden
16	The Tournament for the Bride
17	Wedding and Entry in Ayodhya
	Ayodhyā-kāṇḍ
Dohā 1	After Daśaratha, the Rule of Rāma Mahārāja
	Sundar-kāṇḍ
18	Hanumān's Crossing the Ocean to Find Sītā
19	Hanumān's Song of His Entry in Lanka, His Search for Sītā and Finding Her, the Conversation and Giving Her the Signet-Ring, the Destruction of the Garden, Defeat of the Demon Guard, Audience with Rāvaṇa, Burning the City, Dousing His Tail, Return to and Touching Sītā's Feet (in Farewell)
20–21	The Songs of Her Message, as Told to Hanumān
22	Hanumān's Communiqué upon Approaching Rām
	Yuddha-kāṇḍ
23	A Song at the Time of Raghunātha's Crossing the Ocean
24	Mandodarī's Words to Rāvaṇa
25	Description of Aṅgada's Mission to Rāvaṇa for a Message of Terms
26	Song Where Raghuvīra Speaks Zealously
27	Song of Rāvaṇa's Slaying at the Time of the Battle
28	Meeting with Sītā at Rāma's Triumph
29	Dispatching Hanumān to Bring the Happy News of Imminent Arrival in Ayodhya
30–31	Spotting the Chariot as It Approaches
Dohās 1–2	Envoi: The Harvest of the Poet's Words

DIVINIZING AND DEMONIZING?

This is not your run-of-the-mill *Rāmāyaṇa* as historical imaginaire with a compelling divinizing/demonizing narrative. Those aspects of the story get comparatively little playtime. Sāvant Singh is not cast as Rāma. This is surprising, given that he is so clearly identified with Krishna, in painting. One might have expected him to use the story to legitimize his position, but no bid for his kingship as divinely ordained comes to the fore as the major political message. Neither is there any hint that Durrānī's troops were the model behind the demons in this narrative. Listening to this *Rāmāyaṇa*, one does not come away with the impression that there is a divine world order that needs protection from demonic intruders. What we have instead is a loving meditation on the character of Rāma and the love felt for him by those around him. This is not a blueprint for a political agenda but, rather, an exploration of love, a document of *bhakti*.

Rāma-Rasika elements are very prominent, as the story develops. Recalling the account of the pilgrimage he undertook at the time, that is not surprising. Sāvant Singh, on his way to Braj, had just visited the Rāmānandī monastery at Galta, where he was much impressed with the abbot Hari Ācārya (TĀ 6–8). He may have gone there to seek military help from Rāmānandī Nāgās for his succession war, but if unsuccessful in that purpose, he certainly enjoyed the *satsaṅga* of the abbot with whom he had a lot in common. Hari Ācārya was a Rāma-Rasika poet, interested in the intimacy of the love-play of Sītā and Rāma. Nāgarīdās specifies that the abbot's farewell gift was "meditation on Raghunātha" (*Raghunātha dhyāna*; TĀ 8). It may not be coincidence that he starts out *Garland of Rāma's Romance* with the verb derived from the same root as that noun (*dhyāya*): "Let me meditate on the feet of Sītā and Rāma, soft as a fresh lotus" (RCM 1). While such invocations are rather generic, still the visit to Galta and the charisma of the abbot may have been a source of inspiration. The term *dhyāna* had a particular importance in the Rasika-Sampradāya and figures for instance in the title of Agradās's seminal work *Handmaiden of Meditation to Rāma* (Rām-dhyān-mañjarī).[15] Reading Nāgarīdās's *Rāmāyaṇa* against this background of his pilgrimage account thus provides perspective on the Rāma-Rasika interpretations.

OMISSIONS TOWARD A HAPPY ENDING

Given his personal circumstances, one might have expected Nāgarīdās to dwell on the injustices suffered by his divine hero. Yet he studiously avoids all references to the story of Rāma's brother's usurpation of the throne and the exile, omitting the entire *Ayodhyā* and *Āraṇya-kāṇḍ*. He even skips most of *Kiṣkindhā-kāṇḍ*, along with its main theme, the story of strife between the Vānara brothers Sugrīva and Vālin. This de-emphasis of strife is in tune with Vālmīki's *Rāmāyaṇa*, where the message does not promote discord between brothers but instead highlights the exemplary scenario of the chivalrous humans' resolution of the conflict for the throne in a nonconfrontational way. This is contrasted with the parallel cases in the monkey and demonic worlds. The violence is transferred outside the family. While the Vālmīki *Rāmāyaṇa* starts out in the world of strife in the family, it shifts the focus to the threat coming from outside that dwarfs the internal rivalries.

Even while Sāvant Singh tried to raise an army to fight his brother, he showed himself a good student of the epic: instead of expressing bitterness about fraternal rivalry, his *Rāmāyaṇa* does the opposite. It dwells not on *karuṇā*, or the tragic circumstances of the exile, but on moments of peace and reconciliation. Nāgarīdās seems to say as much in the *Dohā* quoted at the beginning of this chapter, explicitly skipping the stories of *karuṇā*, to move on to the heroic mood (*vīra rasa*) instead (RCM *Dohā* 1). At one level this statement is about choice of poetic mood, the *rasa* the author chooses to develop in his artistic creation. However, there may be more to it. Perhaps Nāgarīdās chose to omit the contests over royal thrones because the stories hit too closely home. Or, to give him more credit, perhaps the transformative power of the *Rāmāyaṇa* worked its magic with him. As he sought alliances with the Marathas, did it dawn on him that it was a major faux pas to invite outsider interference into his kingdom, compared to which the "mere" internal rivalry with his brother was relatively innocuous?

Nāgarīdās concludes the work on a happy note with Rāma's victory over Rāvaṇa and his triumphant return to Ayodhya. He was not the first to do so, of course; the most famous model for this way of retelling the story is Tulsīdās's *Rāmāyaṇa*. Toward the end of the work, Nāgarīdās briefly describes the reaction of Bharata, the brother who ruled in Rāma's stead, as he hears the good news of his brother's return:

> Daśaratha's son sent the Son of the Wind to quickly bring the joyful news.
> Alighting from the flower-chariot, the hero monkey ran off in
> human guise.
> He told the news to Guha and then went to Bharata to report.
> "Sītā's Lord has killed the Lord of Lanka. The Raghu King is coming home."
> Overjoyed on hearing this, staring in amazement, Bharata was
> left speechless.

Heart, vow, breath, and eyes, all collapsed as he became all ears.
Finally Bharata's river, which flowed from devotion, would meet that
  Ocean of Grace.
Nāgarīdās says: the servants of Rāma's feet will attain bliss, nothing less.
(RCM 29)

This is one of the poems Nāgarīdās composed for the anthology and hence can be read as replete with his personal experience. It might be seen as an example of wishful thinking, of the happy ending of the Rāma story giving him hope that his own brother, too, would welcome him back in Kishangarh. It would not be correct, though, to call it escapist, because, at this point, Sāvant Singh was still actively engaged in efforts to regain his throne. But again, we can see here a salutary effect of working through the *Rāmāyaṇa* story: the happy ending of the myth may have helped him keep the faith that eventually he, too, would cope with the difficulties he faced. The ideal scenario of chivalrous brothers in the myth may have inspired him to hold no personal grudge against his brother, but instead to envisage a reconciliation scenario, whereby matters could be resolved relatively peacefully. The image Nāgarīdās uses is of a river flowing into the ocean. Although it would take several more years, a peace treaty and motion of understanding were eventually signed. Nāgarīdās's *Rāmāyaṇa*'s happy ending became a self-fulfilling prophesy.

HAPPY CHILDHOOD MEMORIES

The Rāma-Rasika elements in the story are closely intertwined with Nāgarīdās's personal experience. Proportionally, Nāgarīdās devotes most poems to Rāma's childhood: seventeen of the thirty-one poems cover the events of the *Bāla-kāṇḍ*, of which ten focus on Rāma's youth in Ayodhya. Nāgarīdās begins with a self-composed song for Rāma's birthday (*janma-badhāī*):

Let us go! Today auspicious songs are sung in the palace of King Daśaratha.
A handsome prince of dark body was born: Śrī Rāma.
Artists receive abundant rewards of gold and jewels, and necklaces
  of pearls.
Nāgarīdās: all bad luck is reversed, immense good fortune floods the world.
(RCM 1)

This sounds very similar to Nāgarīdās's songs for Krishna's birthday and may have been performed for the ritual occasion of Rāma-navamī, Rāma's birthday festival. We know this was celebrated in the Rupnagar temple, since there is a whole rubric devoted to it in Nāgarīdās's collection of festival songs, though none of those poems overlap with the ones he includes here.[16]

Some of the most felicitous parts of this *Rāmāyaṇa* are the fond evocations of Rāma's youthful play, several from Tulsīdās's *Gītāvalī* poems on the topic. Nāgarīdās selects for his anthology poems of little Rāma and his brothers playing with bow and arrow (RCM 3–5). Preshadowing later events, Rāma and Bharata's brotherly rivalry in adolescent games figures importantly. Nāgarīdās selects four poems about their competition in polo (*aśva-genduka-līlā*), two from Tulsīdās's *Gītāvalī*, complemented by two he composed himself (RCM 6–9). This theme is lesser known and does not occur in Tulsī's *Rāmāyaṇa*. Nāgarīdās foregrounds Rāma's ability to lose graciously:

> Rāma and Lakshmana on one team, Bharata and the subduer of enemies (Shatrughna) on the other.
> On the bank of the Sarayū, all have counted and divided up the players into teams.
> Adept in ball handling, they all mount their horses, spurring them on. They are more handsome than Kāmadeva!
> With their lotus hands they begin an extraordinary polo game; they become engrossed in their play
> . . . .
> Those winning hesitate, lowering head and eyes; those losing flee in the dust, shedding tears of love.
> Full of delight and love, one side advances while the other turns away.
> Some say, "Rāma has been defeated." Others say, "Bharata has won."
> The Lord makes donations of elephants, horses, and harnesses, as the sky resounds with the beat of the drums
> . . . .
> Tulsī says: this same abundance awaits all those who immerse themselves in the Lord's own passions.[17]
>
> (RCM 6)

Notably, Rāma does not begrudge his younger brother his victory at all. Is Nāgarīdās working through his enmity with his brother here?

Next, Nāgarīdās includes a poem he himself composed on Daśaratha's anguish at having to let Rāma go off to heroic exploits with Viśvāmitra:

Viśvāmitra arrived at the royal palace.
Hardly had he sat down to have his feet washed, when he demanded, as holy men do:
"Vile and evil demons give me great trouble as I carry out my sacrificial rites.
Send with me that prince Rāma, with his beautiful dark body."[18]
Daśaratha was plunged into a sea of despair. He could not bring himself to consent to the holy man's request.
He knew that if he did not comply with the command, the Brahmin's mind would erupt in anger—
Throbbing lips, red eyes . . . the court was left in fear.
It was as if for the sake of destroying the world, agitated Rudra had emerged:
Trees falter on the earth, stars explode, the elephants upholding the world lose their grip[19] . . .
Finally, the king of Avadh gave in at Vaśiṣṭa's urging.
Still of tender age and sweet-faced were the dark and fair-bodied brothers,
Nāgaridās: yet the two princes were allowed to accompany the sage (*tapasvin*).

(RCM 10)

The stress on parental love (*vātsalya*) acquires a poignant existential value if we remember that Nāgarīdās's father had passed away very recently. The impending threat of the guru's possible anger at the king's refusal prompts an anticipatory vision of the apocalypse (*pralaya*), with Shiva's destructive dance. Possibly, Sāvant Singh himself had these feelings upon learning of his father's demise, in a reversal of the mythological situation. The political events at the time must have seemed quite apocalyptic to Sāvant Singh, both on a personal and a political level.

The next poem, again a quotation from Tulsīdās, is a flashback of Rāma and Lakshmana's adventures together in the company of Viśvāmitra. These are framed as relayed in the letter sent to Ayodhya informing the family back home of the wedding proposal from the Mithila king:

Bharata and his brother ran off to the palace,
Overjoyed to report to their mothers the news they had heard at their father's feet.

Voices choked, hairs on end, quivering lips—look at such endearing love!
Kauśalyā pressed them against her breast, then asked keenly, "Is there some news?"
"The king of Tirhut has sent Śatānanda, his *purohit*,
With a welcome letter of news of Rāma and Lakshmana's welfare.
'They crushed Tāḍakā, killed the demons, safeguarded the sacrifice, and liberated a woman.[20]
They earned praise and went to Janaka's city, where they are thriving under the guru's protection.
There many kings had gathered their armies. Stringing the Pināka bow was the condition for Janaka's daughter's wedding.
In that assembly of kings, Raghuvara, broke Shiva's bow like a lotus stalk.'"
Hearing that adoring report from the brothers, the mothers embraced them,
Kissing and caressing their faces over and over. They arranged to donate garments.
In every house of Avadh, there were joyful congratulations when they heard of the felicitous proposal.
Tulsī: in the queens' quarters, the ladies-in-waiting rapturously sang auspicious songs.

(RCM 11)

Tulsīdās masterly packs all the action in just a few lines. The action is doubly framed: relayed in a letter, the contents of which are reported by the two brothers who stayed home to their mothers. This allows for maximum indulgence in the emotions of brothers and mothers, a *rasika* approach to the heroic exploits of Rāma and Lakshmana. There may again be a personalized element, as the poem celebrates the family, in particular maternal and fraternal love, something Nāgarīdās's own life circumstances had led him away from. The poem seems filled with nostalgia.

The next few poems are by Nāgarīdās, who in his own words fills out Rāma's feats of killing demons (RCM 12) and quotes a poem on the liberation of Ahalyā (RCM 13). The latter is framed as relayed by a character in the story, the ferryman, who refuses to let Rāma step in his boat for fear of the amazing power of his feet. The story of the ferryman is further elaborated in a verse by the Nimbārkan guru Paraśurām:

The holy dust of Rāma's feet—
One touch of his feet and a stone changes shape: it becomes alive with a body divine.[21]

The ferryman had brought his boat, but shouted to Rāma, "Lord, please remain standing on the river shore!"
He fled and did not look back, for fear of patient Rāma.
He received the highest reward: the treasure of grace from the Lord, who ferries sinners across the strife of life.
The boat went straight to heaven, and with it the low-caste man, his wife and family aboard.
Even Śeṣa, Maheśa, and Nārada the Vedic sage would need the help of Brahmā, the vazir.
Parasā says: Śuka and Sanaka and his brothers, hearts full of love, sing praise of Rāma's virtues.[22]

(RCM 14)

Nāgarīdās was fond of this song, which he also quoted in *Garland of Stories and Songs* (PPM 23). There the miraculous power of the song itself was stressed, as a villager, Murārīdās from Balonda in Marwar, went straight to heaven as he sang it. Here Nāgarīdās has included it as part of the childhood cycle of Rāma. The saving power of Rāma is misunderstood by the ferryman as possibly costing him his boat, thus spelling financial ruin. Yet it turns out to be his good fortune, as together with his family he will be saved thanks to Rāma. This irony, the simple *bhakta* running away from God but still being saved for the purity of his sentiments, fits well in the *bhakti* worldview, and the focus on emotion is again in sync with the *rasika* interpretation of events.

Strikingly, Nāgarīdās composed or chose to quote poems about a happy, idyllic youth of fraternal and paternal love. They seem imbued with the author's own nostalgic, wistful memories. Possibly in these poems he was working through his own childhood memories of his now estranged brother. Significantly, he dwells on beautiful moments of harmony rather than ill feelings.

FIRST LOVE

Next, Nāgarīdās celebrates how Sītā and Rāma fall in love in the flower garden. That seems natural for a Krishna devotee, and one who had recently been in communication with the Rāma-Rasika abbot of Galta:

Janaka's daughter has entered the garden.
She is on her way with a group of friends to worship the bow with flowers.
. . . .

From the other side come the handsome Raghu-heroes, sent by the sage
to collect flowers.
All of a sudden they meet each other, their eyes wide with the
purest beauty.
His eyes and hers fill with tears, like drops on lotus petals. They only can
behold each other.
Kāmadeva hesitates to take aim with his arrows: both have been
struck already!
As they remember respect for their elders, they each turn their heart away
reluctantly.
Through their eyes, their hearts have tasted the sublime, suffused with
wondrous love—
A passion without rules of modesty (*maryādā*), even though the lovers are
modesty incarnate.
For the purpose of tasting that passion, he shall be born in Nanda's house
as the dance master (Naṭanāgara, that is, Krishna).[23]

(RCM 15)

In this portrayal of the Rāma-Sītā romance, Nāgarīdās pays special attention to their eyes, as he does in that of the Rādhā-Krishna story, and as is the hallmark of the Kishangarhi style of painting. The poem ends with the observation that strong passionate love is out of character for Rāma, who is after all the highest moral ideal (*maryādā puruṣottama*); he will have to return as Krishna to taste such passion in full. This explicitly connects with the poetry Nāgarīdās is more famous for. That he here betrays a marked Krishna chauvinism perhaps indicates the limits of the Rāma-Rasika abbot's influence.

Next, Nāgarīdās selects some of the longest poems of his anthology for the tournament, or Svayaṃvara (RCM 16), and the wedding ceremonies (RCM 17). These poems, too, evoke the ones he composed on the topic of Rādhā and Krishna's marriage. These were also favorite subjects of the Rāma-Rasikas. Moreover, they lend themselves to dramatic enactment:

To arrange for Sītā's marriage, Janaka has planned a tournament—
The spectacle is amazing to behold, a balm to the eyes of all.
In every country, when young princes hear the news, they dress in
their finery.
With elephants and horses, armies and armaments, they march across the
land, gathering in Mithilā.

. . . .

Behind them follow patient Raghuvīra and Laghuvīra (his younger brother).
When the sun rises, in house after house the oil lamps dim, as if uncovered.
The kings gaze on as if marveling at elephants in rut. The Kāmadevas' bravado has vanished.
Handsome like a young lion, standing out in comportment, Rāma is the darling of all.
It takes one hundred and eight great and strong men and much effort to bring out the bow into the assembly

. . . .

A herald stands up in the assembly of kings, and announces thus:
"This is the condition Janaka has set: 'Whoever can draw the bow will marry his daughter.'"
Some only look at that bow and turn back with various excuses.
Some try to lift it, but fall flat onto the ground; some encourage others to lift it . . .
Our two heroes look at each other with a smile—how pleasing they look!
Then Raghuvara, splendid like a dark rain cloud, smiles as he turns to Śrī Sītā.[24]
In a flash of lightning, he tucks up his loincloth and approaches the bow.
At that moment, the blind and the aged, men and women, gods and sages, kings and queens,
Beholding this spectacle of the hero of the Raghu race—all start to ululate in unison.
Forthwith he grasps it! Instantly he lifts it! Crack!—and he breaks the bow and throws it down.
Janaka is relieved, the young girls rejoice, Sītā now feels her life-breath return.
All shout "Bravo" over and over; the immortals in the sky shower down flowers.
Nanddās surrenders himself (*bali*) again and again to that event. Auspicious songs are sung in every house.

(RCM 16)

This poem can be taken as a mini-script for a Rām-līlā, starting with a procession culminating in a tableau (*jhāṅkī*) of the two brothers at the end of the procession, allowing for the audience's *darshana*. The theatrical device of the contest includes elements of comedy (*hāsya rasa*) and builds up to the climax of Rāma's lifting the bow, which again invites audience participation in the ululation that all join at that moment. The poem, then, can be read as the blueprint for one of the processional plays that promote participation in the mythological realm.

The same can be said for the much longer wedding poem. The author, named in the last line, is Vrindāban Ācārya, the abbot of Salemabad, who was very influential with the Kishangarh palace women. Nāgarīdās's own mother and stepmother held him in high esteem, and some say he even gave his blessings at their weddings. There may thus be a very personal link between Nāgarīdās, the compiler, and Vrindāban Ācārya, the author of this particular poem. The description contains several elements typical for Rajput weddings, as may have been witnessed by the author. It is indicative of the close interchange between Krishna- and Rāma-Rasika milieus at the time that this influential Rādhā-Krishna guru composed a moving and lovingly crafted poem on Rāma and Sītā's wedding. Perhaps Nāgarīdās recited this poem for the abbot of Galta. In several ways, this poem is reminiscent of the popular Rām-līlās on the theme, called *Rāma-Sītā-vivāha*. The excerpt abounds in tableaux that allow for the audience's auspicious *darshana*, such as the ceremonial reception of the grooms, the various marriage rituals themselves, the brides' and grooms' first gazing on each other's face, the good-bye in Mithilā, and the reception back home in Ayodhya. It also is set up for audience participation in the mythical events, notably in the processional arrival and return of the grooms' party. Perhaps a play based on this "script" was staged by Hari Ācārya at Galta. In that case, the influence may have run both ways, with Nāgarīdās also inspiring the Rāmānandī abbot.

GIANT LEAPS AND A MOMENT TO PAUSE AND HEAR SĪTĀ'S VOICE

The quotation at the beginning of this chapter showed how Nāgarīdās bypassed in just one distych (RCM *Dohā* 1) all the pathos, or *karuṇā*, of the *Ayodhyā-* and *Araṇya-kāṇḍs*. That includes omitting the crucial story of Sītā's abduction. While Nāgarīdās announced that he would focus on heroism, or *vīra rasa*, in fact he jumped right into the marvel, or *adbhūta rasa*, of Hanumān's exploits in *Sundara-kāṇḍ*. Appropriately, he started with a Sūrdās poem on Hanumān's giant leap (RCM 18). Then, in his own poem he had the monkey leap through all the action before taking leave from Sītā (RCM 19). As with the "letter to Ayodhya" above, this poem furthers the narrative by summarizing many events, some of which are then elaborated on in the following poems.

Nāgarīdās then pauses, dwelling on two poignant poems by Sūrdās expressing *karuṇā*, but that of Sītā's message for her husband as conveyed via the monkey. This interest in Sītā's feelings in exile again has its counterpart in the Krishna universe where the longing in separation, or *viraha*, of the Gopīs and Rādhā is ubiquitous. We hear Sītā's desperate voice translated through the categories of Krishna *bhakti*. In the first poem, she laments her plight:

> "This creature looks like a monkey! How can I convey my message to him?
> Hear me, monkey, how much longer can I keep (for Rāma's sake) my life-breaths (*prānani*) from slipping away?[25]
> They are so unpredictable—when they wish to leave, they don't stop to think.
> Again and again I try hard to stop them at life's main gate, threatening them with God's Name.
> Hanumant, in my despair, I repeat again and again, 'I'm so afraid.'[26]
> Sūr: Has Rāma ever heard anyone sorrowing like this, my beloved Rāma, who is so compassionate?"
>
> (RCM 20)

Sītā's desire for suicide is counterbalanced by a sense of duty to preserve her life for her husband. It is a vivid picture of the "suicidal quandary" she finds herself in. For the corresponding Vālmīkian episode, Sītā's feelings are well summarized in her reflection on a woman's helplessness, as she curses her plight: "*dhig astu paravaśyatām*," or "How wretched to be under the power of another."[27] Vālmīki's Sītā in despair wishes to take her life, yet she realizes that it is not hers to take; it belongs to her husband, whose permission she cannot obtain. In the Vālmīki version, she reasons about her plight and blames herself. She worries what may delay her husband's rescuing her, whether perhaps he has forgotten her or has been killed. She is carried along by the downward spiral of her own logic through the "trauma of abandonment" into the ultimate despair that she has nothing left to stay alive for.[28] In the above-quoted poem by Sūrdās, she splits herself up into her instinct-driven and her duty-conscious selves. On the one hand, she says, her life-breaths, which she characterizes as "slippery" (*capala*), seek to slip away and escape, and, on the other, her conscious self is "guarding" them (*pahiro deta*), stationed at the "main gate" or the mouth (*mukha dvāra*) to keep them in. She casts this guarding task as an impossible mission in the service of Rāma, whose name she constantly invokes to keep her wayward breaths in place. Yet she despairs of her ability to keep doing so. In the last line, she uses one of Rāma's names or epithets, "full of compassion" (*karunāmaya*), hinting that Rāma should live up to his fame and come and release her from this plight.

In Vālmīki's version, this is a soliloquy, ending with the arrival of Hanumān, who brings her hope. In this vernacular version, it takes the form of a message to the monkey. This framing is explicit in the refrain of the song that captures the impossibility of the situation: what can a monkey understand of this quandary? An extra layer of irony thus is added when her message comes mediated through the monkey's report, questioning the Vālmīkian frame. Can we really hear Sītā's voice here?

The second poem is also by Sūrdās:

> "Please put in a good word for me.
> First invoke Raghunātha's name and fall at his feet. Then hand this jewel over to him.
> On the bank of the Mandākinī, on a crystal rock, rubbing face-to-face, we made a *tilaka*.
> How can I even speak about this to you, monkey? Even though I must tell you now, as I remember our love, my chest tightens.[29]
> You are Hanumant, the holy son of the wind. Could you tell him what I have just conveyed to you?
> Sūr: Show the jewel as you come before Rāma's eyes; his presence extinguishes all sin and sorrow, which is so hard to endure."[30]
>
> (RCM 21)

This poem contains an allusion to an intimate moment Sītā and Rāma shared during their exile. It is not clear what the story behind it is, but the incident took place on the bank of the Mandākinī and involved a *tilaka*. Perhaps Sītā's *tilaka* had gotten wiped off and Rāma lovingly made her a new one;[31] the verse seems to say they rubbed their faces together. Or perhaps in lovemaking, her *tilaka* rubbed off on his chest.[32] This is the kind of secret (*rahasya*) that the Rāma-Rasikas are fond of. Sītā tells the monkey about it so that Rāma will know she has really been found, as no one but Sītā and Rāma know of the incident. Again, she feels self-conscious about telling this detail of human love to a monkey. But she also envies him, as he shortly will see Rāma, whom she herself longs so much to behold. The bittersweetness of remembering adds an element of poignancy, something cultivated in the Rāma-Rasika view of things.

RĀMA'S RESPONSE

Hanumān perceives the essence of Sītā's meaning and delivers the message. In his military communiqué (*vijñapti*), he urges Rāma to act quickly: *vega* (quickly!) is repeated thrice in the first three lines of the song (RCM 22) and comes back in the refrain again and again. In the fifth line, he reveals why: Sītā's tears will cause a much bigger ocean to flow, much harder to cross than the mere "watering hole" (*pau*) they now have to deal with. The Lord, himself an ocean (of mercy), should surely be able to appreciate this time-sensitive information. He has to stem the flood before it gets out of hand. Thus, even in the military planning, Sītā's tears and the love of the divine pair are what drive the story, decidedly a Rāma-Rasika approach.

After he receives the message, it is Rāma's turn to cross the ocean, and again Nāgarīdās chooses a Sūr poem:

> Rāma, the gracious one, descends to the ocean shore.
> In an outburst of anger, the darling of the Raghu race acts counter to his nature.
> Mountains on ocean, sky on mountains; clouds—in the shape of monkeys—
> Rumble and shout as they tear things apart, fire burning like lightning.
> The waters surge—the rivers cannot contain them and currents run backward.
> The Lord of the Raghus towers as the ocean cowers like a husband sending his wife back to her father's house.
> The army's bridge carves out a path in the sky, spewing all water creatures up into the air.
> Through Sītā's good influence (*saguna*), auspiciousness returns, as the Lord alights at the other side of the ocean.
>
> (RCM 23)

This poem foregrounds Rāma's anger when the ocean is not cooperative in helping him across to his Sītā. This moment in the epic has been relatively neglected, perhaps because of Rāma's uncharacteristic anger, which is here described as "behavior contrary to his nature" (*viparīta vyauhāra*). Indeed, Rāma's true nature is generous and forgiving (*udāra*). Was Nāgarīdās here identifying with his mythological role model? After all, he was a religious man, a devout Krishna *bhakta*, provoked against his nature to violently try and oust his brother. At the very moment he was composing his *Rāmāyaṇa*, he saw himself forced into an alliance with the rapacious Marathas to reach his objective. He must have been frustrated by the prolonged negotiations, just as Rāma was when the ocean failed to respond to his polite entreaties.

Perhaps this is another moment in the retelling where Nāgarīdās was coping with his existential situation, crying out in anger like his Rāma.

The image used to express this reversal of nature is a natural calamity: Rāma angrily causes the ocean to surge, so the rivers back up and streams flow backward. In addition, the poet compares Raghupati's attitude toward the ocean with that of a husband sending his wife (*patnī*) back to her maternal home (*pyausāra*). This can be seen as an instance of foreshadowing: in many versions of the story, Rāma later does just that, speak harsh words to Sītā and send her away, if not exactly to return to her parental home. Nāgarīdās does not tell the story of Sītā's exile, though. Like Tulsīdās he ends with the return to Ayodhya, ignoring the dramatic events of the last book (*Uttara-kāṇḍ*).

In Nāgarīdās's redaction, even this poem where Rāma takes on his frightening form (*raudra-rūpa*) ends on a happy note, with everything restored to auspiciousness thanks to Sītā's interference. The poem as preserved in Sūr's collected poems (*Sūr-sāgar*) ends differently. It adds a couple of lines that continue the image of Rāma as groom, but then it seems to be Lanka who is the bride, and the bridal imagery is equated with violent images: abundant rain, but of spears; auspicious rivers, but of blood; and the *tilaka* that the groom traces on the bride's forehead is the bridge of the invaders. So the poem's ending is more ominous in the original than in Nāgarīdās's redaction. In both cases, the poet has packed a lot of drama into this short poem, but Nāgarīdās has made sure to redact it such that by the end, all reverts to auspiciousness.

DENOUEMENTS

Working up to the climax of the battle in Lanka, Nāgarīdās selected again a series of *Sūr-sāgar* poems. The first one gives voice to a woman's perspective: Mandodarī's plea to Rāvaṇa to change his mind and return Sītā while he still can (RCM 24). The demon's wife tries to convince him that Rāma poses a serious threat, and in the last line, indeed, Rāma appears at their doorstep with his tumultuous army of monkeys. As she appeals to her husband by citing Rāma's famous forgiveness, the poem turns into a eulogy of Rāma, identifying him as Vishnu and describing his wondrous deeds. Maybe this was not the most tactful way to get through to her husband, but Mandodarī's speech surely was dear to the hearts of the Rāma-Rasikas.

The next poem, again by Sūrdās, pictures Rāvaṇa's defiance when Aṅgada arrives as a messenger from Rāma (RCM 25).[33] This incident appeals to heroic sentiments: the monkey taunts and is in turn ridiculed, but his bravado humiliates Rāvaṇa in his own mighty court. The dialogue is lively, full of taunts and threats. Rāvaṇa even takes an oath by Shiva to send all those misguided monkey-allies of Rāma to monkey heaven. The poem mixes the main heroic sentiment with amazement (*adbhūta*) and comedy (*hāsya*) as the monkey snatches the crown from Rāvaṇa's head, just before flying back unscathed to Rāma's camp, leaving a furious Rāvaṇa foaming. Perhaps Nāgarīdās appreciated this poem as a fond fantasy of getting back at his own enemies in his helplessness.

Next, it is again Rāma's turn to be angry, and he takes a vow to kill all the demons with just one arrow (RCM 26). Since they are Shiva worshippers, they will be dispatched to Shiva's heaven. Like Rāma's one arrow, Nāgarīdās selects just one *pada* to dispatch with the demon and his army:

> Today Rāma's anger flared on the battlefield.
> The gods in their chariots, Brahmā in front, were watching the fight
> . . . .
> The ocean becomes turbulent, Śeṣa's heads tremble, the wind's
> breath ceases.
> Indra laughs, Shiva smiles, though in pain, as he knows his promise will
> be broken.[34]
> Broken lie flags, banners, parasols, chariots, bows, discs, helmets.
> Brave heroes keep fighting, even with their arms severed, like fire burning
> trees without branches.
> Arrows like rays shining through thick clouds, spread to all corners of
> the sky.
> It seems the end of the world is nigh: six suns have risen on both sides.
> Fountains of blood shoot up to the sky, as elephants and horses
> are beheaded.
> The city looks ablaze in a fire, as if ignited from a blade of straw in house
> after house.
> Headless warriors collapse, suddenly overcome with fear, and are jolted off
> their horses.
> Jackals roam around, dragging off body parts, gleaning the field. In a flash,
> they run off with heroes' heads.
> The Lord of the Raghus' anger has become a blazing fire, fanned by
> Sītā's sighs.
> Rāvaṇa, his whole family and all other heroes steadfast on the battlefield,
> like a dense wood of bamboo—

> All reduced to ashes in an instant, like worn cloth consumed by a flame.
> In a flash, Sūrdās's Lord, by the power of his muscular arm, turned them into worm-infested corpses.
>
> (RCM 27)

This is a song of triumph, stressing the utter annihilation of the demons. Its sentiments include *vibhatsa*, or "disgust," in its graphic description of the battle's gory aspects, the battlefield, with its corpses strewn about and jackals carrying off the carrion. To some extent such descriptions are formulaic, but possibly Nāgarīdās was guided in his choice by the slaughter he witnessed all around him in the wake of the Marathas crushing the Rohillas. Perhaps this confrontation with the gory side of battle and war had started to turn him away from his war-plans.

Nāgarīdās then moves to the reunion of Sītā and Rāma, which he describes in his own words as an occasion of joy:

> The people's joy reaches a climax today.
> Moon-faced Sītā is on her way to meet the spotless Moon of the Raghu race.
> Conch shells and drums resound, the sound of auspicious songs fills the air.
> Vibhīṣaṇa and Hanumān in front, the chamberlains, all devotees,
> They all come running, overjoyed as they hear the tumult.
> The mighty army of monkeys and bears surges forward for *darshana*.
> In front are the rod-carriers striking blows when their way is obstructed.
> Then from the Lord came the command in front of all: "Hanumān, bring them to a halt."
> Sītā then left the palanquin and walked as she had been ordered.
> She looked like lightning flashing among the clouds of Rāma's army.
> Sand flew up and filled the sky as armies with many heroes thronged together.
> Nāgardās: such is the joy of Jānakī and Raghunātha's reunion.
>
> (RCM 28)

Remarkably, there is no hint of a trial by fire (Agni-parīkṣā), unless one were to read the comparison of Sītā with lightning that way, but that would be far-fetched. Sītā's dismounting from her palanquin is seen not as humiliating but, rather, as a joyous occasion of *darshana* for the army. The refrain of this poem, indeed, stresses bliss: "The people's joy reaches a climax today" (*bāṛhyo āju lokānanda*). Nāgarīdās has in this poem of his own making redacted the sorrow and tension out of this delicate moment of reunion.

This omission of Sītā's fire ordeal elicits the question of the stretchability of the story. When does a *Rāmāyaṇa* cease to be a *Rāmāyaṇa*? When does Sītā stop being Sītā? Can she still be Sītā if she does not prove her loyalty by undergoing the trial by fire? Can a retelling that thus violates "the narrative grammar" of the story still be called *Rāmāyaṇa*?[35] The answer is an affirmative, and it is not just modern versions that thus deviate from what is perceived to be the traditional script. Nāgarīdās's work provides an eighteenth-century example.

To return to the action in Nāgarīdās's version of the Rāma story, next Hanumān takes another leap ahead, informing Guha and Bharata of Rāma's impending arrival back home. Nāgarīdās himself composed this poem, which stresses Bharata's joyful reaction (RCM 29). Describing Bharata's happy anticipation upon seeing his brother again soon, Nāgarīdās may have thought that perhaps his brother might have a change of heart and accord him such a reception. The poem stops there with this happy anticipation. Nāgarīdās refrained from depicting the actual embrace of the two brothers, skipping the iconic climax of the Rām-līlā episode of *Bharat-milāp* (Reunion with Bharata).[36]

For the grand finale, Nāgarīdās again chooses a Sūr poem, this one about the joys of the home-coming from the perspective of Rāma's subjects:

> "Look, there comes the new king, Rāma!
> From afar, it looks like a second moon." The people of the city point out the chariot in the sky.
> The mighty hero becomes visible with Sītā at his side. As they look down, a wave of bliss surges up.
> In front of them is the army of monkeys with its heroes, propelled by the wind like clouds in the sky.
> Near the city he alights. Knowing the lay of the land by heart, he relates the story of the country of his birth.
> "These are my people, this is my retinue, my dear ones," he himself explains to each monkey.
> "This is Vaśiṣṭha, our family priest: touch his feet," so he instructs his friends.
> "These, Svāmī, are Sugrīva and Vibhīṣaṇa, who are dearer to me than even Bharata."
> "Who could have known what happened to Daśaratha's son who had gone to the forest?" They are speechless.

Then and there, the praise of all builds beyond all bounds. As they describe
his beauty, their hearts are joined with his.
"He killed the enemy for the sake of the gods, and all heroes (Sūr) receive
joy and wealth from him alone."
With that in mind, the Ocean of Grace in his compassion enters the city, as
he sings his people's praise.

(RCM 30)

We hear Rāma enthusiastically introduce his people to the monkeys, notably mentioning that Sugrīva and Vibhīṣaṇa please him more than even Bharata. Does this hint at an estrangement between the otherwise exemplary brothers? Did Nāgarīdās select this line because it projects some of the bad blood between himself and his brother onto the divine brothers? But then, in the last line of the song, the roles are reversed: we have Rāma singing the praises of his people, rather than the other way around. Finally, the apotheosis of the narrative has to be a complete resolution of all dramatic tension in a tableau fit for *darshana*. Nāgarīdās describes in his own words Rāma's joyous reentry into Ayodhya (RCM 31). Fittingly, the work ends with a song full of auspicious omens and rites.

By way of envoi, Nāgarīdās invites the audience to share in the bliss. He includes the traditional "fruit of recitation" (*phala-śruti*) in the verse specifying the awards that will accrue. The very last *Dohā* inscribes the story in his own life circumstances, as he gives date and place of composition.

In sum, two trends dominate Nāgarīdās's retelling. One is the Rāma-Rasika interpretation of the story, foregrounding Rāma and Sītā's relationship and their feelings. In general, the interest is not in plot development but in cherishing feelings of all types of love for Rāma, whether conjugal, parental, devotional, or fraternal. This feeds into the second impulse, that Nāgarīdās dwelled on those incidents of Rāma's life that were mimicked in own life situation, foregrounding emotions like love and rivalry between brothers, anger in war, and disgust on the battlefield. Possibly, he experienced these feelings in his campaigns with the Marathas. Perhaps he also brought real-life experience to the descriptions of the fraught relationship with the brother-rival for the throne. While he did not dwell on the rivalry for the throne itself, Nāgarīdās fondly described the divine brothers' youthful rivalry in polo and Bharata's joy upon hearing news of Rāma's adventures and, most of all, the prospect of receiving his brother back home. Nāgarīdās may have been working through the *Rāmāyaṇa* story in a very personal way.

THERAPEUTIC READING

There is evidence elsewhere in his work that shows that Sāvant Singh was working his way through his personal crisis as he wrote his version of the *Rāmāyaṇa* on the road in exile. He was of two minds about whether to regain his throne by military means or to retire peacefully to Braj to pursue his spiritual interests. War or peace? Even though he succeeded in gaining allies, he had his doubts. He wrote a series of *Dohā*s in which he wryly reported on his position negotiating with the Marathas in Kumaon. They are not dated, but two refer to Kumaon, one to the Kauśikī River, and one to the "Deccanis." From these few verses it is clear that he had no illusions about the Marathas after dealing with them up close. He commented on their shamelessness in looting and negotiating, ironically recommending their uninhibited approach as the one to take toward God. Do not hold back, he advised, when it comes to prayer and devotion, just like the Marathas do not hold back when on military campaign:

> Forget about shame, as you praise the Lord. Stop making sense!
> Just as in the campaign of Kumaon: it is just plain looting.
> Those who were shy in *bhajana*, who held back,
> Should join the Deccanis in this world, and learn from their zeal
> in plundering.
> In the strong stream of illusion, it is hard to settle one's mind.
> As in the middle of the river Kauśikī: head under, feet above.
> Everyone is conscribed up to Kumaon, proud with Rāma's name.
> Obsessing about honor, I lost all honor! If I had let go of honor, I would
> have remained honorable.
>
> (*Chūṭak-dohā* 38–41)[37]

In these lines, we glimpse Sāvant Singh's political decision making in process. Because of the reference to Rāma in the last *Dohā*, it seems he made connections with the *Rāmāyaṇa* story that he was working on at the time. Did his working through the epic direct him toward a peaceful resolution? Insisting on one's rights and honor could lead to the opposite result, losing even that. Enlisting the Marathas, even to fight a rightful cause, was not an uplifting experience.

Sāvant Singh did not draw away from politics right away. Perhaps once set in motion, the political intrigue had to be carried out, even though Sāvant Singh became increasingly weary of his own allies. After his return from

Kumaon, Sāvant Singh, though reluctantly, still went to Delhi "swept up by the affairs of the kingdom," presumably to try and find support there for his cause (TĀ 68). He wrote what seem to be his musings on the topic in three folios dated 1752 (1808 VS, Phālgun *badi* 14, *ravivāra*) with stray verse, written sloppily, perhaps scribbled down while on the road. They may well express his quandary at that moment:

> Who else would know, but Shyāma who dwells within?
> Like talk about a poisonous snake, would it please Rāma?
> The saints spoke the truth, "You will be ashamed in front of Govinda,
> If you spend today like yesterday, enamored with royal status."
> If I fall at the feet of the emperor of Delhi and the Marathas,
> The river Kauśikī would boil over in the pretty valley of Kumaon's range.[38]

These lines are somewhat cryptic, but it is clear that Sāvant Singh is expressing his reservations about the allies he was so busy rounding up. Here, too, he makes a connection with Rāma, possibly with reference to his recent *Rāmāyaṇa* compilation.

Eventually, Nāgarīdās settled in Braj and focused uninterruptedly on a year's worth of festivals, celebrated in the "calendar" section of his pilgrimage account. After the trip to Delhi, he had enough of political maneuvering and left it to his son to take part in the Maratha campaigns in Rajasthan, while he himself retired to Braj. He also articulated the dilemma in which he found himself elsewhere in his contemporary poetry. The same manuscript of 1752 features a poem that is also included in the edited volumes under *Stray Verses* (Chūṭak-kavitta):

> "*Bhakti* and *jakta* (worldliness) do not mix," this proverb says it plainly.
> *Jakta* states one thing, and *bhakta*s sing a different tune.
> The gulf between *jakta* and *bhakti* is the Lord's purposeful doing.
> If you follow the world's demands, *bhakti* cannot touch your heart.
> You have to give up the joy of Krishna *bhakti*, to truly please the world.
> Nāgariyā says: with this kind of *bhakti* you are sure to end up sorry.
> (*Chūṭak-kavitta* 106)[39]

The poignancy of the choice between worldly pursuits and religious peace is palpable here. We have precise dates for how he worked through this quandary (*asamaṃjasu*) of conflicting duties also in another work, *The Desire for Vrindavan Fulfilled* (*Vṛndāban-abhilāṣ-pūran-pad-prabandh*; 50.1).

This work was written in 1752, the very year Sāvant Singh returned to Braj to stay. It is divided into two parts: the main tenor of the first is disgust with worldly affairs and longing for spiritual Vrindavan, and the second part describes the joy upon reaching Braj. A manuscript of this work gives the month in which the first part was finished as Āsāṛh, and at the end, after the second part, the month Bhādon is given.[40] This provides us with a very precise window of months, between Āsāṛh (June–July) and Bhādon (August–September) 1752, when Nāgarīdās made his decision and retired to Braj. Some of the songs in the first part seem to refer to his experience with the Marathas. Thus:

If only I had two bodies!
Neither would I tell anyone what to do, nor would anyone tell me!
One body'd stay with the godless, and live in many countries abroad,
Suffer all kinds of sorrow in a world bereft of devotion.
My other body'd revel in good company and enjoy true bliss to the full,
Live in Braj and see life's purpose achieved. Yes, Braj is the true life.
I have no two bodies, I can't do both and life keeps fleeting away.
Nāgarīdās: Now tell me, how to put to use this one body of mine?
(VAPPP 11; *Chūṭak-pad* 59)[41]

In the second part of the work, he finds a solution out of the quandary:

I have reaped both types of harvest!
I sinned, so I roamed from land to land, with only a sinner for friend.
No joy of sharing devotion, not a festival for God in sight.
For a trifling desire I dwelt with the wicked. My misguided greed led others astray.
Now I have settled in Vrindavan and Barsana. O joy! I must have done something good (*puṇya*)!
What treasure of bliss! Loyal Brajvasis embraced me and made me their own.
Showed me in full the passion plays unheard of elsewhere.
Shyāmā and Shyāma graciously granted their servant Nāgar his wish.
(VAPPP 39; *Chūṭak-pad* 108)[42]

This is a rare case where there are fairly precise dates for individual poems. We thus are afforded a glimpse into the poet's circumstances. We can see him worry about reconciling his worldly "duty" to recover his throne (if only for his son), with his desire for spiritual fulfillment by dwelling in Braj. Maybe the "something good" he did was his working through the *Rāmāyaṇa* story. Perhaps he mobilized the myth for his own personal healing.

MOBILIZING MYTH FOR HEALING

As we read through Nāgarīdās's work, we were reading scripture with him, over his shoulder. We could see him make sense of his own reading/listening experiences of the *Rāmāyaṇa*, as he created his own version. To understand this phenomenon we could turn to theories of religious experience that foreground role-playing, such as role theory, developed by Hjalmar Sundén in Sweden from the late 1950s onward.[43] Given Nāgarīdās's interest in Rās-līlā, and his inspiring encounter with the Rās-līlā-staging *mahant* of Galta, this may be a productive way to proceed. Role theory is a psychotherapeutical technique according to which "myths . . . provide models and patterns of meaning that individuals may adopt for themselves by identifying with the roles in the myths." When individuals experience a similarity between their own situation and a particular myth, one can say "a restructuring phenomenon can occur in that person, so that the mythological reality also becomes reality for the individual in question."[44] This works as a way to cope with an existential crisis.

Such a "healing effect" of the *Rāmāyaṇa* story in particular is noted within the *Rāmāyaṇa* tradition itself. One instance is in Bhavabhūti's eighth-century play *Sequel to Rāma's Romance* (Uttara-rāma-carita), in which Rāma himself works through his own story, witnessing visual and theatrical re-creations of it, as he tries to come to terms with his own injustice in exiling Sītā. The play likens this healing process in Rāma, that is, his ability to find compassion for Sītā, with images of "ripening" or "cooking," and specifically the process of preparing medicines. Thus, at the opening of act 3, Rāma's emotional state of pain (*karuṇā rasa*) is likened to "a compress of healing herbs cooked in a clay oven (*pūṭa-pāka*)."[45] In other words, the ability of compassion or empathy comes after a maturation process, which involves fiery stages of suffering. Significantly, it is not until the Rāma story is theatrically performed within the play in the last act that the catharsis can come about with final reconciliation and reunion of the lovers.[46] When the play-within-the-play turns out to be reality itself, all broken pieces fall into place, and Rāma finally becomes himself again. As the play becomes "real," Rāma's self is healed and he can truly recognize his beloved. At this point comes the final benediction, and Rāma's hard-won mercy is mobilized for the audience's benefit.

Perhaps something similar is going on in Nāgarīdās's *Rāmāyaṇa*. At first the work may seem escapist because Nāgarīdās left out the parts about the brothers' rivalry for the throne. Yet instead, Nāgarīdās focused on passages depicting a positive fraternal relationship, most notably fond reminiscences of youthful rivalry in polo and the description of Bharata's emotional reaction upon the news of Rāma's return. Sāvant Singh thus combined nostalgia with a wistful anticipatory scenario of how his own brother might react upon his return. These passages reveal how the author was working through a relationship that had become strained. In between, there are also expressions of anger and frustration with uncooperative allies as well as disgust with war, perhaps in response to the campaign to ally with the Marathas.

Thus there may be reason to speak of a therapeutic "working through scripture." Very little has been written about such religious reading for Hinduism, although there is a whole branch of bibliotherapy (in the sense of using biblical scripture in psychotherapy) for Christianity, mostly prescriptive as part of pastoral care.[47] This aspect of scripture has been little studied within a historical perspective, perhaps due to lack of sources for reader response. For Nāgarīdās, though, there are supporting materials to document his reading's effect. We also have evidence for a similar phenomenon for his stepmother, the queen Braj Kuṃvarī Bāṅkāvatī. She was a poetess in her own right, writing under the pen name Brajdāsī. In the translation she authored of the *Bhāgavata-purāṇa*, called *Brajdāsī-bhāgavat*, she mentions explicitly that she wrote the work to "relieve the civil war in the kingdom."[48] The dates of the work, which was started in 1749 (1806 VS) and finished in 1755 (1812 VS), coincide exactly with the fraternal war. Though perhaps her "real" power to interfere was limited, living as she did at the court of the usurping brother, she managed to carve out for herself a niche where she could take agency of her own through this socially acceptable activity of "working through scripture." Possibly, this afforded her the opportunity to cope with what must have been very difficult circumstances for her personally. And indeed, there was a happy ending to the story.

The case of Nāgarīdās thus alerts us to the therapeutic potential of close scripture reading. Reconstruction of the historical circumstances, and synoptically reading his *Rāmāyaṇa* with his other works, has let us see the poet at work. We get an inkling of some of the soul-searching that may have gone on as he, like many before him, found personal meaning in a sacred text.

KISHANGARHI *RĀMĀYAṆA* PAINTINGS

Most of the famous Kishangarhi paintings feature Rādhā and Krishna, but there are some exquisite ones that depict scenes from *Rāmāyaṇa*. Few had been published until recently, when the publishing house Diane de Selliers in Paris released an illustrated seven-volume *Rāmāyaṇa*, which includes several previously unpublished Kishangarhi Rāma paintings that postdate the middle of the eighteenth century.[49] Contrary to expectation, the Kishangarhi samples do not fit Nāgarīdās's *Garland of Rāma's Romance* in the same way some of the Krishna paintings illustrate his works. In fact, most of the paintings depict scenes that Nāgarīdās had not included in his retelling. While puzzling at first, it makes sense given the estimated dates. They all date from after Sāvant Singh was exiled, when he had presumably lost the means to sponsor paintings. Though it is possible that some of his favorite painters continued to work with him for a while, it must have been difficult to maintain an atelier while constantly on the road.[50] Thus it is more likely that the *Rāmāyaṇa* paintings were actually sponsored not by Sāvant Singh, to illustrate *Garland of Rāma's Romance*, but by his usurper-brother or that brother's son (Sāvant Singh's nephew). Indeed, several of the paintings are estimated to date from after Sāvant Singh's death.

Two images preserved in unspecified private collections seem ready-made for a Rāma-Rasika audience, as they portray Rāma and Sītā engaged in dreamlike pastimes, fitting for an eternal Ayodhya or the idyllic forest retreat of Pañcāvatī. One painting, estimated to date from 1760, depicts Rāma and Sītā relaxing together, with a vina in the foreground.[51] Sītā is pensively looking at what may be a board with game pieces, as if she is considering her next move; or the pair may be testing perfumes, as the object between them could also be a platter with small perfume bottles.[52] The other painting is an idyllic depiction of Rāma and Sītā in the wilderness against the backdrop of a waterfall.[53] Standing next to a tree teeming with parrots, Sītā is feeding peacocks, while Rāma, seated nearby, looks on smilingly, with practically the same facial expression as in the other painting. Likely both paintings are part of a series, as the way the characters are portrayed is very similar, in attire and slender physique, as well as facial features with curved brows, elongated eyes, and long noses and elegant hairstyle. All of these are the hallmark of Nihālcand's style, or perhaps somewhat more stylized, toward that of Sītārām, his son. I am inclined to speculate that these paintings may have Sāvant Singh's inspiration behind them, even though there are no corresponding poems in *Garland of Rāma's Romance*.

For the *Bāla-kāṇḍ*, there is also a possibly related image of Rāma challenged by Paraśurāma (Jāmadagnya) from a private collection.[54] Perhaps one could relate that to the one line of *Garland of Rāma's Romance*, in which Mandodarī reminds Rāvaṇa of Rāma's great deeds, including his defying Paraśurāma (RCM 24). For the *Āraṇya-kāṇḍ*, there is a painting with very similar stylistic characteristics that depicts the two brothers with the demon Virādha at their feet and Sītā between them, watching on in amazement (lifting her index finger at her lips).[55] However, nowhere in *Garland of Rāma's Romance* is there even any allusion to the incident, so there is no connection with Nāgarīdās. If these paintings are from the same series, the link with Nāgarīdās is very tenuous.

Most of the other Kishangarhi *Rāmāyaṇa* paintings are very different and later. For the Āraṇya-kāṇḍa, an image from circa 1760 depicts a scene from Sītā and Rāma's stay at Pañcāvatī (with five trees in the background), featuring Lakshmana bringing an antelope he has shot before the seated Sītā and Rāma.[56] A painting in Mughal style, interpreted to be Sītā gently chiding her husband not to use violence, dates from 1750–75, as does one said to depict Rāma's response, though it is in a very different style.[57] The latter is similar to a painting dated circa 1820, set in a Sambhar-like landscape.[58] The same landscape is seen in the background of another painting depicting the death of Jaṭāyu in Rāma's lap, estimated to date to 1770–80.[59] A painting also from circa 1775 depicts Rāma's chasing the golden deer, while Rāvaṇa approaches Sītā in the form of an ascetic.[60] From circa 1800 is an unfinished drawing of Rāma and Lakshmana visiting Atri's hermitage and Sītā meeting Anasūya.[61] None of the incidents depicted in these paintings correlates with scenes described in Nāgarīdās's *Garland of Rāma's Romance*. They were likely produced at Sāvant Singh's brother's and nephew's courts.

There is one painting that depicts Rāma's welcome upon his return to Ayodhya by Bharata and a delegation of courtiers.[62] This painting is attributed to Sītārām and estimated to have been painted in 1780, thus well after Sāvant Singh's death. It shows the aerial chariot landing, with Rāma, Sītā, and Lakshmana carrying gifts in their hands, while an emaciated Bharata receives them, sandals (*pāḍuka*) in hand, accompanied by Śatrughna and several of Ayodhya's elders. While the actual *Bharat-milāp* is not featured in *Garland of Rāma's Romance*, Bharata's happy anticipation of the reunion is. Still, it fits better with the Vālmīki *Rāmāyaṇa* scenario, where Bharata is also described as emaciated.

These works were commissioned by the usurper, conceivably as a response to Nāgarīdās's religious reading of the *Rāmāyaṇa*, but then in visual expression. Perhaps Bahādur Singh also worked through the *Rāmāyaṇa* to come to terms with his deeds.[63] The last-mentioned picture with Bharata visibly marked by penance might then be interpreted to express some penitence on the usurper's part. In any case, the Rāma paintings do not appear in Kishangarh until the second half of the eighteenth century, not only after the composition of *Garland of Rāma's Romance* but also after the reconciliation, and in several cases only after Sāvant Singh's death. Even though at least some of the paintings appear to form a set, they do not represent illustrations of *Garland of Rāma's Romance*. However, they may represent a sequel (*uttara*), a response from the other party in the Kishangarhi succession strife.

CONCLUSION: A PERSONALIZED *RĀMĀYAṆA*

In Nāgarīdās's reworking of the Rāma story we see some traits to be expected from a Rādhā-Krishna *bhakta*: an emphasis on Rāma and Sītā's romance, in particular their falling in love, their wedding, and their feelings of *viraha* once separated. These elements fit also with the *rasika* approach within Rāma *bhakti*. There is internal evidence that suggests the inspiration for this text came from Hari Ācārya, the Rāma-Rasika abbot of Galta, near Jaipur, whom Nāgarīdās met and was inspired by, as his own words state (TĀ 8). Some of the Kishangarhi paintings may also be seen against such a Rāma-Rasika background.

A significant feature of Nāgarīdās's *Garland of Rāma's Romance* is the total omission of Sītā's Agni-parīkṣā. As Sāvant Singh was a Rajput of the landed aristocracy, one would have expected him to be preoccupied with issues of purity of lineage and keen to make Sītā, symbol of land, undergo the loyalty test. Yet he does not do so. One wonders whether his predilection for the "pastoral narrative" of Rādhā and Krishna has trumped here the "land narrative" of Sītā and Rāma.[64] That would mean that such narratives function irrespective of the social milieu of the author and his audience.

Nāgarīdās's foregrounding of the romantic relationship of the divine pair is in line with the general emphasis in his *Rāmāyaṇa* retelling on feelings rather than heroic feats. Some elements also have a *Sitz im Leben* and a personalized tone. In a self-censoring impulse, Nāgarīdās skips *karuṇā*, perhaps refusing to give in to self-pity. He focuses instead on joyful feelings, first and foremost filial and parental love, as he zooms in on the joys of childhood, the *bāla-līlā*, through birthday celebration, brotherly childhood exploits, adolescent polo games, and the love of Daśaratha, who has a hard time taking leave of his favorite sons as they leave on dangerous adventures. Correspondingly, Nāgarīdās selects a poem on the joy of the family upon receipt of the report of Rāma's exploits under his guru's tutelage. We may see here a more existential angle to the story, as Nāgarīdās, who had just lost his father and been usurped by his brother, must have identified keenly with the emotions of these scenes. Yet the tone is not bitter but, rather, tenderly loving.

Nāgarīdās includes other *rasa*s in his retelling. The feelings of wonder and amazement are pertinent in the passages where the boatman marvels at the power of Rāma's feet, where the audience looks on in amazement at Hanumān's giant leap, and where Aṅgada daringly defies Rāvaṇa. Heroic feelings (*vīra*) and anger (*krodha*) are actually downplayed, limited to a few poems, where Rāma's anger is expressed, first with the ocean and then with Rāvaṇa. In the latter poem, disgust (*vibhatsā*) takes over. Again, this may have existential roots in Sāvant Singh's witnessing the devastations of war all around him as he negotiated with the Marathas fighting the Rohillas.

Especially poignant are the poems upon Rāma's return to his homeland, where his mixed feelings at introducing his new allies to his old friends and relatives are palpable. Again, there is a personal element: Sāvant Singh found himself far away from home, trying to forge new allies. Whereas he swore off his "dry, barren" homeland with its "foolish, irreligious people" at the beginning of *The Pilgrim's Bliss* (TĀ 1), perhaps we see here a softening in this projection onto Rāma of his own feelings of anticipation at returning home in triumph.

The relative wealth of information we have on this *Rāmāyaṇa* can help us to contextualize other retellings. Speculation about authorial intent is always fraught; still, omissions and foregrounding of certain episodes may well tell us something about the author's personal predilections and his existential situation, if we are willing to listen. This idiosyncratic *Rāmāyaṇa* presents us with an opportunity to discover a hitherto little explored way of understanding the "many *Rāmāyaṇa*s" extant. Role theory reminds us that myths provide models and patterns that help people cope with personal crises. Reading a *Rāmāyaṇa* retelling against the background of a crisis in the author's life is recognized within the tradition itself. In the eighth-century Sanskrit dramaturg Bhavabhūti's *Sequel to Rāma's Romance*, Rāma himself finds healing in his own story. The South Indian *cāṭu* stories have it that Kampa<u>n</u>, the Tamil *Rāmāyaṇa* poet, brought a personal touch to his retelling of Daśaratha's death due to his grief at losing his beloved Rāma. At the time of his retelling, the poet himself had just lost his son Ampikāpati, and he composed an anguished verse on the topic.[65] Another *Rāmāyaṇa* that could fruitfully be read against a personal life story is that by the sixteenth-century Bengali poetess Candrāvatī. In her retelling, she focuses on Sītā's sufferings, and Sītā's abandonment may well have resonated with her because of her own experiences: some say she herself was abandoned by her childhood sweetheart on the day of their marriage.[66]

Nāgarīdās's *Rāmāyaṇa*, though, is not a newly composed retelling, but a mixture of compilation and creation. He uses verses of mostly Sūrdās and Tulsīdās to build his own version of the story. This brings us to a deeper understanding of "authorial voice."[67] *Garland of Rāma's Romance* conveys another aspect of the instability of the authorial voice in *bhakti* texts: something of a very close working through the text, a combination of reading and creating.

Nāgarīdās's mid-century works show that at the time he was working through the *Rāmāyaṇa* story, he felt a growing gap between his political aspirations that forced him to travel and pursue alliances, on the one hand, and inclinations to "retire" in his beloved Braj, on the other. He grew increasingly weary of warmongering. His engagement with the myth of Rāma took place exactly as he strove to enlist outsiders to intervene in the internal struggle for the succession of Rupnagar. In the hindsight of the twenty-first century, he might be thought of as seeking an alliance with Maratha "Hindus" who were fighting Rohilla "Muslims." However, there is no evidence that Nāgarīdās conceived of it that way. Rather, from his other poetry we can tell that he had second thoughts about the Maratha outsider-allies. From the irony in his *Dohās*, it appears he was well aware of the rapaciousness of the Marathas. Perhaps he started to foresee the disastrous consequences of allying himself with them to fight against his brother. At the same time, the mythic example of Rāma's chivalry seemed to soften his heart, allowing for fond reminiscences of childhood rivalries and imaginings of a welcome back home. All this seems indicative of a therapeutic effect of the reading/creation of the text. Perhaps what we witness in this early modern work is the postmodern phenomenon of the reader as the author of the text. Nāgarīdās certainly put a very personal, existential stamp on "his" *Rāmāyaṇa*.

As for whether Sāvant Singh had the story illustrated, the Kishangarhi *Rāmāyaṇa* paintings curiously depict nearly exclusively scenes that Nāgarīdās chose to omit from his retelling. They date from later in the eighteenth century and were unlikely to have been commissioned by him. Probably the patrons were his brother or nephew, the party who usurped his throne. Perhaps these paintings could be looked on as a sequel to *Garland of Rāma's Romance*. If Nāgarīdās worked through his dilemma via a religious reading-cum-interpretation of the story, his successors may have commissioned an independent visual *Rāmāyaṇa* for similar reasons. At least the *Bharat-milāp* painting lends itself to support such a thesis. The paintings, then, may represent a visual response (*uttara-pakṣa*) to the challenge (*pūrva-pakṣa*) of Nāgarīdās's creative reworking, which would make it an *Uttar-rām-carit* of sorts. Perhaps we have uncovered evidence of a dialogue in *Rāmāyaṇa bhāṣā*, in the idiom of the ever-relevant story of Rāma. More research on the paintings, as they become available for scholarly investigation, is needed to back up this surmise.

Conclusion

Pilgrimage, Hagiography, and Scripture

THE MAIN INTENT OF THIS BOOK IS TO BRING MOTION INTO THE somewhat static world of *bhakti* studies. This has been accomplished partly by bringing historical perspective to the devotional world, which is sometimes treated as other-worldly and unchanging. Certainly theology and philosophy are important, but even the most esoteric texts are authored by historical agents. Understanding their preoccupations, rivalries, and sympathies is essential to get the full picture. Together with historicizing, this book has worked to inject notions of circulation of people and ideas.

The book's second purpose is to contribute to understanding how the crises of the mid-eighteenth century at the "end of empire" were perceived at the time. In particular, how did vassal Rajputs experience the downfall of Mughal imperial power, and what motivated their decision making? It is commonly assumed that they thought in terms of Hindu opposition to a Muslim imperial formation or Muslim threats from outside. We have seen, however, that at least for the state of Kishangarh, such was not the case. The situation was much more complex. When the Afghan troops of Durrānī attacked in 1748, Kishangarh rallied to support the Mughal emperor, with whom it was on very good terms. However, in the same year the emperor and Kishangarh ruler Rāj Singh died, and Bahādur Singh saw his chance to usurp his elder brother's throne. First on the agenda for Sāvant Singh from then on was regaining his patrimonium. In seeking alliances, both brothers were concerned with finding a strong party to fight their cause, no matter the confessional conviction. They each turned to one of the rival Kacchvāhā princes of Jaipur, who were themselves embroiled in a fight for their throne, as well as to Mughal power brokers, and eventually to the Marathas. Sāvant Singh may also have sought support from warrior ascetics. There is no evidence that either brother conceived of these conflicts and alliances in religious terms; while Sāvant Singh composed a *Rāmāyaṇa* in the period, he did not mobilize the divine justification and demonization potential of the narrative for his own political ends. If anything, he regarded the Marathas as rapacious and irreligious. He ended up regretting his association with them, through which he regained only half his kingdom at huge cost. By then, Sāvant Singh, weary of the fighting, had already retired to Braj. A subtler use of religious thinking was at work. From contemporary evidence, we can reconstruct how, working through the *Rāmāyaṇa*, Sāvant Singh found his peace and retreated in Krishna's world. Forced exile turned into a retreat to a bucolic paradise. Some might call this escapism, others that he ended up coping with the crisis by opting out of politics. The decision did not come lightly, though. Religious paradigms, myth, hagiographical stories, and rituals connected with pilgrimage were mobilized in shaping his political agency.

LESSONS LEARNED FOR RELIGIOUS STUDIES

The Kishangarhi case study contributes insights to religious studies in three fields: pilgrimage, hagiography, and reworking of sacred scripture. First, Nāgarīdās's testimony illustrates vividly that while pilgrims may be in search of a transcendental realm, and stress that in their accounts, their journey happens in real time and place. Notably, the pursuit of pilgrimage sometimes combined with military goals. The case of Sāvant Singh can be amplified with that of other Rajput kings and the Marathas. Pilgrims' paths intersected with those of soldiers, and the former turned into the latter and vice versa. Because of its close location to Delhi, the center of Mughal power at the time, Braj was a popular side excursion on the way to or from the Mughal capital. Rajput kings in Mughal service saw no contradiction in paying their obeisance to Delhi's Mughal ruler and Braj's Krishna in turn. Places of pilgrimage change over time and undergo real estate booms, sometimes fueled by the less than holy activities going on around them. Braj's expansion in the course of the eighteenth century and the shift of its center to the area surrounding Barsana and Nandagaon was made possible by Jat success (some might say rapaciousness) in cleverly exploiting the military conflicts around them. This entailed also an expansion of rituals and festivals connected to the areas popularly frequented at the time. Nāgarīdās's account also shows how the pilgrimage center's rites and theatrical productions were designed to be participatory, allowing for pilgrims to become an "acting audience" to make the myths happen again, then and there. This may be key to understanding the salutary effect of pilgrimage at times of crisis. In participating in rites at the very spot where the myths are situated, pilgrims are transported into the myth itself. They can allow their lives to be hijacked by the mythical scenarios, which become "real life" for them, as the Holī rites of Barsana did for Nāgarīdās. This therapeutic value of pilgrimage was facilitated by rituals, festivals, and theatrical productions staged at places of pilgrimage that also were conduits for the transmission of devotional songs.

What does Nāgarīdās's case teach us about hagiography? Foregrounding circulation, we found that his hagiography is about the travels not just of holy men but, even more, of holy songs. Nāgarīdās's vignettes show how devotional songs circulated via pilgrims on their way to sacred centers, as well as the opposite: via holy men who visited nearby courts or went on promotion tours in rich "recruiting" areas. The pilgrimage center tended to be a somewhat more open forum for exchange than the restricted space of the court or residential temple. To some extent, the devotional songs traveled there less exclusively, across caste and class barriers. Still, the court temple also was a forum for transmission as devotees congregated to enjoy the *darshana* of the day and the corresponding music program and hummed the songs on the way back home, to be overheard by others. Some of the prime channels for such transmission were the ritual contexts of *bhajana* sessions, bathing rituals, festival rites, procession and circumambulation, and theatrical performances. Not all incidences of transmission were successful: sometimes the king forbade a song's performance other than in a sacred space (as in the case of Jayadeva's Aṣṭapadī), or a sectarian group excluded certain songs from being performed in its repertoire (such as Mīrā's songs in the Vallabha sect). Yet, overall, songs traveled. They did not remain exclusively in a Hindu milieu, as exemplified by the fakir who fell from a roof in ecstasy upon hearing Nāgarīdās's song. Nor were they even restricted to religious milieus, as when devotional songs were interpreted by courtesans (as in the story of Krishnadās Adhikārī). However uncomfortable, on occasion actors crossed from devotional to secular performance domains and vice versa. Perhaps we can speak of an early modern public sphere or ecumene. Even hagiographies that seem on the surface removed from historical vicissitudes may mobilize stories and songs for the purpose of criticizing political agendas. Nāgarīdās's hagiography, *Garland of Stories and Songs*, can be construed as a reaction to the Jaipur ruler Jai Singh II's politics of orthodoxy. In the history of the formation of "Hinduism," it represents a temporary break as the latter increasingly defines itself as orthodox Vaishnavism, a trend at work in Jai Singh II's conferences at the beginning of the eighteenth century and later taken up by Bhāratendu Hariścandra in the nineteenth. Nāgarīdās's hagiography retrieves a moment where heterodoxy was, if not celebrated, at least possible, as borne out by the antinomian stories most prominent in the long recension of the text. Eventually, though, the goal was to inspire devotion for God more than participation in religious debate or contestation against worldly powers, as perhaps the "public sphere" would require. In the end, the hagiography we read is a testimony to the transformative power of song. Miraculous potencies are ascribed to individual songs in performance, and central is the liberalizing effect of sacred utterance.

One additional insight gained from studying this hagiography is that singers composed not in isolation but in dialogue, sometimes rivalry, with one another. We saw many cases of intertextuality, with response in song, sometimes with reference to a specific real-life situation. The sectarian milieus were at times keen on promoting themselves by insisting on their orthodoxy, something that Jai Singh II encouraged. Yet on other occasions, that was not the case. There was both inter- and infra-sectarian rivalry at play, but Sāvant Singh was interested less in demarcation than in an ecumenical attitude with room for diversity of points of view. Possibly, his opening up of exclusive Vallabhan milieus to include others had a military motive. The Rāmānandīs, whom he included, had a military branch at Galta, one of the places Sāvant Singh visited on his pilgrimage. The Nimbārkans had a warrior contingent at the seat of Salemabad in the Kishangarhi domain. His rivalry with his brother who favored the Vallabhans may have played a role here.

Finally, as for the rewriting of scripture, we have been able to reconstruct in some detail the historical background for a *Rāmāyaṇa* retelling. The text in this case study provided testimony about how the act of reading involves an act of composition: Nāgarīdās read and collected Rāma devotional poems, spinning his own "thread" from them and filling out the "garland" with poems of his own. It is rare to get such an insight into an early modern author's mind and to be able to understand his personal engagement with scripture. In reading this work of his together with other poems of the period, we can argue that his reading of scripture, too, could be deemed "therapeutic," that is, he worked through his own trauma via scriptural passages that helped the healing process. This function of scriptural reading has been little studied, but it could be a fruitful direction for further research. Rather than escapism, religion can be marshaled for coping with real-life crises.

SPECIFICS: THE YOGI IN THE PICTURE

What have we learned about the yogi-prince in the idyllic Kishangarhi painting we set out with? The prevalent picture in art history is that Sāvant Singh was not inclined toward politics and simply retired to Vrindavan.

Autobiographical parts of his works describe the journey behind his retirement, how he went about recasting his life during the crisis period following his father's death and after losing the throne.

In *The Pilgrim's Bliss* his search for political and military support became transformed as a narrative on a pilgrim's progress. Nāgarīdās cast his peregrinations in exile as an account of bliss, mainly the joy of visiting Braj, interrupted only by the distractions of "business" intruding on the eternal bliss of Vrindavan. God's play, Krishna's *līlā* as enacted in Braj, became the real world for him, whereas the efforts to gather troops and build alliances paled, even as he felt compelled to keep pursuing them for his son's sake. *The Pilgrim's Bliss* is an extended report on Nāgarīdās's attempts to write himself into Krishna's world. In the paintings Nāgarīdās sponsored during happier days, Krishna is depicted enjoying boating (*naukā-vihāra*) like the prince on Lake Gundalao. Now, we see Nāgarīdās going boating in Krishna's realm, on the Yamunā. Whereas he once tried to draw Braj into his courtly world, now he and his courtiers are drawn into Braj. The *bhakta*s who used to visit his court in Rupnagar, and partake in his soirées, now invite him to their huts in Radhakund to partake in all-night *kīrtana* sessions. Not that he lived in poverty; the appellation "yogi" is not to be taken too literally. He settled in the trendy places that were part of the contemporary Jat-driven real estate boom. The areas of Barsana and Nandagaon were happening places, where nobles, successful businesspeople, mercenaries, and shrewd political agents all built residences and came to enjoy religious spectacle. Like so many others, Sāvant Singh was drawn into Krishna's world, but he brought his own world to the area at the same time. He inscribed his own life into myth by participating in the rites enacting Krishna and Rādhā's adventures. The rites of Braj, especially the seasonal ones, were well designed for such participation. Nāgarīdās describes the riotous climax in the carnivalesque Holī celebrations of Barsana and Nandagaon as the moment when he had truly arrived in Braj.

Sāvant Singh used another technique to propel himself into the divine *līlā:* the power of the devotional song. This is celebrated in his *Garland of Stories and Songs*. The theme was anticipated in *The Pilgrim's Bliss*, in the account of his reception in Vrindavan upon first arrival. No one cared about another worldly king, but when the local holy men heard that the *bhakta*-poet Nāgarīdās had arrived, they ran up to welcome him. Sāvant Singh, prince of Kishangarh, was just another visitor, but Nāgarīdās, the composer of songs, elicited an enthusiastic response. The incident celebrates the success of Nāgarīdās's songs among Braj residents, foregrounding his identity as a devotee and poet over that as a royal. While the bulk of *Garland of Stories and Songs* is about the songs of others, it also features Nāgarīdās's songs. They became popular in the pilgrimage center of Braj, where a Rajput amir circumambulating Govardhan sang one that was received favorably in the divine and human world. Back home in Rupnagar, too, his poetry was a success: it produced such ecstasy that a fakir fell from the roof of a *havelī* singing it, and a newly composed song circulated instantly in the divine world, as proved by Muralīdās's immediate access to it, even before its "publication." Nāgarīdās thus incorporated his own songs in the circulation and reception history of those of famous and well-established singers of the previous centuries. As his identity as a poet became more important, he inscribed his own songs among those of the saints of the times. The hagiography gives us also insight into what motivated Nāgarīdās, who inspired him, and what songs in particular struck him and his contemporaries as powerful. Visually, these sources of inspiration are reinforced in the Kishangarhi paintings of saints, most famously Caitanya, Svāmī Haridās, and Mīrābāī. Amid all the sectarian rivalry of the time, at courts as well as in the temple towns, Nāgarīdās's view is remarkably devoid of sectarianism. In contrast to the chauvinist accounts that most hagiographers give, his is ecumenical in spirit. I have argued that *Garland of Stories and Songs* can be seen as a vernacular follow-up of the debates Jai Singh II had started earlier in the century. Whereas those debates led to bitter sectarian rivalry and the production of Sanskrit texts to assert orthodox antecedents, Nāgarīdās's work did the opposite: it celebrated vernacular songs and composers of multiple sectarian affiliations. It stresses the futility of the very markers of *varṇāśrama-dharma*, such as rules of commensuality that Jai Singh had been so concerned to enforce. Socially, too, Nāgarīdās associated with those opposed to Jai Singh's reforms. Thus even in his "retirement," Sāvant Singh was far from retiring. He did not produce his hagiography in isolation, but partook in the important politico-religious debates of the time.

Finally, in *Garland of Rāma's Romance* we have a unique document of a poet using the story of Rāma to work through the *Rāmāyaṇa*-like drama of his personal life. His brother usurped his throne at the very moment that Sāvant Singh was called to Delhi to participate in fighting off the outside invader, one of the Rāvaṇas of his times, Durrānī. Real life was thrown off course and overtaken by a mythical scenario. Rather than compose a *Rāmāyaṇa* in response, to use for propaganda and foreground the divinization/demonization scenario, or follow the ideal scenario and chivalrously step out of his brother's way as his mythological counterpart, Rāma did, he did neither. Instead, he strenuously pursued his duty to regain his kingdom, if only for his son. He initially tried to do so with the help of Īśvari Singh of Jaipur, but he himself was embroiled in a succession war. Perhaps he sought Rāmānandī help, as he visited Galta, but the farewell gift he received from the Rāma-Rasika-inclined abbot was not an army of Nāgās, but the gift of meditation on Rāma. He turned to Delhi power brokers, but there, too, all were preoccupied with their own fights. It was eventually Maratha help that allowed his son to regain half the kingdom and to rule from Rupnagar. Documents indicate that while he was negotiating the terms of the agreement with the Marathas in Kumaon, where they were embroiled in the Rohilla war, Sāvant Singh became increasingly disgusted with the political goals he was pursuing at such cost. Meanwhile, the Galta abbot's farewell gift bore fruit as Sāvant Singh worked through the *Rāmāyaṇa* story. His version was not one that righteously asserted Rāma's rights or harped on the theme of brothers betraying brothers. He consciously left out all the stories of pathos, or *karuṇā*. Instead, he nostalgically reminisced about brothers' polo games where Rāma chivalrously accepted his loss and about a fond father, Daśaratha, who was devastated upon seeing his favorite son depart on a campaign. Conforming to Rāma-Rasika predilections, like those of the contemporary Galta abbot, he focused on Rāma and Sītā's love and her suffering in separation from him, or *viraha*. Their reunion was a joyful one, no trial by fire needed. The apotheosis was the joyful return to the homeland and emotional reception by the brother. Perhaps this was wishful thinking. Nāgarīdās was torn between his royal duty and his lifelong desire to settle in Braj. What prevailed was the spiritual call of Krishna's world of Vrindavan. The precise date was the rainy season of 1752, after four years of roaming around. In the end, via his therapeutic deep reading and re-creation of the Rāma story, Sāvant Singh seems to have found his way out of his political troubles and into the world of Rādhā and Krishna. What we have witnessed is an early modern narration of a transformed self, all cast in the language of mythology.

Methodologically, this undercurrent in the devotional texts was identified through puzzling together the historical circumstances combined with a synoptic reading of Nāgarīdās's work. In the process, we have also gained insight in the world of personal experience that may underlie the seemingly traditional paintings. There is more to mythological depictions than the mythological story.

Through the detour via Rāma mythology, we have come full circle here, to the painting we began with: Sāvant Singh retiring in Krishna's land, like

Krishna himself, portrayed in the painting as the yogi of Braj. In reliving Rāma's forest exile (*banavāsa*), he has finally earned his place in Krishna's eternal forest of Vṛndāvana. As he says in one of his late songs, which remains a favorite in the Rās-līlās staged today:[1]

> Everything has worked out in the end!
> Śrī Kuñjabihārini and Śrī Kuñjabihārī took mercy on me:
> They've kept me safe in their Vrindavan, a place of splendid beauty.
> Constant bliss in their eternal play, to delight in with fellow-*rasikas*.
> A realm apart from the world, devoid of strife and sorrow.
> Let Nāgarīdās live out his life, forever devoted to Braj.
>
> (*Ban-jan-praśaṃśak* 62)[2]

Notes

Introduction

1 By this *mise-en-scène* for the book, I do not mean to subscribe to the "Dark Ages" interpretation of the eighteenth century. My contribution rather takes the form of a further exploration of the cultural efflorescence of the late Mughal empire. For the political situation at the time, see, e.g., Bayly (1983: 35–73). For a lucid overview of the scholarly approaches, see Alavi (2002: 1–56), and for explanations of changing scholarly views, see Barnett (2002: 11–22) and Marshall (2003).

2 The most important book-length English-language publications on Kishangarhi art to date remain Dickinson and Khandalavala (1959) and Mathur (2000). The brilliant 1995 dissertation of art historian Navina Najat Haidar, of the Metropolitan Museum of Art, has unfortunately remained unpublished

3 As borne out by comparing the portraits of the crown prince with contemporaneous depictions of Krishna (compare Randhawa and Randhawa [1980, plate 1 with plate 4] and Mathur [2000, plate 8 with plate 10]).

4 This theory was first advanced by the "discoverer" of Kishangarhi paintings, Eric Dickinson. It is widely repeated in the secondary literature, although it has been forcefully, though perhaps not fully convincingly, contested by the Kishangarhi scholar Faiyāz Alī Khān (1975).

5 Sāvant Singh included several of her poems in his anthologies, the earliest dated being his 1742 *Illumination of the Way to Recite Śrīmad Bhāgavata(-purāṇa)* (Śrīmad-Bhāgavat-pārāyaṇ-vidhi-prakāś; verses 7 and 25 [K. Gupta 1965, 2:413, 418–19]). See also Pauwels, forthcoming-b.

6 While it is not unusual for the heroes in paintings to take on the features of the patron, this conflation of patron with God himself is more far-reaching.

7 Now in the National Museum, New Delhi; Mathur (2000: plate 4).

8 K. Gupta 1965, 1:248.

9 Ibid., 1:310.

10 The intriguing Rasik Bihārī will be the topic of my next monograph.

11 Sāvant Singh is not unique in this respect. For an insightful reflection on the phenomenon of portraying "kings as God," see Huntington (1994).

12 On this technique in the Caitanya-Sampradāya, see Haberman (1988).

13 Quoted in Elliot and Dowson (1964: 21–22).

14 Escapism is how, classically, Goetz assesses the whole of the refined culture of the eighteenth century in his early attempt to correct for the "Dark Ages" view of the times (1938: 10, 13, 15–18). On reassessing such views, see the articles on culture in Barnett (2002).

15 The first book-length study was by the magistrate and collector of Bulandshahr, Frederic S. Growse (1883).

16 See *Oxford Bibliographies Online*, s.v. "Krishna"; one enduringly inspiring book is Kinsley (1979). On the myth in art, see, e.g., Isacco and Dallapiccola (1983). Basic studies of the mystery plays are Hein (1972) and Hawley and Gosvami (1981).

17 The best overview is Hawley and Juergensmeyer (1988). Originals with facing translation are found in Snell (1991b). More recently, see Hawley (2005, 2009), Martin (forthcoming), Sanford (2008), and several articles in Bryant (2007).

18 A notable exception is Peabody (2003), who historicizes the image in Kota, Rajasthan, and its literature. See also Saha (2004).

19 On the *bhakti* movement, see Pechilis (1999) and Hawley (2015). On the transmission of songs, a notable exception is the study about the Marathi saint Nāmdev by Novetzke (2008).

20 The only exception is his brief *Arilla-pacīsī* (trans. Snell 1991b: 177–83) and some individual poems in articles focusing mostly on Kishangarhi art.

21 Studied as an example of pastoral literature by Entwistle (1991).

1. Soldiers Marching

1 Recent studies from different perspectives are Kolff (1990), Saran and Ziegler (2001), E. Haynes (2002), Sreenivasan (2007), Williams (2007), Freitag (2009), and Talbot (2015).

2 See Asher (1992), Horstmann (2009), Talbot (2009), and Sreenivasan (2014).

3 Haidar in her unpublished dissertation (1995) gives a well-documented overview of the history. The two main studies are in Hindi, by Faiyāz Alī Khān, whose unpublished Ph.D. dissertation (1962) reflects the strong Vallabhan bias of his employer, the Kishangarh court, and by his polemical antithesis, the well-respected Nimbārkan sectarian scholar Vrajvallabh Śaraṇ (1966). In the Bikaner Archives, there is nothing until the nineteenth century. The house of Kishangarh kept all its earlier materials private and restricts access. One has to rely on secondary literature produced by those who had access to these archives. The aforementioned Hindi writers quote documents from the Kishangarh State archives and the archives of the Paraśurām Pīṭh in Salemabad. Unfortunately, neither of these collections is currently accessible for cross-checking.

4 See V. Śaraṇ (1972: 251). I am grateful to H. H. Maharaja Brajraj Singh, who is himself very knowledgeable about his ancestors, for kindly directing me to relevant sections in this work and for offering corrections of an early draft of this chapter. Any remaining mistakes are my own responsibility.

5 See Habib (1982: plate 6b); Deloche (1993, 1:54–55 and plate viii); and Deloche (1968: planche xii and xiv). For example, Aurangzeb halted in Kishangarh en route to Ajmer on February 17, 1678 (twenty-second regnal year; *Mā'śir-e 'Ālamgīrī*, chapter 22; Sarkar 1947: 107).

6 Khān 1974: 3–4; H. H. Maharaja Brajrāj Singh, personal communication, August 8, 2012.

7 *Tuzuk-e Jahāngīrī*; trans. Rogers and Beveridge 1909, 1:151, 281, 291–93.

8 Haidar 1995: 24.

9 *Mā'ṣir ul-Umarā*, Beveridge and Prashad 1952: 619–21.

10 Haidar 1995: 22.

11 For details, see ibid.: 22–23.

12 Celer 1971: gh.

13 Whether the daughter of Rūp Singh (Chandra 2002: 61n2) or, as rumor has it, a stand-in (H. H. Brajrāj Singh, personal communication, August 8, 2012). The arrangement was in compensation for the famous Carumatī/Rūpmatī, the Kishangarhi princess who was promised to Aurangzeb but instead married Rāj Singh of Mewar in 1660 (G. Sharma 1962: 139–40).

14 Celer 1973: 53.

15 Mān Singh may have had an atelier, too, as some paintings are from the late 1600s (Dickinson and Khandalavala 1959: 14).

16 Shivdās Lakhnavī's *Shāhnāmah Munavvar Kalām* (1724?) registers gifts presented at festive occasions by and to Rāj Singh Bahādur of Kishangarh (Askari 1980: 119, 120, 123, 194n188; entries from the third regnal year). The painting is attributed to the famous Dalcand, son of Bhavānīdās, who worked at the Mughal court of Muḥammad Shāh. For image and discussion, see Pauwels (2015: 66–68).

17 V. Śaraṇ 1966: 12. This must have been the first unsuccessful attempt to conquer Thun (Chandra 2002: 215; Dwivedi 1989: 61–66). Sāvant Singh distinguished himself in one attack (on Vaiśākh *badi* 6 1774 VS) and was congratulated by the emperor (Rādhākrishnadās 1898: 16–17).

18 Fateh Singh died in 1724 (*Tavārīḳh Fateh Singh jī kī*, p. 7). There is also a portrait of him attributed to Dalcand in the collection of the British Library (1959,0411,0.3 [see Ahluwalia 2008: 108–9, plate 67]), and he is depicted in a painting of Rādhā and Krishna's *Betel Tasting* (Tāmbūl Sevā) (Mathur 2000: 46–47, plate 5).

19 *Tavārīkh Sukh Singh jī kī*, pp. 8 and 2, respectively. As the story goes, Sukh Singh's party asked for the help of Merta's army, but the messenger, Māṇakcand Koṭhārī, was stopped miraculously, through the intervention of Krishna himself (V. Śaraṇ 1972: 245).

20 In one story he bravely subdued a mad elephant (Dickinson and Khandalavala 1959), an event commemorated in a painting (Khān 1974: plate 2). See also Pauwels (2015: 157).

21 Haidar 1995: 118. Compare, e.g., Mathur (2000: 21 and 48) with McInerney (2002: 19, fig. 5). See also K. Singh (2013: 263–64).

22 Extensively discussed in Pauwels 2015.

23 V. Śaraṇ 1966: 12–13.

24 Ibid.: 15. "*Kuñj* of Nagaridas" appears on a mid-eighteenth-century map of Vrindavan, preserved in the Kapad Dwara, Jaipur (Bahura and Singh 1990: 52, no. 352).

25 K. Gupta 1965, 2:9.

26 As stated in the *Administrative History* (p. 39).

27 The ceremony took place possibly in Delhi or on the way to Kishangarh (*Tavārīḳh Sāvant Singh jī kī*, pp. 39–40; Rādhākrishnadās 1898: 18).

28 Mathur 2000: 11. He may not even have attended the funeral, as Bīr Singh, son of Rāj Singh's second wife, performed the last rites (*kapālakriyā*) for the deceased king (V. Śaraṇ 1972: 245).

29 *Tavārīḳh Sāvant Singh jī kī*, p. 31, in connection with a trip of Bahādur Singh to Lahore in 1741. He traveled with Mīr Mannū, who was the governor of Punjab, Mu'īn ul-Mulk (d. 1753), son of Qamar ud-Dīn Ḳhān (Grewal 1990: 87–88). I am grateful to my colleague Purnima Dhavan for this identification.

30 Sāvant Singh was in Delhi for this reason, though he did not partake in the battle (Rādhākrishnadās 1898: 17–18).

31 Muḥammad Shāh died on April 15, 1748 (Vaiśākh *badī* 14; see *Julusi sanehs* [regnal year correspondences] as published by Sinh [1984: 22]), the day after Rāj Singh. For the background, see Malik (2006: 176–84), who gives a different date, without indicating his source.

32 Sarkar 1964, 1:214–31, 231–34, 290–315, respectively.

33 Gordon 1994: 138.

34 Malik 2006: 230–36; Dhavan 2011: 47–73.

35 Dwivedi 1989: 93–118.

36 Ibid.: 128.

37 Sarkar 1964, 1:30–41; Gommans 1995: 125–26.

38 Dwivedi 1989: 119–24.

39 Sarkar 1964, 1:253–58; Dwivedi 1989: 124.

40 Jai Singh II had tried to unite with Marwar, Mewar, Bikaner, Kota, Karauli, and Kishangarh against the Marathas with the Hurda agreement of 1734 (Parihar 1968: 50–51); however, this effort was soon abandoned.

41 B. Gupta 1979: 39–40.

42 Sachdev and Tillotson 2002: 70; Gordon 1994: 137.

43 Jai Singh was careful to remain on good terms with the Peshva. In 1735, he took special care of the Peshva's mother, Rādhābāī, who was undertaking a pilgrimage to Benares (Acharya 1978: 168–70; B. Gupta 1979: 21–24). Another example where pilgrimage and politics were entwined is Bāji Rāo and his wife's 1736 visit to Nathdvara during their stay in Mewar to press for land and money (Acharya 1978: 112–13).

44 Acharya 1978: 99–100; Gupta and Bakshi 2008: 144–48; Sarkar 1964, 1:200–204; B. Gupta 1979: 39–42. Maratha factions vied among themselves for influence: Holkar was the leading chief in Bundi, whereas Scindhia had a representative in Kota.

45 Notably an elephant and two horses (*Tavārīḳh Sāvant Singh jī kī*, pp. 39–40).

46 Maratha sources indicate that he left Sāvant Singh with only a few hundred horsemen under Kripārām (Gupta and Bakhshi 2008: 190; Sarkar 1964, 1:184; SPD 2:17, 23).

47 Gordon 1994: 137. Such demands led to anti-Maratha riots in the country (Sarkar 1964, 1:189–91).

48 Parihar 1968: 58–60; Gupta and Bakshi 2008: 151–55.

49 Dwivedi 1989: 116.

50 Parihar 1968: 61–68.

51 Whether of cholera or poisoned by the Jaipur *rāṇī* (queen) (see Sarkar 1964, 1:200).

52 Some said that Peshva Bāji Rāo I praised him for his bravery in fighting Malhār Rāo in 1736 (1793 VS; Rādhākrishnadās 1898: 17). The Peshva may have stopped near Kishangarh during his journey north to (unsuccessfully) pressure the emperor into an

advantageous treaty in March 1736 and there met with Jai Singh II of Jaipur (Acharya 1978: 114); some say it was in Bhamalao (Parihar 1968: 53) or Bhambhola, a village near Jahazpur (B. Gupta 1979: 23, on the basis of *Vaṃśa bhāskar* 4:3239), considerably south of Kishangarh. The Maratha letter noting the rivalries between Bahādur Singh and Sāvant Singh was sent by Rāgho Nīlkaṇṭh to the Peshva Bāji Rāo and discusses the campaign against the Rohillas (SPD 21: 29, no. 31).

53 Sarda 1911: 170; Parihar 1968: 76–80.

54 Parihar 1968: 83, on the basis of SPD 27: 119–21, no. 107.

55 Sarkar 1964, 4:127.

56 Sarda 1911: 171; Parihar 1968: 80–84.

57 Parihar 1968: 88–90.

58 The itinerary from 1753 to 1755 shows that Raghunāth Rāo was encamped in Rupnagar during March 1755 (SPD 27: 76, no. 79), but perhaps he did not attack.

59 SPD 21: 95, no. 85; Dattaji Scindhia, letter, dated May 9, 1756; Parihar 1968: 90.

60 The date is 1813 VS Āsāṛh *badi* 5 in *Tavārīḳh Sāvant Singh jī kī*, p. 67. See also V. Śaraṇ (1972: 246), but what Śaraṇ's sources are is not clear. He also cites an epic on Sardār Singh, called *Sardār-sujas*, authored by Hīrālāl Sanāṛhya of Karauli in 1816 VS (Śaraṇ 1972: 246).

61 Sāvant Singh's brother and son both wrote to him to come home (Rādhākrishnadās 1898: 5), and he set out in February–March 1757 (in Phālgun 1813 VS; ibid.: 19). The pillaging of the Braj area was reported in gruesome detail twenty-five years later by the eyewitness Samīn (trans. Irvine 1907: 60, 62). Another eyewitness report, by the devotee Cācā Vrindāvandās, describes two different attacks, the second in 1760–61 (see Bangha 1997: 232).

62 V. Śaraṇ 1972: 247.

63 The text is now completely illegible through whitewashing of the *samādhi*. A photo with partially legible text is in R. Śarmā (1996, 1:24 [facing page]). Reconstructions here are based on Śarmā's (ibid., 1:20) and on the transcription kindly provided by H. H. Mahārāj Brajrāj Singh (July 26, 2011).

64 Literally "behaved Tretā-like," that is, as in the era that Rāma of Ayodhya was the exemplary king, perhaps a reference to his *Garland of Rāma's Romance*.

65 K. Gupta 1965, 2:3.

66 Ibid., 2:4.

67 Sāvant Singh wrote *Amusements of Two Devotees* in Kumaon, where he camped with the Marathas during their campaign against the Rohillas (JBV 21; K. Gupta 1965, 1:68).

68 Even as a prince, Nāgarīdās was interested in humor and satire, in his poetry (K. Gupta 1965, 2:133–37) as well as in paintings (Haidar 2000: 89–90).

69 On *śahr āśob*, see Petievich (1990) and Sunil Sharma (2004: 77–81).

70 Sunil Sharma 2004: 80.

2. Gods and Saints Relocated

1 As argued convincingly in Horstmann's well-documented book (2009).

2 See also Pauwels (forthcoming-a). On the formation of the religion covered under the term *Hinduism* in the nineteenth century, see, e.g., Dalmia (1997) and Dalmia and von Stietencron (1995).

3 Likely one took place in 1713 in Vrindavan and another in 1734 in Rajasthan (Horstmann 2009: 57; 2010: 15–16).
4 Clémentin-Ojha 2005: 16–17.
5 Some left in protest (Horstmann 2009: 158–79).
6 For a list of ritual issues that were debated, and insights of what is behind them, see ibid.: 140–46.
7 On warrior ascetics, see Agrawal (2011: 6) and Pinch (1996: 27).
8 Pinch 2000; Lochtefeld 1994; Horstmann 2009: 50; see also Agrawal 2011: 6.
9 See Horstmann (2009: 170–71).
10 Horstmann 2002: 165.
11 Horstmann 2009: 4–9; see also O'Hanlon and Minkowski 2008 and O'Hanlon 2010.
12 Horstmann 2009: 48–49, 59–75.
13 Ibid.: 158–75.
14 Dickinson and Khandalavala 1959, Mathur 2000, Haidar 2011b.
15 Gauḍ 1898, K. Gupta 1965, Khān 1974.
16 For a handy overview, see Barz (2009: 606–8).
17 Vaudeville 1980: 24–26.
18 Details in Ambalal (1987).
19 There are nine deities, called "nine treasures," or *navanidhi* (Barz 2009: 608–13).
20 Jhaveri 1928.
21 Barz 2009: 613; Dalmia 2006; Saha 2006.
22 See the handy overview chart in Peabody (1991: plate 3) (it leaves out Kevalrām, the adoptive son).
23 By the middle of the seventeenth century, Jat peasant revolts were destabilizing the Braj region, leading to punishing campaigns by the Mughal armies in the area and the plundering of local treasures. In Braj, original temples were left behind and the images and their treasures were moved. See Pauwels and Bachrach (forthcoming).
24 Peabody 1991: 739–40.
25 Rādhākrishnadās (1898: 9–10) claims that he was related to Raja Āskaran of Narvargarh, who is mentioned in 252VV 73 (Kṛṣṇadās 1986b: 191–214).
26 Khān 1974: 3–4; Haidar 1995: 24.
27 Haidar 1995: 22–23.
28 See Richards (1995: 132–33); also *Mā'šir ul-Umarā* 619–20.
29 RV 139–42; Celer 1971: 135–37.
30 He is identified as a son of Viṭṭhalnāth's eldest son, Girdhar jī, by the name of Dīkṣit (Gopīnāth Dīkṣit according to Ambalal [1987: 63]; Viṭṭhaleśvar Dīkṣit according to *The Story of the Manifestation of Śrī Nātha jī*).
31 A Śrī Kalyāṇarāya image has also been in the hands of the sixth *gaddī* since the sixteenth century, a consolation prize for the loss of Bālakrishna to the third house (Entwistle 1987: 178).
32 Celer 1971: 138–39.
33 RV 152–62; Celer 1971: 139–43.
34 Throughout, I have retained the Braji honorific *jū*, equivalent to the Hindi *jī*.
35 A legendary king fabled for sponsoring great sacrifices and being a fervent Vaishnava.
36 Celer 1971: 143.

37 Dated as 1706 VS (1649 CE). He went under the command of the future emperor Aurangzeb (MU 620).

38 RV 185–200; Celer 1971: 147–50; MU 620.

39 Mahārāṇā Jagat Singh I (r. 1628–52) was initiated by a Gosvāmī of the third *gaddī*, for which there is evidence in the form of a land grant (Saha 2007: 309). The image of Śrī Nātha jī (of the first house) was installed under Jagat Singh's son Rāj Singh I (r. 1653–80). The third *gaddī*'s *nidhi-svarūpa*, Śrī Dvārkānātha jī, when it left Gokul went first to Ahmedabad in 1670 and came to be installed in 1720 in Kankroli, where it still resides (Ambalal 1987: 57).

40 The same is true for goddess worship: a description of Vijau Daśamī in 1712 VS occurs after his victory of Mandalgarh (Celer 1971: 155–56) and involves distribution of salaries to soldiers and compensation to the wounded and bereft.

41 For nuancing the commonplace blaming on Aurangzeb's iconoclasm, see Pauwels and Bachrach (forthcoming).

42 Peabody 1991: 735–37, 743.

43 In a play on words (*yamaka*), *rūpa* is repeated twice: once in the meaning of "beauty" and once as Rūp's signature.

44 K. Gupta 1965, 1:302. Also quoted in V. Śaraṇ (1966: 10); and trans. Haidar (1995: 24).

45 K. Gupta 1965, 1:311.

46 Ibid., 1:458.

47 Haidar (1995: 24) also notes the role of the king as a *sakhī* in the divine *līlā*, in connection with the first poem.

48 However, the date of the text may well be later; see Pauwels and Bachrach (forthcoming).

49 Trans. Vaudeville (1980: 18–27) (first part only).

50 References below are to the most easily available edition, Ācārya (1968), which is very close to the older one published by Lakshmi Venkateshvar Steam Press in 1905. For more details, see Pauwels and Bachrach (forthcoming).

51 Ācārya 1968: 67–68.

52 Rūp Singh actually died in the succession battle at Samūgarh, where he was on Dārā Shikoh's side. His bravery during the battle was remarked on appreciatively by the foe, Aurangzeb (MU 620–21).

53 Ācārya 1968: 69.

54 Ibid.: 69–70.

55 Khān 1974: 709–10.

56 V. Śaraṇ 1966: 30–31. They are not in the manuscript preserved in the Mathura Janmabhumi Library, which was a gift for the Salemabad *mahant* (MS 13254-361; fol. 40r).

57 Reproduced by Khān (1974: *phalak* 1; discussed on 850). The whereabouts of the painting are not given. The identification of Sāvant Singh is not confirmed.

58 Soni and Relia 2016: 158–59; Navina Najat Haidar thinks it possible, or perhaps attributable to his son, Sītārām (personal communication, April 4, 2017).

59 V. Śaraṇ 1966.

60 Khān 1974.

61 Clémentin-Ojha 2011: 429, 431–32.

62 Also ascribed to Nimbārka is a famous ten-stanza (*Daśaślokī*) summary of his teaching, which his contemporary followers still recite by heart (ibid.: 430–31).

63 Ibid.: 439–40.

64 Ibid.: 433–34.

65 The sect is sometimes called "Harivyāsī" after this important leader (Clémentin-Ojha 2005: 5). The lineage of his eldest disciple, Svabhurāma, is based in Dhruv Tila in Mathura.

66 One was originally in Punjab but moved to Bengal; it also has a Vrindavan offshoot (Clémentin-Ojha 2011: 436–37).

67 Bhm 185; Rūpkalā 1977: 784–85.

68 BRB 522; Rūpkalā 1977: 785–86.

69 Entwistle 1987: 185.

70 In the 1710s; see Horstmann (2009: 159).

71 Clémentin-Ojha 2011: 438.

72 For instance, the succession battle in Bharatpur in 1826 (Clémentin-Ojha 2005: 7–8n24).

73 Perhaps pushed by the Maharashtrian Brahmins at court.

74 Clémentin-Ojha 2005: 17; Horstmann 2009: 169. Jayrām Śeṣ was also supported by the rulers of Bundi, Kota, and Karauli (R. Śarmā 1996, 1:19).

75 The queen mother of Pratāp Singh (r. 1778–1803) built a temple within the palace, Śrī jī kī morī (Clémentin-Ojha 2011: 435), and the powerful queen, known by her patronymicon Bhaṭṭiyānī, who was regent for her minor son (1819–35), donated tax-free lands to Nimbārk Śaran (abbot 1814–38) and built a temple in 1826 in Vrindavan: Śrī jī kī Baḍī Kuñj (ibid.; Clémentin-Ojha 2005: 8). The Salemabad head at this point claimed jurisdiction over all Nimbārkan branches, though that was not unchallenged (Clémentin-Ojha 2011: 435). The Nimbārkan influence in Jaipur came to an end under the infamous Vaishnava persecution of Rām Singh II (1851–80): the then *mahant* saw his lands confiscated and had to flee Jaipur (Clémentin-Ojha 2011: 436).

76 V. Śaraṇ 1966: 11. Based on a commemoration of that abbot, for which Mān Singh sent presents from Delhi in 1700 (1756 VS).

77 This visit is commemorated in a historical document of 1725 (1782 VS), cited by V. Śaraṇ (1966: 14).

78 R. Śarmā 1996, 1:14–18, 27–32.

79 Haidar 2011a: 540, fig. 8; 532.

80 Vrindābandev Ācārya is mentioned in *Brajdāsī-bhāgavat*, v. 48; R. Śarmā 1996, 2:1265. Brijnāth Bhaṭṭ in *Brajdāsī-bhāgavat*, v. 53; R. Śarmā 1996, 2:1265. The edited text is based on a manuscript from 1777 (1834 VS). A manuscript preserved in the Jaipur collection confirms the information on the two gurus (Bahura 1976: 481–82).

81 Bangha 2007: 346. He was possibly the Kavīśvar Vrajnāth who is recorded as earning twelve rupees a month according to the *Mahārājā Rāj Singh jī kā itihās* register (p. 139; according to V. Śaraṇ [1972: 255–56n2]). And/or he was possibly the Brijnāth Bhaṭṭ who took part in a gathering held in Rupnagar in 1742 (ŚBPVP 27; see Pauwels, forthcoming-b]).

82 On Caitra *sudi* 10, 1760 VS, according to a grant document that gifts a yearly income of three hundred rupees to the guru. The baby's name in the document is Krishna Singh, Nāgarīdās's given name (V. Śaraṇ 1972: 241 [on the basis of a Rupnagar *bahī* from 1715–76]). The ceremony may have been a head-shaving, or *muṇḍan* (R. Śarmā 1996: 1:26).

His sister, Fateh Kumārī, also was initiated (R. Śarmā 1996: 1:26). Unfortunately, these documents are currently inaccessible and cannot be verified.

83 V. Śaraṇ 1966: 37–19.

84 V. Śaraṇ says he saw the portraits in Kishangarh in 1946. That they were marked with numbers leads him to speculate they were part of a *pūjā* collection, that is, a group of paintings included in a shrine for worship (1972: 259).

85 The painting is reproduced in V. Śaraṇ (1966: 17).

86 "Lion Hunt," 51–54 and 57, as quoted in V. Śaraṇ (1966: 16).

87 Rāj Singh made a land grant to the messenger conveying the news to him in Delhi (Khān 1974: 7–8).

88 Vrindābandev's Rādhā-Krishna poetry is quoted eleven times in his *String of Song-Pearls* (PMĀ 103, 207, 365, 466, 518, 561, 563, 627, 740, 742, 744). In the same collection, six poems by Śrī Bhaṭṭ jī are also included (PMĀ 373, 471–72, 550, 635, 663).

89 The date of agreement is given as 1814 VS, Āśvin *badi* 9, and the date of his passing as Kārtik *badi* 5 (V. Śaraṇ 1972: 162).

90 See ibid.: 254.

91 R. Śarmā 1996, 1:16–17.

92 Ibid., 1:17.

93 This painting is reproduced in Dickinson and Khandalavala (1959: 18, fig. 4).

94 V. Śaraṇ 1972: 254.

95 This idea is broached in the foreword to *Nāgara-samuccayaḥ* by Bābā Rādhākrishnadās (1898: 21).

96 He authored, inter alia, *The Ocean of the Nectar-Essence of Devotion* (Bhakti-rasāmṛta-sindhu), trans. Haberman (2003).

97 For an extensive study, see Haberman (1988).

98 See Entwistle (1987: 149, 167–68, 252–55).

99 Hawley 2015: 163–64.

100 Mukherjee and Habib 1988, 1989.

101 Case 1996.

102 Entwistle 1987: 166–67.

103 Horstmann 2009: 45–47.

104 Ibid.: 75–98.

105 In particular, Kṛṣṇadeva Bhaṭṭācārya's *Karma-vivṛtti* and Harekṛṣṇa Miśra's *Vaidika-vaiṣṇava-sadācāra*, trans. Horstmann (2009, appendixes).

106 Horstmann suggests that the Navab's interest may have had to do with the Gauḍiyas' influence in trade and banking in Bengal, where they were prized as tax collectors (ibid.: 107–8, 116).

107 Evidenced by several documents (ibid.: 98–120).

108 This sketch is preserved at the National Museum in New Delhi (published in Welch [1976: 122–23, no. 69]).

109 See Pauwels (2015: 71, plate 3).

110 More on this issue in the discussion of *The Pilgrim's Bliss*.

111 Entwistle 1987: 168.

112 Ibid.: 185; Snell 1991a: 4.

113 Ed. and trans. Snell 1991a.

114 Some say he was exiled, but Entwistle doubts this (1987: 194).

115 For Hit Kamalnayan and Hit Anūp(lal), see Snātak 1957: 596; Mītal 1968: 405.

116 Bangha 2007: 319.

117 Pal 2004: 164–65, plate 77. Inscriptions in Devanagari identify Gosvāmī Hit Rūplāl, Gosvāmī Kiśorīlāl, Cācā Vrindāvandās, Gopāldās, Krishnadās, Premdās (who wrote a commentary on *Eighty-Four Love Songs*), and Kāśīrām (deciphered by Haidar in Pal [2004: 186]).

118 Ed. and trans. Rosenstein 1997.

119 For Viṭhal Vipul, see Mītal 1968: 465–66.

120 For Bihāranidas, see ibid.: 466–67; Entwistle 1987: 170–71.

121 See Pauwels (2009a).

122 Entwistle 1987: 179–80.

123 Hargulāl 1971.

124 Entwistle 1987: 194.

125 Kedarnāth 1911, 1915; R. Haynes 1974: 122–24.

126 *Nij-mat-siddhānt, avasān khaṇḍ*, 98. Kiśordās also offended Rādhāvallabhans by publicizing that their disciples had defected to his own group (Gosvāmī 1952, 61).

127 Rosenstein 1997: 16–17.

128 Though his dates (1692–1758 VS) are too early, there may be a connection to his lineage.

129 Mītal 1968: 471–72. The history of the temple and its image is described in Gopāl Kavi's *Vrindāban-dhām-anurāgāvalī*, in the chapter Śrī Rasikbihārī jī ke mandir kā prasaṅga.

130 Published in Okada, Biardeau, and Porcher (2011), the so-called de Selliers *Rāmāyaṇa*.

131 The classical study is Burghart (1978); anthropological work by van der Veer (1988) and historical study by Pinch (1996).

132 Agrawal 2011: esp. 5 and 7.

133 Old Hindi songs are found in the Sikh scripture, Ādi-granth, and in the anthologies of the Dādū-panthī *Sarvāṅgī*s (Vaudeville 1993: 87–88; Agrawal 2011: 5). On the Sanskrit texts, see Agrawal (2011: 4).

134 Bhm 35; Rūpkalā 1977: 281–82.

135 See Agrawal (2011: 4–5). Horstmann reports that the earliest self-referential identification as Rāmānandī in the Galta documents dates from the 1730s (2002: 145).

136 Bhm 36; Rūpkalā 1977: 282. This claim is further pursued by Nābhādās's guru nephew (disciple of another disciple of Nābhādās's guru Agradās), Anantdās, in his hagiographies, called *Parcaī*s.

137 Bhm 35; Rūpkalā 1977: 281–82.

138 Bhm 36; Rūpkalā 1977: 282.

139 His subsisting on milk is confirmed in Bhm 38; Rūpkalā 1977: 302. Residence in Pushkar is asserted in Siṃha 1957: 86. Patronage by the Amer king is in Bhm 116; Rūpkalā 1977: 724.

140 Horstmann 2002: 147, 153–54. Bahura also cites yogic songs attributed to Prithvīrāj (1976: 25–27).

141 Bahura 1976: 25.

142 The Galta Rāmānandīs until recently were appointed the caretakers of the deity, which is now housed in the Sītārāma-dvārā in the City Palace of Jaipur (Horstmann 2002: 145).

143 Loss in battle thus would expose the image to plunderers, as happened in the battle of Gangwana of 1741, where the Jaipur ruler fought against Marwar (he eventually won, thanks to his imperial allies). The image was retrieved in exchange for Bakht Singh's image, Śrī Giridhara jī, which had been captured by the Kacchvāhās (Gupta and Bakshi 2008: 154–55). The image plays a role in processions for religious festivals even now.

144 For example, a grant in the subah, or province, of Ajmer confirmed in 1640 (Horstmann 2002: 156, 188) and one from Maharaja Indra Singh of Nagor in 1705 (Horstmann 2009: 163).

145 Especially during the reign of Jai Singh I (r. 1621–67) (Horstmann 2002: 157).

146 See Siṃha (1957: 379–82). When his *guru-bhāī*, Kīlhadās, succeeded their guru at the Galta monastery, Agradās went to establish a new branch in Raivasa, in the Shekhavati-Jaipur area, which became the center of Rāma-Rasika *bhakti* in Rajasthan. His pupil, the *Garland of Devotees* author Nābhādās, moved with him.

147 McGregor 1983. Agradās may have been influenced by the Krishna *bhakta* Svāmī Haridās, as a poem in praise of the latter is found with the *chāpa* "Agaradāsa Alī" (Rosenstein 1997: 12). He was not alone: Nābhādās, too, wrote works in Braj (e.g., *Rāmcandra-aṣṭayām*; Siṃha 1957: 384–85).

148 Lutgendorf 1991: 228. The intellectual exchange with Braj seems to have continued until well into the nineteenth century. Though by then most went to Ayodhya to find a guru, several spent time in Vrindavan and added the epithet "Vrindāvanī" to their names (Siṃha 1957: 171–72).

149 On the *rās-dhārī* reference, see Horstmann (2009: 165). On his promoting Rāma-Rasika *bhakti*, see Horstmann (2002: 158 [on the basis of nineteenth-century sectarian accounts]).

150 For full lineage details, see Siṃha (1957: 335–36).

151 His *samādhi* is at Govardhan (Horstmann 2010: 10–11).

152 Siṃha 1957: 356. For the use of *chāpas* in the name of girlfriends, see Lutgendorf (1991: 223).

153 Horstmann 2010: 14–17. He was also heavily sponsored by Shekhavat nobility.

154 Now branched out to Madhya Pradesh (Ratlam and Indore) and Gujarat (Dakor) (Siṃha 1957: 336).

155 He is mentioned in *Garland of Devotees* (Bhm 39; Rūpkalā 1977: 308).

156 Kiraṇ 2003: 57–59.

157 Archival research confirms this; for example, in 1730, Vrijānand signed a document promising to conform to the king's stipulations of orthodoxy (Horstmann 2010: 12).

158 His promotion of the link can be derived on the basis of the manuscripts he commissioned (ibid.: 27). He may have played a role in the 1713 conference in Vrindavan and the 1734 one in Rajasthan (Horstmann 2009: 57; 2010: 15–16).

159 The sectarian interpretation is expressed in Siṃha (1957: 388–90). Documentation of the animosity between Shaiva *sanyāsīs* and Vaishnava *vairāgīs* in Lochtefeld (2010: 59–61). On the building of Hanuman Garhi, see Hastings (2002: 107–8).

160 This document was also signed by Sukhrām of Raivasa; trans. Horstmann (2002: 160–61).

161 Siṃha 1957: 137, 398. He also wrote commentaries on *Vālmīki Rāmāyaṇa* to prove the credentials of his *rasika* interpretation (ibid.; Horstmann 2009: 165).

162 Horstmann 2002: 166; 2009: 163–64.

163 Horstmann 2002: 166; 2009: 164. On the issue of forced marriage, see Siṃha (1957: 398).

164 According to an undated document (Horstmann 2009: 165).

165 Horstmann 2009: 165 and n95. There is a posthumous *stotra* (encomium) in his praise (Horstmann 2002: 166).

166 He wrote a Hindi *Aṣṭ-yām* and a Sanskrit *Jānakī-gīta*, modeled after *Gīta-govinda*.

167 Horstmann 2002: 170; Siṃha 1957: 408–9.

168 Nāgarīdās does quote a Krishna devotional song by Agradās in his *String of Song-Pearls* (PMĀ 611).

169 This notwithstanding hagiographical efforts to turn him into a Brahmin (Callewaert 1988).

170 Ibid.

171 *Dādū-janma-līlā* 11.16; Callewaert 1988: 68.

172 Grant of Māgh *badi* 11, 1847 VS; Nārāyaṇdās 1979: 418.

173 Pemārām 1976: 48.

174 Some claim the date of composition is 1660, others 1713 or 1720 (Callewaert 2000: 28–29; Nāhaṭā 1965 and Nārāyaṇdās 1969 [on the basis of late eighteenth- and early nineteenth-century manuscript material]).

175 Hastings 2002: 175.

176 He was a Dādū-panthī Nāgā, whose guru was Santoṣdās in the lineage of Sundardās (Nahaṭā 1965: ṣ).

177 A document from the Kapad Dwara in Jaipur, no. 1282, trans. Horstmann (1994: 62–63).

178 Horstmann 2002: 163, 189n49.

179 Hastings 2002: 153–54.

180 Horstmann 1994: 66. They are mentioned in court records from 1768 (Thiel-Horstmann 1991: 269).

181 On Vasant, see Mayaram (2005: 154). On the shrine's patronage, see Moini (2004: 53–95).

182 Pilgrimage account by Ganesh Sadashiv Shastri Lele Tryambakkar in 1885, analyzed by Glushkova (2006); incidentally, he also passed through Kishangarh (see ibid.: esp. 220 and 228).

183 Moini 2004: 61, 63, 77 (for Jodhpur); ibid.: 62–63, 70 (for Jaipur).

184 In 1741, Abhai Singh of Marwar sent a party including Sāvant Singh's brother Bahādur Singh to successfully attack Kacchvāhā-occupied Ajmer (Sarda 1911: 169).

185 A transcription is published in a collection of royal grants and decrees (*farmāns*, *asnad*), and other documents issued and ratified by Mughal emperors between 1560 and 1850 (Ajmerī 1952: 323–24). I am grateful to Elizabeth Thelen, Ph.D. candidate at the University of California, Berkeley, for sending me a copy of the relevant pages in this rare book.

186 Moini 2004: 61; Currie 1989: 196. However, the evidence is problematic. The seals of the document are of Shāh ʿĀlam II (r. 1759–1806) and Mān Singh Rājkuṃvar (i.e., as royal prince), and the document itself refers to Mān Singh as Maharaja. Mān Singh of Kishangarh reigned in 1658–1706, that is, over a century before the emperor. I am grateful to Purnima Dhavan for helping me decipher the document and alerting me to the problems with the published interpretations.

187 Moini 2004: 67 (on the basis of an Urdu work, *Uhad-e Tauliyat* by Mirza Abdul Qadir Beg, published in Ajmer in 1944 [pp. 36–38, 40, 43, 72–74, 88, 93–94]). Unfortunately, this work is not available to me.

188 All depicted are identified by an inscription. See also Pauwels (2014); for detailed views of the inscriptions, I am grateful to Navina Najat Haidar. More on this below.

189 *Śṛṅgār-śikṣā*, ed. Celer (1971: 35–50). It is more likely that this is another person by that name.

190 This painting, too, identifies all the guests with a Devanagari inscription. Dickinson and Khandalavala 1959: 38; Pauwels 2015: plate 2.

191 This painting is preserved in the India Office collection in London (Prints and Drawings, shelf mark Add.Or.4473).

192 Sometimes the full name Aham Kirdār Sultān Pīr is given, and he is said to have been related to Mīrān Sāhib of Ajmer Taragarh (Ali 2003: 82).

193 Ibid.

194 National Museum, New Delhi, accession no. 48.4/12. Perhaps it was produced in Bhavānīdās's atelier (Haidar 1995: 84).

195 His interests extended to what was at the time the vogue for Urdu (called Rekhtā) poetry in Delhi (Pauwels 2015).

196 Jainism is often seen as a static entity, steadfast in its commitment to extreme nonviolence (*ahiṃsā*) and unchanging over time, but recent scholarship has tried hard to correct for this ahistorical view (e.g., Flügel 2008).

197 Flügel 2002: 1221.

198 Cort 2002: 40–41.

199 They also served as caste gurus for North Indian Khandelvāls (see ibid.: 51).

200 Ibid.: 54.

201 Ibid.: 39–40, 42–48, 63.

202 Ibid.: 40, 48–54; but see also its distinction in ibid.: 63–66.

203 The name may refer to the foundational thirteen-point manifesto, the thirteen rebels undersigning it first, or a thirteenth path superseding all twelve others.

204 According to Cand Kavi's *Kavitta Terā-panth kau*; see Cort (2002: 51–52).

205 Cort 2002: 53–54.

206 Ibid.: 55.

207 Ibid.: 53, 57.

208 Ibid.: 58–59.

209 Ibid.: 62, 76n43.

210 Ibid.: 62. Its origins are unclear; see ibid.: 76n43.

211 Ibid.: 58.

212 Ibid.: 59–60.

213 Ibid.: 61.

214 Horstmann 2010: 7–8.

215 H. H. Maharaja Brajraj Singh, personal communication, August 9, 2012; see also Lodha 2005: 515–18.

216 Kantisagarji 1965: 826–28.

217 Jain 1963: 71.

218 Ibid.: 196–97.

219 Ibid.: 181.

220 Haidar reproduces the colophon (1995: plate 213) and doubts the authenticity mostly due to confusion with Surdhaj Nānāgrām, Nihālcand's descendant, who lived a century later.

221 Bangha 2007: 338.

222 The story also stresses the importance of food restrictions, as the Jaina is keen on inviting Viṭṭhalnāth for breakfast, but the latter refuses to take food from nonbelievers. Another commonality between the two faiths is the strict vegetarian diet.

3. Devotees on the Move

1 This painting (first published in Mathur [2000: 89, plate 26]) shows a handsome youth of bluish skin tone swimming in what may be a pond, or conceivably the Yamunā, toward a group of women fetching water and bathing, evocative of the Gopīs of Braj. He is interpreted to be Krishna, but he could also be seen as Sāvant Singh wading across the river, especially given the equestrian scenes in the background, beyond the water. These may depict a hunt, possibly undertaken by the army that accompanied Sāvant Singh.

2 Lochtefeld 2010: 228.

3 In the wake of the theoretical work on pilgrimage by Victor Turner and Edith Turner (e.g., 1978), the 1980s saw an increase in research on pilgrimage in Hinduism. For a bibliographical overview of the field, see R. Singh (2011).

4 Diana L. Eck's pathbreaking work on Benares (1983) opened the gateway for a host of studies on different pilgrimage centers, incorporating also non-textual data. For Braj, see Entwistle (1987), which has a strong historical approach.

5 For Rajasthan, see Gold (1988).

6 Examples of modern pilgrims are Enugula Veeraswamy, a Brahmin from Madras, who wrote an account of the pilgrimage he undertook to Benares from 1830 to 1831 (Yang 1999: 112–14, 119–20, 129, 134–35, 153–54); the Tanjore Maratha ruler Serfoji Bhosle II, whose pilgrimages in the South (1801–2) and the North (1820–22) have been recorded (Glushkova 2002–3); and Raghunāth Rāo, a prince of Vincur in Maharashtra, whose mid-nineteenth-century pilgrimage was described by Tryambakkar in 1885 (Glushkova 2006).

7 In contrast to the consumerist observations in, for example, the pilgrimage reports of Serfoji II (Glushkova 2002–3: 267).

8 Again, contrasting with the detailed observations of the arrangements made for bivouacs in Serfoji II's pilgrimage reports (ibid.).

9 For example, Raghunāth Rāo was harassed by the pilgrim guides (*paṇḍās*) in Gayā (ibid.: 229).

10 Nāgarīdās's work also differs from Persian first-person accounts by Kāyasthas and Khatrīs, which occasionally include pilgrimage descriptions. For example, Nek Rāy, writing in the seventeenth century, describes a pilgrimage to the Sufi shrine in Kacaucha (Alam and Subrahmanyam 2004: 66) and a visit to Avadh (ibid.: 68), and Ānand Rām "Muḳhlīs" recounts his visit to the Gaṛh Muktesar fair in 1747 (Alam and Subrahmanyam 1996; Irvine 1903). Muḳhlīs's mentor (*ustād*), the Persian poet Bedil, wrote on Mathura (Pellò 2015).

11 An example is the Sanskrit *Mathurā-māhātmya* in the *Varāha-purāṇa*, which may go back to the twelfth century (for other similar works, see Entwistle [1987: 232–35ff.]). Later this tradition became vernacularized with prescriptive itineraries often specifically intended for particular sects (ibid.: 268–69, 271–72).

12 For Braj, especially, the hagiographical pilgrimage accounts of Caitanya, Vallabhācārya, and their followers (ibid.: viz. 256–59, 261–68).

13 For example, the records of the Datiyā kings' visits to Braj in the nineteenth century (ibid.: 273).

14 Glushkova 2002–3: 269.

15 Entwistle 1987: 270. There also are passages in the fourteenth-century account by Jaina Jinaprabhu Sūri (ibid.: 231–33) and by Bilhana in the late eleventh, early twelfth century (ibid.: 226–27). The seventeenth-century autobiography *Ardha-kathānaka* by the Jaina reformer and merchant Banārsīdās also contains descriptions of visits to holy places (e.g., Rohtak, Pārśvanāth, Benares, the Avadh area, and Delhi), but it is more encompassing than just a pilgrimage report (R. Sharma 1970: 56–57, 65, 107, 109, 115).

16 Beyond "it is an amazing *mūrti*" or "it is a magical place" and so on (Nāhaṭā 1959: 115–19 [based on a manuscript from Anūp Sanskrit Library in Bikaner]).

17 Pauwels 2009b; Entwistle 1987: 159.

18 Lochtefeld 2010: 173.

19 Entwistle 1987: 197–98; Irvine 1907: 70.

20 *Kavitta* also collected in *Stray Verses* (*Chūṭak-kavitta* 60; K. Gupta 1965, 2:136).

21 *Savaiyā* also included in *Chūṭak-kavitta* (62; K. Gupta 1965, 2:137).

22 Interpretation of Bābā Rādhākrishnadās (1898: 20–21).

23 Ceremonial offering of fire and incense waved in front of the object of worship, here the Yamunā River (Haberman 2006).

24 Brahmins' wives of the *Bhāgavata-purāṇa* story, who chose to feed Krishna rather than carry out their ritual tasks (BhP 10.23). I thank Swapna Sharma for this interpretation.

25 Likely widows, clad in white.

26 For an overview of these goals, see, e.g., Bhardwaj and Lochtefeld (2004); also Gold (1988: 149).

27 Ann Grodzins Gold's section titled "Troubles Relieved, Well-Being Procured: What Happens at Shrines" (1988: 146–54) foregrounds concerns of physical health and desire for offspring. Bhardwaj and Lochtefeld's categories of "peace" and relieving "mental tension" (2004: 493–94) approach closer to Nāgarīdās's goals.

28 For example, Raghunāth Rāo, in the mid-nineteenth century, embarked on his first pilgrimage after the loss of his wife and daughter (Glushkova 2006: 218).

29 India's biggest inland salt lake to which Nāgarīdās refers in his poetry, contrasting it unflatteringly with Prem Sarovar in Braj (*Chūṭak-pad* 82; K. Gupta 1965, 1:100–101, also 2:66).

30 Khān 1974: 364.

31 The pond was dry when I visited on July 27, 2011, and the site seemed inactive as a pilgrimage center.

32 Sarkar 1984: 236–38.

33 Īśvarī Singh fought on the side of the beleaguered Rām Singh against Bakht Singh and his supporter, the Mir Bakhshi Salābat Ḳhān.

34 Orr 1947: 199–201 (sources not given).

35 Nath 1996: 180–81. Possibly one of the shrines that the Govindadeva image had temporarily resided in on his way to Jaipur about a half century earlier and where, afterward, a "memorial image" had been installed; for example, Rupahera (also known as Govindapura), situated southwest of Galta (ibid.: 174).

36 Sarkar 1964, 1:184.

37 Perhaps this refers to the *gomukha* through which the natural water supply streams.

38 He reports Sakaran as his first minor entry point. This site is depicted on a contemporaneous map of the Govardhan area, possibly by Nihālcand, preserved in the collection of Jagdish Mittal in Hyderabad. I am grateful to Navina Najat Haidar for sending me an image of the map (personal communication, September 17–18, 2014).

39 Nāhaṭā 1959: 115–16.

40 According to sectarian sources, Śrī Nātha jī left in 1669 and was officially installed in Mewar first in 1672 (see Pauwels and Bachrach, forthcoming). On *darshana* in Braj by the time of Jai Singh, see Entwistle (1987: 186). Maheśvarī gives a full description of the *parikramā*, including a Shiva image (Mahādeva jī Raṅgeśvara with Pārvatī) on top of Govardhan (Nāhaṭā 1959: 116), which may be the Rūpeśvara (*Rupesuram*) that Nāgarīdās mentions while visiting Radha- and Krishnakund.

41 Summarizing: "So many places in Holy Mathura are miraculous" (Nāhaṭā 1959: 117).

42 Other deities named "Bihārī" include one near Nagari Kunj and the old residence of Śrījī Mahārāj on Bihar Ghat, originally worshipped by Aṭalbihārī, a Nimbārkan Nāgā mentioned in *Garland of Devotees* (Bhakt-māl). This deity seems to have been prominent for the Bharatpur Jats in this period (Entwistle 1987: 140).

43 Cīrabihārī jī and Kuñjabihārī jī (Nāhaṭā 1959: 118–19).

44 Entwistle 1987: 270 (Maheśvarī).

45 The party also included the young prince's grandmother, Jambāvatī, Jagat Singh's mother, who also went on pilgrimage to Dvarka in 1641 (S. R. Sharma 1971: 16–17). On the illustrated text, see Topsfield (2000: 29).

46 Entwistle 1987: 190.

47 Sarkar 1964, 1:253–58.

48 Gommans 1995: 41–42, 82.

49 This is possibly the village of Kampil (southeast of Soron), which has been associated with Kapila (Jacobsen 2008: 177–78). There is also a Rāmeśvara temple at the site (Dallaporta and Marcato 2011: 13, picture 17). Kampilya was on the southern branch of the Grand Trunk Road (Filippi and Marcolongo 1999: 35), on the right bank of the Ganges, so that would fit with Sāvant Singh's description of crossing the Ganges afterward. Alternatively, it may be a reference to the site of Kapileshwar, southeast of Almora.

50 Though the reference could also be just to "lions and tigers" in this desolate area. Narsingh Badri is one of the so-called Pañc Badrī in the Alakananda valley on the way to Badrinath at 1,861 meters (Kaur 1985: 94, map on 95), depicted in a scroll by a Garhwali artist of the pilgrimage route for the Alakananda River from the early eighteenth century (Galloway 2014: 20–22).

51 Kaur 1985: 93, map on 31.

52 The reference is probably not to Dhaulagiri, now in Nepal, but is more likely to one

of the bright white peaks in the neighborhood of Badrinath, such as Gauriparbat (6,727 m) or Dunagiri (7,066 m).

53 *Jugal-bhakt-vinod* 21; K. Gupta 1965, 1:177.

54 Entwistle 1987: 371–72.

55 *Vrindāban-abhilāṣ*'s colophons give 1809 VS Asāṛh–Bhādon.

56 Dwivedi 1989: 128.

57 Entwistle 1987: 370–71.

58 Ibid.: 271.

59 *Sujān-caritra* (7.1.60; Rādhākrishnadās 1902: 207–8). I am grateful to Ankur Mittal of D.K. Agencies for providing me with a photocopy of this rare text. See also Entwistle (1987: 271).

60 Bhardwaj 1997: 9.

61 Contemporary description in Haberman (2006: 102). Nowadays there is both morning and evening āratī, but Nāgarīdās may just not have experienced the morning āratī.

62 Entwistle 1987: 416.

63 A Vaṃśīdās is mentioned in one of the VRI documents regarding the theological debates about *svakīyā* and *parakīyā*. He was a second-generation follower of Rūpa Kavirāja of the Sauramya-mat (Horstmann 2009: 75–86, 121).

64 That is, when they heard his devotional name, by which he signed his poetry.

65 Recently published in Del Bontà (2014: 18–19, plate 8), as *A Yogini at Her Retreat*.

66 On this genre, see Vaudeville (1986).

67 Ibid.: 40–41.

68 The Gwalior Maharaja built the *chatrī* under which the image is now placed (Entwistle 1987: 375).

69 In the temple of Dāūjī, it is celebrated on the sixth of the bright half of Bhādon (Baldeo Chaṭ; ibid.: 487). At Uncagaon, perhaps it was celebrated on this earlier date because of Balarāma's association with snakes.

70 Ibid.: 369.

71 As well as a walled garden and a monument to his brother (ibid.: 375–76).

72 It is unclear whether this rite was performed on images or on human actors.

73 Collections of devotional songs organized by festivals (*Varṣotsav-pad-saṅgrah*) tend to start with this festival (Rousseva-Sokolova 2000: 515), including Nāgarīdās's own *Garland of Festivals* (K. Gupta 1965, 1:117). In his *Pilgrim's Bliss*, Nāgarīdās is instead following the *bārahmāsā* tradition.

74 Entwistle 1987: 378–79.

75 Ibid.: 383.

76 Ibid.: 372.

77 Ibid.: 487.

78 Ibid.: 387.

79 Ibid.: 386–87.

80 Ibid.: 369.

81 See Pauwels (2015, plate 14).

82 In his *Vrindāban-dhām-anurāgāvalī*. The fair at Brahmakund took place for five evenings in the month of Śrāvaṇ, when poems composed by Nāgarīdās were recited before Rādhā-Krishna images placed under two *chatrī*s beside the tank (Entwistle 1987: 412).

83 Entwistle 1987: 285, 488; author's observation in 1986.

84 Nāhaṭā 1959: 117. The pilgrim visited shortly before, in Asoj (Āśvin), and so was not an eyewitness.

85 Entwistle 1987: 282–84, 488.

86 Nāgarīdās says everyone goes to "Gokul," but it is clear that he means Nandagaon, as at the end the pilgrims are said to return to Nandagaon (TĀ 159).

87 Again, this may be Sonehara ki Kadamkhandi or any grouping of Kadamba trees.

88 The festival in Vrindavan is described in Lodrick (1981: 114–18).

89 I come back to this interesting participatory eyewitness account below, this chapter, under "Mythical and Worldly Realms Interpenetrating."

90 Hawley and Goswami 1981: 104.

91 Anuradha Kapur (1990: 24) about the audience of the Rām-līlā.

92 Case 2000.

93 As explained above (in chapter 2, under "Other Krishna Devotional Sects"), Acintya-bhedābheda is associated specifically with the Gauḍīya-Sampradāya, but the other sects have similar theories.

94 The last line of the work says it was composed in 1752 (Holī VS 1808; see PV 48, K. Gupta 1965, 2:264) at the banks of the Ganges.

95 These may have been part of the *būṛhī līlā* cycle, still performed there today (Entwistle 1987: 369).

96 On contemporary Rām-līlās, see Kapur (1990: 6, 11–12, 23–24).

97 Entwistle 1987: 487; Thielemann 2002: 12–14.

98 For a contemporary description, see Entwistle (1987: 374).

99 As reported in *Vrindavan Today*, "Sankari Khor Lila," September 8, 2014, http://news.vrindavantoday.org/2014/09/sankari-khor-lila.

100 There is a pond (*kuṇḍa*) by that name in between Nandagaon and Barsana (Entwistle 1987: 382).

101 Entwistle suggests that this may be a reference to the four lion-like monster statues in gray stone on the west side of the pond (1987: 381–82).

102 Implied is that any mother has responsibility for her children and her instincts are to protect them.

103 Kadamkhandi could be the aforementioned wooded area Sonehara ki Kadamkhandi near Barsana or any place in Braj where there is a cluster of Kadamba trees.

104 See also Pauwels (2015: 231–32).

105 Mason 2009: 115–41.

106 Ibid.: 134.

107 Bakhtin compares the participatory aspect of the medieval carnival with modern-day Mardi Gras, which has degenerated into a mere spectacle (1984: 7).

4. Legends Mobilized

1 Or "Stories about Songs," if the first two words can be read as a determinative (*tatpuruṣa samāsa*), rather than a coordinative compound (*dvandva*).

2 Khān, who organizes his edition chronologically, includes it as one of the last works (1974: 567–615).

3 For more on these religious specialists, see Lutgendorf 1994: 66.

4 Nāmdev's songs have few Marathi characteristics, but his oeuvre in general as preserved in North India has marked Rajasthani and Braj features (Callewaert and Lath 1989: 6–7).

5 On the history of the term and its applicability to the Indian context, see Mallison (2001: vii–xx).

6 See, inter alia, W. H. McLeod's pioneering work on Sikh hagiography, Phyllis Granoff's on Jaina religious biography, David N. Lorenzen's on Hindu *bhakti* and William L. Smith's on North Indian hagiography. Important overview volumes are edited by Winand M. Callewaert and Rupert Snell (1994) and Françoise Mallison (2001).

7 For more on these characteristics, see Pauwels (2002).

8 See Hare (2011).

9 Attributed to Vallabha's grandson Gokulnāth and arranged by Gokulnāth's nephew Harirāy. The earliest manuscript of 84VV dates to 1640 and of 252VV to 1730, close to the time *Garland of Stories and Songs* was composed (Hawley 2015: 365n105).

10 Saha 2006: 237–39, 341.

11 Pritchett 1994: chapter 5.

12 On the vogue for Urdu poetry in Delhi, see Pauwels (2015). Perhaps the earliest Tazkirah, certainly the most influential, is Mīr Taqī "Mīr"'s Persian *Nikāt al-Shu'arā*, estimated to have been written in 1752 (Naim 1999: 8).

13 Rao and Shulman 1998: 7.

14 Ibid.: 186–87. Rao and Shulman remark that "these [*cāṭu*] verses circulated in what we might call a premodern cultural public space, somewhat similar to the public space of the European bourgeoisie, as defined by Habermas" (ibid.: 8).

15 See, e.g., ibid.: 14–15, 168–69, 176–81.

16 Ibid.: 135–48 and 159–68, respectively.

17 Ibid.: 148–59 (language) and 168–90 (critique of authority).

18 Rao and Shulman remark on similarities with the contemporaneous Mughal Persian poetic milieu (ibid.: 185–90).

19 For in-depth studies, see Dalmia-Lüderitz (1992) and Dalmia (1997).

20 Dalmia-Lüderitz 1992: 289.

21 Khān 1974: 2.

22 Dalmia-Lüderitz 1992: 288.

23 See Pauwels (forthcoming-b).

24 Dalmia-Lüderitz 1992: 295n26.

25 Dalmia 1997: 124–25.

26 As argued convincingly in ibid.: 338–439, esp. 379–81.

27 Ibid.: 380–81.

28 Another instance of individual authorial intent rather than collective creation is articulated in the introductory section, where the author says *liṣ(y)auṃ hauṃ*, or "I have written."

29 See the JCPM MSS 2210, fol. 72v, and 3904, fol. 114r, both dated 1792; also MS 903, fol. 37r, which is undated.

30 The differences with *Garland of Stories and Songs* are that it is in verse (*Caupāī*); it is meant to be sung (designation of tune [*rāga*] and rhythm [*tāla*] are given at the beginning); its title indicates the author saw it as a *parcaī* rather than a *prasaṅga*; its structure

does not allow for quotation of songs by Govindsvāmī; and it is also more sectarian Vallabhan: in the story as well as in the invocation and envoi, it expresses devotion for Viṭṭhalnāth (K. Gupta 1965, 2:190–92; Khān 1974: 503–6; not in V. Śaraṇ 1966).

31 See the front cover of Caturvedī (1983). Both images are discussed below.

32 The Kishangarh Royal Collection has a manuscript with *Garland of Stories and Songs* (Peṭī 6B) that includes an illustrative sketch, on the page following the *prasaṅga* of Paramānand (fols. 155ff.).

33 On the basis of published catalogs (and the Internet manuscript base of the National Mission for Manuscripts), I have traced manuscript copies preserved in Agra (B. R. Ambedkar Viśvavidyālaya 1032.1); Bharatpur (RORI 256 and 4077.24); Jaipur (City Palace Museum 731, 903, 1484, 2210, 3905); Jodhpur (RORI 155); and Vrindavan (VRI 17136-I; VRS 968 and 1019). Two that I was unable to trace are reported to be in Benares (Nāgarī Pracāriṇī Sabhā collection; originally from the private collection of Yājñik of Lucknow [see K. Gupta 1965, 2:16 and 1:103, MS "yā"]), and Datia (according to the manuscript searches carried out at the beginning of the twentieth century [see K. Gupta 1965, 1:87]).

34 JCPM MS 3904, fol. 114r.

35 JCPM MS 2210, fol. 173r.

36 Phaḍke 1974. Mahīpati (1715–1790) contextualizes the story mythologically, stating that it was by the wish of Krishna that Jayadeva was born (*Bhakt-vijay* 2.1; Abbot and Godbole 1982: 11). Nāgarīdās does not frame it that way. The Bengali work *Jaydeb-caritra* by Banmālī Dās stresses as its main agenda the importance of the pilgrimage center of Kenduli (Smith 2000: 12).

37 Kedarnāth 1915: 17, v. 38.3.

38 Mītal 1968: 361.

39 The story is told by Bābā Priyāśaraṇ in Śrī Ācārya-caritāvali, which dates from 1942 (1999 VS) (K. Śaraṇ 1979: 187–79). There is indeed a Rādhāmādhava temple in Radhakund, the deities of which are considered "replacement" (*pratibhu*) mūrti of Jayadeva. However, it is said to have been a stop on the exodus from Vrindavan to Jaipur in 1670, not to Salemabad in 1713.

40 They can also be read as propaganda for the continued performance of Jayadeva's *Gīta-govinda* in the Jagannātha temple in Puri, which may have been under attack in this period (see Dash 2004: 332–41).

41 Krishna's suggestion that Rādhā place her foot on his head implies a role reversal, as to do so would indicate an admission of the other's superiority. This unorthodox sentiment is what makes Jayadeva hesitate.

42 Priyādās: BRB 147; Rūpkalā 1977: 347–48. Kiśordās: Kedarnāth 1915: 31–32, vv. 69–70.

43 *Gīta-govinda Sarga* 10, *Prabandha* 19; Siegel 1978: text 304–5, trans. 273–74.

44 BRB 150; Rūpkalā 1977: 35–31.

45 BRB 151; Rūpkalā 1977: 351–52.

46 BRB 159–62; Rūpkalā 1977: 359–62. Mahīpati also tells this story, specifying that Jayadeva sings *Rādhā-vilāsa* to revive his wife (*Bhakt-vijay* 2.235; Abbott and Godbole 1982: 28).

47 Bhm 108; Rūpkalā 1977: 673–74. BRB 429–55; Rūpkalā 1977: 674–95. Hawley 2005: 55–60; Mallison 2013.

48 Mallison 1986: 17–18.

49 Mallison 1998: 271.

50 *Māhero* in Rājasthānī: the ritual gift-giving on the occasion of the seventh month of one's daughter's first pregnancy, observed strictly within the Brahmin community Narsī Mehtā belonged to (Mallison 1986: 18).

51 Ibid.: 269. The king is named Maṇḍalīk in the poem; Rā Māṃḍalika III ruled Junagarh in 1432–70 (ibid.: 29, esp. n89).

52 See *Bhakt-vijay* chapter 30; Abbott and Godbole (1982: 457–64). On the commemoration of Narsī, see Mallison (1998: 269).

53 Not in the shorter redaction of the work.

54 On Anantdās's *Parcaī*s, see Callewaert and Sharma (2000).

55 According to Nābhādās, Nāmdev and Tilocan were both disciples of Jñāndev in Viṣṇusvāmī's lineage (together with Vallabha) (see Bhm 48; Rūpkalā 1977: 380).

56 See Smith (2000: 100). The incident of God appearing in a dog is also hinted at by Harirām Vyās and Anantdās and related in the 1693 *Pothī Prem Ambodh* (Callewaert and Lath 1989: 18, 24).

57 See Pauwels (2002, 2009a).

58 Here *Moghol* means simply "a high-ranking, powerful Muslim." Nāmdev, because of his low caste, could be forced to do labor for those of higher status.

59 This story is also alluded to by Nābhādās and told in full by Anantdās (Callewaert and Lath 1989: 17–18). Mahīpati does not elaborate.

60 The king uses the familiar second-person pronoun *tum* for the Brahmins (which they also used to address him), but the respectful plural third-person pronoun *ve* for the saint.

61 *Prasaṅga* 4.11–16; Callewaert and Sharma 2000: trans. 314–20, 341–46.

62 For Priyādās, see Callewaert and Friedlander (1992: 31–32). The song Nāgarīdās quotes is found in all the seventeenth-century manuscripts consulted by Callewaert and Friedlander, though not in the *Ādi-granth* and the Fatehpur manuscript (ibid.: 44).

63 Upon initiation, the devotee is given a necklace of basil-beads (*tulsī kaṇṭhī*).

64 For Anantdās: Lorenzen 1991: 191–97; trans. 118–21; Callewaert and Sharma 2000: text 85–89. For Priyādās: BRB 281; Rūpkalā 1977: 490–91.

65 So does the textbook *Hindee and Hindoostanee Selections*, published in 1827 by William Price and Tarinee Churun Mitr (Hare 2011: 189). The song must have been popular and circulating widely by that time.

66 The refrain is similar to *Kabīr-granthāvalī* 287 (a poem attested in a 1681 MS), with the refrain "Now my heart has tasted Hari's rasa, so I am drunk with devotion" (Callewaert 2000: 395), and reminiscent of the *Ādi-granth* song with the refrain "Oh Hermit Yogī, my mind is intoxicated" (ĀG 969 Rāmkalī Kabīr 2).

67 Pauwels 2002: 162–68, 186–96.

68 This is remarkable, because around this time, in 1715, in the region (at the Naraina Dādū-panthī seat) a manuscript was prepared that includes, inter alia, an image of Kabīr and Rāmānanda (reproduced in Friedlander [1996: 601; details 449–50]).

69 Khojī is one of the *bhakta*s enumerated in Nābhā's hagiography (*Bhakt-māl* 97; Rūpkalā 1977: 635), and this is elaborated in Priyādās's *ṭīkā* (BRB 399–400; Rūpkalā 1977: 636–38). The stories are about reaching Rāma in the hereafter.

70 Kañjar is a low-caste group in Rajasthan (Lavania et al. 1998: 498–500; for Uttar Pradesh, see Hasan, Rizvi, and Das 2005: 701–8). Kol is a tribe from Central India (ibid.: 833–36).

71 The general idea is that the low-caste, laden with leftovers, still asking for more, was very polluting.

72 Manuscripts in the longer redaction: JCPM 903 and 2210.

73 Lutgendorf 1994.

74 Nor for that matter in the Rāmānandī *Bhakt-māl* or its commentary (see Paramasivan 2010: 11–12).

75 Otherwise, Nāgarīdās does not include any of the features of these "spurious" hagiographies: he does not delineate a canon of Tulsī's works or establish a link between Tulsī's life and his works, nor does he focus on legitimation of the vernacular scripture; he does not assert interpretive traditions, that is, *paramparā* lineages of *Rām-carit-mānas* interpreters, or etiological stories providing the origin of popular practices of recitation.

76 Priyādās refers to a non-specified *Dillīpati pātasāha*.

77 BRB 120–21; Rūpkalā 1977: 762–64.

78 The Tulsīdās story is also told in Mahīpati's hagiography (*Bhakt-vijay* 3.69–148; Abbot and Godbole 1982: 36–41), where Tulsī dismisses the passing Rāma and his army as "some Muslims" (*avindha*). Still, the story has a happy ending, because Hanumān relents and asks Rāma to appear in his "true form" for Tulsī.

79 Both are also told by Priyādās (BRB 514; Rūpkalā 1977: 767–68).

80 *Bhakt-vijay* 3.245–313; Abbot and Godbole 1982: 49–54.

81 Mentioned in *Tuzuk-e Jahāngīrī* as Anīrā'ī Singh-dalan, the title of Anūp Rāy (TJ 185–88, 263, 336, 373). I am grateful to Purnima Dhavan for this reference. Since he is first mentioned in *Tuzuk-e Jahāngīrī* as having saved Jahāngīr during a tiger hunt, she also speculates that he might have been a Ban Gujjar, a caste frequently used as guides for armies and for tracking game (personal communication, June 15, 2012).

82 Metcalfe 1843: fol. 16v.

83 Yet later it was even briefly a prison for the last emperor, Bahādur Shāh Zafar.

84 Chatterjee 2013: 24–26.

85 As argued by Chatterjee (ibid.: 28).

86 BRB 517–18; Rūpkalā 1977: 771–72. Mahīpati in his hagiography also reports a visit by Tulsīdās to the Braj area (*Bhakt-vijay* 3.315–19; Abbot and Godbole 1982: 54–55), but notes neither his hesitation to bow before Krishna images nor the Vallabhan connection, though he mentions Gokul (besides Mathura and Vrindavan). Mahīpati's Tulsīdās meets Priyādās (*Bhakt-vijay* 3.320–39; Abbot and Godbole 1982: 55–56).

87 252VV 4.3; trans. Pauwels 2008: 66–67.

88 84VV 89.2; Barz 1976: 151–3l; Kṛṣṇadās 1986a: 278–79.

89 84VV 89.1; Barz 1976: 142–51, 265–77.

90 84VV 90.1.

91 84VV 90.6; Barz 1976: 184–86; Kṛṣṇadās 1986a: 305–6.

92 The song quoted refers to the down on Krishna's cheek, which is reminiscent of Persian homoerotic poetry.

93 252VV 3.8; Kṛṣṇadās 1986b: 31–33.

94 Mānikcand: 252VV 29; Kṛṣṇadās 1986b: 107–8.
95 252VV 2.1; Kṛṣṇadās 1986b: 19–21.
96 This story is found only in some manuscripts of the shorter recension.
97 252VV 2.3; Kṛṣṇadās 1986b: 22–23.
98 That is, the curtain that hides the image from view while it is being prepared for *darshana*.
99 There is a pun here: *hari* stands for Krishna and is also a verb meaning "having taken away."
100 84VV 92.5; Barz 1976: 228–33; Kṛṣṇadās 1986a: 323–25.
101 252VV 243; Kṛṣṇadās 1986b: 486–91.
102 252VV 243.1; Kṛṣṇadās 1986b: 486–88.
103 252VV 243.2; Kṛṣṇadās 1986b: 488–89.
104 252VV 243.3–4; Kṛṣṇadās 1986b; 489–91.
105 His initiation is not related, but the link is asserted in the introductory and final remarks of 252VV 245 (Kṛṣṇadās 1986b: 492–93).
106 BRB 417–18; Rūpkalā 1977: 659–69.
107 Hawley 1984: 3–22.
108 On the Vārtā story, see ibid.: 8; 84VV 88.1; Barz 1976: 112–13.
109 Likewise questioned by Hawley (2005: 248–63).
110 84VV 88.3; Barz 1976: 114.
111 84VV 92.4; Barz 1976: 227–28; Kṛṣṇadās 1986a: 321–23.
112 *String of Song-Pearls* includes three, six, and nine poems by each of the three, respectively.
113 BRB 523–24; Rūpkalā 1977: 787–88. Priyādās quotes the first three words of the song, whereas Nāgarīdās gives the full version.
114 PPM 46; BRB 498; Rūpkalā 1977: 746–47.
115 The district (*pargana*) of Sandila was in the district of Hardoi, south of the Gomti River (Benett 1878, 3:298–304). It is interesting that a Brahmin is the administrator, as traditionally the district was administered by Sayyids; for a brief time, under Humayūn, it was administered by Chandels.
116 BRB 500–501; Rūpkalā 1977: 748–49.
117 BRB 499; Rūpkalā 1977: 747–48.
118 BRB 502; Rūpkalā 1977: 749–50.
119 This custom would constitute a reversal of normal social hierarchy where the son-in-law and his family are on the receiving side of ritual gifts.
120 PMĀ, fol. 193v; in a manuscript dated 1746 (1803 VS), preserved by Faiyāz Alī Khān's descendants.
121 Pauwels 2015: plate 3.
122 V. Śaraṇ asserts that it is in Rupnagar, but there is no lake there (1966: facing p. 90).
123 For detailed views of the inscriptions, I am grateful to Navina Najat Haidar.
124 *Rasik-ananya-mālā, parcaī* 2; see Pauwels 2002: 203–4, 252–56.
125 *Rasik-ananya-mālā, parcaī* 1; Purohit 1986: 1–3.
126 *Rasik-ananya-mālā, parcaī* 24; Purohit 1986: 66–67.
127 *Rasik-ananya-mālā, parcaī* 15; Purohit 1986: 38–40.
128 Delvoye 1997: 238–55.

129 252VV 237; Kṛṣṇadās 1986b: 475–77.
130 In *Nij-mat-siddhānt*, see Rosenstein (1997: 15–16); Kedarnāth (1915: 89–95).
131 Delvoye 1997: 247. Alternatively, Mathur dates it to circa 1775 (2000: 98–99, plate 31).
132 Delvoye 1997: 248; Datta 1977: 107. Datta stresses that the *tilaka* of Svāmī Haridās in the National Museum painting (also shown in a portrait of his in Bhārat Kalā Bhavan in Benares) is Nimbārkan and not what contemporary Haridāsīs typically wear (1977: 105–6). The Mughal copy of the detail is now in a private collection (see Pal 1997: 224–25, plate 135).
133 See also Pauwels (2010: 183–95).
134 Bhm 115 and BRB 471–80, respectively; Rūpkalā 1977: 712–23.
135 BRB 479; Rūpkalā 1977: 721.
136 BRB 473–75; Rūpkalā 1977: 716–18.
137 BRB 476–77; Rūpkalā 1977: 718–19.
138 BRB 480; Rūpkalā 1977: 722.
139 A reference to the *Mahābhārata*, where Krishna saved Draupadī from humiliation.
140 A reference to the story of the devotee Dhruva, who defied his godless father Hiraṇyakaśyapu.
141 A reference to the story where Vishnu came to the rescue of the elephant king, killing the crocodile that attacked him (BhP 8.2).
142 Perhaps as a substitute for the image of Krishna, in front of which he would usually dance.
143 Pauwels 2010: 192–94.
144 Krishnadās Adhikārī: 84VV 92.1; Barz 1976: 213–14. Rāmdās: 84VV 54: Kṛṣṇadās 1986a: 189–90.
145 The same is found in the Braj commentary to *Śikṣā-patra*, the Sanskrit advice of Harirāy to his younger brother (at the same time, Bīrbal also is depreciated as *anyāśrayī*; commentary to 18.15; Śrī Subodhinī Sabhā 1936: 207).
146 Mallison 1991: 202.
147 Mukta 1994: 1–3.
148 For the full argument, see Pauwels (2010).
149 V. Śaraṇ says the manuscript is dated 1883 (1940 VS) (1966: 26), presumably referring to KRC Peṭī 6B, no. 67, a volume in red velvet that contains all of Nāgarīdās's works, written in 1884 (1941 VS), by a Brahmin Mathurādās in Kishangarh. The Royal Collection in Kishangarh also has an undated and unnumbered big red volume that looks to be from the same period (where PPM starts on fol. 155, and the Mīrā chapters on fol. 179r). Intriguingly, KRC 67 does have some passages erased on fol. 179v.
150 The Mewar historian Shyāmal Dās compiled a counter-colonial history (*Vīr-vinod*), in which Mīrā was rehabilitated (Martin 2000).
151 *Mīrābāī kā Jīvancaritra* by Munśī Devīprasād.
152 This is also how Mīrā is portrayed in the Amar Citra Kathā comic books (Hawley 1995: 108–20).
153 BRB 478; Rūpkalā 1977: 720.
154 In Nāgarīdās's story, the persecuting Rāṇā is Mīrā's older rather than younger brother-in-law. Academic works of this period often portray the younger Ratan Singh or Vikramāditya in the villain role.

155 Tivārī 1974; on which see Hawley (2005: 100–101). Notwithstanding the similarities, the *Garland of Stories and Songs* does not totally fit the late nineteenth-century picture. For example, Mīrā's natal family does not figure importantly. Like Priyādās, Nāgarīdās begins with the name of her birthplace, Mertau, but none of the Rathor Merta rulers, Dūdā, Vīramdev, or Jaimal, are mentioned.

156 Preserved in the Jaipur City Palace Museum Library (MS 2210; fols. 33r–43r).

157 Another old manuscript that includes the Mīrā *prasaṅgas* (fols. 13r–15v) is Rādhāvallabhan and estimated to date from 1800 (1850 VS); it is preserved in the Ras Bhāratī Sansthān (collection of Jayesh Khandelval in Vrindavan 968).

158 Haidar 1995: 138–39, plate 125 (photo by R. Skelton; I am grateful to Haidar for providing me with a colored copy of the plate in her dissertation). A detail of the painting is reproduced on the cover of a popular edition of Mīrā's work (Caturvedī 1983), and a detail of Mīrā's bust was redrawn and issued as a postage stamp by the Government of India in 1954 as part of a saints-poets series (Haidar 1995: 139n143).

159 Alternatively, the cloth held by the accusing woman may be the one on which the cup had been offered.

160 Or, alternatively, the painting may depict the dramatic climax of Mīrā's story in Dvarka, her final desperate plea to God in the temple to save her, as the servants of the Rāṇā and the *purohit* were about to take her back home to Rajasthan (PPM 17). Mīrā is not alone in the temple, as she is in the story, but the entering man in the background could be the *purohit*, and the women standing nearby, holding the pillars, her "Vaishnava girlfriends on the porch." The item in the hands of the woman in front of the image might be a book manuscript, in which Mīrā's songs are collected.

161 Haidar 1995: 139 (confirmed by personal communication with the Mukhiyā of the Śrī Kalyāṇarāya temple in 2003 and 2011 and Hīrālāl Kīrtaniyā in 2011).

162 Most of the authors enumerated here are celebrated in the vignettes of *Garland of Stories and Songs* and/or have been introduced in chapter 2. The two Nāgarīdāses are the one named Nehī (mentioned in PPM) and the pupil of Bihārīdās (McGregor 1984: 93). Dāmodar may be Harivaṃś's disciple, better known as Sevakjī (McGregor 1984: 90). Poems with the *chāpas* "Ali Bhagvān" and "Caturbihārī" are included in Nāgarīdās's *String of Song-Pearls*. Prītam Rasik may be the Rādhāvallabhan or Haridāsī Rasikdās (ibid.: 408 and 470, respectively). Mādhav may refer to Mādhavdās Jaganāthī, a contemporary of Caitanya (ibid.: 94). Āskaran is remembered as a Vallabhan and uncle of the founder of Kishangarh (Entwistle 1987: 210n417). Rāmdās could be Mīrā's *purohit*, the Sikh Guru, or the Marathi saint of that name, who is now commonly associated with Śivājī.

163 K. Gupta 1965, 1:115.

164 This Sanskrit Śloka from *Padma Purāṇa*, Kārtika Māhātmya, Bhakti Sandarbha 269.827, is often quoted by Gauḍīya theologians, for example, Gopāla Bhaṭṭa and Jīva Gosvāmī (Shrīvatsa Gosvami, personal communication, August 6, 2012).

165 A reference to the myth of the origin of the Gaṅgā: Vishnu's feet started to melt as he heard Shiva's flute play, and Brahmā collected the water and formed the Gaṅgā from it.

166 Novetzke 2008: 74–85.

167 For example, Śrīnivās Ācārya "toured tirelessly all parts of Bengal to initiate and then maintain his network of devotees" (Stewart 2010: 282).

168 On the circulation of kings, see Pouchepadass (2003).

169 84VV 90, *prasaṅga* 6; Kṛṣṇadās 1986a: 305; Barz 1976: 184.

170 84VV 92 *prasaṅga* 1; Barz 1976: 213–14.

171 Habermas 1974: 49; see also Orsini 1999.

172 Bayly 2000: 180.

173 Agrawal 2009: 49.

174 Novetzke 2008: 16–18; Bayly 2000: 181–82.

175 Bayly 2000: 195–96.

176 Ibid.: 185–86.

177 Ibid.: 189–99.

178 Ibid.: 207–8.

179 As demonstrated for the nineteenth century by Clémentin-Ojha and Ojha (2009: 163–64).

180 The situation is complicated by the vexed question of what constitutes the state.

181 Perhaps this is more in line with the contesting of "public reputations of big men," in the light of arguments that mobilized social groups are less likely than influential local people to be seen as pushing for representation of their views (Bayly 2000: 187 [based on Mattison Mines's research in Tamil Nadu]).

182 In 1722–37 and again in 1740 (Horstmann 2009: 43).

183 Curiously, though, the first dated manuscript of the longer version was written for Pratāp Singh in Jaipur.

184 Term from Dalmia (1997: 7).

5. Myth Retold

1 K. Gupta 1965, 2:138; RORI Jaipur, fol. 3v.

2 On this genre, see Rao and Shulman (1998).

3 It is included in manuscripts of his complete works, for example, KRC Peṭī 6B, no. 9, fols. 94b–107b.K. Gupta reports that he was unable to locate any separate manuscript of this work (1965, 1:105–6). A copy of *Garland of Rāma's Romance* is preserved (together with other works by Nāgarīdās) as catalog no. 9 in the Bālmukund collection of the Śrī Naṭnagar Śodh Sansthān in Sitamau. See the institute's web page, accessed September 21, 2016, http://natnagarsitamau.com.

4 Richman (1991) is the classical collection of articles on the topic, but many others have appeared since.

5 For both, there are several articles in Richman (2001) and Bose (2003, 2004). See also Hess (1999) and Kishwar (2001).

6 Pollock (2004 [first published in the *Journal of Asian Studies* in 1993]) has generated a lively scholarly debate on the topic.

7 Ibid.

8 Griffiths 1999: 97–98.

9 252VV 21; Kṛṣṇadās 1986a: 96–97.

10 The song quoted is from his *Gītāmṛt-gaṅgā* (13.93).

11 Most of the poems are attested in other collections of the poets' works, but Nāgarīdās's quotations, when compared with the standard editions, frequently show significant differences ascribable to oral transmission.

12 The quotations make up less than the three-quarters that Griffiths suggests in his formal definition (1999: 98).

13 Term from Griffiths (ibid.: ix–x).

14 Smagorinsky 2001: 137.

15 Cf. also Siṃha 1957: 212–13. Agradās is also quoted in Nāgarīdās's *String of Song-Pearls*.

16 For the festival songs, see V. Śaraṇ (1966: 317–18) and Khān (1974: 706–8). They are also in the manuscript preserved in Mathura, Shrī Krishna Shodhpīṭh Pustakālay (Janmabhūmi Library, MS 13254-365138 [undated], fol. 35r–v). Compared to the poems included in the *Garland of Rāma's Romance*, two have a similar rhyme: UM 7 and RCM 2, UM 8 and RCM 3.

17 Meaning that on earth, too, men can expect the same abundance as the gods above.

18 The sage is asking for Rāma's help in safeguarding his Vedic sacrifice.

19 The mythological elephants stationed at the quarters of the sky to uphold the earth.

20 Reference to the killing of a fierce demoness and the (perceived) adulteress Ahalyā's redemption.

21 Again a reference to the incident where Ahalyā was liberated by the touch of Rāma's feet.

22 The reference to Śuka, Sanaka, and his brothers strengthens the attribution to the founder of the Salemabad Pīṭh, where the Sanakādis were worshipped prominently.

23 This cleverly contains also the poet's signature, Nāgar.

24 This stresses the identity of Sītā as Śrī, Vishnu's wife, and implies that Rāma was aware of who she was to him.

25 Sītā is too timid to state that she wants to die and is transferring agency to her life-breaths, claiming they are slipping away from her watchful eye.

26 In using the Sanskritic form of the monkey's name, Hanumant, Sītā accords him with more respect.

27 S. Goldman 2001: 223.

28 Ibid.: 232–36.

29 An alternative reading is: "he'll remember it became stuck to his chest in love-play."

30 Sītā is trying to allay Hanumān's fears that Rāma might be upset upon hearing this intimate information repeated by a monkey. At the same time, she wistfully envies him the privilege of seeing Rāma, whereas she would long for a glimpse of her husband to help her through this difficult time.

31 References to the *tilaka* mark of red mineral powder (*manaḥsīlāyās tilaka*) are already in Vālmīki's version. In *Sundara-kāṇḍa*, Sītā says: "You must surely remember the *tilaka* mark of red mineral powder that you placed on my forehead when my regular *tilaka* mark had been rubbed off" (38.5; Goldman and Goldman 1996: 224 and 538n21), and Hanumān mentions it when he renders the message to Rāma (63.21; Goldman and Goldman 1996: 290).

32 See the alternative meaning for this half-line. An incident of the transferal of a *tilaka* mark to Rāma's chest is alluded to in some versions, but the southern and western recensions omit it (Goldman and Goldman 1996: 455n14).

33 Cf. *Sūr-sāgar* 9.573; Vājpeyī 1978, 1:192–93.

34 This line makes light of the Vedic gods as they react to Rāma's feat. Shiva is torn, presumably because, on the one hand, Rāvaṇa is his devotee, but, on the other, the greater cosmic good has to prevail.

35 Questions by Rao (2004).

36 Kapur 1990: 11–12, 199–202.

37 K. Gupta 1965, 2:5–6.

38 I discovered these in the Kishangarh Royal Collection, in Peṭī 6B, no. 9 (a red volume, measuring approximately 10 × 20 cm, of three folios).

39 K. Gupta 1965, 2:147.

40 As reported by Khān (1974: 340).

41 K. Gupta 1965, 1:95.

42 Ibid., 1:104.

43 Mason 2009: 128–32.

44 Ibid.: 128.

45 Shulman 2001: 74.

46 Ibid.: 58–60, 63, 76.

47 For Hinduism, perhaps the only study is Jarow's on coping with death in the *Bhāgavata-purāṇa*, but this is from the perspective of the story within the text (2003).

48 *Maṅgalācaran* of the second *skandha*, *Chappay* 1, R. Śarmā 1996, 1:84.

49 The illustrated multivolume work is by Okada, Biardeau, and Porcher (2011). For those previously published, see Mathur (2000: plates 20 and 32).

50 Mathur states that no painting activity took place during the period of turmoil. After the peace treaty was signed, Nihālcand and his sons worked in Rupnagar for Sardār Singh, but after Sāvant Singh's death they migrated to Kishangarh (2000: 26).

51 Okada, Biardeau, and Porcher 2011, 1:33.

52 The scene seems to have been painted over, as a silhouette of what looks like an ascetic figure is still visible in the green behind Rāma.

53 Okada, Biardeau, and Porcher 2011, 1:48–49.

54 Okada, Biardeau, and Porcher 2011, 1:208–9. This image seems to be from the same series as the one with the vina, as it has a similar blue border with golden floral motive, and there is a striking similarity in the facial features of Rāma.

55 Ibid., 3:18–19. Like the image with the vina, this one, too, seems to have been painted over.

56 National Museum, New Delhi, accession no. 63.807; see Mathur 2000: 76–77, plate 20.

57 The first painting is in the collection of Navin Kumar in New York; Okada, Biardeau, and Porcher 2011, 3:28. The second is in the Government Central Museum in Albert Hall, Jaipur; ibid., 3:30–31.

58 *Rama, Sita, and Lakshman Seated by a Rocky Shore*, San Diego Museum of Art (accession no. 1990.771). It can be viewed online at the museum's website, www.sdmart.org/collections/Asia/item/1990.771, accessed September 12, 2015.

59 Formerly in the collection of Sven Gahlin in London; Okada, Biardeau, and Porcher 2011, 3:156–57.

60 National Museum, New Delhi, accession no. 59.284/9; see Mathur 2000: 100–101, no. 32.

61 *Rama, Lakshmana, and Sita at a Hermitage*, Los Angeles County Museum of Art (accession no. M.79.252.1). It has not yet been published, but can be viewed online at the museum's website, http://collections.lacma.org/node/242198, accessed July 3, 2013.

62 Okada, Biardeau, and Porcher 2011, 6:7.

63 At his court, a *Rāmāyaṇa* was composed in 1775 by Haricaraṇ Dās (Friedlander 1996: 254).

64 Terms from Rao (2004).

65 Rao and Shulman 1998: 146–47.

66 Sen 2000: 183–84. An example from the more recent past is Narendra Kohli's 1974 novel *Abhyudaya*, which has been studied for its political agenda by Phyllis Herman (2003: 135–38).

67 In line with what John Stratton Hawley has so pertinently drawn attention to in a celebrated essay (1988).

Conclusion

1 For the modern setting, see Thielemann (1998: 78–83).

2 K. Gupta 1965, 1:29.

Bibliography

Abbreviations Used in Documentation

84VV	*Caurāsī Vaiṣṇavan kī Vārtā*
252VV	*Do Sau Bāvan Vaiṣṇavan kī Vārtā*
Bhm	*Bhakt-māl*
BhP	*Bhāgavata-purāṇa*
BRB	*Bhakti-ras-bodhinī*
JBV	*Jugal-bhakt-vinod*
JCPM	Jaipur City Palace Museum: Khās Mohor Collection
KRC	Kishangarh Royal Collection
MĀ	*Mā'sir-e 'Ālamgīrī* (Sarkar 1947)
MM	*Manorath-mañjarī*
MU	*Mā'sir ul-Umarā* (Beveridge and Prashad 1952)
OHED	*The Oxford Hindi-English Dictionary* (McGregor 1993)
PMĀ	*Pad-muktāvalī*
PPM	*Pad-prasaṅg-mālā*
PV	*Phág-vihār*
RCM	*Rām-carit-mālā*
RORI	Rajasthan Oriental Research Institute
RV	*Rūp-vacanikā*
ŚBPVP	*Śrīmad-Bhāgavat-pārāyaṇ-vidhi-prakāś*
SPD	*Selections from the Peshwa Daftar* (Sardesai 1930–34)
TĀ	*Tīrthānand*
TJ	*Tuzuk-e Jahāngīrī* (Rogers and Beveridge 1909–14)
VAPPP	*Vṛndāban-abhilāṣ-pūran-pad-prabandh*
VRI	Vrindavan Research Institute
VRS	Vrindavan, Ras Bhāratī Sansthān

Editions of Nāgarīdās's Works (Order of Publication)

Gauḍ, Śrīdharātmaja Kisanlāl. 1898. *Nāgara-samuccayaḥ*. Bombay: Jñānsāgar.

Gupta, Kiśorīlāl. 1965. *Nāgarīdās Granthāvalī*. 2 vols. Benares: Nāgarī Pracāriṇī Sabhā.

Śaraṇ, Vrajvallabh. 1966. *Śrī Nāgarīdāsjī kī Vāṇī: Nāgarīdāśjī ke jīvanvṛtta evaṃ vāṇiyoṃ kā sanśodhit sanskaraṇ*. Vrindavan: Śrī Sarveśvar Press.

Khān, Faiyāz Alī. 1974. *Nāgarīdās Granthāvalī*. New Delhi: Kendrīya Hindī Nideśālay.

Secondary Sources

Abbott, Justin E., and Narhar R. Godbole. 1982 (1933). *Stories of Indian Saints: Translation of Mahipati's Marathi Bhaktavijaya*. 2 vols. in one. Delhi: Motilal Banarsidass.

Ācārya, Govindlāl, ed. 1968. *Śrīnāthjī kī Prākaṭya Vārtā: Go. Śrī Harirāy mahānubhāv kṛt*. Nathdwara: Vidhya Vibhag.

Acharya, K. A. 1978. *Maratha-Rajput Relations from 1720 to 1795 A.D.* Akola: Sitabai Arts College.

Agrawal, Purushottam. 2009. *Akath Kahānī Prem Kī: Kabīr kī Kavittā aur unkā Samay*. New Delhi: Rājkamal Prakāśan.

———. 2011. "In Search of Ramanand: The Guru of Kabir and Others." *Pratilipi*, November. Accessed May 22, 2012, http://pratilipi.in/2008/10/in-search-of-ramanand-purushottam-agrawal.

Ahluwalia, Roda. 2008. *Rajput Painting: Romantic, Divine, and Courtly Art from India*. London: British Museum Press.

Ajmerī, Khvājah Sayyid 'Abdulbārī Ma'nī. 1952. *Asanid-us-Sanadid*. Ajmer: n.p.

Alam, Muzaffar, and Sanjay Subrahmanyam. 1996. "Discovering the Familiar: Notes on the Travel Account of Anand Ram Mukhlis." *South Asia Research* 26, no. 2: 131–54.

———. 2004. "The Making of a Munshi." *Comparative Studies of South Asia, Africa and the Middle East* 24, no. 2: 61–72.

Alavi, Seema, ed. 2002. *The Eighteenth Century in India*. Delhi: Oxford University Press.

Ali, Faiyāz "Azad." 2003. "Sabhī sampradāyoṃ ke āsthā kā sthal: Sultān pīr kā mazār." In *Rūpkiraṇ*, edited by D. C. V. Kiraṇ, 82–83. Rupnagar: Kiraṇ Publications.

Ambalal, Amit. 1987. *Krishna as Shrinathji: Rajasthani Paintings from Nathdvara*. Ahmedabad: Mapin.

Asher, Catherine. 1992. "The Architecture of Raja Man Singh: A Study of Sub-imperial Patronage." In *The Powers of Art: Patronage in Indian Culture*, edited by Barbara Stoler Miller, 183–201. Delhi: Oxford University Press.

Askari, Syed Hasan, trans. 1980. *Shāhnāma Munawwar Kalām by Shiv Dās Lakhnawi*. Indian Council of Historical Research. Patna: Janaki Prakashan.

Bahadur, S. P., trans. 1978. *Complete Works of Gosvami Tulsidas*. Benares: Prachya Prakashan.

Bahura, Gopal Naryana. 1976. *Literary Heritage of the Rulers of Amber and Jaipur*. Jaipur: United Printers.

Bahura, Gopal Naryana, and Chandramani Singh. 1990. *Catalogue of Historical Documents in Kapad Dwara, Jaipur*. Part 2, *Maps and Plans*. Jaipur: Jaipur Public Charitable Trust.

Bakhtin, Mikhail. 1984 (1965). *Rabelais and His World*. Translated by Hélène Iswolsky. Bloomington: Indiana University Press.

Bangha, Imre. 1997. "The Harikalā Belī and Ānandghan's Death." *Annali—Instituto Universitario Orientale, Napoli* 57: 231–41.

———. 2007. "Court and Religious Communities as Centres of Literary Activity in Eighteenth-Century India." In *Indian Languages and Texts through the Ages*, edited by Csaba Dezsö, 307–53. New Delhi: Manohar.

Barnett, Richard B., ed. 2002. *Rethinking Early Modern India*. New Delhi: Manohar.

Barz, Richard K. 1976. *The Bhakti Sect of Vallabhācārya*. Faridabad: Thomson Press.

———. 2009. "Vallabha Sampradāya." In *Brill's Encyclopedia of Hinduism*, edited by Knut A. Jacobsen, Helene Basu, Angelika Malinar, and Vasudha Naryanan, 1:606–16. Leiden: Brill.

Bayly, Christopher. 1983. *Rulers, Townsmen, and Bazaars: North Indian Society in the Age of British Expansion, 1770–1870*. Cambridge: Cambridge University Press.

———. 2000. *Empire and Information: Intelligence Gathering and Social Communication in India, 1780–1870*. Cambridge: Cambridge University Press.

Benett, William Charles. 1878. *Gazetteer of the Province of Oudh*. 3 vols. Allahabad: North-Western Provinces and Oudh Government Press.

Beveridge, Henry, trans., and Baini Prashad, rev. and annotator. 1952. *The Maāthir-ul-Umarā, Being Biographies of the Muḥammadan and Hindu Officers of the Timurid Sovereigns of India from 1500 to about 1780 A.D. by Nawwāb Ṣamṣām-ud-Daula Shāh Nawāz Khān and His Son 'Abdul- Ḥayy*. Vol. 2. Calcutta: Asiatic Society.

Bhardwaj, Surinder Mohan. 1973. *Hindu Places of Pilgrimage in India (A Study in Cultural Geography)*. Berkeley: University of California Press.

———. 1997. "Geography and Pilgrimage: A Review." In *Sacred Places, Sacred Spaces: The Geography of Pilgrimages*, edited by Robert H. Stoddard and Alan Morinis, 1–23. Geoscience and Man 34. Baton Rouge, LA: Geoscience Publications.

Bhardwaj, Surinder Mohan, and James G. Lochtefeld. 2004. "Tīrtha." In *The Hindu World*, edited by Sushil Mittal and Gene Thursby, 478–503. New York: Routledge.

Bose, Mandakranta, ed. 2003. *The Rāmāyaṇa Culture: Text, Performance, and Iconography*. New Delhi: D. K. Printworld.

———, ed. 2004. *The Ramayana Revisited*. New York: Oxford University Press.

Bryant, Edwin, ed. 2007. *Krishna: A Sourcebook*. New York: Oxford University Press.

Burghart, Richard. 1978. "The Founding of the Ramanandi Sect." *Ethnohistory* 25, no. 2: 121–39.

Callewaert, Winand M. 1988. *The Hindī Biography of Dādū Dayāl*. New Delhi: Motilal Banarsidass.

———, ed. 2000. *The Millenium Kabīr Vānī: A Collection of Pad-s*. New Delhi: Manohar.

Callewaert, Winand M., and Peter G. Friedlander. 1992. *The Life and Works of Raidās*. New Delhi: Manohar.

Callewaert, Winand M., and Mukund Lath. 1989. *The Hindī Padāvalī of Nāmdev: A Critical Edition of Nāmdev's Hindi Songs with Translation and Annotation*. New Delhi: Motilal Banarsidass.

Callewaert, Winand M., with Swapna Sharma. 2000. *The Hagiographies of Anantadās: The Bhakti Poets of North India*. Richmond, UK: Curzon Press.

Callewaert, Winand M., and Rupert Snell, eds. 1994. *According to Tradition: Hagiographical Writing in India*. Khoj: A Series of Modern South Asian Studies 5. Wiesbaden: Otto Harrassowitz.

Case, Margaret H., ed. 1996. *Govindadeva: A Dialogue in Stone*. New Delhi: Indira Gandhi National Centre for the Arts.

———. 2000. *Seeing Krishna: The Religious World of a Brahman Family in Vrindaban*. New York: Oxford University Press.

Caturvedī, Ācārya Paraśurām, ed. 1983. *Mīrā kī Padāvalī*. Allahabad: Hindī Sāhitya Sammelan.

Celer, Janardan Rāo, ed. 1971. *Vṛnd Granthāvalī*. Agra: Vinod Pustak Mandir.

——. 1973. *Vrind aur unkā Sāhitya*. Agra: Vinod Pustak Mandir.

Chandra, Satish. 2002. *Parties and Politics at the Mughal Court, 1707–1740*. New Delhi: Oxford University Press.

Chatterjee, Kumkum. 2013. "Goddess Encounters: Mughals, Monsters, and the Goddess in Bengal." *Modern Asian Studies* 47, no. 5: 1435–87.

Clémentin-Ojha, Catherine. 2005. "Ascetics' Rights in Early Nineteenth Century Jaipur (Rajasthan)." Accessed March 2013, http://ceias.ehess.fr/docannexe/file/2381/ascetics_rights_2005_online_since_march_2012.pdf. Forthcoming in *Asceticism and Power in South and Southeast Asia*, edited by Peter Flügel and Gustaaf Houtman (New York: Routledge).

——. 2011. "Nimbārka Sampradāya." In *Brill's Encyclopedia of Hinduism*, edited by Knut A. Jacobsen, Helene Basu, Angelika Malinar, and Vasudha Naryanan, 2:429–43. Leiden: Brill.

Clémentin-Ojha, Catherine, and Sharad Chandra Ojha. 2009. "The Royal Patronage of Roving Ascetics in Mid-Nineteenth Century Rajputana." In *Patronage and Popularisation, Pilgrimage and Procession: Channels of Transcultural Translation and Transmission in Early Modern South Asia*, edited by Heidi Rika Maria Pauwels, 149–66. Wiesbaden: Otto Harrassowitz.

Cort, John E. 2002. "A Tale of Two Cities: On the Origins of Digambar Sectarianism in North India." In *Multiple Histories: Culture and Society in the Study of Rajasthan*, edited by Lawrence A. Babb, Varsha Joshi, and Michael W. Meister, 39–83. Jaipur: Rawat Publications.

Currie, P. M. 1989. *The Shrine and Cult of Mu'īn al-Dīn Chistī of Ajmer*. New Delhi: Oxford University Press.

Dallaporta, Annamaria, and Lucio Marcato. 2011. *Kampil: Archaeological Study of a Site in the Ancient Kingdom of Panchala*. New Delhi: Munshiram Manoharlal.

Dalmia, Vasudha. 1997. *The Nationalization of Hindu Traditions: Bhāratendu Hariśchandra and Nineteenth-Century Banaras*. New Delhi: Oxford University Press.

——. 2006. "The Other in the World of the Faithful." In *Bhakti in Current Research, 2001–2003: Proceedings of the Ninth International Conference on Early Devotional Literature in New Indo-Aryan Languages, Heidelberg, 23–26 July 2003*, edited by Monika Horstmann, 115–39. New Delhi: Manohar.

——.*See also* Dalmia-Lüderitz, Vasudha.

Dalmia, Vasudha, and Heinrich von Stietencron, eds. 1995. *Representing Hinduism: The Construction of Religious Traditions and National Identity*. New Delhi: Sage.

Dalmia-Lüderitz, Vasudha. 1992. "Hariścandra of Banaras and the Reassessment of the Vaiṣṇava Bhakti in the Late Nineteenth Century." In *Devotional Literature in South Asia: Current Research, 1985–1988*, edited by R. S. McGregor, 281–97. Cambridge: Cambridge University Press.

Dash, Gaganendra Nath. 2004. "*Gita-Govinda* Traditions: A Medieval Debate and Its Impact on Modern Oriya Identity." In *Text and Context in the History, Literature, and Religion of Orissa*, edited by Angelika Malinar, Johannes Beltz, and Heiko Frese, 331–59. New Delhi: Manohar.

Datta, Gopāl. 1977. *Svāmī Haridās kā sampradāya aur uskā vāṇī-sāhitya*. New Delhi: National Publishing House.

Del Bontà, Robert. 2014. *Art Passages: Indian and SE Asian Art*. San Francisco: Art Passages.

Deloche, Jean. 1968. *Recherches sur les routes de l'Inde au temps des Mogols (Étude critique des sources)*. Publications de l'École française d'Extrême-Orient 67. Paris: Adrien-Maisonneuve.

———. 1993. *Transport and Communications in India prior to Steam Locomotion*. Translated by James Walker. Delhi: Oxford University Press.

Delvoye, Françoise "Nalini." 1997. "The Image of Akbar as a Patron of Music in Indo-Persian and Vernacular Sources." In *Akbar and His India*, edited by Irfan Habib, 188–214. New Delhi: Oxford University Press.

Dhavan, Purnima. 2011. *When Sparrows Became Hawks: The Making of the Sikh Warrior Tradition, 1699–1799*. New York: Oxford University Press.

Dickinson, Eric, and Karl Khandalavala. 1959. *Kishangarh Paintings*. New Delhi: Lalit Kalā Academy.

Dwivedi, Girish Chandra. 1989. *The Jats: Their Role in the Mughal Empire*. Bangalore: Arnold Publishers.

Eck, Diana L. 1983. *Banaras, City of Light*. Princeton, NJ: Princeton University Press.

Elliot, H. M., and John Dowson, trans. and eds. 1964 (1877). *The History of India, as Told by Its Own Historians*. Vol. 8. Reprint, Allahabad: Kitab Mahal.

Entwistle, Alan W. 1987. *Braj: Centre of Krishna Pilgrimage*. Groningen Oriental Studies 3. Groningen: Egbert Forsten.

———. 1991. "The Cult of Krishna-Gopāl as a Version of Pastoral." In *Devotion Divine: Bhakti Traditions from the Regions of India; Studies in Honour of Charlotte Vaudeville*, edited by Diana L. Eck and Françoise Mallison, 73–90. Groningen Oriental Studies 8. Groningen: Egbert Forsten.

Filippi, Gian G., and Bruno Marcolongo, eds. 1999. *Kāmpilya: Quest for a Mahābhārata City*. Delhi: D. K. Printworld.

Flügel, Peter. 2002. "Sthanakavasi Jain Tradition." In *Religions of the World: A Comprehensive Encyclopedia of Beliefs and Practices*, edited by J. Gordon Melton and Martin Baumann, 6:1221–23. Santa Barbara, CA: ABC-CLIO. Downloaded August 22, 2012, www.soas.ac.uk/staff/staff30946.php.

———. 2008. "The Unknown Lonka: Tradition and the Cultural Unconscious." In *Jaina Studies, edited by* Colette Caillat and Nalini Balbir, 181–279. Papers of the Twelfth World Sanskrit Conference, vol. 9. Delhi: Motilal Banarsidass. Downloaded August 22, 2012, www.soas.ac.uk/staff/staff30946.php.

Freitag, Jason. 2009. *Serving Empire, Serving Nation: James Tod and the Rajputs of Rajasthan*. Leiden: Brill.

Friedlander, Peter G. 1996. *A Descriptive Catalogue of the Hindi Manuscripts in the Library of the Wellcome Institute for the History of Medicine*. London: Wellcome Trust.

Galloway, Francesca. 2014. "Asia Week New York (14–22 March)." Accessed May 18, 2014, www.francescagalloway.com/usr/documents/exhibitions/list_of_works_url/15/awny2014.pdf.

Glushkova, Irina. 2002–3. "Moving God(s)ward: The Idea of *Tīrtha-yātrā*." In "Professor Ashok R. Kelkar Felicitation Volume," *Bulletin of the Deccan College Research Institute* 62–63: 265–83.

———. 2006. "Moving God(s)ward, Calculating Money: Wonders and Wealth as Essentials of a *Tīrtha-yātrā*." *Journal of South Asian Studies* 29, no. 2: 215–34.

Goetz, Hermann. 1938. *The Crisis of Indian Civilization in the Eighteenth and Early Nineteenth Centuries*. Calcutta: University of Calcutta.

Gold, Ann Grodzins. 1988. *Fruitful Journeys: The Ways of Rajasthani Pilgrims*. Berkeley: University of California Press.

Goldman, Robert P., and Sally J. Sutherland Goldman, trans. 1996. *The Rāmāyaṇa of Vālmīki: An Epic of Ancient India*. Vol. 5, *Sundarakāṇḍa*. Princeton, NJ: Princeton University Press.

Goldman, Sally J. Sutherland. 2001. "The Voice of Sītā in Vālmīki's *Sundarakāṇḍa*." In *Questioning Ramayanas: A South Asian Tradition*, edited by Paula Richman, 223–38. Berkeley: University of California Press.

Gommans, Jos J. L. 1995. *The Rise of the Indo-Afghan Empire, c. 1710–1780*. Leiden: Brill.

Gordon, Stewart. 1994. *Marathas, Marauders, and State Formation in Eighteenth-Century India*. Delhi: Oxford University Press.

Gosvāmī, Vāsudev. 1952 (2009 VS). *Bhakta kavi Vyāsjī*. Mathura: Agravāl Press.

Grewal, J. S. 1990. *The Sikhs of the Punjab*. Rev. ed. Cambridge: Cambridge University Press.

Griffiths, Paul J. 1999. *Religious Reading: The Place of Reading in the Practice of Religion*. New York: Oxford University Press.

Growse, Frederic S. 1883 (1873–74). *Mathurā, a District Memoir*. 2nd ed. Mathura: North-Western Provinces and Oudh Government Press.

Gupta, Beni. 1979. *Maratha Penetration into Rajasthan: Through the Mukandara Pass*. New Delhi: Research Publications in Social Sciences.

Gupta, R. K., and S. R. Bakshi, eds. 2008. *Rajasthan through the Ages*. Vol. 4, *Jaipur Rulers and Administration*. Studies in Indian History. New Delhi: Sarup.

Haberman, David L. 1988. *Acting as a Way of Salvation: A Study of Rāgānugā Bhakti Sādhanā*. New York: Oxford University Press.

———, trans. 2003. *The Bhaktirasāmṛtasindhu of Rūpa Gosvāmin*. New Delhi: Indira Gandhi National Centre for the Arts and Motilal Banarsidass.

———. 2006. *River of Love in an Age of Pollution: The Yamuna River of Northern India*. Berkeley: University of California Press.

Habermas, Jürgen. 1974. "The Public Sphere: An Encyclopedia Article (1964)." Translated by Sara Lennox and Frank Lennox. *New German Critique*, no. 3: 49–55.

Habib, Irfan. 1982. *An Atlas of the Mughal Empire: Political and Economic Maps with Detailed Notes, Bibliography, and Index*. Aligarh: Centre of Advanced Study in History, Aligarh Muslim University; New Delhi: Oxford University Press,

Haidar, Navina Najat. 1995. "The Kishangarh School of Painting, c. 1680–1850." Ph.D. diss., Oxford University.

———. 2000. "Satire and Humour in Kishangarh Painting." In *Court Painting in Rajasthan*, edited by Andrew Topsfield, 78–91. Mumbai: Marg Publications.

———. 2011a. "Bhavanidas." In *Masters of Indian Painting*, edited by Milo C. Beach, Eberhard Fischer, and B. N. Goswamy, 2:531–46. Supplementum 48. Zurich: Artibus Asiae Publishers.

———. 2011b. "Nihal Chand." In *Masters of Indian Painting*, edited by Milo C. Beach, Eberhard Fischer and B. N. Goswamy, 2:595–606. Supplementum 48. Zurich: Artibus Asiae Publishers.

Hare, James P. 2011. "Garland of Devotees: Nābhādās' *Bhaktamāl* and Modern Hinduism." Ph.D. diss., Columbia University.

Hargulāl. 1971 (2028 VS). *Sarvopari nityavihāriṇī ras-sāgar (Aṣṭācāryoṃ kī Vāṇī)*. Vrindavan: Śrī Prem Hari Press.

Hasan, Amir, B. R. Rizvi, and J. C. Das. 2005. *People of India*. Vol. 42, *Uttar Pradesh*. Mumbai: Popular Prakashan.

Hastings, James M. 2002. "Poets, Saints, and Warriors: The Dadu Panth, Religious Change, and Identity Formation in Jaipur State, circa 1562–1860 CE." Ph.D. diss., University of Wisconsin–Madison. ProQuest (3049346).

Hawley, John Stratton. 1984. *Sūr Dās: Poet, Singer, Saint*. Publications on Asia of the Henry M. Jackson School of International Studies, University of Washington, 40. Seattle: University of Washington Press.

———. 1988. "Author and Authority in the *Bhakti* Poetry of North India." *Journal of Asian Studies* 47, no. 2: 269–90.

———. 1995. "The Saints Subdued: Domestic Virtue and National Integration in *Amar Chitra Katha*." In *Media and the Transformation of Religion in South Asia*, edited by Lawrence A. Babb and Susan S. Wadley, 107–34. Philadelphia: University of Pennsylvania Press.

———. 2005. *Three Bhakti Voices: Mirabai, Surdas, and Kabir in Their Time and Ours*. New Delhi: Oxford University Press.

———. 2009. *The Memory of Love: Sūrdās Sings to Krishna*. New York: Oxford University Press.

———. 2015. *A Storm of Songs: India and the Idea of the Bhakti Movement*. Cambridge, MA: Harvard University Press.

Hawley, John Stratton, and Shrivatsa Goswami. 1981. *At Play with Krishna: Pilgrimage Dramas from Brindavan*. Princeton, NJ: Princeton University Press.

Hawley, John Stratton, and Mark Juergensmeyer. 1988. *Songs of the Saints of India*. New York: Oxford University Press.

Haynes, Edward S. 2002. "Lineage, State, and Symbolism of Rule in Late-Eighteenth-Century Eastern Rajputana." In *Rethinking Early Modern India*, edited by Richard B. Barnett, 33–83. New Delhi: Manohar.

Haynes, Richard. 1974. "Svāmī Haridās and the Haridāsī Sampradāya." Ph.D. diss., University of Pennsylvania. ProQuest (7502738).

Hein, Norvin. 1972. *The Miracle Plays of Mathurā*. New Haven, CT: Yale University Press.

Herman, Phyllis. 2003. "Remaking Rama for the Modern Sightseer." *South Asian Popular Culture* 1, no. 2: 125–40.

Hess, Linda. 1999. "Rejecting Sita: Indian Responses to the Ideal Man's Cruel Treatment of His Ideal Wife." *Journal of the American Academy of Religion* 67, no. 1: 1–32.

Horstmann, Monika. 1994. "Ein Kapitel nordindischer Religionspolitik im 18. Jahrhundert: Jai Singh II. und die religiösen Orden." *Zeitschrift für Religionswissenschaft* 2, no. 1: 49–68.

——. 2002. "The Rāmānandīs of Galtā (Jaipur, Rajasthan)." In *Multiple Histories: Culture and Society in the Study of Rajasthan*, edited by Lawrence A. Babb, Varsha Joshi, and Michael W. Meister, 141–97. Jaipur: Rawat Publications.

——. 2009. *Der Zusammenhalt der Welt: Religiöse Herrschaftslegitimation und Religionspolitik Mahārājā Savāī Jaisinghs (1700–1743)*. Wiesbaden: Otto Harrassowitz.

——. 2010. "Rāmānandī Nāgas: Politics and Bhakti." Paper presented at the Twenty-First European Conference on Modern South Asian Studies, Bonn, July 26.

——. *See also* Thiel-Horstmann, Monika.

Huntington, Susan L. 1994. "Kings as Gods, Gods as Kings: Temporality and Eternity in the Art of India." *Ars Orientalis* 24: 30–38.

Irvine, William, trans. 1903. "Garh Muktesar Fair in 1747; or, A Thirteen Days' Trip." *Indian Magazine and Review*, June, 66–71, 102–6, 116–21, 151–56, 169–72.

——. 1907. "Aḥmad Shāh, Abdālī, and the Indian Wazīr, 'Imād-ul-Mulk (1756–1757)." *Indian Antiquary* 36: 10–18, 43–51, 55–70.

Isacco, Enrico, and Anna L. Dallapiccola, eds. 1983. *Krishna, the Divine Lover: Myth and Legend through Indian Art*. Boston: David R. Godine.

Jacobsen, Knut A. 2008. *Kapila: Founder of Sāṃkhya and Avatāra of Viṣṇu*. New Delhi: Munshiram Manoharlal.

Jain, Kailash Chand. 1963. *Jainism in Rajasthan*. Jivarāja Jaina Granthamālā 15. Sholapur: Jaina Saṃskṛti Saṃrakshaka Sangha.

Jarow, E. H. Rick. 2003. *Tales for the Dying: The Death Narrative of the Bhāgavata-Purāṇa*. Albany: State University of New York Press.

Jhaveri, Krishnalal Mohanlal. 1928. *Imperial Farmans (A.D. 1577 to A.D. 1805) Granted to the Ancestors of His Holiness the Tilakayat Maharaj*. Bombay: News Printing Press.

Kantisagarji, Muni. 1965. "Ajmer Samiparvī kṣetra ke Katipay Upekṣit Hindī Sāhityakār." In *Hajārimalmuni Smṛti Granth*, edited by Shobhachad Bharilla. Byavar (Rajasthan): Hajārimalmuni Smṛti Granth Prakashan Samiti.

Kapur, Anuradha. 1990. *Actors, Pilgrims, Kings, and Gods: The Ramlila of Ramnagar*. Oxford, UK: Seagull Books.

Kaur, Jagdish. 1985. *Himalayan Pilgrimages and the New Tourism*. New Delhi: Himalayan Books.

Kedarnāth, Caraṇsevak Lālā Vaiśya, ed. 1911. *Nijmat Siddhānt: Śrī Mahant Kiśordāsjī kṛt. Vol. 1, Ācāryya Khaṇḍ*. Lucknow: Anglo-Oriental Press.

——. ed. 1915. *Nijmat Siddhānt: Śrī Mahant Kiśordāsjī kṛt*. Vol. 2, *Madhya Khaṇḍ*. Lucknow: Anglo-Oriental Press.

Khān, Faiyāz Alī. 1962. "Bhaktavar Nāgarīdās." Ph.D. diss., University of Rajasthan, Jaipur.

——. 1975. "Kishangarh Painting and Bani Thani." *Roopa Lekha* 40, nos. 1–2: 83–88.

Kinsley, David. 1979. *The Divine Player: A Study of Kriṣṇa Līlā*. New Delhi: Motilal Banarsidass.

Kiraṇ, D. C. V. 2003. "Atīt ke sitāre: Tīlāvat vaṃś (gautra) ke ādya pravartak evaṃ Rāmāvat Sampradāy ke pramukh Ācārya Jagadguru Śrī Sāketnivāsācārya ṭīlā svāmījī mahārāj." In *Rūpkiraṇ*, edited by D. C. V. Kiraṇ, 57–60. Rūpnagar: Kiraṇ Publications.

Kishwar, Madhu. 2001. "Yes to Sita, No to Ram: The Continuing Hold of Sita on Popular Imagination in India." In *Questioning Ramayanas: A South Asian Tradition*, edited by Paula Richman, 285–308. Berkeley: University of California Press.

Kolff, Dirk. 1990. *Naukar, Rajput, and Sepoy: The Ethnohistory of the Military Labour Market in Hindustan, 1450–1850*. Cambridge: Cambridge University Press.

Kṛṣṇadās, Gaṅgāviṣṇu, ed. 1986a (1958). *Caurāsī Vaiṣṇavan kī Vārtā*. Reprint, Bombay: Lakshmi Venkateshvar Steam Press.

——, ed. 1986b (1958). *Do Sau Bāvan Vaiṣṇavan kī Vārtā*. Reprint, Bombay: Lakshmi Venkateshvar Steam Press.

Lavania, B. K., D. K. Samanta, S. K. Mandal, and N. N. Vyas, eds. 1998. *People of India*. Vol. 38, *Rajasthan*, pt. 2. Mumbai: Popular Prakashan.

Lochtefeld, James G. 1994. "The Vishva Hindu Parishad and the Roots of Hindu Militancy." *Journal of the American Academy of Religion* 62, no. 2: 587–602.

——. 2010. *God's Gateway: Identity and Meaning in a Hindu Pilgrimage Place*. Oxford: Oxford University Press.

Lodha, Chanchal Mal. 2005. *History of Oswals*. Jodhpur: Panchsil Prakashan.

Lodrick, Deryck O. 1981. *Sacred Cows, Sacred Places: Origins and Survivals of Animal Homes in India*. Berkeley: University of California Press.

Lorenzen, David N. 1991. *Kabir Legends and Ananta-Das's Kabir Parachai*. Albany: State University of New York Press.

Lutgendorf, Philip. 1991. "The Secret Life of Rāmcandra of Ayodhya." In *Many Rāmāyaṇas: The Diversity of a Narrative Tradition in South Asia*, edited by Paula Richman, 217–34. Berkeley: University of California Press.

——. 1994. "The Quest for the Legendary Tulsīdās." In *According to Tradition: Hagiographical Writing in India*, edited by Winand M. Callewaert and Rupert Snell, 65–85. Khoj: A Series of Modern South Asian Studies 5. Wiesbaden: Otto Harrassowitz.

Malik, Zahir Uddin. 2006 (1977). *The Reign of Muhammad Shah, 1719–1748*. New Delhi: Icon Publications.

Mallison, Françoise. 1986. *Au point du jour: Les prabhātiyāṁ de Narasiṁha Mahetā, poète et saint vishnouite du Gujarat*. Paris: École française d' Extrême-Orient.

——. 1991. "Lorsque Raṇachoḍarāya quitte Dwarka pour Dakor, ou comment Dvārakānātha prit la succession de Daṅkanātha." In *Devotion Divine: Bhakti Traditions from the Regions of India; Studies in Honour of Charlotte Vaudeville*, edited by Diana L. Eck and Françoise Mallison, 197–207. Groningen Oriental Studies 8. Groningen: Egbert Forsten.

——. 1998. "Le discours hagiographique dans les hagiographies du saint-poète gujarati Narasiṁha Mahetā (XVème siècle, Inde occidentale)." *Bulletin de l'École française d'Extrême-Orient* 85: 265–83.

——, ed. 2001. *Constructions hagiographiques dans le monde indien: Entre mythe et histoire*. Bibliothèque de l'École des Hautes Études, Sciences Historiques et Philologiques 338. Paris: Librairie Honoré Champion.

——. 2013. "Devotion Rewarded: The Attitude towards Wealth in the Religious Literature of Medieval Gujarat." In *Bhakti beyond the Forest: Current Research on Early Modern Literatures in North India, 2003–2009*, edited by Imre Bangha, 137–51. New Delhi: Manohar.

Marshall, P. J. 2003. *The Eighteenth Century in Indian History: Evolution or Revolution?* Delhi: Oxford University Press.

Martin, Nancy. 2000. "Mīrābai in the Academy and the Politics of Identity." In *Faces of the Feminine in Ancient, Medieval, and Modern India*, edited by Mandakranta Bose, 162–82. New York: Oxford University Press.

———. Forthcoming. *Mirabai*. New York: Oxford University Press.

Mason, David. 2009. *Theatre and Religion on Krishna's Stage: Performing in Vrindavan*. New York: Palgrave Macmillan.

Mathur, Vijay Kumar. 2000. *Marvels of Kishangarh Paintings from the Collection of the National Museum, New Delhi*. Delhi: Bharatiya Kala Prakashan.

Mayaram, Shail. 2005. "Living Together: Ajmer as a Paradigm for the (South) Asian City." In *Living Together Separately: Cultural India in History and Politics*, edited by Mushirul Hasan and Asim Roy, 145–71. New Delhi: Oxford University Press.

McGregor, R. S. 1983. "The *Dyān-Manjarī* of Agradās." In *Bhakti in Current Research, 1979–1982: Proceedings of the Second International Conference on Early Devotional Literature in New Indo-Aryan Languages, St. Augustin, 19–21 March 1982*, edited by Monika Thiel-Horstmann, 237–44. Berlin: Dietrich Reimer.

———. 1984. *Hindi Literature from Its Beginnings to the Nineteenth Century*. A History of Indian Literature, edited by Jan Gonda, vol. 8, fasc. 6. Wiesbaden: Otto Harrassowitz.

———, ed. 1993. *The Oxford Hindi-English Dictionary*. Oxford: Oxford University Press.

McInerney, Terence. 2002. "Mughal Painting in the Reign of Muhammad Shah." In *After the Great Mughals: Painting in Delhi and the Regional Courts in the Eighteenth and Nineteenth Centuries*, edited by Barbara Schmitz, 12–33. Mumbai: Marg Publications.

Metcalfe, Sir Thomas. 1843. "Reminiscences of Imperial Delhi." Manuscript in British Library. Shelfmark Add.Or.5475. Accessed May 22, 2012, www.bl.uk/onlinegallery/onlineex/apac/addorimss/v/019addor0005475u00016vrb.html.

Mītal, Prabhudayāl. 1968. *Braj ke dharma sampradāyoṃ kā itihās*. Delhi: National Publishing House.

Moini, S. Liyaquat H. 2004. *The Chishti Shrine of Ajmer: Pirs, Pilgrims, Practices*. Jaipur: Publication Scheme.

Mukherjee, Tarapada, and Irfan Habib. 1988. "Akbar and the Temples of Mathura and Its Environs." In *Indian History Congress: Proceedings of the Forty-Eighth Session, Goa University, Bambolim, 1987*, 234–50. New Delhi: Indian History Congress.

———. 1989. "The Mughal Temple Administration and the Temples of Vrindavan during the Reigns of Jahangir and Shahjahan." In *Indian History Congress: Proceedings of the Forty-Ninth Session, Karnataka University, Dharwad, 1988*, 287–300. New Delhi: Indian History Congress.

Mukta, Parita. 1994. *Upholding the Common Life: The Community of Mirabai*. New Delhi: Oxford University Press.

Nāhaṭā, Agarchand. 1959. "Braj yātrā ke kuch prācīn vivaraṇ." In *Braj aur Braj-yātrā*, edited by Govinddās and Rāmnārāyaṇ Agravāl, 112–19. Delhi: Bhāratīya Viśva Prakāśan.

———, ed. 1965. *Rāghavdās kṛt Bhaktamāl: Caturdās kṛt ṭīkā sahit*. Rājasthān Purātan Granthmālā 78. Jodhpur: Rājasthān Prācyavidyā Pratiṣṭhān.

Naim, C. M. 1999. *Zikr-i Mir: The Autobiography of the Eighteenth Century Mughal Poet, Mir Muhammad Taqi "Mir."* New Delhi: Oxford University Press.

Nārāyaṇdās, Svāmī, ed. 1969. *Śrī Svāmī Rāghavdāsjī viracit Bhaktmāl: Svāmī Caturdāsjī kṛt padya ṭīkā tathā bhakticaritra prakāśikā gadya ṭīkā sahit*. Pushkar: Dādūdayālū Mahāsabhā.

———. 1979 (2036 VS). *Śrī Dādūpanth Paricay*. Vol. 3. Jaipur: Śrī Dādū Dayāl Mahāsabhā.

Nath, R. 1996. "Śrī Govindadeva's Itinerary from Vṛndāvana to Jayapura, c. 1534–1727." In *Govindadeva: A Dialogue in Stone*, edited by Margaret H. Case, 161–83. New Delhi: Indira Gandhi National Centre for the Arts.

Novetzke, Christian Lee. 2008. *Religion and Public Memory: A Cultural History of the Saint Namdev in India*. New York: University of Columbia Press.

O'Hanlon, Rosalind. 2010. "Letters Home: Banaras Pandits and the Maratha Region in Early Modern India." *Modern Asian Studies* 44, no. 2: 201–40.

O'Hanlon, Rosalind, and Christopher Minkowski. 2008. "What Makes People Who They Are? Pandit Networks and the Problem of Livelihoods in Early Modern Western India." *Indian Economic and Social History Review* 45, no. 3: 381–416.

Okada, Amina Taha Hussein, Madeleine Biardeau, and Marie-Claude Porcher. 2011. *Le Ramayana de Valmiki illustré par les miniatures indiennes du XVe au XIXe siècle*. 7 vols. Paris: Diane de Selliers Éditions.

Orr, W. G. 1947. *A Sixteenth-Century Indian Mystic: Dadu and His Followers*. London: Lutterworth.

Orsini, Francesca. 1999. "What Did They Mean by 'Public'? Language, Literature, and the Politics of Nationalism." *Economic and Political Weekly* 34, no. 7: 409–16.

Pal, Pratapaditya, ed. 1997. *Dancing to the Flute: Music and Dance in Indian Art*. Sydney: Art Gallery of New South Wales.

———. 2004. *Painted Poems: Rajput Paintings from the Ramesh and Urmil Kanoria Collection*. Pasadena, CA: Norton Simon Museum; Ahmedabad: Mapin.

Paramasivan, Vasudha. 2010. "Between Text and Sect: Early Nineteenth-Century Shifts in the Theology of Ram." Ph.D. diss., University of California, Berkeley. ProQuest (3449047).

Parihar, G. R. 1968. *Marwar and the Marathas (1724–1843 A.D.)*. Jodhpur: Hindi Sahitya Mandir.

Pauwels, Heidi Rika Maria. 2002. *In Praise of Holy Men: Hagiographic Poems by and about Harirām Vyās*. Groningen Oriental Studies 18. Groningen: Egbert Forsten.

———. 2006. "Hagiography and Reception History: The Case of Mīrā's *Padas* in Nāgrīdās's *Pada-prasaṅga-mālā*." In *Bhakti in Current Research, 2001–2003: Proceedings of the Ninth International Conference on Early Devotional Literature in New Indo-Aryan Languages, Heidelberg, 23–26 July 2003*, edited by Monika Horstmann, 221–44. New Delhi: Manohar.

———. 2008. *The Goddess as Role Model: Sita and Radha in Scripture and on Screen*. New York: Oxford University Press.

———. 2009a. "Imagining Religious Communities in the Sixteenth Century: Harirām Vyās and the Haritrayī." *International Journal of Hindu Studies* 13, no. 2: 143–61.

———. 2009b. "The Saint, the Warlord, and the Emperor: Discourses of Braj Bhakti and Bundelā Loyalty." *Journal of the Economic and Social History of the Orient* 52, no. 2: 187–228.

——. 2010. "Rāṭhaurī Mīrā." *International Journal of Hindu Studies* 14, nos. 2–3: 177–200.

——. 2014. "Cosmopolitan Soirées in Eighteenth-Century North India: Reception of Early Urdu Poetry in Kishangarh." *South Asia Multidisciplinary Academic Journal* (Centre d'Études de l'Inde et de l'Asie du Sud, Paris). http://samaj.revues.org/3773.

——. 2015. *Cultural Exchange in Eighteenth-Century India: Poetry and Paintings from Kishangarh.* Studies in Asian Art and Culture 4. Berlin: EB-Verlag.

——. 2016. "Rewriting the Sītā-Rāma Romance: Nāgarīdās' *Rām-Carit-Mālā* (1749)." *Journal of Hindu Studies* 9, no. 3: 351–72.

——. Forthcoming-a. "Canonization of Bhakti Gurus: A Missing Link between Jai Singh II (Early Eighteenth Century) and Harischandra (Mid-Nineteenth Century)." In *Generating the Guru: Genealogies of Religious Authority in South Asia*, edited by István Keul and Srilata Raman.

——. Forthcoming-b. "Śrīmad-Bhāgavata-Pārāyaṇa-Vidhi-Prakāś: An Early Modern Poetry Workshop?" *International Journal of Hindu Studies.*

Pauwels, Heidi Rika Maria, and Emilia Bachrach. Forthcoming. "Aurangzeb as Iconoclast? Vaishnava Accounts of the Krishna Images' Exodus from Braj." *Journal of the Royal Asiatic Society.*

Peabody, Norbert. 1991. "In Whose Turban Does the Lord Reside: The Objectification of Charisma and the Fetishism of Objects in the Hindu Kingdom of Kota." *Comparative Studies in Society and History* 33, no. 4: 726–54.

——. 2003. *Hindu Kingship and Polity in Precolonial India.* Cambridge: Cambridge University Press.

Pechilis, Karen. 1999. *The Embodiment of Bhakti.* New York: Oxford University Press.

Pellò, Stefano. 2015. "Persian as a Passe-Partout: The Case of Mirzā 'Abd al-Qādir Bīdil and His Hindu Disciples." In *Culture and Circulation: Literature in Motion in Early Modern India*, edited by Thomas de Bruijn and Allison Busch, 21–46. Leiden: Brill.

Pemārām. 1976. "Rājasthān ke śāsakoṃ par Dādūpanthī Sampradāy kā prabhāv." *Journal of the Rajasthan Institute of Historical Research* 12, no. 1: 40–48.

Petievich, Carla R. 1990. "Poetry of the Declining Mughals: The Shahr Āshob." *Journal of South Asian Literature* 25, no. 1: 99–110.

Phaḍke, Viśvanāth Keśav, ed. 1974. *Śrībhakta Vijaya.* Pune: Yaśvant Prakāśan.

Pinch, William R. 1996. *Peasants and Monks in British India.* Berkeley: University of California Press.

——. 2000. *Warrior Ascetics and Indian Empires.* Cambridge: Cambridge University Press.

Pollock, Sheldon. 2004. "Ramayana and Political Imagination in India." In *Religious Movements in South Asia, 600–1800*, edited by David N. Lorenzen, 153–208. New Delhi: Oxford University Press. Originally published in *Journal of Asian Studies* 52, no. 2 (1993): 261–97.

Pouchepadass, Jacques. 2003. "Itinerant Kings and Touring Officials: Circulation as a Modality of Power in India, 1700–1947." In *Society and Circulation: Mobile People and Itinerant Cultures in South Asia, 1750–1950*, edited by Claude Markovits, Jacques Pouchepadass, and Sanjay Subrahmanam, 240–74. New Delhi: Permanent Black.

Pritchett, Frances. 1994. *Nets of Awareness: Urdu Poetry and Its Critics.* Berkeley: University of California Press.

Purohit, Lalit Prasād. 1986 (1960). *Rasik Ananya Māl: Mūl evaṃ gadya rūpāntaraṇ.* Reprint, Vrindavan: Veṇu Prakāśan.

Rādhākrishnadās, Bābā. 1898. "Śrī Nāgarīdāsjī kā jīvan caritraṃ." In *Nāgara-samuccayaḥ*, edited by Śrīdharātmaja Kisanlāl Gauḍ, 1–25. Bombay: Jñānsāgar. Originally published in *Nāgarīpracāriṇī Sabhā Patrikā* 2 (1897): 105–30.

———, ed. 1902. *Sūdan Kavi kṛt Sujān Caritra.* Benares: Nāgarī Pracāriṇī Sabhā.

Ramanujan, A. K. 1989. "Talking to God in the Mother Tongue." *Manushi*, nos. 50–52: 9–17.

Randhawa, Mohinder Siṃh, and Doris Schreiner Randhawa. 1980. *Kishangarh Painting.* Bombay: Vakils Feffer and Simons.

Rao, Velcheru Narayana. 2004. "When Does Sītā Cease to Be Sītā? Notes toward a Cultural Grammar of Indian Narratives." In *The Ramayana Revisited*, edited by Mandakranta Bose, 219–41. New York: Oxford University Press.

Rao, Velcheru Narayana, and David Shulman. 1998. *A Poem at the Right Moment: Remembered Verses from Premodern South India.* Voices from Asia 10. Berkeley: University of California Press.

Richards, John F. 1995. *The Mughal Empire.* The New Cambridge History of India, pt. 1, vol. 5. Cambridge: Cambridge University Press.

Richman, Paula, ed. 1991. *Many Rāmāyaṇas: The Diversity of a Narrative Tradition in South Asia.* Berkeley: University of California Press.

———, ed. 2001. *Questioning Ramayanas: A South Asian Tradition.* Berkeley: University of California Press.

Rogers, Alexander, and Henry Beveridge, trans. 1909–14. *The Tuzuk-i-Jahāngīrī; or, Memoirs of Jahāngīr.* 2 vols. London: Royal Asiatic Society.

Rosenstein, Ludmilla. 1997. *The Devotional Poetry of Svāmī Haridās: A Study of Early Braj Bhāṣā Verse.* Groningen: Egbert Forsten.

Rousseva-Sokolova, Galina. 2000. "The Tradition of *Varṣotsav-pad-saṃgrah*: A Different Perspective on Brajbhāṣā Devotional Poetry." In *The Banyan Tree: Essays on Early Literature in New Indo-Aryan Languages; Proceedings of the Seventh International Conference on Early Literature in New Indo-Aryan Languages, Venice, 1997*, edited by Mariola Offredi, 2:513–22. New Delhi: Manohar.

"Rūpkalā," Sītārām Śaraṇ Bhagvānprasād, ed. 1977 (1903–9). *Gosvāmi Nābhājī kṛt Śrī Bhaktmāl: Śrī Priyādāsjī praṇīt ṭikā-kavitta, Śrī Sītārāmśaraṇ Bhagvānprasād Rūpkalā viracit Bhaktisudhāsvād tilak sahit.* Reprint, Lucknow: Tejkumār Book Depot.

Sachdev, Vibhuti, and Giles Tillotson. 2002. *Building Jaipur: The Making of an Indian City.* London: Reaktion Books.

Saha, Shandip. 2004. "Creating a Community of Grace: A History of the Pushti Marga in Northern and Western India (1479–1905)." Ph.D. diss., University of Ottawa. Library and Archives Canada.

———. 2006. "A Community of Grace: The Social and Theological World of the *Puṣṭi* Mārga Vārtā Literature." *Bulletin of the School of Oriental and African Studies* 69, no. 2: 225–42.

———. 2007. "The Movement of *Bhakti* along a North-West Axis: Tracing the History of the Puṣṭimārg between the Sixteenth and Nineteenth Centuries." *International Journal of Hindu Studies* 11, no. 3: 299–318.

Sanford, Whitney. 2008. *Singing Krishna: Sound Becomes Sight in Paramānand's Poetry.* Albany: State University of New York Press.

Śaraṇ, Kunjabihārī, ed. 1979. *Śrī nikunj ras prakāśak Śrī Ācārya Caritāvali.* Calcutta: Śrī Rādhā Krishna Prakāśak Sansthān.

Saran, Richard D., and Norman P. Ziegler. 2001. *The Mertiyo Rathors of Merto, Rajasthan: Select Translations Bearing on the History of a Rajput Family, 1462–1660.* 2 vols. Ann Arbor: Centers for South and Southeast Asian Studies, University of Michigan.

Śaraṇ, Vrajvallabh. 1966. *Śrī Nāgarīdāsjī kī Vāṇī: Nāgarīdāśjī ke jīvanvṛtta evaṃ vāṇiyoṃ kā sanśodhit sanskaraṇ.* Vrindavan: Śrī Sarveśvar Press.

———. 1972. *Śrī Nimbārkācārya aur unkā sampradāy.* Vrindavan: Śrī Sarveśvar Press.

Sarda, Har Bilas. 1911. *Ajmer: Historical and Descriptive.* Ajmer: Scottish Mission Industries.

Sardesai, Govind S., ed. 1930–34. *Selections from the Peshwa Daftar.* 46 vols. Bombay: Government Central Press.

Sarkar, Jadunath, trans. 1947. *Maāsir-i-Ālamgiri of Sāqī Must'ad Khān: A History of the Emperor Aurangzib-'Ālamgir (Reign 1658–1707 A.D.).* Bibliotheca Indica 269. Calcutta: Royal Asiatic Society of Bengal.

———. 1964–72 (1932–50). *Fall of the Mughal Empire.* 4 vols. 3rd ed. Calcutta: M. C. Sarkar.

———. 1984. *A History of Jaipur.* Rev. ed. Hyderabad: Orient Longman.

Śarmā, Nārāyaṇdatt. 1978. *Nimbārka sampradāya aur uske Kṛṣṇa bhakta Hindī kavi.* Mathura: Aśok Prakāśan.

Śarmā, Rāmprasād. 1996. *Śrī Brajdāsī Bhāgavat.* 2 vols. Salemabad: Śrī Nimbārk Mudraṇālay.

Sen, Nabaneeta Dev. 2000. "Candrāvatī Rāmāyaṇa: Feminizing the Rāma-Tale." In *Faces of the Feminine in Ancient, Medieval, and Modern India,* edited by Mandakranta Bose, 183–91. New York: Oxford University Press.

Sharma, G. N. 1962. *Mewar and the Mughal Emperors.* Agra: Shiva Lal Agarwala.

Sharma, Ramesh Chandra, trans. 1970. "The *Ardha-Kathānak*: A Neglected Source of Mughal History." *Indica* 7, nos. 1–2: 49–73, 105–20.

Sharma, Sri Ram. 1971. *Maharana Raj Singh and His Times.* Delhi: Motilal Banarsidass.

Sharma, Sunil. 2004. "The City of Beauties in Indo-Persian Poetic Landscape." *Comparative Studies of South Asia, Africa and the Middle East* 24, no. 2: 73–81.

Shulman, David. 2001. "Bhavabhūti on Cruelty and Compassion." In *Questioning Ramayanas: A South Asian Tradition,* edited by Paula Richman, 49–82. Berkeley: University of California Press.

Siegel, Lee. 1978. *Sacred and Profane Dimensions of Love in Indian Traditions as Exemplified in the Gītagovinda of Jayadeva.* Delhi: Oxford University Press.

Siṃha, Bhagavatī Prasād. 1957. *Rāmbhakti meṃ Rasik Sampradāy.* Rasik Granthmālā 1. Balrāmpur: Avadh Sāhitya Mandir.

Singh, Kavita. 2013. "A Knowing Look: Appropriation and Subversion of the Mughal Idiom in Rajput Paintings of the Eighteenth Century." In *Synergies in Visual Culture—Bildkulturen im Dialog,* edited by Manuela de Giorgi, Annette Hoffmann, and Nicola Suthor, 257–68. Paderborn, Germany: Wilhelm Fink.

Singh, Rana P. B. 2011. "Holy Places and Pilgrimages in India: The Emerging Trends and Bibliography." In *Holy Places and Pilgrimages: Essays on India*, edited by Rana P. B. Singh, 7–57. New Delhi: Shubhi Publications.

Sinh, Raghubir. 1984. *The Julusi Sanehs of the Mughal Emperors of India, 1556–1857 A.D.* Sitamau, Madhya Pradesh: Shri Natnagar Shodh-Samsthan.

Smagorinsky, Peter. 2001. "If Meaning Is Constructed, What Is It Made From? Toward a Cultural Theory of Reading." *Review of Educational Research* 71, no. 1: 133–69.

Smith, William L. 2000. *Patterns in North Indian Hagiography*. Stockholm Studies on Indian Languages and Literature 3. Stockholm: University of Stockholm.

Snātak, Vijayendra. 1957 (2014 VS). *Rādhāvallabha sampradāya: Siddhānta aur sāhitya*. Delhi: National Publishing House.

Snell, Rupert. 1991a. *The Eighty-Four Hymns of Hita Harivaṃśa: An Edition of the Caurāsī Pada*. Delhi. Motilal Banarsidass; London: School of Oriental and African Studies.

———. 1991b. *The Hindi Classical Tradition: A Braj Bhāṣā Reader*. London: School of Oriental and African Studies.

Soni, Sonika, and Anil Relia. 2016. *Rajputana Nayak: Portraits from the Royal Courts of Rajasthan, 1660–1940 CE*. The Indian Portrait 8. Ahmedabad: Archer. Accessed September 28, 2016, www.theindianportrait.com/the-indian-portrait-8-paintings-from-the-royal-courts-of-rajasthan.

Sreenivasan, Ramya. 2007. *The Many Lives of a Rajput Queen: Heroic Pasts in India, c. 1500–1900*. Seattle: University of Washington Press.

———. 2014. "Faith and Allegiance in Mughal India: Perspectives from Rajasthan." In *Religious Interactions in Mughal India*, edited by Vasudha Dalmia and Munis D. Faruqui, 157–91. New Delhi: Oxford University Press.

Śrī Subodhinī Sabhā, ed. 1936. *Śrī Harirāyjī kṛt Baḍe Śikṣāpatra*. Rev. ed. Bombay: Jagadīśvar Printing Press.

Stewart, Tony K. 2010. *The Final Word: The Caitanya Caritāmṛta and the Grammar of Religious Tradition*. Oxford: Oxford University Press.

Talbot, Cynthia. 2009. "Becoming Turk the Rajput Way: Conversion and Identity in an Indian Warrior Narrative." *Modern Asian Studies* 43, no. 1: 211–43.

———. 2015. *The Last Hindu Emperor: Prithviraj Chauhan and the Indian Past, 1200–2000*. Cambridge: Cambridge University Press.

Thielemann, Selina. 1998. *Rāsalīlā: A Musical Study of Religious Drama in Vraja*. New Delhi: APH Publishing.

———. 2002. *Divine Service and the Performing Arts in India*. New Delhi: APH Publishing.

Thiel-Horstmann, Monika. 1991. "On the Dual Identity of Nāgās." In *Devotion Divine: Bhakti Traditions from the Regions of India; Studies in Honour of Charlotte Vaudeville*, edited by Diana L. Eck and Françoise Mallison, 255–71. Groningen Oriental Studies 8. Groningen: Egbert Forsten.

Tivārī, Bhagvān Dās. 1974. *Mīrāṃ kī prāmāṇik Padāvalī*. Allahabad: Sāhitya Bhavan.

Tod, James. 1920. *Annals and Antiquities of Rajasthan*. 3 vols. London: Oxford University Press.

Topsfield, Andrew. 2000. "The Saving Power of Soron: Sahibdin of Udaipur and the *Sukarakshetra Mahatmya*." In *Court Painting in Rajasthan*, edited by Andrew Topsfield, 26–40. Mumbai: Marg Publications.

Turner, Victor, and Edith Turner. 1978. *Image and Pilgrimage in Christian Culture.* New York: Columbia University Press.

Vājpeyī, Nanddulāre, ed. *Sūrsāgar*. 2 vols. Nāgarīpracāriṇī Granthmālā 25 and 35. Benares: Nāgarīpracāriṇī Sabhā.

Van der Veer, Peter. 1988. *Gods on Earth: The Management of Religious Experience and Identity in a North Indian Pilgrimage.* London: Athlone Press.

Vaudeville, Charlotte. 1980. "The Govardhan Myth in North India." *Indo-Iranian Journal* 22, no. 1: 1–45.

——. 1986. *Bārahmāsā in Indian Literature: Songs of the Twelve Months in Indo-Aryan Literatures.* Delhi: Motilal Banarsidass.

——. 1993. *A Weaver Named Kabir.* Delhi: Oxford University Press.

Vrindābandevācārya, Mahārāj. 1998 (2055 VS). *Śrī Gītāmṛt Gaṅgā.* Salemabad: Akhila Bhāratīy Śrīnimbārkācāryapīṭh.

Welch, Stuart Cary. 1976. *Indian Drawings and Painted Sketches, Sixteenth through Nineteenth Centuries.* New York: Asia Society.

Williams, Joanna, ed. 2007. *The Kingdom of the Sun: Indian Court and Village Art from the Princely State of Mewar.* San Francisco: Asian Art Museum.

Yang, Anand A. 1999. *Bazaar India: Markets, Society, and the Colonial State in Gangetic Bihar.* Berkeley: University of California Press.

Illustrations

Figures

I.1. (Also on cover) *Radha Offering Flowers to Yogi Krishna,* Kishangarh School, ca. 1750–60 2
I.2. *Portrait of Maharaja Savant Singh with Consort, Bani Thani,* attributed to Nihālcand, Kishangarh School, mid-1700s 4
1.1. Kishangarh fort 14
1.2. *Rāj Singh Receiving Fateh Singh,* attributed to Dalcand, ca. 1730s 16
1.3. Nagari Kunj, residence of the Kishangarh house at Vrindavan 17
1.4. *Bahādur Singh Showing off his Skill at Archery,* attributed to Dalcand, ca. 1750 19
1.5. *Portrait of Sardar Singh, Son of Savant Singh,* Kishangarh School, ca. 1760 23
1.6. Sāvant Singh's samādhi at Vrindavan 27
2.1. Temple of Śrī Kalyāṇarāya Jī at Kishangarh fort 34
2.2. Nimbārkan monastery at Salemabad 43
2.3. *Vrindābandev Ācārya Teaching Sāvant Singh and Others,* painting framed in living quarters of Śrī jī in Salemabad 46
2.4. Water tank at Galta 55
2.5. Guru-Lineage of Krishnadās Payohārī in his cave at Galta 56
2.6. Krishnaite wall paintings on the exterior of the Gopāla jī Mandir at Galta 57
2.7. Wall painting of *bhajana* at Galta 60
2.8. Dādū Pīṭh monastery at Naraina 61
2.9. Tomb of Sultān Pīr at Rupnagar fort 64
3.1. *Krishna Swimming,* Kishangarh School, ca. 1770–1775 72
3.2. Chatri at Kupghat in the pilgrimage center of Devyani 81
3.3. The shrine for Gālava Rishi at Galta 83
3.4. Approaching Barsana 86
3.5. *A Yogini at her Retreat,* attributed to the atelier of Bhavānīdās, Kishangarh School, ca. 1725–50 91
3.6. The narrow passage at Sankari Khor in Barsana 93
3.7. *Krishna's Nuptials,* Kishangarh School, late eighteenth century 100
3.8. *Go-dhūli at Gopāṣṭamī,* Kishangarh School, ca. 1760 103
4.1. *Jayadeva Worships Rādhāmādha,* painting framed in the Salemabad temple 117
4.2. *Disguised Akbar with Tansen Visit Svami Haridas,* Kishangarh School, ca. 1760 140
4.3. A Two-Storeyed *Havelī* in Rupnagar 156

Tables

1.1 Chronological Overview of the Second Part of Nāgarīdās's Life 24
3.1 Overview of the Pilgrimage Trajectory of *The Pilgrim's Bliss* 80
4.1 Comparison of Long and Short Recension of *Garland of Stories and Songs* 114
5.1 Overview of the Headings of *Garland of Rāma's Romance* 167

Index

Adhyātma (spiritual Jaina movement), 65–66
Ādi-granth, 214n133, 225nn62,66
Afghan, 3, 7, 15, 18, 36, 164, 197
Agra, 9, 14, 39, 50, 51, 66, 75, 84, 133, 158, 224n33
Agradās, 57, 168, 214n136, 215nn146,147, 216n168, 231n15
Agravāl (caste), 66
Aḥmad Shāh (emperor), 19, 22
Ajmer, 14, 22, 25, 63–64, 67, 206n5, 215n144, 216nn184,185, 217nn187,192
Akbar, 14, 50, 53, 56, 114, 116, 128, 131, 134, 139–40, 141, 154
'Ālamgīr II, 20
Amarcand (painter), 64
Amer, 15, 29, 44, 50, 56, 61, 62, 65, 120, 214n139
Ānandghan, 67
Anantdās, 121, 123–24, 214n136, 225nn54,56,59,64
āratī, 78, 87, 102–3, 141–42, 221n61
ascetic, 5–6, 50, 53, 66, 69, 90, 124–25, 136, 150–51, 157–58, 215n59; warrior, 30–31, 44–45, 48, 57–59, 62–63, 77, 82, 197, 210n7
Aṣṭadaś-siddhānt-pad (*Eighteen Songs of Instruction*), 52
Aṣṭ-chāp, 33, 112, 130
Aurangzeb, 15, 33, 36, 41, 129, 206n5, 207n13, 211nn37,41,52
Ayodhya: historical, 58, 84, 215n148; mythical, 163–65, 167, 169–70, 172, 177, 181, 185, 191–92, 209n64
'Azīm ush-Shān, 15
Baḍ Gūjar, 128–29
Bahādur Shāh (Mu'ammad Mu'azzam Shāh 'Ālam), 15, 17, 18, 226n83
Bahādur Singh (of Kishangarh) and the Marathas, 22–23, 209n52, 216n184; financial dissatisfaction, 208n29; peace treaty with, 25–26; religious dissidence, 48–49, 52, 54, 146, 193; siege against, 82–83; usurpation, 18–19, 197
Bakht Singh (of Jodhpur), 22, 215n143, 219n33
Bālājī Bāji Rāo ("Nānāsāhib"), 21, 81
Bālānand, 44, 58, 62
Balarāma (Baladeva), 34, 80, 95, 102–3, 221n69
Balkh, 15, 37, 149
Banī-ṭhanī, 5, 53–54, 77–78, 112, 133, 205n10
Bāṅkāvatī. *See* Brajdāsī
Bansīdās, 51, 89, 221n63
bārahmāsā, 91–92, 221n73
Benares, 31, 33, 54–5, 84, 111, 113, 140, 208n43, 218nn4,6, 219n15, 224n33, 228n132
Bengal, 15, 31, 34, 49, 91, 117, 129, 135, 152, 158, 195, 212n66, 213n106, 224n36, 229n167
Bhagavad Mudit, 138
Bhagavān ("Hit Rāmrāy"), 51, 108, 114–15, 133, 135, 158
Bhagavāndās (of Amer), 61
bhakti: ananyatā (exclusivity), 110, 129–30, 163; compatibility of Krishna and Rāma *bhakti*, 129–30, 163, 174–75, 177–78, 215n147; compatibility with politics, 186–89, 198; devotional songs,

137, 148–57; devotional sects (*see* Dādū-panth; Gauḍīya-; Haridāsī-; Mādhva-; Nimbārka-; Rādhāvallabha-; Rāmānandī-; Vallabha-Sampradāya); devotional story cycles, 109–11; Jaina interest in Rādhā-Krishna *bhakti*, 67–68; joyful aspects of Rādhā-Krishna *bhakti*, 27–28; methodological approach in this book, 7–10, 203; *Rāgānugā*, 7, 49; Rāma *bhakti* modeled after Krishna *bhakti*, 57–60, 83; Rāma-Rasika *bhakti*, 57–59, 168, 170, 174–75, 177, 179–81, 185, 191, 215nn146,149; *rasika* approach not conflicting with military, 57–58, 69; research, 206n19; *sakhī-bhāva*, 37–39, 40, 52; Sants and Krishna *bhakti*, 125

Bhakti-ras-bodhinī (*Illumination of Devotional Emotion*), 44, 109, 112

Bhakt-māl (*Garland of Devotees*): by Nābhādās, 44, 60, 109, 112, 118, 126, 143, 215n146; by Rāghavdās, 62

Bhakt-vijay (*Victory to the Devotee*), 117, 121–22, 126, 128

Bharata, 169–72, 184–85, 190, 192–93, 196

"Bhāratendu" Hariścandra, 111–13, 199

Bharatpur, 212n72, 220n42, 224n33

Bhavabhūti, 189, 194

Bhavānīdās (painter), 45, 90–91, 206n16, 217n194

Bhīm Singh (of Kota), 36–37

bhītariyā (temple servant), 37, 115, 155

Bihāranidās (Bihārīdās), 52, 147, 214n120, 229n162

Bijai Singh (of Jodhpur), 22–23

Birad Singh (of Kishangarh), 26

Bīrbal, 114–15, 131, 228n145

Brahma-sūtra, 30, 44

Braj, 6, 8–12; circulation of songs in, 150–52, 186–89; connection of mythical and earthly realms in, 96–99, 104–5; hagiographical stories about, 108, 129–30, 133, 137–38, 143, 147–48, 155, 158, 226n86; itinerary to, 79–80, 83–84; Jai Singh and, 31, 84; Jat brigands-landlords in, 20, 85–86, 105, 138, 210n23; Kishangarh connections with, 15; marauding armies in, 25, 52, 54, 209n61, 214n117; Nimbārkans and, 44, 48; Rāma-Rasikas and, 58–59, 215nn147–8; *rasika* Krishna Sampradāyas and, 48–51, 53–54; real estate boom in eighteenth century, 85–87; renaissance in sixteenth century, 74–75; research on, 219nn11–15,29; Sāvant Singh's attraction to, 17–18, 75–76, 79, 88–89, 186–89, 195, 198; Sāvant Singh's pilgrimages to, 24–25, 71–73, 83–88, 89–96; seasonal poems on, 74; transforming cities into, 35–37; Vallabhans and, 33–35, 36–39, 41. *See also under* festivals

Braj sites: Barsana, 24, 77, 80, 85–87, 91–106, 136, 138, 188, 198–99, 201, 222nn100,103; Gokul, 33, 42, 82, 84, 101, 131, 133, 211n39, 222n86, 226n86; Govardhan, 33, 42, 80, 83, 88–89, 94–95, 129, 131–32, 149–51, 156, 202; Jāvak Vaṭ, 80, 94; Kadamkhandi, 80, 86, 93, 95, 100, 102, 222nn87,103; Karhara, 80, 86, 90, 92, 100; Kokila Ban, 80, 93–94; Krishnakund, 80, 84, 89, 137; Lārilījī temple (Barsana), 85, 92; Mānasī Gaṅgā, 80, 94; Mathura, 20, 24–25, 44, 73, 77–78, 80, 84–85, 87, 90, 131, 136; Nandagaon, 24, 37, 80, 86, 91–92, 94–98, 101–2, 104–6, 198, 201, 222n86; Prem Sarovar, 80, 92, 219n29; Radhakund, 49–51, 80, 84, 87–89, 94, 118, 159, 224n39; Sakaran, 87, 220n38; Sāṅkarī Khor, 80, 93–94, 101; Uncha-gaon, 80, 86, 94, 99; Vishram Ghat (Mathura), 73, 77, 80, 84

Brajdāsī, 26, 45, 189–90

Brajdāsī-bhāgavat, 46, 191, 212n80

Braj Kuṃvarī. *See* Brajdāsī

Brijnāth Bhaṭṭ, 46, 212nn80,81

Bundi, 21, 37, 39, 58, 208n44, 212n74

būṛhī līlā, 93, 100, 222n95

Caitanya (Mahāprabhu), 31, 49, 51, 133, 136, 202, 205n12, 219n12, 229n162
Candrāvatī, 195
Carumatī, 207
caste orthopraxis. See *varṇāśrama-dharma*
cāṭu, 111, 194, 223n14
Catuḥ-sampradāya, 30, 68, 112, 147, 158
Caturbhujdās, 33, 114, 131, 147, 152
Caturdās (Dādū-panthī), 62
Caturdās Khojī, 60, 114, 126, 128, 157, 159
Catur Kuṃvarī (Nāgarīdās's mother), 45
Caube, 73, 131
Caurāsī Vaiṣṇavan kī Vārtā (*Story of Eighty-Four Disciples*), 33, 109, 223n9, 226nn88–91, 227nn100,108,110,111, 228n144, 230nn169,170
Chītsvāmī, 33, 114–15, 131, 147
Citaur, 36

Dadhi-kādauṃ, 92–94
Dādū (Dayāl), 61, 66, 216n271
Dādū-panth(ī), 31, 60–63, 82, 214n133, 216n176, 225n68
Dalcand (painter), 16, 207nn16,18
Dān-keli, 80, 93–94, 100–101
Dārā Shikoh, 211n52
Daśanāmī, 31, 58
Dattaji Scindhia, 23, 25, 209n59
Deccan(i), 15, 34, 186
Delhi: Braj and, 9–10, 36–37, 50, 74–75, 198; hagiography set in, 131, 136, 153; Jainas in, 66–67, 131, 219n15; Kishangarh and, 63; literature and, 28, 111, 217n195, 223n12; Mughal politics and, 17–20; Salimgarh in, 129; Sāvant Singh and, 6, 24, 65, 71–72, 80, 83, 85, 105, 111, 163–64, 187, 202–3, 207n27, 208n30, 212n76, 213nn87
Devī (Goddess), 69, 129, 211n40
Devyānī, 63, 77, 80–82, 87
ḍhāṛhīs (genealogical specialists), 92–94
dhrupada, 52–53
Dhruv(dās), 52, 147
Dhyān-mañjarī (*Handmaiden of Meditation*), 57, 168

Do Sau Bāvan Vaiṣṇavan kī Vārtā (*Story of Two Hundred Fifty-Two Vaishnavas*), 33, 109, 210n25, 223n9, 226nn87,93, 227nn94,95,97,101–5, 228n129, 230n9
Durrānī, Aḥmad Shāh Abdālī, 18–20, 24–25, 52, 54, 75, 164–65, 168, 197, 202
Dvarka, 122, 131, 141–42, 220n45, 229n160

ecumenical, 110, 125, 156, 157, 159–60, 199–200, 202
ekādaśī (fast on the eleventh day of the fortnight), 31

fakir, 107, 112, 115, 155, 199, 202
Fateh Singh (prince of Kishangarh), 16, 207n18
Faiyāz Alī Khān, 43, 205n4, 206n3, 227n120
festivals: Annakūṭa, 36, 80, 94; Balarāma's birthday festival, 92; Dādū *melā*, 61; Divālī, 17, 94; Gopāṣṭamī, 80, 95, 101; Hindorā, 93, 100; Holī (Phāga), 75, 78–80, 95–99, 103–4, 106, 131, 134, 153, 199, 201; Jaina, 66; Kārtik, 36, 80, 89, 94; Krishna's birthday festival (Janmāṣṭamī), 92, 155, 171; Lalitā birthday festival, 80, 92, 100; and the public sphere, 157; Rādhā's birthday festival (Rādhāṣṭamī), 80, 93, 100; Rakṣā-bandhana (Salono), 80, 92, 99; Rāma's birthday festival (Rāma-navamī), 162, 170–1; Sāñjhī, 80, 94; Śarad Pūrṇimā, 80, 94, 150; Sāvan, 92; Swinging festival, 154; Tīj, 80, 92; Vasant (in Ajmer), 63; wedding celebration (*Rādhā-Krishna-vivāha*), 100; wedding celebration (*Sītā-Rāma-vivāha*), 48, 59, 83, 175–77

Gadādhar Bhaṭṭ, 51, 114, 135, 147, 150
Gaṅgā (Ganges), 24, 80, 87–88, 96–98, 141, 163, 229n165
Galta: conference at, 62; history of, 54–9, 214nn135,142, 215n146; visit by Sāvant Singh, 77, 79, 80, 82–83, 87, 168, 174
Gauḍīya-Sampradāya: history of, 49–51, 152; influence in Bengal, 213n106; Jai

Singh's attitude towards, 31, 69, 89, 159; philosophy, 222n93, 229n164; Sāvant Singh's attitude towards, 54, 133, 135–37, 149, 159
Gīta-govinda, 108, 117–20, 149–50, 216n166, 224nn40,43
Gītāvalī (String of Songs), 59, 166, 171
Gokulnāth, 39, 223n9
Gopāl Kavi, 94, 214n129
Govinddev Ācārya, 26, 48
Govindsvāmī, 33, 115–16, 139, 147, 224n30
gṛhastha, 30, 158

hagiographical topoi: *ananyatā* (exclusive devotion), 129–30, 141, 143; completing verses of others (*para-pūrita*), 111, 118–19; death of devotee, 133, 138, 141, 142–43; etiology of place, 128–29; explanation of liturgy, 134, 152, 153; feeding holy men, 136; God's help in times of need, 120–21, 128–29, 135, 141–42; God loves low-caste devotees, 122–23, 126; God responds to devotees, 148; initiation/conversion, 112, 130, 131–32, 133, 134, 138; (king's) test of the holy (wo)man, 119–20, 121, 123, 124, 128–29, 133, 134; persecution of the holy (wo) man, 141; power of song, 119–20, 138, 139, 150–51, 154; rivalry amongst holy men, 134; sage and the Pharisee, 123, 133; unexpected visions of God, 121–22, 126, 127; worldly occurrences seen in divine light, 136–37, 154, 155
hagiography: audience of, 107–8; author as saint, 111–12; circulation of, 148–57; collective authorship of, 113–16; countering orthodoxy, 157–60; court and temple, 108; devotional story cycles, 109–11; about female devotees, 141–46; about Gauḍīya devotees, 135–37; about Gujarati devotees, 120–21; methodological approach in this book, 11–12, 107–13; mobilization of, 116–17; modern, 111–13; non-sectarian, 146–48; about Rāma devotees, 126–30; about Rasika-trayī, 137–40; research on, 109, 223nn5–8; about Sanskrit devotees, 117–20; about Sants, 121–26; sectarian appropriations of, 109–10, 130–35, 135–37, 139; summary findings, 199–200; about Vallabhan devotees, 130–35
Hanumān, 58, 94, 127–29, 167, 177–79, 183–84, 194, 226n78
Hāpaujī (Hari Singh), 62
Hari Ācārya (Harisevak), 59, 82–83, 168, 177, 193
Haridās, 52, 114, 116, 137, 139–40, 147, 202, 215n147, 228n132
Haridāsī-Sampradāya, 39, 52–53, 54, 118
Harirāy, 39, 223n9, 228n145
Harivaṃś, Hit, 51–52, 114, 137–38, 147, 229n162
Harivyāsdev Ācārya, 44, 212n65
Hīrālāl Sanāṛhya, 209n60
Hit-caurāsī-pad (*Eighty-Four Love Songs*), 51, 138, 214n117
Holkar, 21–22, 84, 208n44

intertextuality, 9, 60, 117, 200
Īśvarī Singh (of Jaipur), 21–22, 24, 46, 58, 66, 81–83, 163, 203, 219n33

Jahāngīr, 14, 34, 127–29, 226n81
Jaina, 65–68, 131, 138, 217n196, 218n222, 219n15, 223n6
Jaipur, 15: alliance with Sāvant Singh, 21–24, 163, 203; Dādū-panthī influence in, 62; deities, 50, 54, 82, 118, 215n143, 220n35, 224n39; dynastic struggle, 21–22, 81–83; Jaina movements in, 65–67; manuscript collections in, 113, 116, 144, 212n80, 214n142, 216n177, 224n33, 229n156, 230nn183,1, 232n57; meddling in Ajmer, 63–64; Nimbārkan influence in, 44–45, 48, 212n75; orthodoxy promoted by court, 30–32, 54, 68–69, 157–59, 160–61, 199; Rāmānandī influence in, 57–58, 82
Jai Singh I (of Amer; Mirzā Raja), 50, 215n145

Jai Singh II (of Jaipur; Savāī): building activity, 92; conferences, 30, 44, 53, 62, 199, 210n3, 215n158; close relation with Kishangarh, 15, 46; close relation with Gauḍīyas, 50; death and succession, 21, 46; governor of Agra, 51, 84; interference in Bundi, 21; involvement in Braj, 20, 85–87, 92–93, 105, 138, 198, 201, 210n23, 220n42; Jat fortress of Thun besieged, 15; orthodoxy countered by Sāvant Singh, 51–52, 54, 70, 89, 157–59, 160–61, 199–202; orthodoxy enforced by, 30–32, 44–45, 48, 50–51, 53, 58–59, 62–63, 68–69, 70, 113, 147, 209n52; pilgrimage to Soron, 84; Rāmānandī influence, 44, 58–59; Vedic sacrifices, 58, 160
Jayadeva, 108, 111, 114, 117–20, 138, 199, 224nn36,39–41,46
Jayappa Scindhia, 21–24, 84
Jayrām Śeṣ, 45, 48, 212n74
Jīva Gosvāmī, 118, 135, 141
Jodhpur, 14, 22, 45, 48, 62–63, 216n183

Kabīr, 55, 60, 62, 66, 110, 114, 121–25, 225nn66,68
Kācariyā Pīṭh, 48
Kali Yuga, 18, 26, 152
Kaman, 50–51, 65–66
Kampan, 194
Kapila, 80, 85, 87, 90, 220n49
Kauśikī, 80, 85, 98, 186–87
Khwājā Mu'īn ud-Dīn Chistī, 63
kīrtaniyā, 107, 113, 115, 154
Kishangarhi school of painting
—atelier, 15, 232n50
—eyes, 6
—hallmarks, 3
—modeled after royalty, 5, 7, 218n1
—paintings: *Bahādur Singh worshiping Vallabhan deities*, 48, 213n93; *Betel Tasting (Tāmbūl Sevā) with Fateh Singh*, 207n18; *Boat of love*, 5; *Kishangarhi Raja and Sufi*, 65, 217n194; *Krishna as yogi*, 4–6, 29, 108; *Krishna Swimming*, 218n1; *Lion Hunt of Sāvant Singh*, 47, 213n93; *Mīrābāī performing pūjā*, 145–46, 229n158; *Moonlight party in Rupnagar*, 64, 217n190; *Night in the Hot Season*, 51, 63, 137; *Portrait of Fateh Singh*, 207n18; *Portrait of Vallabha*, 42, 211n58; Portraits of Nimbārkans, 46, 213n84–5; *Rādhāvallabhans at the court of Bahādur Singh*, 52, 214n117; *Rāj Singh Approaching a Temple*, 45; *Rāj Singh and Jai Singh with Muḥammad Shāh and courtiers*, 15, 207n16; *Rāmāyaṇa* theme paintings, 191–3; *Return of the Cattle in the Evening* (Go-dhūli), 102–3; *Sāvant Singh subdues an elephant*, 207n20; *Sāvant Singh worshiping*, 42, 211n57; *Six Sufis*, 64, 217n191
—sketch: *Caitanya Mahāprabhu and disciples*, 51
See also this book's list of illustrations
Kishan Singh (Rathor of Kishangarh), 14, 34, 61, 67
Kiśordās, 53, 118–19, 214n126
Kisorīdās, 114, 138, 149
Kosi. *See* Kauśikī
Kota, 36–37, 39, 206n18, 208nn40,44, 212n74
Krishna: actors impersonating, 95–96, 99–101, 103–5, 157; birthday festival (Janmāṣṭamī), 92, 171; as brahman, 32; myth in real life, 96–99, 105–6; pastoral (Krishna Gopāla), 8–9, 43, 193, 206n21; research approach of this book, 10–11; research on, 9, 205nn16–8; subordinates himself to Rādhā, 118–19, 224n41; as yogi, 4–6
Krishnadās (Adhikārī), 114–15, 131–33, 134–35, 143, 147, 149–50, 152–53, 166
Krishnadās Kaṭahariyā, 166
Krishnadās Payohārī, 55–56, 61, 214n139
Krishna devotional sects, 32–54. *See also* Gauḍīya-, Haridāsī-, Mādhva-, Nimbārka-, Rādhāvallabha-, Vallabha-Sampradāya
Krishna images

—deities: Bihārī (Bāṅke), 53, 77, 80, 84, 220n42; Govindadeva, 31, 50, 82, 133, 220n35; Madanamohana, 50; Jagannātha, 118–19, 224n40; Śrī Brajanātha jī, 37; Śrī Dvārkānātha jī, 33, 211n39; Śrī Kalyāṇarāya jī, 15, 34–37, 42, 48, 146, 153, 229n161; Śrīnātha jī, 26, 33–34, 35–36, 39–41, 42, 50, 84, 110, 113, 129, 131, 153, 163, 211n39, 220n40; Rādhādāmodara, 118; Rādhāmādhava, 117–18, 224n39; Rādhāvallabha, 51
—miracles, 37–38, 39–41
—worship of images, 33
Kumbhandās, 33, 114, 130–31, 152

Loṅkāgaccha, 65, 67

Mādho Singh (of Jaipur), 21–22, 24, 62, 67, 81, 83
Madhukar Shāh, 114, 133, 138
Mādhva-Sampradāya, 159
Māhātmya, 73
Maheśvarī (pilgrim from Bikaner), 74, 84, 94, 220n40
Mahīpati, 117, 121–22, 128, 224nn36,46, 226nn78,86
Malhār Rāo, 22, 39, 84, 86, 208n52
Maṅgal-kāvya, 129
Mān Singh (of Amer), 62, 129
Mān Singh (of Kishangarh), 15, 40–41, 63, 207n15, 212n76, 216n186
Marathas: connection with Rām-carit-mālā, 183–88, 190, 194–95; in history, 15, 20–21, 58, 71, 74, 81–82, 84–86, 121; Sāvant Singh and, 21–26, 76, 121, 159, 163, 169, 180; Smārta Brahmins in Jaipur, 159
Marwar, 22–23, 25, 41, 66, 81, 116, 126, 128, 174
Mā'sir ul-Umarā, 207n9, 210n28, 211nn37,38,52
Merta, 45, 48, 62, 81, 207n19, 229n155
Mewar, 14, 21, 34, 36, 50, 84, 144, 152, 207n13, 208nn40,43, 220n40, 228n150
Mīrā(bāī), 108, 114, 116, 141–46, 147–49, 152, 160, 199, 202, 228nn149–54, 229nn155–60,162
Muḥammad Shāh (emperor), 7, 15, 17, 19, 20, 37, 207n16, 208n31
Muralīdās, 51, 89, 114–15, 137, 149, 154, 159, 202

Nābhādās, 44, 55, 60, 62, 109–10, 112–13, 118–20, 130, 141, 143, 147
Nāgarīdās (for life of *see under* Sāvant Singh)
—penname, 26, 87
—Rāma-Rasika influence on, 82–83, 110, 168, 170, 174–75, 177, 179–81, 185, 191, 193
—works of, 17; Arilla-pacīsī (*Twenty-five Arillas*), 206n20; Bāl-vinod (*Childhood Amusements*), 28; Ban-jan-praśaṃs (*Praise of the Woodland People*), 25, 204; Bihār-candrikā (*Love-Play's Moonlight*), 5; Braj-vaikuṇṭh-tulā (*Weighing Braj and Vaikuṇṭha*), 18, 76; Chūṭak-dohā (*Stray Dohās*), 27, 186; Chūṭak-kavitta (*Stray Kavittas*), 162, 187; Chūṭak-pad (*Stray Songs*), 147, 188; Govind jī kī Parcaī (*Introduction to Govind jī*), 115; Jugal-bhakt-vinod (*Amusements of Two Devotees*), 28, 209n67, 221n53; Kali-vairāgya-vallarī (*Dejection's Vine in Corrupt Times*), 18; Manorath-mañjarī (*Blossoming Wish*), 18; Pad-muktāvalī (*String of Song-Pearls*), 5–6, 37, 48, 51, 52, 69, 144, 227n112, 229n162, 231n15; Pad-prabodh-mālā (*Garland of Songs of Awakening*), 146–47; Pad-prasaṅg-mālā (PPM; *Garland of Stories and Songs*), 11, 42, 47, 51–53, 67, 86–87, 99, 107–61, 165, 174, 201–2, 223nn9,30, 224n32, 229n162; Phāg-vihār (*Celebration of Holī*), 24, 98, 222n94; Rām-carit-mālā (*Garland of Rāma's Romance*), 11, 48, 59, 162–96, 202–3, 230n3, 231n16; Śrīmad-Bhāgavat-pārāyaṇ-vidhi-prakāś (*Illumination of the Way to Recite Śrīmad Bhāgavata [-purāṇa]*), 44, 109, 112, 205n5, 212n81;

Sujan-ānand (*Gaiety on the In-Laws' Get-Together*), 28; Tīrthānand (TĀ; *The Pilgrim's bliss*), 22, 51, 59, 71–106, 112, 137, 165, 168, 187, 193–94, 201; Utsav-mālā (*Garland of Festivals*), 42, 162, 221n73, 231n16; Van-vinod (*Amusements in the Woodland*), 28; Vr̥ndāban-abhilāṣ-pūran-pad-prabandh (*The Desire for Vrindavan Fulfilled*), 187–88, 221n55
Nāgarīdās (Nehī), 52, 87, 114, 138
Nagari Kunj, 17, 26, 84, 207n24, 220n42
Nāgās, 58, 82, 216n176, 220n42. *See also* warrior ascetics
Nagor, 23, 65, 67, 215n144
Nāmdev, 114, 121–23, 148, 156–57, 206n19, 225nn55,58
Nanddās, 11, 33, 130, 147, 166, 176
Naraina, 60–63, 82, 225n68
Nārāyaṇ Bhaṭṭ, 49, 92
Nārāyaṇdās Naṭvā, 142–43, 153
Narsī Mehtā, 108, 114, 120–21, 147–48, 225nn50–52
Narvāhan, 114, 138
Nathdvara, 34, 36, 84, 152, 208n43
Nihālcand (painter), 4–5, 42, 47, 140, 145, 220n38, 232n50
Nij-mat-siddhānt (*Our Sect's Theology*), 118, 140, 214n126
Nimbārkācārya, 43–44, 211n62
Nimbārka-Sampradāya, 42–49, 118, 146

Oswal, 67, 131

Padmāvatī, 119–20
Paramānanddās, 33, 114, 130, 147, 224n32
para-pūrita (completing verses of others), 111, 118–19
Paraśurām (Ācārya), 44, 47, 58, 166, 173
Parcaī, 121, 123–24, 214n136, 225n54
Peshva, 21–2, 81, 208nn42,53
philosophy: Acintya-bhedābheda (hard-to-fathom difference in non-difference), 49, 96, 222n93; Advaita (monism), 32, 44, 52, 55, 67; Bhedābheda (difference in non-difference), 110; Dvaita (dualism), 3; Śuddhādvaita (pure monism), 32; Svabhāvika-bhedābheda (natural difference in non-difference), 44; Viśiṣṭādvaita (qualified monism), 44, 55
pilgrimage: building activity in places of, 85–87; festival cycle, 91–96; itineraries, 79–85; methodological approach in this book, 11–12, 71–75; mythical connections, 96–9; performances in centers of, 99–105; pleasure and, 75–79; research on, 73, 218nn2–6, 219nn11–15,26; rites at centers of, 87–90; summary findings, 198–99; *tīrtha*, 69, 71, 74, 77, 87
Pītāmbardās, 53
Pratāp Singh (of Jaipur), 116, 144, 212n75, 230n183
Pratāp Singh (of Kishangarh), 61
Prithvīrāj (of Amer), 56, 214n140
Priyādās, 44, 109, 119–20, 123–24, 127, 129, 133, 135–36, 141, 144, 225nn62,69, 226n86, 229n155
procession, 87–90, 95, 100–105, 176–77, 199, 215n143
public sphere (Habermasian), 137, 156–57, 160, 199–200, 223n14
Puri, 49, 54, 118, 150, 224n40
Pushkar, 23, 56, 69, 214n139

Qandahar, 15, 35–36

Rādhā: actors impersonating, 95–96, 99–101, 103, 157; birthday festival (Rādhāṣṭamī), 80, 93, 100; Braj sites sacred to (*see under* Barsana; Jāvak Vaṭ; Radhakund; Sāṅkarī Khor); earliest worship (perhaps), 43–44; eyes, 5–6, 175; invitation to Sāvant Singh to stay in Braj, 97; joyful aspects of Rādhā-Krishna devotion, 27–28, 49–54; in Kishangarhi painting, 3–5, 15–16, 175, 191, 207n18; Krishna subordinates himself to, 118–19, 224n41; parental home, 136–37; pastoral narrative, 193; poetry, 213n88, 221n81; *sakhī-bhāva* for, 37–39,

52; *svakīya-parakīya*, 50; *viraha*, 178; visions of, 138; wedding, 100, 175
Rādhāvallabha-Sampradāya, 51–52, 54, 100, 138, 214n126
Rāghavdās, 62
Raghunāth Rāo (Maratha general), 22–23, 25, 209n58
Raghunāth Rāo (of Vincur), 63, 218n6, 219n28
Rahīm Khānkhānā, Abdur, 51
Raidās, 55, 60, 62, 114, 121–24, 157
Rāj Singh (of Kishangarh), 15–16, 19, 45, 197, 207n16, 208n28, 212n81, 213n87
Rāj Singh (of Mewar), 84, 207n13, 211n39
Rāma: anger of, 179–81, 182–83; *Bharat-milāp* (Reunion with Bharata), 184; birthday festival (Rāma-navamī), 162, 170–71; brotherly rivalry and love, 169–70, 171, 173, 184; childhood, 170–74; devotional sect, 54–60; first love, 174–75; Krishna poets on, 48, 166; love for his people, 184–85; as low-caste hunter, 127–28, 159; modeled after Krishna *bhakti*, 57–60; as Moghol, 110; Śrī Sītārāma jī (deity), 56, 214n124; wedding, 59, 83, 175–77
Rāmānanda, 54, 125–27, 159, 225n68
Rāmānandī-Sampradāya, 31, 54–60, 61–62, 82, 110, 121, 159, 177, 214nn135,142
Rāmānuja, 44, 55, 60, 126, 159
Rāmāyaṇa, 159; divinizing/demonizing agenda, 164–65, 168; land narrative, 193; mobilized for healing, 189–90; paintings in Kishangarh, 191–93, 195–96; *Rāmāyaṇa*-like scenario in Sāvant Singh's life, 6, 11, 163–65, 170, 172, 177, 180, 183, 186–87, 193–95, 209n64; retelling by Nāgarīdās, 48, 162–96, 202–3
Rām-carit-mānas (*Holy Lake of Rāma's Romance*), 166
Rāmgaṅgā, 80, 85, 87
Rām-līlā, 100, 176–77, 184, 222nn91,96
Rāmprapanna (Madhurācārya), 57, 59
Rām Singh (of Jodhpur), 22–23, 219n22
rasa: adbhūta, 177, 182; *hāsya*, 28, 176, 182; *karuṇā*, 123, 162, 169, 177–78, 189, 193, 203; *krodha/raudra* (*rasa*), 180–81, 182–83, 194; *mādhurya* (erotic), 57, 136; *vātsalya*, 172; *vibhatsa* (*rasa*), 183, 194; *viraha*, 91, 130, 131, 178, 203; *vīra rasa*, 162, 169, 172–73, 177, 182, 194
Rasik Bihārī. *See* Banī-ṭhanī
rasika: Krishna-rasika, 49–54, 88–89, 101, 111, 124–25, 153–54; Rāma-Rasika, 57–59, 168, 170, 174–75, 177, 179–81, 185, 191, 215nn146,149; Rasika-trayī, 53, 137–40; soldier and, 69
Rasik-ananya-mālā, 227nn124–27
Rasikdās (or -dev), 53, 229n162
Rās-līlā, 9, 11, 59, 68, 75, 83, 92–94, 96, 99–105, 157, 189, 204
Rathor, 14, 61, 63, 144, 146, 161, 229n155
Rāvaṇa, 162, 164–65, 167, 169, 181–82, 192, 194, 202, 231n34
Rohilla, 20, 22, 24, 84, 183, 194–95, 203, 209nn52,67
role theory (Hjalmar Sundén), 189, 194
Rūpa Gosvāmī, 49–51
Rūpa Kavirāja (*vairāgī*), 50, 159, 221n63
Rūplāl, 52, 214n117
Rūpmatī, 207n13
Rupnagar: atelier, 232n50; capital, 45, 51; foundation, 15; Jaina presence, 67–69; in Pad-prasaṅg-mālā, 107–8, 113–15, 118, 137, 149–50, 153–56, 159; siege, 21, 23–26, 48, 82, 209n58; Sufi presence, 63–64; temple-town, 35–37, 171
Rūp Rām, 85–86, 92, 94
Rūp Singh (of Kishangarh), 15, 37–41, 64, 112, 114, 149, 211nn47,52
Rūp-vacanikā (Exposition on Rūp/Beauty), 15, 112

śahr āśob (The City Destroyed), 28, 209n69
Sakhī-Sampradāya. *See* Haridāsī-Sampradāya
Salābat Ḳhān, 19, 22, 219n33
Salemabad, 25–26, 42–49, 58, 62, 117–18, 166, 177, 206n3, 212n75
Sambhar, 61, 79, 81–82, 192

sandhyā-bhāṣā (Twilight-idiom), 125
Śaṅkara, 32, 44, 55, 68
Sanyāsī. *See* ascetics
Śaraṇ, Vrajvallabh Vedāntācārya, 43, 206n3, 207n19, 209n60, 212nn76,77,82, 213nn84–85,89
Sardār Singh (of Rupnagar), 22–26, 64, 209n60, 232n50
Sardār-sujas, 209n60
Śārdul Singh (of Kishangarh), 62
satī, 141, 144
satire, 209n68
satsaṅga, 37, 59, 69, 88–89, 125, 132, 168
Sauramya-mat, 50–51, 54, 159, 221n63
Sāvant Singh (for works of *see under* Nāgarīdās): battle of Thun, 15–16, 207n17; ceremonies of peace with brother, 25–26; close early connection with Braj, 17–18; concubine Banī-ṭhanī, 5, 53–54, 77–78, 112, 133; coronation, 18; father's death, 18, 201; Krishna bhakti chauvinism, 177; lion hunt, 47; Maratha contacts, 74–75, 84–85; mother's death, 17; Nimbārkan affiliation, 46–49; patron/likeness in painting, 7, 168, 205nn3,6, 105; pilgrimage to Braj, 71, 74–79, 82–84, 88–90; pilgrimage to Soron, 88; Rāmānandī contacts, 59–60, 75, 82–83, 168, 177, 200; reception in Vrindaban, 89; *samādhi*, 26–27; search for allies, 18–22; selection as crown prince, 16; settles in Braj, 27–28, 85–87, 91–96, 147, 187–89; stepmother, 26, 45, 189–90; usurped by brother, 18; Vallabhan affiliation, 41–42
scripture (rewriting): compiler as reader, 165–66; deliberate omissions, 168–69; divinizing/demonizing narrative, 168; methodological approach in this book, 11–12, 164–68; political relevance, 164–65; Rāma-Rasika elements, 170–85; real-life significance, 163, 180–81, 185–89, 190; religious reading, 166; research on, 164, 230nn4–6; rewriting conclusion, 169–70; summary findings, 200; therapeutic reading, 186–90.
sectarian orthodoxy. *See* Catuḥ-sampradāya
Serfoji Bhosle II (of Tanjore), 74, 218nn6–8
Shāh ʻĀlam II (emperor), 15, 63, 216n186
Shāhnāmah Munavvar Kalām, 207n16
Shiva, 110, 148, 172–73, 182, 220n40, 229n165, 231n34
Shivdās Lakhnavī, 207n16
Siṃh-śikār (Lion Hunt), 47, 213n86
Sītā, 167; Agni-parīkṣā, 183, 193; dialogue with Hanumān, 177–79, 231nn26,30; eternal sporting with Rāma, 57; exile, 189; falling in love, 174–75; in Kishangarhi *Rāmāyaṇa* paintings, 191–92; message to Rāma, 177–79; *rahasya*, 179–80, 231nn29,31; reunion with Rāma, 183–84; as Śrī, 231n24; suicide wish, 179, 231n25; Svayaṃvara (tournament), 175–77; symbol of land, 193; viraha, 177–79; wedding (*vivāha*), 48, 59, 83
Sītārām (Kishangarhi painter), 191–92, 211n58
Smārta Brahmin, 31, 159
Soron, 80, 84, 87–88, 96
Śrī Bhaṭṭ, 44, 147, 213n88
Śrīnātha jī kī Prākaṭya Vārtā (*The Story of the Manifestation of Śrīnātha jī*), 39, 41, 210n30
Sudān (author), 86
Sufi, 29, 63–65, 69, 218n10
Sukh Singh (prince of Kishangarh), 16, 207n19
Sultān Pīr, 64, 217n192
Sūraj Mal, 20–21, 24, 81, 85–86, 92
Sūrdās, 11, 33, 114, 134–35, 150, 166, 177–79, 181, 183, 195
Sūrdās Madanmohan, 51, 114, 135–37, 149–51, 154
Sūr-sāgar, 181, 231n33
svāmī-bhakti, 37
svarūpa, 33–34, 40, 132, 153, 211n39
Śvetāmbara scribes, 67

Tānsen, 53, 114, 116, 134, 139–40
Tavārīkh Maḥkamah (*Administrative Chronicle*), 14, 47, 206n4, 207nn18, 26, 27, 208nn29,45, 209n60, 212n81
Tazkirah, 110–11, 157, 223n12
Terah-panth, 66
Ṭīlācārya (Ṭīlā Svāmī), 58
Tilakāyat, 33
Tilocan, 114, 121–22, 225n55
Tod, James, 13, 146
Tulsīdās, 11, 59, 67, 110; hagiography about, 126–30, 147, 159, 163, 226nn75,78,86; poetry on Rāma, 166, 169, 171–73, 181, 195
Tuzuk-e Jahāngīrī, 207n7, 226n81

Udaipur, 53, 62, 66
utsava. *See* festivals
Uttara-rāma-carita (*Sequel to Rāma's Romance*), 189, 194
Uttarārdh-bhaktmāl (*Sequel to the Garland of Devotees*), 111–13

Vallabhācārya, 32–33, 42, 46, 47, 48, 50, 130, 219n12, 213n9, 225n55
Vallabha-Sampradāya: and Bahādur Singh, 48, 149; bias of Kishangarh court, 47, 206n3; hagiographical accounts, 68, 109–10, 113, 115, 130, 133–35, 139, 214n30, 229n162; historical sketch, 32–42, 50, 226n86; at Jaipur court, 31, 46, 67; poems included in Rām-carit-mālā, 166; promotion tours, 152; redaction of Pad-prasaṅg-mālā, 158–59
Vallabhrasik, 51, 135, 147
Vaṃśīdās. *See* Bansīdās
varṇāśrama-dharma, 30–31, 45, 50, 62, 157–58, 160, 202
Vārtā, 33, 39–42, 109–10, 115, 130–34, 139, 143, 152
Viṣṇusvāmī-Sampradāya, 30, 53
Viṭṭhalnāth, 33, 110, 113, 129–31, 133–34, 152, 156, 224n30
Viṭhal Vipul, 52, 147
Vrijānand, 57–58, 82, 215n157
Vrind, 15, 35, 64, 112
Vrindābandev Ācārya (Vrindāban Prabhu), 44–48, 166, 209n61, 212n80, 213n88
Vrindavan: Brahmakund, 94; deities and temples in, 50–53, 118, 212n75; in hagiography, 110, 124–25, 130, 133, 135, 137–41, 149–52, 158; Jai Singh conferences in, 210n3, 215n158; Jñān Gudarī, 78, 80, 84, 88, 90; Kabīr in, 110, 124–25; map of, 207n24; marauding armies in, 25, 52, 54, 209n61, 214n117; Rāmānandīs in, 57, 215n148; Sāvant Singh in, 5, 17–18, 24–27, 69, 73, 77, 87, 89–90, 94–95, 147, 187–88; sects in, 44, 49–53; Seva Kunj, 51
Vrindāvandās, Cācā, 52, 209n61, 214n117
Vyās, Harirām, 52–53, 114–15, 125, 137–38, 147, 157–58, 159–60, 225n56

Yamunā, 9, 71, 76–78, 83, 87, 96. 105, 219n23
Yashodakund, 95, 101
yogi/yogini. *See* ascetics

GLOBAL SOUTH ASIA

Padma Kaimal

K. Sivaramakrishnan

Anand A. Yang

SERIES EDITORS

Global South Asia takes an interdisciplinary approach to the humanities and social sciences in its exploration of how South Asia, through its global influence, is and has been shaping the world.

A Place for Utopia: Urban Designs from South Asia, by Smriti Srinivas

The Afterlife of Sai Baba: Competing Visions of a Global Saint, by Karline McLain

Sensitive Space: Fragmented Territory at the India-Bangladesh Border, by Jason Cons

The Gender of Caste: Representing Dalits in Print, by Charu Gupta

Displaying Time: The Many Temporalities of the Festival of India, by Rebecca M. Brown

Banaras Reconstructed: Architecture and Sacred Space in a Hindu Holy City, by Madhuri Desai

Mobilizing Krishna's World: The Writings of Prince Sāvant Singh of Kishangarh, by Heidi R. M. Pauwels

www.ingramcontent.com/pod-product-compliance
Lightning Source LLC
Chambersburg PA
CBHW030613230426
43661CB00053B/1961
* 9 7 8 0 2 9 5 7 4 2 2 3 6 *